THIS WILL
NOT PASS

Trump, Biden, and the Battle for America's Future

JONATHAN MARTIN &
ALEXANDER BURNS

Simon & Schuster
New York   London   Toronto   Sydney   New Delhi

Simon & Schuster
1230 Avenue of the Americas
New York, NY 10020

First Simon & Schuster hardcover edition May 2022

SIMON & SCHUSTER and colophon are registered trademarks of
Simon & Schuster, Inc.

For information about special discounts for bulk purchases, please contact
Simon & Schuster Special Sales at 1-866-506-1949 or business@simonandschuster.com.

The Simon & Schuster Speakers Bureau can bring authors to your live event. For
more information, or to book an event, contact the Simon & Schuster Speakers
Bureau at 1-866-248-3049 or visit our website at www.simonspeakers.com.

Interior design by Wendy Blum

Manufactured in the United States of America

1   3   5   7   9   10   8   6   4   2

Library of Congress Cataloging-in-Publication Data has been applied for.

ISBN 978-1-9821-7248-0
ISBN 978-1-9821-7250-3 (ebook)

For MJ and Penelope

—A.I.B.

For Betsy and Ella

—J.L.M.

CONTENTS

A Note to Readers

THIS BOOK IS based on hundreds of interviews with people at every level of government in Washington, scores of American states and cities, and several foreign capitals. These interviews were conducted on a range of terms: Some people agreed to speak on the record, meaning that they could be cited by name, while others insisted on some degree of anonymity in order to share the most sensitive elements of their experiences in this time of crisis.

Some sources relayed confidential documents to confirm or expand upon their recollections. Others shared audio or video tapes taken at crucial times, including recordings of private meetings with White House officials and congressional leaders. These materials represent a crucial contribution to the historical record, allowing the authors to narrate some of the most important and disturbing moments of this period in thorough detail.

Where quotations are attributed directly to individuals, using quotation marks, it is because they reflect the verbatim language used in interviews, text messages, emails, documents, or in recorded material, or were relayed by authoritative sources soon after the fact. In other situations, this book renders conversations and scenes in paraphrased form, without quotation marks.

Interviews for this book are quoted in the present tense to reflect that the speaker was looking back on events from a distance; conversations and remarks that unfolded in real time are quoted in the past tense.

In every instance, the authors have endeavored to tell the story of these tumultuous years in our history as vividly as possible, and with the highest degree of precision and fidelity to the facts.

Introduction

A Recognizable Target

ABIGAIL SPANBERGER AND Alexandria Ocasio-Cortez were not close friends.

Though they both claimed House seats in 2018, an election year that elevated a vanguard of Democratic women, the two had little in common. Spanberger had been an operative with the Central Intelligence Agency before running for the House as a down-the-middle centrist in the red-tinted suburbs of Richmond, Virginia. Ocasio-Cortez, a decade her junior, was an organizer on the 2016 Bernie Sanders campaign and then defeated an incumbent member of the Democratic leadership, campaigning as a socialist in New York City.

In some respects, the two women represented the enormous gulf within the Democratic Party, separating the young left-wingers who made up the party's grass roots from the moderate suburban constituencies whose votes had delivered Democrats a majority in the House in 2018 and then elected Joe Biden to the presidency.

But in the first days of 2021, Spanberger and Ocasio-Cortez were not thinking much about their differences. Spanberger placed a call to her colleague on a more urgent subject.

In just a few days, Congress would be tasked with certifying the results of the 2020 election. In a normal year, it was a pro forma exercise. The popular vote had already been tallied and the Electoral College had carried out its arcane duties in the middle of December. The role of the House and Senate was mostly ornamental.

Things were shaping up differently this year. President Donald Trump had refused to concede the election, and he had instead spent the two previous months peddling increasingly outlandish conspiracy theories about election fraud. His complaints were ungrounded in fact, and lawsuits brought on his behalf had been all but laughed out of court.

But many of his followers had bought into Trump's claims, and a good number of them were planning to gather in Washington for a demonstration outside the Capitol on January 6. The president was clinging to a bogus theory that his obsequious vice president, Mike Pence, could use his status as the presiding officer in the Senate to block certification of the election.

As a former intelligence officer, Spanberger was concerned about the possibility of violence—particularly violence targeting her fellow Democrats, and most especially the handful of highly recognizable progressive women who had been demonized by the right. She reached out to Ocasio-Cortez to urge her to take some unusual precautions, counseling an American lawmaker to approach the physical space of the Capitol—and the ritual of certifying a free and fair election—with the same caution she may have used with an intelligence asset in a dangerous foreign country.

"You are a very recognizable target," Spanberger recalls telling Ocasio-Cortez. "Drive to work, and make sure that you dress in a way where you are as less recognizable as you could possibly be."

"Wear sneakers, dress down—don't look like you."

That extraordinary conversation was one of many rippling through Congress in those tense days before January 6. In the aftermath of the insurrection, it would become clear that the national security apparatus of the United States and the police leaders responsible for defending the Capitol had failed to anticipate and prepare for the scale of the threat at hand. But to the lawmakers charged with completing the transfer of power between presidents, the mood of menace was pervasive.

To them, it was apparent enough that the basic institutions of American democracy had been strained almost to the breaking point.

In late December, Maxine Waters, the senior Democrat from Los Angeles, had spoken up on a video call with other lawmakers to inquire about security measures for January 6. Waters, one of the most recognizable Black women in Congress and a frequent target of the conservative media, was alarmed about one far-right organization in particular. In the first presidential debate, Trump had pointedly declined to denounce the extremist group known as the Proud Boys—"Stand back and stand by," he told them—and now some of its members appeared to be headed to Washington.

What, Waters asked, is being done about that?

On January 3, Democratic leaders issued guidance to lawmakers on keeping a low profile. Worried about a potential altercation with pro-Trump demonstrators on January 6, they advised the rank and file to conceal the special pins that identified them as members of Congress and to use a network of tunnels that runs under the Capitol to move around that day, rather than going outside. Lauren Underwood, a young lawmaker from Illinois, later paraphrased the safety advice with frustrated sarcasm: "It'll be fine, but in case you're worried just take the tunnel."

Andy Kim, a House Democrat from New Jersey, had intended to bring his wife and two sons down to Washington to see him sworn in for a second term. A former National Security Council official who had worked in Afghanistan, Kim and his wife, Kammy, decided to err on the side of caution.

"I told her, 'You know, I'm a little concerned about some of the chatter that we're hearing about this protest,'" Kim says. "'So, I mean, I want you and the kids to stay up in Jersey.'"

Before Kim returned to Washington alone, his wife said goodbye with a message Kim did not recall her giving him at any other time.

"Her last words to me were: 'Be careful,'" he says.

Another Democrat, Jason Crow of Colorado, had brought his family to the nation's capital for his swearing in and had hoped they would stay until January 7—the day after Congress would certify Biden's victory and drop the curtain on the Trump era. But those plans changed. A former army ranger who did three tours in Afghanistan and Iraq, Crow says he sent his family home on the eve of the certification vote.

"My wife and I made the decision for them to leave on the fifth, which they did for safety," he says.

Crow was not the only veteran of America's twenty-first-century wars to recognize an incipient breakdown in political order.

The previous summer, Mikie Sherrill of New Jersey, who flew helicopters in the navy before winning a wealthy suburban district in 2018, had pressed the country's top general to confirm that the armed forces would not be used to thwart an orderly transition from one president to the next. The Trump administration had used the military in a brazen political stunt in early June, when the president marched through Lafayette Park to brandish a Bible outside St. John's Church, flanked during the short walk by the secretary of defense, Mark Esper, and the chairman of the Joint Chiefs of Staff, Mark Milley.

Both men had expressed regret afterward, but Sherrill was deeply dismayed. Concerned that the armed forces could be used in even more sinister ways, she pressed Milley by phone to commit that there would not be "some sort of military coup."

"He assured me in private that he understood his constitutional duties, as did our military," Sherrill says. "And he felt very secure that the military would carry out its constitutional duties."

But as the certification vote rapidly approached, questions of military neutrality and public order were looming as large as ever. Milley, an army general whose relationship with the president was in tatters, was among those broaching exceptionally delicate subjects in preparation for the long day ahead.

On January 4, the general placed a call to Tom Cotton, the Republican senator from Arkansas. A hard-line conservative and a close ally of the president, Cotton had announced he would vote to certify the election results, and he was working closely with Mitch McConnell, the Senate majority leader, to counter a group of senators who intended to object.

Milley had taken note of Cotton's statement, and reached out to ask for help.

Could you explain, he asked Cotton, how the certification process on January 6 is supposed to work?

He was worried, the general explained, that Washington was poised to explode. It was not that he feared an insurrection, exactly. But Milley had seen the scenes of violence in American streets the previous summer, and he feared that in a tinderbox environment there could be an outbreak of street violence between extreme forces on the right and left.

That turned out to be a fatally misguided read on the threat at hand.

Even House Republicans were alarmed. On the eve of the vote, the GOP Conference gathered in the Capitol Visitor Center to debate how they should handle the process, with some members beaming in remotely. It was obvious that a large number of conservatives would vote to object to the election results, some of them out of an earnest belief in election-fraud conspiracies but most out of fear that doing the opposite would bring down the wrath of President Trump and his MAGA army. A small few acknowledged that fear openly and fretted about the implications of indulging a paranoid horde.

"Those people coming to D.C. in droves, praying that tomorrow, we are going to overturn the election and make Donald Trump the president for four more years—are we going to satisfy those concerns with what we do tomorrow?" asked Mike Gallagher, a young Marine veteran representing Wisconsin's Eighth Congressional District.

"How long," Gallagher demanded to know, "are we prepared to tell these people that the election is not over?"

Debbie Lesko of Arizona, a pro-Trump conservative, said she had asked House leaders to "come up with a safety plan" because there could be hundreds of thousands of people pouring into Washington. Expressing fear about the left-wing group Antifa, she wondered aloud: Should members get special transportation or police escorts back to their homes?

But Lesko wasn't just musing about threats from the far left.

"We also have, quite honestly, Trump supporters who actually believe that we are going to overturn the election," she said, "and when that does not happen—most likely will not happen—they are going to go nuts."

Kevin McCarthy, the Republican leader, assured Lesko that he was in touch with the sergeant at arms and "they're preparing ahead of time" on the security front. A conciliatory character by nature—far more of a cheerleader than an arm-twister, as congressional leaders go—McCarthy had forged a tight political alliance with Trump, and he was eager not to let the certification debate strain that bond or divide the GOP Conference.

"I do not judge anybody on how they vote," he said in wrapping up the tense discussion, adding: "What I'd like to do is get through tomorrow."

On the day of the certification vote, the potential for violence was so clear that Brendan Boyle, a House Democrat from Philadelphia, heard from some labor union leaders back home with an unusual offer. The officials with the building trades, including associates of the longtime boss John "Johnny Doc" Dougherty, had followed the news reports suggesting things could get rough on January 6. Would it be helpful to Boyle, they wondered, if they sent down some of their guys to be by his side?

To the whole assortment of lawmakers and officeholders bracing for the worst on January 6—or what they imagined might be the worst—there was no real debate about the immediate cause of the threat of violence. There were larger forces in American politics swirling around that date, great currents of social division and cultural change, of decaying trust in shared institutions and eroding confidence in the democratic process.

But those forces had converged on January 6 for a reason, and Adam Smith, the chairman of the House Armed Services Committee, knew what it was.

A matter-of-fact moderate from Washington State with close ties to the nation's military establishment, Smith had told his fellow Democrats he believed there was zero chance of a coup, in part because Trump seemed to lack the intellectual wattage and administrative wherewithal to carry one out. In Smith's reckoning, the president was far more interested in branding his new "shiny Space Force" and repainting Air Force One, than in drawing up plans for an American junta.

After all, Smith says of Trump, "my perception is, he is a fucking moron."

Smith says he discouraged his colleagues from even speculating publicly about the concept of a military takeover, lest anxious Democrats inadvertently supply the dim president with inspiration for a crazy plan he did not already have.

Still, the Armed Services Committee chairman had spoken numerous times with military leaders about how they might handle things if Trump tested the limits of his powers as commander in chief. Mark Milley had told Smith that he knew he did not have to follow illegal orders—a reassuring enough sentiment, should Trump prove more devious than Smith believed him to be.

* * *

By the early afternoon of that day, the House and Senate had been evacuated, with the top leaders of both chambers sequestered at Fort McNair, a waterfront military base in Washington, D.C., and hundreds of other lawmakers locked down in an assortment of Capitol Hill offices and hearing rooms.

The evacuation had followed a large and angry rally outside the Capitol, where Trump urged a raucous mass of supporters to "fight like hell" and demanded that Pence "stand up for the good of our Constitution" or face Trump's personal repudiation. Taking those words to heart, thousands of Trump's supporters had soon overrun the flimsy barricades outside the Capitol complex. The mob included doctors and small business owners, cops and military veterans, seasoned radicals and angry newcomers to the far-right cause. Some aped the vigilantism of the Wild West and Jim Crow South, raising a cry: "Hang Mike Pence!"

Pence had been plucked from the Senate chamber by the Secret Service and sequestered inside the Capitol. For once defying the president in public, the vice president had refused to indulge Trump's fantasies of blocking the election results, and he had declined to leave. According to Marc Short, Pence's chief of staff, the vice president did not want to create the image of his motorcade fleeing the seat of government in the world's greatest democracy.

The exodus from the Senate had been a confusing, hectic affair, with lawmakers young and old, Democrats and Republicans, ordered hastily away from the chamber by Capitol Police as they struggled to figure out what was going on. Some of them knew that the complex had been breached. Few understood that there was a rampaging mob on their heels.

"Do not run, just walk!" yelled out a police officer, hoping to stop a senatorial stampede.

Patrick Leahy, the Senate's senior Democrat, was rushed toward the tunnels out of the Capitol by a uniformed officer as fast as the eighty-year-old Vermonter could walk. Lisa Murkowski of Alaska, a Republican who had broken repeatedly with Trump, and whom the president had marked down as a target for political retribution, clasped arms in the hall with Dan Sullivan, her state's junior senator, recognizing the threat far more seriously than some of her colleagues.

"I got my Marine," she said, alluding to Sullivan's status as a colonel in the Marine Corps reserve.

Not far off was Josh Hawley, the Missouri senator and former Supreme Court clerk who had been the first Republican to announce plans to challenge the election results in the Senate. A number of his conservative colleagues thought Hawley's objection was little more than a play for publicity—an act of gratuitous pandering to Trump, who knew little of constitutional law but was always eager to accumulate allies and enablers.

As the senators, reporters, staffers, and cops went down an escalator and toward the Senate subway that connects the Capitol to a labyrinth of office buildings, Hawley was no longer gaming out the political impact of his procedural stunt. Nor did he cut the same rabble-rousing pose he had adopted hours earlier when he was famously photographed holding a clenched left fist in solidarity with onlooking pro-Trump protesters.

Now the mob was out of control, and Hawley was simply trying to figure out what had happened and what to do.

"They just said, 'Go to Hart 216,'" he all but shrugged, naming a spot that would come to be known as the "secure location."

His Senate colleague Kevin Cramer, an affable North Dakotan, wondered aloud in his Plains patter about just what was afoot.

Cramer had been a trusty Trump ally and, like many Republicans, thought the president's inflammatory behavior was mostly harmless, just the antics of an entertainer-politician. The senator loved telling a story about Trump's priorities from a North Dakota stop the president made on Cramer's behalf. Trump had wanted to know in advance: What kind of crowd had Elton John drawn at the Fargodome, and could he outdo the English piano man?

The last few weeks had been different, though, and Cramer thought Trump had behaved in a grossly irresponsible way in the run-up to January 6. Cramer had felt the sting of that anger: He had announced a few days earlier that he would vote to certify the election, because there were simply no grounds for doing otherwise.

"The most damaging thing the president has done yet was the way he talked about Pence and his responsibilities," Cramer said.

The senators were converging on their secure location, an expansive conference room in the Hart Senate Office Building best known as a site of Supreme Court nomination hearings and the explosive testimony of James B. Comey Jr., the former FBI director, against Trump. And as they approached Hart 216, their predicament began sinking in. Pictures were popping up on their phones showing the rioters pillaging the Capitol, including one man toting a Confederate battle flag just outside the Senate chamber.

"Oh, wow," Cramer exclaimed, striding through the Hart basement. "That's right there, all right. How the heck did they get in?"

His mind, though, kept returning to the president.

"Sometimes I'm not even certain what his end goal is," he said of Trump, adding, "As you know, I'm one of his top loyal people in the Senate. He's never called me, none of his attorneys have ever called me. Sometimes I wonder if he even really—what the real motive is."

Five and a half years after Trump rode down the Trump Tower escalator to announce his campaign for president, his own allies were still wrestling with the same question: Just what is he doing?

Mitt Romney knew precisely what his nemesis had done.

The former Republican presidential candidate had been one of Trump's harshest Republican critics since the president sailed down that escalator in Trump Tower in June of 2015. Romney had eschewed a third presidential bid of his own that year, opting instead to bombard Trump from the sidelines. After the election, he had attempted a rapprochement with the president-elect, interviewing for the job of secretary of state over dinner at Jean-Georges in New York, only to be passed over for a former Exxon executive with no government experience.

Not long after, Romney had relocated to Utah, the official seat of his Mormon faith, and in 2018 he had taken a Senate seat there. Soon, he became the only Republican senator to vote for Trump's impeachment on the charge of pressuring the Ukrainian government to smear the Biden family.

Romney was every bit a politician, and throughout his career he had displayed a streak of opportunism that was pronounced even by the standards of that profession. But now, in the winter of his political life, he was free to speak his mind about a political figure who offended him to his core. In Mitt Romney's eyes, Donald Trump was a moral atrocity—as a man, father, husband, and president.

And Romney had never been so visibly and publicly angry as when he strode into Hart 216.

Just minutes earlier, he had exited the Senate chamber in fury upon hearing that the Capitol had been breached. He had been directed away from the mob by a fast-acting cop, Eugene Goodman, and by mere seconds he had escaped colliding with a throng of insurrectionists who would certainly have recognized him on sight. In Hart, Romney would call his home-state governor, Spencer Cox, to seek help protecting members of his family in Utah.

As he caught up with his colleagues, Romney's eyes were lit with rage, his face flushed.

"Unbelievable," he said of what was clearly now a dark day in American history.

"This is what the president has caused today, instigating this—this insurrection," he spat out.

It was a national humiliation.

"It's what this says to the country and the world," Romney said. "The only time this ever happened before was in the Civil War."

Then he stormed off, joining his dazed colleagues in the hangar-size room as they were phoning aides and relatives to tell them they were, at least for the moment, all right. Others could not avert their gaze from the pictures on their phones: The Senate chamber had been breached. There would be no peaceful transfer of power in America in 2021.

*   *   *

This book is an account of a political emergency in the United States—the story of how the country reached and survived a moment when carrying out the basic process of certifying an election became a mortally dangerous task.

During a period of two years, stretching from the onset of the coronavirus pandemic through the crucial legislative battles of the new Biden administration, Americans saw their nation's two-party system and the electoral process itself put to an extraordinary test. Not since 1968—a year of political assassinations and mass riots at home, and calamity on the battlefield abroad—has American democracy endured such a period of crisis.

In this time, it became inescapably clear that American politics had become not just a contest between parties or factions or regions, or even between the left and the right. The basic elements of American democracy—campaigning and voting and legislating—had been transformed into so many fronts in an existential battle for the survival of the democratic system. Many lawmakers had become mere tribunes for their radicalized constituents, only exacerbating the internal tribalism that was menacing the country more than any foreign foe.

The two parties were not merely adversaries, but enemies in a domestic cold war that had started to run hot. And one of those two parties was in thrall to an authoritarian demagogue who chose to attack the Congress rather than gracefully relinquish power.

Well before shots rang out at the Capitol on January 6, American political leaders were confronting a set of dire questions. In the face of multiple overlapping threats—including a once-in-a-century pandemic—could the basic institutions of American government function?

In spite of the country's profound divisions, could the United States still manage to hold a free and fair election and then usher in a new government that would faithfully carry out the people's business?

The answer to both questions has been a resounding: sort of.

Considered from a hopeful angle, the events of this period are indeed an affirmation of American political resilience amid an unheard-of assault from within.

The country, after all, did not collapse. A would-be strongman *was* defeated. The transfer of power from one White House to the next *did* happen. A new yet familiar president *has* sought to be a leader for all Americans in a way his predecessor never even feigned. The two parties *have* negotiated across the aisle in an attempt to improve the lives of their constituents.

But that triumphant narrative is not the only important vantage point on this period. Alongside those encouraging events, another timeline has unfolded in dark parallel.

Donald Trump has not been banished from national life, but instead remains the dominant force in his party and is bent on purging those few Republicans who won't bow to him.

The country's bitter political and social divisions have not eased, but have instead proven so pernicious as to undermine the distribution of miraculous vaccines against the coronavirus, badly worsening the spread of more contagious strains.

In contrast to past crises, the pandemic has not united the country but become a deadly new front in the culture wars.

Joe Biden and the Democratic leaders in Congress, Nancy Pelosi and Chuck Schumer, have only fitfully managed to rally their own ungainly coalition in the job of governing, let alone unite the country as a whole. Far from presiding as a soothing and self-assured national healer, Biden has appeared too often captive to the arcane internal politics of his own party, prone to undermining his own arguments, and too tangled in indecision about his priorities to speak plainly to the country about what they are.

And the next election, one that may well return Trump loyalists to power in Congress, is now only months away.

The former president's delusions about a stolen election—the fictions that inspired a riot on January 6—have lingered with corrosive force, warping his own party and catalyzing a wave of red-state voting restrictions aimed at cracking down on election fraud that did not happen. The fantasies of a Trump restoration have only deepened since his departure from the White House.

In May of 2021, about four months after leaving office, Trump telephoned the conservative editor Rich Lowry to tell him his magazine, *National Review*, would take off like a rocket if it recognized that he had actually won the election. In fact, Trump told Lowry, he expected to be reinstated by August, and Republicans would be put back in charge of the Senate once the supposedly pervasive corruption of the 2020 election was exposed.

It was beyond belief, Trump said, that Mitch McConnell did not seem to understand this.

The former president's comments were pure madness.

As central a figure as Trump is in America's political crisis, however, he is hardly the only consequential character in this period, and his aberrant conduct alone does not illustrate the depth of the country's challenge. Nor was his ascent unique to America—right-wing nationalism has been menacing liberal democracy around the globe. This is a more complicated, still-ongoing story that didn't end with one election.

* * *

The reporting for this book involved hundreds of interviews with senators, governors, members of the House, diplomats, lawyers, political strategists, entrepreneurs, foreign leaders, and officials at the highest ranks of both the Biden and Trump administrations. It is based on hundreds of pages of confidential documents and recordings of some of the most powerful people in the land, including Trump, Pelosi, Schumer, and McCarthy, speaking in unguarded candor to colleagues and friends.

The sources and voices in this story represent a great multiplicity of perspectives that agree on a single reality: that the future of American democracy is at risk.

This story unfolds in three parts. First is the pre-election phase: the period in which President Trump was mismanaging the coronavirus pandemic, terrorizing the nation's governors while offering medicine-wagon remedies for a catastrophic respiratory plague, and flailing in his efforts to define a message for his own upended campaign. Biden, meanwhile, was laboring to unify the Democratic Party, seeking a running mate and an agenda that could bring together a vast set of constituencies that shared a deep antipathy to Trump and little else.

Second is the period stretching from Election Day to the inauguration of President Biden and the (second) impeachment of former President Trump. In this stage, it was apparent that the country had rejected Trump, but the ultimate balance of power in Washington was very much in doubt. Democrats were contemplating the possibility of Biden's agenda smashing on the rocks of a Republican-controlled Senate, while Republicans were cowering in fear as Trump began to turn on his own party. It took an attack on the Capitol and a second Republican defeat in Georgia to complete the transition away from the Trump presidency.

Third, there was the phase from February onward, as President Biden attempted an acrobatic feat of leadership: pushing a liberal policy agenda of titanic ambition with the thinnest of majorities, while reaching across the aisle on other matters to show the country that bipartisan governance was still possible.

In this stage, it became grimly apparent that the two-party system remained dangerously unstable. One side—the Republican Party—was collapsing into a faction animated by their disgraced leader and a reflexive contempt for anything associated with the Democrats, including basic public-health precautions. Meanwhile, the Biden-led Democrats spent much of 2021 wrestling with their own roiling ideological and cultural divisions, as the coalition that ejected Trump from the White House proved full of challenging contradictions that frustrated Biden's ability to govern.

By the end of 2021, Biden had enjoyed one of the most productive first years of any new president, sweeping a multitrillion-dollar coronavirus relief bill into law, achieving a major bipartisan deal on infrastructure, and coming tantalizingly close to groundbreaking deals on family-welfare policy and climate change. Yet those achievements came at a price, as painstaking negotiations strained the cohesion of Biden's party and tested the patience of an electorate detached from the Washington wrangling and increasingly alarmed by the resurgent pandemic and the rising cost of consumer goods.

In many respects, Biden's landmark achievements appeared to be the work not of a rising new electoral majority, but of long-entrenched Democratic leaders who came of age in the 1960s and found their last great opportunity to legislate in the present crisis. And, as the year wore on, the limitations of those leaders and their mastery of Washington became increasingly clear. Their methods and instincts appeared in many cases painfully mismatched to the merciless politics of 2021.

Far from quickly erasing the Trump era, leaders in both parties have found the shadow of the last presidency has been longer and darker than they anticipated, coloring every major political decision and legislative negotiation of the Biden administration and shaping even the perceptions of American democracy overseas. Not long ago, Senator Chris Murphy of Connecticut recalled speaking in his office with the Egyptian ambassador to the United States and seeking to lobby him on matters of democratic reform and the human rights of political prisoners.

Look at what's going on in your own country, the envoy had fired back. You want to preach to us about democracy? I saw what happened on January 6.

Other accounts of this period have emphasized the tactical political decisions that shaped the outcome of the election, or the degree to which unelected elements of the country's government stood up to Donald Trump. During his short presidency, a cult of hero worship sprang up around a succession of non-politicians: lawmen like Robert S. Mueller III and physicians such as Anthony

Fauci; jurists such as Ruth Bader Ginsburg and John G. Roberts; and military men like James Mattis and, most recently, Mark Milley.

But in the end, a democracy can only succeed if its elected leaders are determined to sustain it, and if the voters to whom they answer maintain their faith in the system.

As of this writing, it is difficult to say with confidence that either the American elite or the American electorate has what it takes to defend the principles of free and representative government.

It is beyond the scope of this narrative to fully catalog the forces that have driven the United States to this baleful point. But even a simple timeline of the last quarter century in American life speaks powerfully to the reasons why many voters may have lost faith in the system.

In less than a third of an average American lifetime, the country endured a contested presidential race in 2000; the terror attacks of September 11, 2001; the long and disastrous wars in Iraq and Afghanistan; the financial crisis of 2008 and the Great Recession; the election of Donald Trump in 2016; and the devastation of the coronavirus pandemic in 2020. That is a catalog of failure and failure and failure.

It is a great irony of this time that it has fallen to Joe Biden, a man implicated in some of those failures, to pull the country back from the brink. In a dark hour, American voters turned not to a messianic outsider or to a man on horseback, but to a man of the gavel—a former Senate committee chairman before he was vice president—to redeem the worn-out system in which he toiled for half a century.

*　*　*

Joe Biden did not predict the events of January 6, but the fear of American system failure—of a breakdown in the institutions and values of democracy—haunted him throughout the 2020 election. He felt in his bones that his campaign against Donald Trump was a fight for American survival.

On the Sunday before Election Day, he said as much to Hakeem Jeffries, a

Brooklyn congressman who joined Biden on the campaign trail outside Philadelphia. Biden was upbeat about his chances, telling Jeffries that he felt good about the energy he was seeing on the trail. He believed he would win on November 3. Jeffries agreed: Democrats just needed to keep their foot on the gas through Election Day, he said.

It was the sort of small talk—equal parts rah-rah optimism and nervous energy—common at the end of campaigns.

Then Biden said something entirely uncommon in American political campaigns, Jeffries recalls.

"I certainly hope this works out," the future president said. "If it doesn't, I'm not sure we're going to have a country."

Chapter 1

Reciprocity

IT WAS HOURS before dawn in California when Gavin Newsom's phone rang. The fifty-two-year-old governor was accustomed to early calls from the East Coast, but under normal circumstances a 4:30 a.m. wake-up call from the White House was unusual.

These were anything but normal: The coronavirus pandemic had struck Newsom's state and the president of the United States wanted to talk about it.

Newsom, a Democrat, enjoyed a strange relationship with President Donald Trump. The two had known each other since long before Trump's election in 2016: When he was merely a celebrity real-estate developer, Trump had donated money to one of Newsom's campaigns, and Newsom's ex-wife, the television personality Kimberly Guilfoyle, was dating the president's eldest son. Trump and Newsom had dealt with each other in office a number of times, mainly around natural disasters like wildfires.

They had a disaster on their hands now.

It was the very beginning of March, and the respiratory pathogen that had already ravaged parts of China and Italy was in increasingly abundant evidence in the United States. The first case had been confirmed on January 21, in Washington State, and six weeks later West Coast governors and mayors were moving toward embracing strict clampdowns on public activity and commerce in order to slow the spread of the disease.

Trump had something more specific on his mind. The president was concerned about the *Grand Princess*, a cruise ship anchored off San Francisco. Passengers on the ship had been exposed to the coronavirus, and it was not yet clear what the local, state, or federal government would do with the people on board.

If we bring them ashore, Trump complained to Newsom, that could increase the total number of coronavirus cases in the country.

Trump's tone was equal parts flippant and frustrated. It was the kind of offhand remark Newsom had learned to expect from a president who routinely hectored him about why California did not do a better job "raking" its forests to clear out flammable debris—an almost comically reductive view of the state's complicated forest-management challenge.

The president was not a student of policy, Newsom knew, and sometimes he just sort of said stuff. You had to wait him out and then ask for what you wanted—which in this case, Newsom told him, was federal cooperation with bringing the boat into dock and processing the passengers for medical treatment or quarantine.

"Whatever you guys need," Trump said, according to Newsom's memory. "Let's bring it in."

On March 6, Trump blurted out in public what he'd told Newsom on the phone. While visiting the headquarters of the Centers for Disease Control and Prevention in Atlanta, he was asked a question about the cruise liner and replied that he would leave the decision to others, but added: "I don't need to have the numbers double because of one ship."

The media coverage was merciless. Here was the president of the United States, at the onset of a global pandemic, musing openly about massaging the infection stats by keeping a cruise ship at sea.

For a governor like Newsom, there was no free political capital to be spent on outrage. The difficult reality of the situation was that a world-historic threat to public health was under way, and the man in the Oval Office was a shallow political provocateur. Donald Trump was not interested in negotiating the fine points of legislation or learning the details of his public-health powers.

Indeed, as the House and Senate swept a $2.2 trillion aid package, known as the CARES Act, into law, Trump was not even on speaking terms with the top Democrat in Congress, House Speaker Nancy Pelosi. (In conversations with Newsom, Trump typically called her "your friend Nancy," while the Speaker would refer to "your friend Trump" in her own chats with the governor.)

The state, local, and federal officials tasked with managing the day-to-day response to the pandemic could choose to vent outrage about the lamentable realities of the Trump White House, or they could do their best to extract what they needed from the Trump administration by staying on the right side of Donald Trump.

And the president, a notoriously vengeful man, made it more than apparent that he was keeping track of who treated him like a friend and who did not.

Trump was watching, he told Newsom, for "the reciprocity."

"He used to say that even privately—that it was one of his favorite words," Newsom says. "It says everything and nothing at the same time."

* * *

That transactional worldview defined Donald Trump's presidency, including his response to the coronavirus pandemic. A proudly divisive leader who saw the executive branch as an extension of his own personality, he had governed for three years as a factional president before the pandemic struck—a champion of "his people" and a scourge of the other side, however he chose to define those groups at any given moment.

There had never been a pretense that Trump was a leader for all Americans, or that the White House saw no distinction between red states and blue states. He was the leader of his own coalition: a largely white, largely rural, largely working-class voting base that relished Trump's reactionary cultural politics, soldered to a largely white, largely urban, extremely wealthy donor base that valued his hostility to taxes and regulation.

If other constituencies factored into Trump's week-to-week thinking as president, they only did so because he thought they might be politically useful for one reason or another.

It was not the governing style of a president suited to pulling the country together in a crisis. But then, for three-quarters of his term, Trump had faced no crisis on the scale of the worst his immediate predecessors confronted. There had been no 9/11, no global economic collapse, no new foreign war, no truck bombs aimed at an American barracks in Beirut or a federal building in Oklahoma City. There had been episodes of horror, like the caging of migrant children on the Southern border, but for the most part those had been authored by the president and his aides rather than inflicted on the country from above or abroad.

When the pandemic struck, Trump did not have a plan for crushing it, or even a general theory of how to handle a public-health crisis.

After all, Trump had spent his whole term preparing to ask voters to give him another one based on a promise of continued peace and prosperity. For the first three-quarters of his presidency, unemployment had been way down. The stock market had been way up. Yes, Republican officials acknowledged, the president was thinly versed in the details of governing. Yes, he occasionally derided major American cities as vermin-infested hellholes and demonized people on the basis of their race or national origin. And, to be sure, his personality was problematic: Haley Barbour, the former Mississippi governor and Republican Party chairman, had taken to joking of Trump: "Narcissistic asshole syndrome is incurable after seventy."

But, Republicans insisted and mostly believed, many voters had decided to look past that and found Trump more palatable than the Democrats. Besides, their argument went, even if he was a factional leader, he was a factional leader who wound up creating wealth for everybody.

The coronavirus pandemic shattered that argument. The unemployment rate soared to nearly 15 percent by April. Trading on the stock market had to be repeatedly paused due to steep plunges. Entire sectors of the economy—restaurants, hotels, airlines, movie theaters—effectively collapsed overnight. And at the outset of the 2020 general election, there was no end in sight.

Reciprocity

Donald Trump needed a new plan—a plan to win a difficult campaign.

The president had anticipated that the 2020 race would be an easy one. He had dismissed many of his Democratic challengers in private conversations and lapped up rosy prognoses fed to him by solicitous advisers who went to great pains to keep bad news away from him.

There was no apparatus in place to give Trump a tougher prognosis about his chances of winning reelection, let alone one shaped by an unpredictable public-health crisis.

Long before 2020, some Republican leaders—people outside the White House—had feared that Trump would face a challenge from a mainstream, moderate Democrat who could win the election simply by making it a referendum on Trump's personality. The person many of them feared most was Joe Biden, the former vice president with an affinity for the blue-collar whites whose support Trump needed in overwhelming numbers.

But Trump did not fear Biden. Indeed, at a dinner with Chris Christie, the former governor of New Jersey, before the 2018 midterm elections, Trump belittled Biden as a joke, a weak old man—hardly someone to be feared. When Christie suggested Trump might be underestimating the grandfatherly Delawarean, the president scoffed at the idea. He told Christie he was more concerned about Elizabeth Warren or Bernie Sanders, since they would promise the voters huge new government benefits.

That, Trump said, would be popular.

Not that he would ever really admit to being concerned about any of his potential rivals.

Flying to California on Air Force One in September of 2019, shortly after Elizabeth Warren had drawn a massive crowd to Manhattan's Washington Square Park, Trump boasted to the White House press corps that he could have commanded the same numbers in the heart of one of America's most liberal cities.

"If I stood there, you'd have twenty thousand people," he insisted.

As Trump rambled on during the off-record session with reporters, his staff encouraged his bravado by applauding his stamina.

"Would Joe Biden do this?" Trump asked.

"We've been going on forty minutes," responded Stephanie Grisham, then the White House press secretary.

Trump's court of sycophants appalled more clear-eyed Republicans. In 2019, the president summoned the Senate majority leader, Mitch McConnell, to the White House, and instructed his aides to walk the Kentucky Republican through their presidential polling. They were forecasting a Trump romp from coast to coast, though there were still a few delicate strategic decisions for the campaign to resolve.

"Go get the hats," Trump told his assistant, Madeleine Westerhout. She returned, to McConnell's visible dismay, with one hat emblazoned with the slogan "Make America Great Again," and another hat reading "Keep America Great." Which one, Trump wanted to know, should he go with? And should he put an exclamation point on the end?

The Republican National Committee chair, Ronna McDaniel, took a strong position on that last point. A former member of the party establishment who had gone by her full family name, Ronna Romney McDaniel, until her affiliation with the Romney clan became inconvenient, McDaniel curried favor with Trump by ridiculing another humbled dynast. "It reminds us of 'Jeb!'" she said, according to a person in the room, alluding to Jeb Bush's campaign-sign punctuation. "No exclamation point."

Trump instantly agreed. McConnell remained impassive through the meeting.

Telling Trump what he wanted to hear had become a way of life for an entire political party. Brian Jack, the White House political director, told Senate strategists not to share their swing-state polling information with Trump, lest he react badly to the numbers. When Republicans approached the White House early in 2020 to express concern that Trump could be vulnerable in Georgia, a once-red state in the midst of a rapid demographic transformation, Jack responded: "There is no way you can convince the president he will win Georgia by less than ten points, let alone that he might lose."

But of course, few people were trying to dissuade Trump from thinking that way. After a meeting at the White House in July 2020, McConnell expressed bewilderment to an aide about the stream of happy news Trump's advisers were feeding to him. It was one of the bleakest periods in the campaign for Trump, but no one could have known it from the cheerful prognoses presented by the president's political team.

One Trump adviser in particular surprised McConnell—a fair-haired and sharp-featured man who offered only sunny forecasts to the president. McConnell wanted to know: Who was that guy?

Learning that it was Bill Stepien, Trump's new campaign manager, McConnell grumbled: He just tells Trump what he wants to hear.

There was a horde of accomplices in this presidential-level coddling, at every tier of the Republican Party, driven by an accurate conviction that Trump was a singularly popular figure on the right and that keeping his good favor was simply the cost of doing business.

Kevin McCarthy, the House minority leader, stood out from the pack as perhaps the most ingratiating major figure in the GOP. Having failed in a previous bid for Speaker of the House amid opposition from the right wing, McCarthy had no anchorage in his party's ideological waters—he was simply determined not to be outflanked on the MAGA wing.

He had worked in politics nearly his entire adult life, first as a junior aide to his predecessor in Congress, then as a state legislator before winning his House seat in 2006. In an early meeting with national party strategists during that campaign, McCarthy was up front about the scale of his ambitions: He was running for Congress, McCarthy said, because he planned to be the Speaker of the House.

Even as he rose, though, McCarthy retained the nose-against-the-glass style of a Bakersfield kid who wanted to make it big, always gazing longingly at the famous. In his case, that frequently meant quite literally showing off pictures of himself with movie stars. It also meant he was particularly vulnerable to the force field of political celebrity, first in Sacramento when Arnold Schwarzenegger became governor of California and then when Donald Trump became president of the United States.

McCarthy was always determined to be part of the in crowd, and so it came as no surprise, but rather as a source of amusement to his fellow Republicans when he sent Trump a jar of Starburst candy containing only the president's two favorite flavors. He was just as determined to present a menu of House candidates to the president that fit his tastes.

He made a habit of briefing Trump on McCarthy's own favored congressional recruits, making sure the president knew of the many nice things they had said about him in the past. On rare occasions when McCarthy wanted to enlist a candidate who had been critical of Trump, he would orchestrate displays of loyalty to appease the president. He instructed Carlos Gimenez, the mayor of Miami-Dade County and a former Trump critic, to tweet an expression of admiration for Trump in order to secure the support of the White House, and Gimenez had quickly obliged as he entered a crucial House race.

In sessions with House and Senate strategists, Trump would veer back and forth between issuing edicts of intimidation and playing the class clown to a chortling audience. In meetings with McConnell and his advisers, the president would rail against Martha McSally, the appointed Arizona senator who was running for election in her own right. A former fighter pilot and survivor of sexual assault, McSally had denounced Trump after the 2016 publication of the *Access Hollywood* tape that showed the future president bragging about groping women. Like most Republicans, McSally had run back to Trump soon after, and she was campaigning in 2020 as a supporter of the White House. But Trump himself had not forgotten.

"She's a horrible candidate," Trump would say. "Just terrible. No one likes her."

McConnell would try to speed through the races where he knew Trump didn't like the leading Republican Senate candidates, often attempting to skip discussion of Maine entirely, where Susan Collins was running for reelection and had not endorsed Trump for a second term. But in several meetings Trump could not resist weighing in with what he might call locker-room talk about Collins's challenger, Sara Gideon, the telegenic Speaker of the Maine House of Representatives.

"Sara Gideon—very attractive. Very attractive," Trump said in one session, according to a person in the room.

Then he added a joke at the first lady's expense: "Not that I've looked at a woman that way in five years—five years at least." (He and Melania Trump were married in 2005.)

But the president's threats were no joke. Republicans who had stepped out of line in more memorable ways usually found themselves defeated, driven into retirement, or pleading for forgiveness. As he prepared to run for reelection to the Senate in North Carolina in 2020, Thom Tillis recognized he had to make up with Trump for a severe infraction: In February 2019, he had written a column in the *Washington Post* criticizing the president's use of emergency powers to repurpose federal money for a wall on the Mexican border. Trump had not forgiven him, and voters at home had noticed. Tillis was consistently running behind Trump on the ballot in polling for both parties.

"What am I supposed to do? Like go in and just, like, grovel?" Tillis had asked an adviser.

The answer had been, basically, yes. If Tillis—or any other politician—wanted to avoid the wrath of the country's most powerful Republican politician, or if they wanted the speedy cooperation of the White House on matters of substance, then they needed to show the president he could count on them to behave with lasting gratitude and extreme deference.

It was the logic of a protection racket, more or less. You could be on Team Trump, with some modest guarantee of political safety, or you could be against the president.

That, in Donald Trump's mind, was the meaning of reciprocity.

* * *

The president's operating style took on new significance with a deadly illness sweeping the country. Scores of governors were desperate to secure support and resources from the federal government, many of them Democrats who either had no relationship with Trump or a purely hostile one. As they scrambled to connect with the White House, they quickly ran into Newsom's calculus: Trump was most interested in helping people he got along with, and regions of the country he saw as Trump country.

By 2020, this had become predictable to those in the political arena, and it was easy to grow inured to his zero-sum outlook. But it represented a jarring break from civic tradition in a country where presidents usually put the full weight of the federal government behind communities in crisis. It did not matter to Bill Clinton after the Oklahoma City bombing that he had no chance to carry the state, any more than it mattered to George W. Bush on September 11, 2001, that New York would never vote for him.

Trump was different. In 2020, the American president and his advisers had no compunction about inserting politics, personal grievances, and public-relations gimmicks into urgent matters of state. As the coronavirus struck, governors found it difficult to secure the resources they needed urgently from the federal government.

JB Pritzker, the Democratic governor of Illinois, spoke to Trump on March 23 to plead with him to ramp up production of personal protective equipment. His state needed millions of masks; like many other governors, he wanted to Trump to invoke the Defense Production Act, a Korean War–era law that allowed the federal government to mandate the manufacturing of materials required for national defense.

Trying to connect with Trump on a personal level, Pritzker, a wealthy investor, told him: Mr. President, I'm a businessman and I don't like the government interfering with the commercial market, but right now we're dealing with chaos in the market for these goods. The federal government needs to act.

The president heard him out, but when the call was over Pritzker told an aide he was unsure he had gotten through to Trump at all.

Even as some of the country's largest states were locking down virtually all public activity in the hope of saving their hospital systems from collapse, Trump declared on March 24 that he wanted the United States "opened up and just raring to go" by Easter Sunday, April 12—a fantastical timeline that appealed to the president for reasons of bravado and branding.

Then on March 28 Trump announced he was considering a drastic action to contain the coronavirus. He hoped to treat it, effectively, as a blue-state illness, imposing a federal quarantine on the states of New York, New Jersey, and Connecticut. Speaking to reporters at the White House, Trump explained he had been urged in that direction by "a lot of the states that are infected but don't have a big problem." He mentioned the governor of Florida, the enthusiastically pro-Trump Republican Ron DeSantis, as someone he had spoken to that day.

"They're having problems down in Florida," Trump said, with "heavily infected" people arriving there from other states.

The announcement sent a shock wave through the tristate area, enraging the local Democratic authorities who were already overwhelmed with coronavirus cases and now feared that an unenforceable federal quarantine decree would be inflicted on their beleaguered administrations. Andrew Cuomo, at the time a national hero to Democrats for his showy pandemic briefings as governor of New York, publicly warned the measure would amount to a "declaration of war."

In New Jersey, Phil Murphy, a first-term governor, was scrambling to reach the incoming White House chief of staff, Mark Meadows. A former leader of the hard-line House Freedom Caucus who had insinuated himself into Trump's inner circle, Meadows had barely started on the job when the pandemic crashed into what would become the final year of the Trump administration. As the president was floating draconian movement restrictions on the country's largest population center, Meadows struggled to understand how such an order could even be carried out.

Murphy's answer to him was simple: It could not.

Ned Lamont, the governor of Connecticut, was pleading the same case with Meadows. A quarantine, he argued, would be a total disaster. "We've got, you know, five hundred roads going in and out, trains—you can't shut this down," he recalls saying.

A few hours later Lamont got a call from the president. He was backing off the quarantine idea.

"We're just going to ask you to voluntarily limit traffic between your communities, something like that," Trump told him, by Lamont's account.

"I think it's the right thing to do," Lamont answered, with bounteous gratitude. "I appreciate you doing this."

The whole uproar followed a familiar pattern from the first three years of the Trump presidency: a hugely disruptive proposal introduced casually by the president, only to be quickly abandoned once predictable backlash and practical reality set in. But the stakes were higher now, and Trump's impulsive, highly political pronouncements had the potential to do damage on an entirely different scale.

Like their colleague in California, Murphy and Lamont knew they could not afford to be cut off from the White House, or to live in perpetual, helpless fear of whatever Trump's next edict might be. And in the early days of the pandemic, the president was all over the map—one day endorsing lockdowns, another calling for a swift return to life as usual, sometimes seemingly dependent on whom he had last spoken to or what state he was focused on.

Yet most governors did not have Newsom's easy cell-phone relationship with the president. So Murphy chose to communicate with him by other means: He went on Fox News, tangling with Tucker Carlson for fifteen minutes over New Jersey's crackdown on the pandemic and what Carlson called "the suffering that this lockdown has caused."

Without the lockdown, Murphy countered, the "alternative would have been multiples of this."

It was not a terribly rewarding interview, but the next morning Murphy found it had had the desired effect. His phone rang, and it was the president of the United States. Trump had seen the interview and he wanted Murphy to know he agreed with him. The Fox guys, he said, were bonkers about the pandemic—Hannity especially, Trump said.

That guy is obsessed with "the Swedish model" of looser public-health restrictions, the president told Murphy.

"Listen, he's wrong," Trump said, according to Murphy's memory.

The very next day, on April 17, Trump showed why it was dangerous for governors to stray from his good side. Even as he privately assured Murphy and Newsom that they could count on his support for their pandemic-management strategies, he publicly spewed venom at another pair of Democrats who were taking essentially the same approach to the crisis.

News media had begun to cover protesters in Michigan, Virginia, and Minnesota who were defying the governors' public-health policies, and Trump was only too glad to amplify their angry complaints against the Democratic governors in all three states: Gretchen Whitmer, Ralph Northam, and Tim Walz.

"LIBERATE MICHIGAN!" he thundered on Twitter. "LIBERATE VIRGINIA, and save your great 2nd amendment. It is under siege!" . . . "LIBERATE MINNESOTA!"

Walz, the Minnesota governor, experienced Trump's sudden attack as more than a social-media broadside.

"It brought armed people to my house," Walz says. "It put the security folks a little bit more on high alert."

But he, too, calculated that he could not afford to escalate a conflict with Trump. In phone calls with the president, the governor says he tried to engage Trump on what, exactly, he was demanding from Minnesota.

"I just really, really want to clarify," Walz told Trump. "What do we mean 'liberated' from?"

Trump talked past the question, Walz says: "I never got a response."

Trump was not only burdening Democratic governors with his wildly careening approach to the pandemic. In private, Republican governors had begun holding conference calls where they shared their strategies for the pandemic away from the eyes and ears of White House aides. Asa Hutchinson of Arkansas, a sober conservative who had served in Congress in the Clinton era, blames Trump to this day for sabotaging his own battle with the coronavirus at the state level.

"President Trump's comments, his rhetoric, and his almost flippant attitude in some contexts made it difficult for a governor like me to really push the seriousness of the medical emergency that we're in," Hutchinson says.

One Republican governor drew Trump's personal ire. When Brian Kemp, the Republican governor of Georgia, announced in mid-April that he was allowing businesses to reopen with certain masking requirements, the White House responded with fury. While Trump was generally impatient to return to life as usual, he and his aides disliked Kemp for political reasons and treated his pandemic-management plans with a skepticism they did not apply to other Republicans.

Kemp had been nominated for governor in 2018 thanks to Trump's personal support, a fact of which the president never tired of reminding him. But Trump had long since soured on him, in part because Kemp declined to appoint a trusted Trump lieutenant in Congress, Doug Collins, to an open Senate seat.

When Kemp's name came up from that point on, Trump would often repeat a sour refrain. "He's fucking weak, he's just a terrible governor, and I'm the guy who got him there," the president would say, according to one strategist who heard the rant repeatedly.

As Kemp prepared to reopen his state, Trump conveyed his displeasure in a phone call, commanding the governor to rescind his reopening plans. Trump's pandemic-response adviser, Dr. Deborah Birx, had been pushing hard internally against Georgia's plan, and for once Trump seemed to be listening to her. "I got you elected," Trump reminded Kemp, according to one person present for the conversation. When the tense call was over, Trump instructed two aides, Brian Jack, the political director, and Kayleigh McEnany, the press secretary, to follow up with Kemp and "figure this out."

In a second call, the two aides pressed Kemp further, with McEnany taking the lead. A thirty-two-year-old former cable TV pundit, McEnany told Kemp, the fifty-six-year-old chief executive of a major American state, to withdraw his reopening order. Kemp protested, reminding McEnany that Trump himself had been urging governors to reopen. McEnany told Kemp that if he did not bend to Trump's preferences, then the president would come out against his plans in public.

On April 22, the president made Kemp pay a price for his disobedience. "I disagree with him on what he is doing," Trump said at a press briefing. "I think it's too soon."

On April 30, Murphy was welcomed to a meeting in the Oval Office. There was no attempt to strong-arm him into hastening the end of lockdowns. After the meeting, Trump pulled the governor aside and led him into the old private dining room adjacent to the Oval. There, he showed the Democrat a precious document.

"Did you see what happened in 2016?" Trump asked him, presenting the Democrat with a copy of the electoral map from that year.

When Murphy answered in the affirmative, the president probed: "Do you think I can win New Jersey?"

Murphy, a gregarious former Goldman Sachs executive, paused to contemplate his options. Should he flatter the president further and say yes? Maybe, Murphy recalls thinking, he could goad Trump into burning money on the fool's errand of competing in deep-blue New Jersey.

The stakes were too high.

"You know what, I don't see it," he told the president.

Trump did not mind. For whatever reason—perhaps Murphy's sizable personal fortune—the president had long ago decided this guy was one of the good ones. There would be no "LIBERATE NEW JERSEY" tweets that day. Instead, Trump led Murphy and two of his aides into another adjoining room, one that the wide-eyed governor was shocked to find full of MAGA gear—hats, cuff links, trays, the works. The display, Murphy says, "looked like the gift shop at Disney."

"They literally hand you a shopping bag," the governor recalls, "and you took anything you'd like."

That same week, the American death toll from the coronavirus topped sixty thousand.

As the spring progressed, Trump's interest in managing the pandemic only waned further. He stopped showing up for weekly calls with the nation's governors, leaving that job to his vice president, Mike Pence, who was managing the White House's coronavirus task force. The president's attention was on other matters, like how quickly he could resume holding large public events on the campaign trail.

But the president's Cosa Nostra–adjacent operating style remained.

Looking ahead, Trump was determined not to let the pandemic turn his nominating convention into a pale version of the spectacular, glitzy MAGA-fest it deserved to be.

The Republican convention was set to be in Charlotte, North Carolina, but the city's Democratic mayor and the state's Democratic governor had grave concerns about allowing the events to proceed. Roy Cooper, the governor, told the Republican National Committee in no uncertain terms that there could be no dense, unmasked, indoor gathering in his state. On May 29, the president called up Cooper directly to tell him that was a problem.

Trump opened the call with a nakedly partisan taunt. "You'll be thrilled, as a Democrat, to know we're up to almost two hundred and seventy judges, can you believe it?" he began, referring to his latest slate of conservative nominations to the federal bench. Then he brought up the subject at hand.

"I know that you are a little bit of a shutdown type," Trump told Cooper. "I understand both sides of that equation, as you can understand, but—how are you doing toward the arena, toward the convention?"

Cooper, a former small-town lawyer with the voice and demeanor of a likable high school principal, explained to Trump that the state was in "Phase Two" of its reopening, which meant there were still strict limitations on mass gatherings and commercial activity.

"We've been talking to the RNC, and we've been talking about the fact that, you know—we know we've got to scale back with people inside, and we wanted to get options for what the RNC wanted," Cooper said.

Cooper simply would not guarantee a nineteen-thousand-person indoor rally in his state's largest city in the middle of the summer. He did not understand why Trump could not grasp the urgent public-health reasons for his hesitation. Didn't Trump want to protect his supporters who would flock to the arena in Charlotte?

"Aren't you worried about them, particularly?" Cooper asked.

"No, no, I'm not," Trump said.

The president told Cooper they had both been right to support lockdowns early on, bragging that his administration had probably saved 2 million lives. But there came a point where enough was enough.

"What people don't realize," the president explained, "it's a tiny percentage of 1 percent of the people that really get hit, and they're generally older people and older people with a bad heart problem, or diabetes or something. But it's really a tiny percentage."

Trump was uninterested in a scaled-down event. It was essential, he said, to "fill up the arena—otherwise we'll cancel the whole damn thing.

"I've never had an empty seat, from the day I came down the escalator," Trump said, adding, "I don't want to be sitting in a place that's, you know, 50 percent empty or more."

Cooper thought he still had an opening to press his case, stroking the president's ego. "But you've been smart since this pandemic began," he said, "and you haven't been playing to large crowds since this pandemic began."

"No, I haven't been playing to any crowds—no, I gave it up," Trump said, in a tone that conveyed that that was part of the problem. "I'd like to—I think we'll start very soon, because there are many arenas that will accept that."

"You have other states where the numbers are lower," the president went on, joking about the Chinese province where the virus originated: "Hey, Roy—the Wuhan numbers are better."

Trump stressed to Cooper he had plenty of other options for siting his convention.

"There's a lot of Trump country out there," he said.

The president closed the call by reminding Cooper that his administration had done much for North Carolina during the pandemic, and telling Cooper that he could expect to hear from the RNC to follow up on his convention requests.

"We got you the ventilators, testing—we got you a lot, and that's okay," Trump said, making clear enough that it wasn't just "okay," and he could use something for the effort. "We've been good to you. We gave you the National Guard—gave you a lot."

The president's worldview, dividing the nation into Trump country and everybody else, pervaded the administration, and it afflicted even governors who tried hard to navigate Trump's towering ego. When Ned Lamont's blue state of Connecticut was competing to host a major pharmaceutical production facility against a site in Canada, the Democrat called up a number of senior Trump administration officials to ask for help. The facility would ultimately produce vaccines, Lamont argued. It should be in the United States.

It was Peter Navarro, the volatile America-first trade adviser, who gave Lamont the most direct signal on the administration's interest in the thorny details of international business competition. In a phone call, Lamont says, Navarro told him he was not interested in helping the governor navigate a negotiation against "the fucking Canucks."

Lamont, a patrician businessman whose great-grandfather had run J.P. Morgan, responded in a level deadpan.

"Well, Mr. Navarro, you say it so well, maybe you should send a message to the head of the pharmaceutical firm," he recalls saying.

But Navarro did not want to help Connecticut. His prickly retort told Lamont everything he needed to know about the White House's view of the divided and suffering country.

"I don't want to get involved with blue-state politics," Navarro said, according to Lamont.

* * *

On March 12, a few days after President Trump complained to Gavin Newsom about bringing the *Grand Princess* ship ashore, Elizabeth Warren got a phone call of her own.

The progressive senator was standing in her dining room in Cambridge, Massachusetts, in the dimming light of a late winter afternoon, when she found herself speaking with Joe Biden.

The two had been declared rivals for nearly a year, battling for the 2020 Democratic presidential nomination as two of the party's leading candidates. But they had been competitors for far longer than that: Their respectful but hard-fought rivalry dated back nearly two decades, to Warren's days as a bankruptcy-law professor strenuously opposing Biden's quest to tighten the bankruptcy code on behalf of the credit card companies that made his home state their headquarters.

Biden had won that old fight—his tough-on-debtors bill passed over Warren's impassioned objections in 2005—and only a week before this phone call he had all but triumphed in the Democratic presidential primary. Warren had ended her campaign on March 5, after Biden romped through the Super Tuesday states. Only Bernie Sanders remained as an increasingly token opponent to Biden's coronation.

"I've decided I want to adopt your approach on bankruptcy," Biden told Warren, by her recollection. "Are you okay with that, if I do that?"

"Okay?" Warren replied. "I'm over the moon."

Biden went further, discoursing at some length to Warren about the importance of the bankruptcy code and what adopting Warren's approach would mean to families living on the economic margins of American society. Given the intensity of their past clashes on the subject, and Biden's seemingly immovable commitment to his home state's credit card industry, it was a staggering reversal—a bit like Donald Trump calling up a liberal immigration activist and making the case for mass amnesty.

When the call was over, Warren, a skeptical character by nature, was pleased but not quite sure what to make of it. "Sweetie," she called out to her husband, the Harvard Law professor Bruce Mann. "Guess who just called."

It was nice to hear Biden finally moving in her direction, Warren thought. But of course, he was after her endorsement, and he had not exactly said what it would mean for him to take up her approach on bankruptcy. Maybe—only maybe, she thought—he would actually do something real on the issue.

The next day, on March 13, Warren was delighted to see in the news that Biden had endorsed her plan for bankruptcy reform during a virtual event with voters in Illinois. Biden said he hoped voters on the left would come to see "there's a whole range of things we agree on."

That moment, Warren says, was when you could "hear the music starting to change" from the Biden campaign.

The Biden soundtrack, up to that point, had been a pretty bland assortment of tunes. The former vice president had stuck close to one message throughout the primary, about restoring the country's soul and proving that Donald Trump was an aberration in the American presidency. Unlike his top rivals, Sanders and Warren, Biden had not electrified large parts of the Democratic coalition by promising a root-and-branch overhaul of the American economy. Indeed, in his early days as a presidential candidate, he had promised a room of wealthy donors that "nothing would fundamentally change" for them under a Biden presidency.

But the cautious monotony of the Biden campaign was not driven only by a resistance to left-wing ideas. He had not campaigned as a fierce progressive, but neither had he waged his primary bid as an articulate centrist with an inventive set of ideas from the political middle. When he clashed with left-wing opponents during debates, Biden had typically questioned not the substance of their ideas but their political viability: He had not, like Pete Buttigieg, delivered a detailed critique of the mechanics of socialized medicine, but had instead stressed that there was no path through Congress for the progressives' grandly expensive plan.

Other moderate Democrats had introduced signature policy initiatives into the conversation: Cory Booker's proposal for "baby bonds" to wipe out child-hood poverty, or Michael Bennet's "Medicare X" plan for an aggressive public health insurance option. The Biden campaign had put out white papers on pol-icy, many of them focused on expanding the achievements of the Obama admin-istration (or, as his campaign dubbed it, the "Obama-Biden administration"). But when Biden was on the stump, he seldom talked about them in detail.

Joe Biden's signature idea was defeating Donald Trump and bringing the country back together, and Democratic primary voters had rewarded him for it.

In the space of a month, Biden had gone from back-to-back humiliations in Iowa and New Hampshire to dominating the Democratic pack in South Carolina and the Super Tuesday primaries. Some of it had been luck: Biden could not have planned on a split decision in Iowa between Sanders and Butti-gieg, or on Warren cleanly decapitating the then-surging Bloomberg campaign on a Las Vegas debate stage, or on Sanders strangely choosing to spend the run-up to South Carolina litigating his views on the Castro regime in Cuba.

But a lot of it had been the basic wisdom of Biden's campaign strategy. He and his advisers understood that the Democratic Party was obsessed with beat-ing Trump, and that the party's leftward lurch had been overstated in the media. There was only one candidate in the race who was known to every Democrat in the country, liked by the bulk of them, especially African Americans, and seen overwhelmingly as a strong bet to beat Trump in the fall. That was Joe Biden.

Sometimes politics is not all that complicated.

Yet Biden's lightning victory in the Democratic race presented a new set of challenges, every one of them compounded by the onset of the pandemic. The disease had frozen the nation's public life, effectively snuffing out Sanders's ability to mount a drawn-out underdog candidacy for the nomination. But it had also complicated Biden's ability to reach out to the left and unify his own party. There could be no great unity rally with Sanders or Warren, no laying on of hands from the chiefs of the progressive movement to show the grass roots that Biden was now their guy.

And Biden's spare policy agenda was now transparently unequal to the political moment. He could not simply campaign on beating Trump, buffing up the Affordable Care Act, and restoring American alliances around the world. The economy was a smoking crater, and mobile morgues were being deployed to manage the dead in major American cities. A return-to-normalcy campaign was no longer an option.

In other words, Donald Trump wasn't the only presumptive nominee who needed a whole new approach to the race.

*　*　*

Warren was not the only former Biden rival eager to see him drive an ambitious message in the general election. Cory Booker, the New Jersey senator who had pulled out of the primary fight in mid-January, urged Biden in March to embrace his status as a transitional figure in American politics—not in the sense of being a placid caretaker, but as someone who could heal the country and address some of its most urgent policy needs before passing the baton to others.

During a car ride between Flint, Michigan, and Detroit, on the day he endorsed his onetime opponent, Booker urged Biden to present himself as a "bridge to the next generation" who could unify the country. (That night, at Biden's final rally before the next day's primary, the former vice president would do just that, standing with Booker, Kamala Harris, and the state's governor, Gretchen Whitmer, and calling himself "a bridge.")

But Booker also told Biden that being a transitional president did not have to mean going small on policy.

"If you just stood for the American public, and said I'm only going to do things that 70 percent of Americans want—that's what we need, is a sense that our president is fighting for all of us," Booker recalls telling Biden, offering mainstream gun-control policy as an example.

Locked down only days later at his Delaware home, a sixty-eight-hundred-square-foot lakefront estate, Biden set about mastering two parallel challenges: uniting the Democratic Party and mastering the complexities of the coronavirus pandemic.

It was an almost entirely virtual exercise. Unlike Trump, Biden was in no mood to be cavalier about his personal safety in the pandemic. Then seventy-seven, he was unambiguously part of a high-risk group. His brainstorming sessions on policy and his efforts at intra-party diplomacy took place over endless phone calls and Zoom sessions, including hours-long, near-daily sessions with a team of health and economics experts counseling him on the mechanics of pandemic response.

For all his public avuncularity, Biden had developed a reputation over decades as a hard-driving, unforgiving boss, who would surround himself with highly credentialed experts and then push their expertise to the point of exhaustion. Briefing the former vice president could become what some aides called a game of "stump the staffer"—a sustained effort by Biden to query and query and query and query until whatever unfortunate adviser he chose to test that day admitted he had asked something they could not answer.

During his pandemic briefings, Biden did not just want to know how much money Congress was allocating for economic relief, but the exact paths that money would follow from the federal treasury into state-level agencies, and from there into the hands of businesses and consumers. He did not just want to know how many coronavirus cases there were, and where, but how the federal government was distributing protective equipment, where it was getting it from, and how it was moving around the country.

It was painstaking preparatory work—work that kept Biden out of public view, and that did not necessarily bring him any closer to the imaginative vision of American recovery he now needed for the campaign.

But Biden knew he needed that vision, and he said as much to another one of his former presidential rivals.

One of the Biden campaign's short-lived ideas for putting its candidate back in public view, without leaving his Wilmington property, was launching a podcast hosted by Biden himself. And on May 4, two months into lockdown, Biden taped an episode with Andrew Yang, the nonprofit executive who had run a quixotic campaign for the Democratic nomination as a champion of a universal basic income program that would pay out a chunk of cash to every American on a monthly basis.

Before the recording began, according to Yang, Biden told him the country was at a decisive juncture. During the primary, Yang says, Biden had not been associated with "big, bold, transformative change." The Biden who spoke with him that day struck a different tone.

The country, Biden told Yang in private, needed "a new New Deal"—an update on the colossal program of public works, social-welfare benefits, and business regulation introduced by Franklin Roosevelt during the Great Depression.

"It got me thinking," Yang says, "about how Joe recognized what the country needed was something big and transformative."

The question for Biden was what that something should be.

The task of pulling together the Democratic coalition was just as complicated. Biden had won the nomination by marshaling a diverse alliance of voters on the center-left, from older Black voters in the South to wealthy suburban whites in the North and the vestiges of the Democratic white working class in the Midwest. All saw him as the best bet to beat Trump, and to hold back the excesses of what they often called "the Bernie wing."

But if Biden's base represented a strong majority of the party, there was another 40 percent or so to be reckoned with: younger and more liberal voters, including younger people of color and Latino voters of all ages, who had leaned toward Sanders in the final weeks of the primary. Biden did not know these voters as well, nor did he know many of their heroes in Congress.

It was not that Biden did not have relationships with a younger generation of Democratic leaders. He did. He had campaigned hard for many of them in the 2018 midterm elections, draping his arm around Conor Lamb and comparing the young prosecutor to his own beloved, deceased son, Beau, on the way to lifting Lamb to victory in a Pittsburgh-area House district. He had invited Lauren Underwood, a thirty-two-year-old nurse who became the youngest Black woman to serve in Congress after winning a tough Illinois race in 2018, to meet with him at his Washington office. There, he had counseled her on how to navigate a Congress that was inhospitable to young people, as it had been to him nearly a half century earlier.

It was not that Biden had not thought about how to excite liberal Democrats in the general election. He had. In a meeting with Lisa Blunt Rochester, the House member from Delaware, before announcing his campaign, Biden had told her that he was strongly considering the idea of a female running mate. He seemed to know that his identity—his age, race, and gender—meant he would need a very different kind of partner in the fall.

But the ideological and cultural gulfs in the Democratic Party were persistent and serious, and there was no question on which side of them Biden and his inner circle resided. At one point in the general election, Mike Donilon, one of Biden's closest advisers, expressed bewilderment to a friend about the cultural attitudes he saw even among the younger staff on the Biden campaign: "These kids," Donilon complained, "don't even want us putting Thomas Jefferson references in speeches!"

In what became a defining political choice of his general-election candidacy, Biden tried to solve two problems at once: Under pressure to rally support on the left and to come up with a new set of ideas to match a moment of national crisis, he opted for an approach that was at once highly efficient and thoroughly unconventional. Flipping the traditional approach of hewing to the base in the primary and running toward the middle in the general election, Biden moved left after claiming the nomination. He decided he would adopt many of the policies of his progressive rivals to unite his party and flesh out his own comparatively bare-bones governing plans.

Exactly how far left he would move—well, there would be a gradual process for figuring that out.

That March call to Warren was only the beginning: In May, Biden empaneled a slate of policy task forces, bringing in centrists like Lamb to work alongside progressives like Alexandria Ocasio-Cortez, with a mandate to craft a more daring agenda that both broad wings of the party could embrace. If it ultimately became an agenda that conflicted with certain other Biden campaign themes—restoring national unity, reaching across the aisle, and working with Republicans—well, that was a tension he could work out later.

To some people close to the Biden campaign, the months and months of introspection and policy negotiation, carried out in no small part from Biden's literal basement, felt like a dangerously passive posture at the outset of a campaign against a beast of an opponent. From their perspective, the Biden campaign staff seemed all too willing to leave Biden indoors, keeping him away from the cameras and boom mics that could offer him daily opportunities for verbal miscues.

And Biden himself seemed to grow sensitive, as time went on, to the limits of his public profile. As he began to review campaign polling in preparation for selecting a vice-presidential candidate, one consistent trend popped out of the numbers. People liked Biden, but their impressions of him were pretty vague.

Biden asked one adviser with concern: "People don't really know that much about me, do they?"

It was a grave worry for some of Biden's oldest advisers, and by the late spring, Ron Klain, Biden's once and future chief of staff, had taken to sending blunt, repetitive notes to the Biden campaign high command. He often typed in all-capital letters, banging away again and again at the same impatient message:

GET HIM OUT OF THE BASEMENT. YOU ARE LOSING THE ELECTION.

*　*　*

Klain was wrong about that. As passive and invisible as Biden's campaign was on most days, he still had the upper hand by late spring over a president who was badly bungling not one but two national crises.

The murder of George Floyd on May 25 profoundly changed the character of the presidential race, thrusting issues of race, policing, and social justice to the heart of the political debate as in no other campaign since the civil rights era.

A forty-six-year-old Black man in Minneapolis, Floyd had been brutally killed by a police officer, Derek Chauvin, who knelt on his neck for nine minutes in the course of arresting him on a trivial charge. The entire killing was captured on video, and as the nation watched Floyd lose his life it reacted with volcanic moral indignation. Tens of millions of protesters filled the streets and parks and plazas of major cities and tiny towns, shattering pandemic-era restrictions on public gatherings and jolting Congress into a new set of talks on a federal police-reform law. In Minneapolis, the site of the murder, police struggled to maintain control of the city as demonstrations turned violent and a police precinct building was set aflame.

Biden even left his basement: In Delaware, Blunt Rochester saw a darkening mood in Wilmington and believed the moment demanded leadership from the state's favorite son. The congresswoman was one of only a few Black women with clout in the Biden campaign, an operation dominated by the former vice president's overwhelmingly white circle of longtime advisers. Blunt Rochester bombarded those people with phone calls, warning that an ugly kind of upheaval could be at hand. Biden knew the potential consequences of that, she told them. He had lived through the 1968 riots in Wilmington, and the long occupation of the city by National Guard troops afterward.

Her message was simple, Blunt Rochester says: "We've got to get out."

On Sunday, May 31, Biden visited an area of Wilmington that had been the site of large protests the previous night and was photographed kneeling and speaking to a young Black man and his child there. "We are a nation in pain right now," he tweeted, "but we must not allow this pain to destroy us."

President Trump was delivering a very different message.

Reciprocity

* * *

If the murder of George Floyd spurred Biden into a slightly more active mode of campaigning, it seemed to trigger something else entirely in Trump. The president had long since tired of managing—or even pretending to manage—a virus that was obstructing his reelection campaign, and he had stopped giving daily briefings on the pandemic after recommending off-the-cuff that Americans try injecting bleach or sunlight as a cure for the pathogen. One of his close allies, Jim Justice, the governor of West Virginia, had pleaded with the president to return to the briefing room and try speaking frankly to the country about the disease again, but Trump rebuffed the idea.

The president was tired, it seemed, of feeling like the victim of forces beyond his control. He wanted to be in charge, and he wanted the public to know he was in charge.

On June 1, the day after Biden's outing to downtown Wilmington, Trump convened the nation's governors on a call. It was ostensibly one of the state executives' weekly gatherings to discuss the coronavirus with the administration, but when the governors logged on that Monday it was immediately clear they were in for a different kind of meeting. Trump was on the call, joined by a team of advisers that included Bill Barr, the attorney general, and Mark Esper, the secretary of defense.

Savaging the racial-justice protesters around the country as "terrorists," Trump urged the governors to exact "retribution" while demanding a swift return to public order. Esper, a buttoned-down West Point graduate and former Raytheon executive, advised the governors that they should seek to "dominate the battlespace" in their states. In the Rose Garden later that day, Trump threatened to deploy federal troops if the governors did not move swiftly enough.

The executives were in shock. Up early at the governor's residence in Salem, Oregon, the Democratic governor, Kate Brown, called out to her husband in a nearby room: You've got to hear what this guy is saying.

"You can't make this shit up," Brown remembers telling her husband. "You cannot believe that this is happening in the United States of America."

At her State Capitol office in Maine, Governor Janet Mills called out to a security agent. "You gotta sit here and listen to this because I think the president of the United States is having a nervous breakdown or something, and it's scary," she recalls saying.

The day would only grow more surreal. And the president put a camouflage-patterned exclamation point on it when he staged a cinematic photo op marching through Lafayette Square, outside the White House, and hoisted a borrowed Bible over his shoulder outside St. John's Church, where every president since Madison has worshiped. Marching behind him were Esper, Barr, Meadows, and perhaps most remarkably, Mark Milley clad in military fatigues. Coming after police cleared out protesters with tear gas and horses, the episode had the odor of an epaulet-wearing dictator asserting his authority—at least, if the caudillo had a taste for campy reality television.

Many of the men involved in those back-to-back displays of strongman-style machismo quickly regretted it, and some said as much in public. Both Esper and Milley contemplated resigning, but decided to stay on the job lest their departure leave Trump's autocratic impulses even more unchecked.

But in the moment, the whole production was an extraordinary act of menace by a sitting president and the cadre that surrounded him in government, and an unmistakable sign that the president saw his political interests being closely bound up with official threats of violence and displays of force.

The next week, Trump invited Phil Murphy and his wife, Tammy, the first lady of New Jersey, to dinner at his golf club in Somerset County. The invitation itself presented a kind of test for the Democratic governor: Trump was in the midst of one of the most incendiary periods in his presidency, and he was asking a leading member of the opposition party to dine with him. But could a governor afford to say no, when the president was still in charge of the federal government's public-health powers, along with billions of dollars in other resources that could help his state?

On the patio at Bedminster, the Murphys found a very different Trump at dinner than the one who had marched across Lafayette Square. In New Jersey, the president was happily ensconced in his circle of yes-men, regaling the state's first couple with stories about Mike Tyson (the boxer, Trump said, had been convinced at one point that Trump was having an affair with Robin Givens, Tyson's wife at the time) and Tom Brady (the football star, Trump said, had not been the same after marrying Gisele Bündchen, who insisted on cooking him a painstakingly health-conscious diet).

Far from a would-be dictator or even a ruthless partisan, Trump came off for much of the evening as a kind of Catskills comedian, ridiculing fellow Republican Marco Rubio for his robotic meltdown in a 2016 presidential primary debate and even making light of his own uptight vice president.

Did you know, Trump asked the Murphys, that Mike Pence won't even have dinner with a woman who isn't his wife?

This duality to Trump—the ugly demagogue and the snickering jokester—confounded Democrats and Republicans alike. How serious were the threats of a man who, in private, often seemed more Friars Club than führer?

The Murphys did not have much time to ponder this question at the time, as an upbeat Trump rambled about his reelection campaign. The president's daughter Ivanka and son-in-law were there to egg him on. Jared Kushner was delighted to show the Democratic governor the app they were using to organize a triumphant return to the campaign trail in Tulsa, Oklahoma, the following week. The crowd, Kushner said, was going to be out of this world.

The stadium can accommodate twenty-five thousand, Trump boasted. The convention center nearby can take the rest. We'll do two stops.

The only hitch, Trump said, was that the rally was scheduled the same day as something called Juneteenth. It was an occasion commemorating the enforcement of the Emancipation Proclamation and the end of slavery, and while it was not yet a federal holiday, it had been celebrated for years in the Black community. It was not a day that meant something to Donald Trump.

Can you imagine, Trump asked the Murphys, "changing the day of the rally in Oklahoma to accommodate *these people*? Have you ever heard of such a ridiculous thing?"

It was a display of raw disdain for a population of Americans already in great pain after George Floyd's murder, and another sign that Donald Trump simply did not see himself as a president for everyone.

At the end of the night, Trump showed Phil Murphy once again why reciprocity was important to him. The president summoned a press aide to show the New Jersey governor a tweet he had drafted endorsing an infrastructure project crucial to the state. Murphy had lobbied him at dinner to support a new rail bridge across the Hackensack River, and now Trump was prepared to send his guest home with a reward for his attendance. The Portal North Bridge now had his personal seal of approval.

"You want to go out and do a press conference right now?" Trump asked. "The press is always here."

Fortunately for Phil Murphy, the press was not there. There was no need to face the cameras with one of the most hated figures in his state.

Trump's desire to restore his own sense of dominance and control—to show the electorate that he was not cowed or contained by some virus—drove him into a series of embarrassing conflicts and errors throughout the early summer. On the same June 1 call with governors when he threatened to deploy troops to their states, Trump berated Mills, the Maine governor, for asking him to avoid touring a medical facility in her state out of concern for "security problems." He went ahead with the visit and attacked Mills as a "dictator."

The next day, Trump lashed out at another Democratic governor whom he saw as obstructing his campaign. On Twitter, he announced he was pulling the Republican convention out of Charlotte because Roy Cooper was "still in Shelter-in-Place mode."

Forging ahead with the planned Tulsa rally, Trump put local authorities there into a state of terror about the possibility of disease or public disorder.

On the eve of the rally, the country got a sobering reminder of the pandemic's rampant spread: On June 18, the confirmed American death toll from the disease surpassed one hundred thousand. In Tulsa, the city's Republican mayor, G. T. Bynum, texted a colleague: I just hope we can avoid a riot.

There was no riot. Nor was there the record-shattering crowd Kushner had promised. The campaign had not anticipated that fear of the coronavirus would depress turnout even among Trump's supporters. Nor did it understand that, in an unusual act of digital-age political sabotage, countless Korean pop-music fans had signed up for the rally to inflate the turnout number, only to leave much of the arena empty for the president's great return to the trail. It was an embarrassing flop.

But as the summer proceeded, the president would only intensify his intimidation tactics with state and local leaders he saw as standing in his way. There was simply no distinction in his mind between his personal political urges and the powers of his office of state.

In Chicago, Mayor Lori Lightfoot found herself harassed repeatedly by Trump after she issued an acid rebuke to the president for his violent threats against demonstrators. (Her message to Trump, Lightfoot told reporters, "starts with an 'F' and ends with 'you.' ") Trump had long made a habit of denigrating Chicago, but from that point on Lightfoot says he seemed to make a point of savaging her and her city in especially harsh terms—language that would echo for days on Twitter and Fox News. Every time he did, the president stirred up ugly and dangerous forces in her city.

"I'd have people calling: 'I'm going to come to City Hall and shoot her, I'm gonna kill her, I hope she dies,'" Lightfoot says. "You could see a spike every time he said something about me personally."

She was one of numerous public officials—governors, mayors, and members of Congress—who began to step up their personal security arrangements during this period, as a reckless president inflicted his own fury on a nation already seething with frustration and fear. In her case, Lightfoot says marked police cars took up positions in front and behind her house.

Trump's tools for bullying extended beyond incitement and verbal abuse. In July, top officials in Trump's administration blurred the line between politics and government, deploying federal officers for a camera-ready crackdown on rioters in Portland, Oregon. Chad Wolf, the acting secretary of homeland security, tweeted out photos of himself addressing camouflage-clad agents there in a scene that could have been staged for an action movie.

Kate Brown, the governor, had reached out to Mike Pence to ask for his help calming the situation, and the vice president had interceded to encourage a withdrawal of federal agents. But while negotiations between state and federal authorities were still in progress, a senior official at the Department of Homeland Security warned Brown's chief of staff, Nik Blosser, that people close to the president were just fine with an ongoing clash in Portland.

"Not everyone wants to de-escalate this," the official told Blosser.

Trump's protection-racket antics continued deep into the summer. To the shock of governors in both parties, the president even played political favorites with the emergency-response money the federal government was handing out to distressed states. Since the start of the pandemic, Trump's administration had been picking up the full cost of state-level National Guard deployments in response to Covid. But in early August, Trump announced that the federal government would no longer be quite so generous. His administration would now only reimburse states for 75 percent of their National Guard expenses.

Two states, however, would continue to get reimbursed at the 100 percent rate: Texas and Florida, the two biggest states with pro-Trump governors.

Larry Hogan, the Republican governor of Maryland, says Trump spoke more or less openly about the preferential treatment he was giving a few chosen states. A frequent critic of Trump who was chair of the National Governors Association at the time, Hogan had spent months lobbying the administration to keep up the flow of federal money into the National Guard in all fifty states. He was stunned when Trump extended the 100 percent reimbursement for two states only.

Hogan recalls Trump saying that for the other forty-eight governors—everyone besides his allies Ron DeSantis of Florida and Greg Abbott of Texas—getting that extra money would require an extra conversation.

"You have to call me and ask me nicely," Trump said, according to Hogan.

Ned Lamont, the Connecticut governor, found out much closer to Election Day that Trump was not joking. After an early August storm that knocked out power around his state, Lamont petitioned the White House for an extra boost in federal emergency-response funding.

Lamont's phone rang in the evening, as he was sipping his second glass of wine and awaiting a reply from the White House. It was the president.

"There's something you want to ask me about FEMA?" Trump prompted him, according to Lamont's memory.

Yes, Lamont said, there was.

"Well," Trump said, in a not-quite-serious tone. "Ask me nicely."

By then, Lamont knew the drill. The president insisted on some display of fealty to make things move smoothly in his administration. Trump's words were not exactly a threat. But in the moment, Lamont says, he felt like the Ukrainian president whom Trump had urged to "do us a favor, though" in return for American aid.

Still, Lamont had a job to do, and so he asked nicely.

"We're in incredible distress," he recalls saying, "and it would mean a lot to the people that I represent every day if you could bring it upon yourself for 100 percent FEMA reimbursement."

The magic tone worked.

"You got it," Trump replied.

Chapter 2

Fire and Forget

IT WAS EARLY in the summer of 2020 and Jill Biden was frustrated. Speaking in confidence with a close adviser to her husband's campaign, the future first lady posed a pointed question.

There are millions of people in the United States, she began.

Why, she asked, do we have to choose the one who attacked Joe?

The person she meant was Kamala Harris, and the looming choice was her husband's decision on a running mate.

Jill Biden was not the only person in Biden's inner circle to be annoyed, even angry, at Harris's prominence in the search for a running mate. The California senator's presidential campaign the previous year had been a stumbling disappointment, marred by infighting among her staff, indecision about her message, and an unsteady performance by the candidate herself. Its high point had come in the very first debate of the Democratic primary process, when Harris had delivered a finely scripted, theatrical smackdown of Biden for reminiscing fondly about his past work with segregationists.

That moment had wounded Joe Biden and enraged his family. They had regarded Harris as a personal friend, owing to her political relationship with Beau Biden during their overlapping terms as the attorneys general of California and Delaware. Before announcing his own campaign, Biden had fretted to his advisers about the possibility of a nasty primary race that could turn personal: In one conversation, he had mentioned Harris's past romantic relationship with Willie Brown, the former San Francisco mayor who had appointed Harris to a pair of minor political positions, as the kind of thing that should be off-limits.

Biden had not been prepared to compete with Harris as a combative adversary, and it had showed on that Miami debate stage. The former vice president had looked gobsmacked and offered only a halting, stilted defense of his own long record.

Now, a year later, the author of that humiliation was the leading candidate to be Biden's running mate and one of his closest partners in government.

And his wife wanted to know why.

The answer was at once complicated and simple: For most of Biden's advisers, the selection of a running mate was a supremely tactical decision, all about doing whatever Biden needed to keep his advantage over Donald Trump and win the election. Kamala Harris was neither the candidate who most greatly impressed Biden's vice-presidential search committee, nor the person his advisers saw as most immediately prepared for the presidency. Yet she was the one they concluded would do the most to help secure victory in an election Biden and his party viewed as having near-apocalyptic stakes.

That conclusion, however, was not easy in coming, least of all to the Biden family.

The vice-presidential search is traditionally a source of gleeful speculation and reportorial competition, as the ups and downs of the process slowly leak out into public view. In a normal campaign year, it fills the void between the end of the primaries and the party conventions that kick off the most intense phase of the general election. And in a typical campaign, the vice-presidential process is forgotten almost as soon as it is completed.

In 2020, the choice was weightier than that: For Biden, selecting a running mate represented the most important test of his ability to unite his sprawling party across fault lines of generation, age, and ideology. He had won a decisive victory in the Democratic primaries on the strength of his kindly, mainstream public image, and his argument to a complex cross-section of Democratic voters that he was the candidate best equipped to beat Trump. He was leading Trump in the polls, and he needed a running mate who would do nothing to endanger that.

But the tumult of the coronavirus pandemic, followed by the killing of George Floyd, had put new pressure on Biden to show he was not merely a candidate of inoffensive nostalgia. Could Biden, in filling out his ticket, simultaneously preserve his center-left base—an array of older African Americans, suburban professionals, moderate white women, and disaffected former Republicans—while appearing responsive to the impatience and outrage that had filled the streets with demonstrations from coast to coast?

Biden's age added to the stakes of the decision. If Biden won the election, he would be the oldest president ever inaugurated, taking office two years shy of his eightieth birthday. John McCain's old joke that the vice president has just two responsibilities—breaking tied votes in the Senate and inquiring daily about the health of the president—was not entirely a laugh line in that context. Biden could not contemplate choosing someone for the job who might look to voters like a junior trainee, given that the president would spend most of his term past the age of life expectancy for the average American male.

One prominent Democrat expressing interest in the job was dismissed almost from the start for that reason. Anita Dunn, one of Biden's closest advisers, told a political ally that Stacey Abrams, the former Georgia gubernatorial candidate, simply did not pass that test. Abrams had become a heroic figure to Democrats around the country with a 2018 campaign that fell just short of achieving a historic breakthrough: the election of the country's first Black woman governor—and in the Deep South, no less.

Biden's advisers did not see that as a sufficient qualification for the ticket.

We're going to choose someone with governing experience, Dunn said in the spring of 2020, according to this ally.

Then there was Biden's personal view of the vice presidency, shaped during his two consequential terms in the job. He had been, by all accounts, a close adviser to Barack Obama, but both men had encouraged a gauzy mythology about their relationship that only somewhat resembled reality. Biden knew well that much of Obama's political brain trust had seen him as a figure to be tolerated more than admired—as a windy old creature of Washington with the political instincts to match. After eight years, Obama and his political machine had thrown their clout behind Hillary Clinton's candidacy before Biden ruled out a bid of his own, a wounding slight that Biden wrote about with unconcealed resentment in a 2017 memoir.

It had been thirty-two years since a former vice president ascended to the Oval Office. The last time it happened, another figure with deep government experience, George Herbert Walker Bush, had chosen a younger, more telegenic, more ideological, not-especially-deep running mate in Dan Quayle. That choice showcased Bush's determination to freshen his party's ticket—and to ensure he and his close circle of advisers would not be overshadowed during the campaign or face a rival power center in government.

Would Biden—having paid his dues as a grateful subordinate, quietly advising the president while absorbing condescension and mockery from West Wing aides—demand the same of his eventual running mate?

In public, Biden had articulated only two nonnegotiable characteristics for his running mate: that she be female, and that she be ready for the job. In the spring of 2020, Democratic opinion researchers were already picking up signs that swing voters were skeptical of the gender-based criterion. In focus groups, they found voters asking why Biden had not even considered male options, if his ultimate goal was to choose the best person for the job? It was a reminder of the ingrained sexism of the electorate and the burden on Biden to choose a partner of unquestionable credentials.

To some of Biden's advisers, Harris was the obvious choice from the start, a happy-enough medium between all the conflicting imperatives in the choice. She was decades younger than Biden, but not young enough to risk appearing underqualified. She would make history by virtue of her gender and race, but she was otherwise a conventional politician who had risen in California by touting her experience as a prosecutor and working comfortably within the established system. She had tacked far to Biden's left as a presidential candidate, but it had not been a convincing display of ideological fervor. Biden's advisers believed she would just as readily move back to the center if called upon to do so.

Ron Klain, who was tasked with vetting vice-presidential candidates, told Biden early on he believed Harris was the best choice for the job. His reasoning had little to do with Harris's distinctive political strengths and vulnerabilities. Klain's calculus was more elementary and pragmatic: As things stood in the spring of 2020, Biden was on track to win the election, and he could not afford to do anything that would put that at risk. In Klain's view, recent history showed that the safest choices for the vice presidency were people who had run for president themselves. Even an unsuccessful past presidential candidate, like Harris, was more prepared for the rigors of a general election than a talented newcomer.

That filter alone sharply narrowed the list of potential running mates. Only three people under consideration had run for president themselves: Harris, Elizabeth Warren, and Amy Klobuchar. Harris was the only person of color on that short list, a consideration that would come to dominate the Biden campaign's thinking after George Floyd's murder.

But Klain offered another argument to Biden, too. Yes, Harris had attacked Biden more harshly than any other major candidate in the Democratic primaries. Yes, the Biden family had seen it as a smear and a betrayal. In Klain's assessment, that would work to Biden's advantage.

Choosing Harris will show people that you are magnanimous and forgiving, Klain told Biden. It will show the country just what a unifying leader you can be.

At that early stage in the process, Biden was not yet fully persuaded. There was a long list of women he wanted to consider for the vice presidency—senators and governors and mayors, women with experience in the military and in finance, in street-level law enforcement and overseas diplomacy—each of them with a set of strengths that could help Biden assemble a winning coalition against Trump. In terms of biography, ideology, race, and political experience, it was certainly the most diverse vice-presidential vetting list ever assembled.

As Biden's self-imposed deadline for choosing a running mate slipped further into the summer, the job of beating Trump loomed ever larger. The president was only growing more combative and irresponsible as the pandemic wore on and a summer of protest yielded outbursts of rioting and public disorder. Biden was still ahead in the polls, but he could not afford to give Trump an opening for a comeback. The vice-presidential process would test Biden's appetite for risk, his political imagination, and his feel for the mood of 2020.

He could not afford to make the wrong choice.

* * *

Three groups of Biden advisers steered the search. He empaneled a committee of four Democratic dignitaries to screen candidates: Chris Dodd, his former Senate colleague; Lisa Blunt Rochester, the congresswoman from Delaware; Eric Garcetti, the mayor of Los Angeles; and Cynthia Hogan, Biden's former legal counsel in the vice presidency. They would conduct extensive interviews with the main contenders and report back to Biden.

Separately, a team of lawyers would conduct the formal vetting of the candidates, covering their financial entanglements, political records, medical histories, and more. Biden's core political advisers—Dunn, Klain, and the rest—would offer counsel throughout.

When Biden named his vice-presidential search committee at the end of April, his inner circle of advisers had already drafted a list of more than a dozen women on whom the screening team were to focus their efforts.

Some candidates on the list faded quickly: Jeanne Shaheen and Catherine Cortez Masto, the senators from New Hampshire and Nevada, took themselves out of the running. Keisha Lance Bottoms, the mayor of Atlanta and an early Biden supporter in the Democratic primary, was seen as a treasured ally but too new to the national stage. Abrams fought hard to win real consideration but never overcame the experience issue Dunn had identified.

A popular Latina governor, Michelle Lujan Grisham of New Mexico, got a close look from the Biden team but seemed uneasy about competing hard for the job. A no-nonsense former state health secretary buried in managing the pandemic on the ground, Lujan Grisham found the vetting process tiresome—"It is insane," she says—and she was blunt about her reservations with Biden when he interviewed her for the job.

"He asked me to sell him on vice president: 'Why should you be the vice president?' " Lujan Grisham says.

"I didn't ask to be the vice president," Lujan Grisham told Biden, by her account. "You asked for me to be vetted—you tell me why you think I would make a good vice president. This was not my idea."

Biden, she says, "seemed amused by that." She did not become a top contender.

Governor Gina Raimondo of Rhode Island was an early standout in the interview process. A former venture capitalist who was an articulate leader of her party's centrist wing, the forty-nine-year-old Raimondo had earned the lasting enmity of some Biden advisers during the Democratic primaries, when she endorsed Michael Bloomberg's eleventh-hour candidacy and became a co-chair of his campaign. But away from public view, Raimondo had gone further than backing Bloomberg: At a gathering of governors in early February—weeks before Biden's comeback in South Carolina—she approached a prominent Biden ally with a startling entreaty.

Biden has to get off the stage, Raimondo told this person, arguing that Biden was sinking fast in the race and keeping moderate voters divided. If Biden ended his campaign soon, she suggested, it could allow Bloomberg to stop Bernie Sanders from seizing the nomination.

Things had not quite worked out that way, and at the start of the vice-presidential search Raimondo was still carrying the baggage of having supported a campaign that wound up as a billion-dollar embarrassment. But her performance with the search committee was exemplary, and Hogan in particular was taken with the Harvard-, Yale-, and Oxford-educated daughter of an Italian Catholic watch factory worker. Since the 2016 election, Raimondo had been scathing in her criticism of the Democratic Party's failure to speak realistically about the needs of ordinary people, and if Biden wanted a partner who would help him rebut economic populists on the left and right he could do no better.

Garcetti later told the presumptive Democratic nominee that Raimondo was the closest thing he would get in a running mate to "a female Joe Biden."

Biden liked Raimondo, but the University of Delaware alum disagreed with that characterization. "We're not all that alike," he said, pointing to Raimondo's Ivy credentials.

While Raimondo cleansed herself of the Bloomberg stain during the vice-presidential search, she did not get close to joining the ticket. She had a combative relationship with major unions in Rhode Island and was viewed in antagonistic terms by national progressives. To choose her could have provoked a revolt in the house of labor, and that was a risk Biden and his advisers were not prepared to take.

Another white moderate, Amy Klobuchar, withdrew from consideration after the murder of George Floyd. Once seen as a leading contender, she found herself under suddenly intense scrutiny because of her background as a former district attorney in Hennepin County, where she had handled cases involving abuse by the Minneapolis Police Department. In a preemptive, face-saving move, she pulled out of the search in June and publicly called on Biden to name a woman of color as his running mate.

It was a clever enough public-relations trick for Klobuchar, but it was one that rankled some in the Biden camp. The former vice president wanted to make up his own mind on the best choice for his ticket, without being pressured by his friends. And besides, two of his friends who had a more intimate view of the politics of race were guiding him differently.

One was Jim Clyburn. The South Carolina congressman who had helped deliver the Democratic nomination to Biden had extracted an ironclad promise that Biden would appoint a Black woman to the Supreme Court. But when it came to the vice presidency, Clyburn took a more accommodating approach. A Black woman, he said, was "not a must." The only imperative was for Biden to choose someone who would help him win.

A second voice of caution was Barack Obama. Though the former president kept a wary distance from matters of campaign strategy, he offered Biden a delicate word of advice at the start of his search for a running mate.

If Biden were to pick a woman of color for the ticket, Obama told him privately, he should not underestimate the potential for a racist backlash that would harm him in November. It was a word of warning that could not be taken lightly, coming from the first Black president—a man who had been forced to surrender the Oval Office to a demagogue who had propagated the racist "birther" attack on him.

* * *

Trump's willingness to smear people of color as less than fully American loomed over another Illinoisan in the vice-presidential search.

Of all the people on the search team's long list, none came close to matching the sterling political biography of Tammy Duckworth. The senator was a military veteran who grew up in poverty, relying on food stamps to make ends meet so she could graduate high school. She joined the army and deployed to fly helicopters in Iraq; in 2004, a rocket-propelled grenade attack downed her aircraft, nearly killing Duckworth and inflicting grievous injuries that required the amputation of both legs.

After a long recovery at the Walter Reed military hospital in Washington, Duckworth had charted a jagged path into Illinois politics before winning a Senate seat in 2016. At the 2008 Democratic convention, Duckworth had given a brief speech introducing Beau Biden—an important sentimental link to the Biden family. In 2018 she became the first senator to give birth while in office.

When Duckworth told her story to the vice-presidential search team, they were enraptured. It was clear that Duckworth, uniquely among the vice-presidential candidates, would reinforce Biden's message of optimistic patriotism and national resolve. Her view of the vice presidency, too, made a deep impression on her interviewers: She said it was a job that was all about loyalty—loyalty to Biden and loyalty to a shared mission.

When he interviewed Duckworth, Biden told her he wanted a vice president to whom he could assign sensitive and important tasks, with confidence they would be carried out faithfully. Duckworth supplied him with a military term to capture the spirit of that job description. In military jargon, there is a kind of hardware known as a "fire-and-forget" missile: one that gets pointed toward a target and launched and needs no further navigation.

What Biden wanted, Duckworth told him, was a "fire-and-forget vice president."

It was an apt description of what Biden's political advisers wanted, too: a running mate who could be announced with minimal controversy, excel in a few key moments in the general election, and otherwise do little to change the course of the race.

For a moment, it seemed like that running mate might be Tammy Duckworth.

There were downsides to her, too. Duckworth was not as politically practiced as other candidates and prone to making unhelpful mistakes on television. In the midst of the search, she fumbled a question on CNN about whether statues of George Washington should be taken down as part of the country's reckoning with its slaveholding roots; Duckworth said on television that "we should listen to the argument" before clarifying on Twitter than she did not support removing statues of Washington. While the vice-presidential search was examining Duckworth closely—she actually turned over the results of a colonoscopy to the vetting team—she had not been through the gauntlet of national politics yet like Harris and the other former presidential candidates.

Then there was the matter of her birthplace.

Duckworth had spent part of her youth in Hawaii, but she was born in Thailand to a Thai mother and an American father. And that made Joe Biden's lawyers very nervous.

Were Duckworth chosen for the ticket, they predicted, the Trump campaign or its outside allies would instantly challenge her eligibility for the presidency. The Constitution required that a president be a "natural-born citizen" of the United States, and by any fair interpretation Duckworth met that standard. John McCain had been born outside the country, too, as a child of two Americans in the Panama Canal Zone, and it had not harmed his legitimacy as a candidate in the 2008 general election.

But Biden lawyers, including Robert Bauer, the former White House counsel, worried about the implications of an unfair interpretation. It would only take one rogue judge, these lawyers warned, to throw Duckworth off the ballot in a key state, possibly taking Biden with her. An extended court battle would likely work out in favor of a Biden-Duckworth ticket. But did they really want an extended court battle?

Was there any doubt Trump and his lawyers would attack Duckworth on those terms, if given the chance?

Biden had raised the issue with her gingerly.

"Tammy, you're great," he told her, before adding: "But there's this one thing . . ."

Duckworth pushed back hard on the Biden team, arguing that they should not preemptively surrender to the threat of birther-style litigation. She reminded them that she had been attacked in racist and xenophobic terms in past campaigns, and that she had prevailed.

"I've beaten every asshole who's come after me with that," she said.

Biden's reply was rueful. It's not a question of whether you're eligible, he said. It's just a question of whether we want this to become a distraction in the campaign.

The senator got the sense that Biden felt bad about the message he was conveying to her. His campaign was about to engage in a preemptive surrender to the most vicious of Donald Trump's political tactics—to a version of the same lie that had made Trump a celebrity folk hero to the paranoid right. The imperative of defeating Trump in November meant retreating from a confrontation with that lie.

Or so Biden told himself.

* * *

In early June, Joe Biden boarded a plane for the first time in months and traveled to Houston for a meeting with the Floyd family. It was his first long-distance trip since the coronavirus pandemic locked down the country and his campaign in March. He and Jill were there on a mission of consolation, to share in the grief of people who had seen their loved one murdered.

But the Floyd family was delayed en route to their rendezvous with Biden, and the former vice president and second lady found themselves stalling for about forty-five minutes in a holding location with the Reverend Al Sharpton. The subject of the vice presidency was unavoidable.

Sharpton was among the most prominent national figures who had called on Biden to put a Black woman on the ticket, and it had been reported that he was leaning toward Stacey Abrams as his favorite. Biden mentioned to Sharpton that he had read as much in the press, but he had another woman on his mind.

"What do you think of Val Demings?" Biden asked.

A member of Congress from Central Florida, Demings had been one of the Democratic managers in Trump's first impeachment trial earlier in the year. A former cop, she had become one of a tiny number of Black women to lead a big-city police department as Orlando's police chief. Still in her second term in the House, she was fairly new to electoral politics. But at age sixty-three and with a varied and distinctive résumé, Demings was no wide-eyed novice.

Sharpton said he liked Demings very much. Then the presumptive Democratic nominee for president made a remark that Sharpton took as a kind of coded message.

I haven't committed to choosing a Black woman, Biden told him, before adding: "But I don't hold grudges."

Who else could he be alluding to, Sharpton thought, except for Kamala Harris?

If Biden seemed to be grappling with the implications of choosing Harris, he was still far from making up his mind. Race had become a prime qualification in the search, and several other Black women were major contenders, including Demings and Susan Rice, the former national security adviser.

Most significant and unexpected among them was Karen Bass.

Bass's name had not been on the initial list of women for the search team to review, and Biden's political advisers had strongly discouraged the committee from introducing new names into the process.

But Chris Dodd had smarted at that restriction, and he made a concerted push to give Bass a shot. The widely respected chair of the Congressional Black Caucus, Bass had gotten to know Dodd more than half a decade earlier, when he was the top lobbyist in Washington for the motion picture industry and Bass was becoming an influential force in the House on Africa policy. They had met together about the problem of pirated films in Nigeria, and a mutual admiration had quickly developed.

Dodd insisted on offering Bass the chance to be vetted and she accepted, with reservations.

A former health-care activist and Speaker of the California State Assembly, Bass had spent much of her career in the progressive politics of the West Coast. There were aspects of her background that the vetting committee should know about, she said. Chief among them was a trip she took to Cuba in the 1970s, organized by a leftist group known as the Venceremos Brigade.

Bass had never hidden her support for warmer relations with the repressive island nation, and had traveled there with President Obama in 2016. But Bass knew her record would be scrutinized in a different way now. Given the political influence of Cuban-American émigrés in Florida, she worried that it could become a liability for Biden.

The search committee was not deterred. They interviewed her anyway, and Dodd's colleagues came away intrigued. Bass had risen to a position of influence in the House for a reason: She was a person of deep policy expertise and congenial manners, a natural legislator who despite her more liberal inclinations shared Joe Biden's preference for governing by compromise.

Of all the candidates under consideration, she was by far the most involved in crafting a legislative response to the ongoing killings of Black people by police. At a moment of pitched national conflict over matters of race, a Biden-Bass ticket might offer a picture—literally, as Biden would say—of what it would mean to heal the land.

In one conversation with the search team, Bass indicated she had no real interest in running for president herself, a potentially valuable selling point for a campaign worried about the top of the ticket being upstaged by an ambitious partner.

After a wide-ranging interview with her House colleague, Blunt Rochester told one person involved in the search: I think she's the one.

When Bass's name leaked to the press, a groundswell of support for her rose on the left. Perhaps more importantly, leading Democrats in California reached out to the Biden campaign to vouch for Bass's credentials. Dolores Huerta, the legendary labor leader, endorsed her for the ticket, alarming supporters of Harris. In some cases, California Democrats explicitly pressed for Bass as an alternative to Harris. Biden was startled by the ferocity of some of the intra-state factional attacks on Harris by her fellow Democrats, including members of the state's large congressional delegation.

David Crane, a California Democrat who had been one of Arnold Schwarzenegger's closest advisers while Bass was a powerful legislative leader in the state, was among the voices lobbying for her over Harris. "In contrast to Kamala Harris," Crane told Biden's advisers, "Karen cares about something greater than herself."

Working against Bass was Biden's lack of personal familiarity with her. Many of the other top candidates had worked with Biden directly at some point in their careers, or if not with him then with Jill or Beau. For a politician like Biden, who often operates on gut instinct, that kind of thing mattered. And for the candidates who did not already know him, the pandemic-driven restrictions on travel and socializing left them with few options for building a relationship in real time.

Then the Cuba stories started.

There was the fact of her youthful trip there, to start with. Then there was the matter of Bass's statement on the death of Fidel Castro, including an uncomfortably respectful reference to the socialist dictator as the "*Comandante en Jefe*," and a description of his passing as a "great loss to the people of Cuba." Those comments began circulating on social media, then made the leap to American television and even British tabloids.

Then the digging into her past went beyond the Cuba issue. A video popped up on the *Daily Caller*, a conservative website, showing Bass generously praising the Church of Scientology at a 2010 event in her Los Angeles–based House district. Bass, busy with police reform negotiations and lacking a large political operation to aid her, struggled to mount a response.

In a private conversation, Garcetti told Biden that Bass had real strengths as a running mate and governing partner, but that she might cost him badly in Florida. Still, the two men agreed that was not necessarily disqualifying: With or without Bass on the ticket, they believed, Biden's best path to the presidency probably ran through the Midwestern swing states rather than Florida.

But Biden's campaign was spooked. The do-no-harm rule that had governed the vice-presidential process from the start seemed to count against Bass. She had simply not been tested sufficiently for Biden's advisers to see her as a safe choice.

Notably, Bass was not the only Black woman to reach an advanced stage of the vetting process only to face a sudden onslaught of negative information from her past. For Demings, there had been a series of news articles detailing her uneven record of confronting police abuse in Orlando. For Rice, there were questions raised about her personal wealth and investments, and her supporters became aware of a dossier of unclear provenance circulating that cataloged past criticism of her hard-driving management style.

To some of these women and their close allies, the sudden attention to their defects did not seem organic. Tough scrutiny is inevitable in any vice-presidential search, but something about this seemed more deliberate, even targeted—and aimed at all of the most formidable Black women under consideration, except for Kamala Harris.

Even Joe Biden wondered aloud: Was Harris's team driving this? Her campaign had been notorious during the Democratic primary for circulating scorching opposition research on other candidates—"oppo" files—to the press. Were they doing the same thing now?

When Biden voiced that concern to a close adviser, he was urged not to count it against Harris. After all, even if her former campaign consultants were operating that way, that did not necessarily mean Harris herself was involved.

Former Harris competitors, like Bass, seemed to reach a similar, wary but equivocal conclusion.

"I wasn't surprised by the arrows, that's part of the process," Bass says, adding of Harris: "Look, she gets nine hundred arrows thrown at her every day."

Bass's friends told her that veterans of the Harris campaign were behind the onslaught, pointing to a San Francisco–based consulting firm, SCRB Partners, that had shepherded Harris's career for a decade. The journalist Edward-Isaac Dovere, in a narrative of the 2020 election, reported later that Rice called Harris personally during this time to tell her to call off her hatchet men.

But in the absence of hard proof, Bass says she opted not to blame the future vice president.

"I know the firm that she's worked with," Bass says. "I did hear that, too, but I never saw any evidence of it."

* * *

Did that leave Harris as the safest choice? If Duckworth and Bass and Demings were all compromised or risky in some way, was Biden's last, best choice the woman who dealt him the most humiliating setback of his primary campaign?

Biden's search committee believed she was. The group of four—Dodd, Blunt Rochester, Garcetti, and Hogan—had not been instructed to report back with a single name as their recommendation. But when Garcetti laid out their conclusions to Biden, he voiced the consensus view of the group: Harris was not necessarily the strongest option on every score, but she was clearly the option who served Biden's near-term political interests most comprehensively.

The search team had some quantitative evidence for that assessment. During the vice-presidential search, a secret Democratic polling project was operating with the backing of Reid Hoffman, the tech billionaire and a major backer of the Democratic Party. The initiative had tested voters' initial impressions of ten vice-presidential candidates, then showed them clips of the candidates speaking and subjected voters to snippets of positive and negative information about each of them. It was a person-by-person stress test.

The results were bracing: None of the women did much to move the presidential race in Biden's direction, but some crumbled against sharp criticism. Demings's favorability plunged when voters found out about scandals in the Orlando Police Department under her watch. So did Duckworth's when voters learned about allegations of mismanagement at the Illinois Veterans Affairs Department when she was in charge there. And so, too, did Rice's when the pollster reminded voters of her role in the Obama administration's handling of the 2012 attack on the American consulate in Benghazi, Libya. In a sign that Obama's warning to Biden was well founded, the women of color in the poll appeared markedly more vulnerable to criticism than the two white women it tested.

Harris was somewhat more resilient, however, likely owing to her higher profile and better-defined image. Voters disliked the negative information they learned against her—the charge that she was a flip-flopper with no core, the facts of her relationship with Willie Brown, and her record of prosecuting marijuana offenses—but her favorability dropped by 15 to 18 points for each argument, compared with 30-point swings against some of the other candidates. Among the Black women tested in the poll, only Bass held up as well under attack.

The polling was not conducted for the Biden campaign, but Hoffman's political operation shared it with Garcetti, who in turn shared it with the search team. While they did not cite the specific numbers in their presentation to Biden, they were part of the backdrop for the analysis.

As for Harris's attack from primary season, Garcetti told Biden it would make for some unpleasant coverage and then it would be forgotten.

Biden gave a sighing response: "I guess I would see that clip everywhere for about a week," he said.

The primary-season hangover came to define coverage of Harris's vice-presidential prospects in the final weeks of the search, especially after it was reported that Dodd had found Harris inadequately contrite in her interview. He privately disputed that characterization, but it was enough to enrage Harris's substantial network of supporters and spark allegations of sexism in the search.

Biden told a senior adviser late in the search that he personally understood the strong arguments for choosing the California senator, but that his family remained unconvinced. For Jill and others, there was a serious question of trust.

There was a question, too, of Harris's political skills. She had entered the presidential race in 2019 as perhaps the most heralded candidate besides Biden himself, kicking off her candidacy with a huge rally in Oakland that served as a show of force. Even before she entered the race, Harris was perceived by political professionals, in America and abroad, as a warhorse contender. About a month before entering the race on the Martin Luther King Jr. holiday in 2019, she was approached in a New York City restaurant by Israel's former premier, Ehud Olmert, who half-jokingly offered—in full view of two people he did not realize were reporters—to serve as a surrogate campaigner with Jewish voters.

A compelling candidate in certain contexts, Harris had seemed adrift for much of the Democratic presidential race, rotating through a series of slogans and carefully prepped sound bites that never amounted to a coherent message. Her campaign team was divided against itself from the start, torn between California-based consultants, who wanted her to embrace her record as a tough-on-crime prosecutor, and more progressive advisers—including her sister, Maya—who urged Harris to shift leftward with the times.

Having spent most of her career in the law, Harris found it disorienting to have her deep expertise suddenly treated as a matter of embarrassment by some members of her own campaign. In less-familiar areas, like the progressive litmus-test subject of socialized medicine, she often seemed to be guessing at the answers her party's activist class wanted to hear.

Even her admirers saw her presentation in the primary as self-defeating. Lori Lightfoot, the Chicago mayor, says she got to know Harris during the Democratic race and they bonded over their shared background as prosecutors. Harris, Lightfoot says, had been an empathetic but "tough" officer of the law: "She was for the people and locking up bad guys." That was not the message Harris conveyed as a presidential candidate.

"She ran in a really tough primary, where at that time the fervor to be as far left as possible was real," Lightfoot says. "I don't think that's really who she is in her heart of hearts."

Harris's future running mate had the same intuition. During the primary, Biden privately and repeatedly shared versions of a common observation about Harris: She doesn't seem to know who she wants to be.

Harris's tortured relationship with her past record as a prosecutor had fatal political consequences in a primary debate in July of 2019, when Tulsi Gabbard, a far-left candidate, lambasted her for her tangled position on the death penalty and her record of locking people up for minor drug crimes. Harris floundered in response.

Few relished that moment as thoroughly as Joe Biden's political advisers.

Yet the legacy of Harris's presidential campaign had been more than a feud with the Biden family and the disorder of her political operation. For the first time in history, a Black and South Asian woman had been a viable candidate for a major party's presidential nomination. Alone among the Black women on Biden's vice-presidential short list, Harris had a large national constituency who saw her as a path-breaking figure. When Harris marched in street demonstrations after the killing of George Floyd, she had been received as a political celebrity.

Many of her admirers—including other Black women—had preferred Biden in the presidential primary. But since the outset of the nominating contest, there had been speculation about a package deal from political elites and activists alike.

Clyburn heard those murmurs about a Biden-Harris ticket. Black voters in his Columbia-to-Charleston district wanted Biden for president, Clyburn says. And they wanted something more than that, too.

"It was obvious to me that people wanted Biden, and they wanted a Black woman," Clyburn says. "They wanted Biden, and they wanted Harris."

To some of Harris's allies, it seemed inevitable all along that she would be the pick. Cory Booker, who was short-listed for vice president himself in 2016, joked to Harris at the time that she had to promise when it happened that she would let him swim in the pool at the Naval Observatory, the vice-presidential residence. She was so clearly the right pick for the job, he says.

"It was so obvious," Booker says.

Even people within Harris's campaign had seen her as a potential running mate for Biden. It was such a natural pairing, at least on paper, that her political advisers convened a meeting with the California senator before the first debate to discuss one possible consequence of taking on Biden so forcefully. Would Harris be comfortable attacking the front-runner, they wondered, if she knew it could cost her in a future vice-presidential search?

Harris's response had been as direct as the question.

I'm running for president, she said. If we have to worry about VP later, we'll worry about VP later.

That decision amounted to a bet that either her attack on Biden would work, or that Biden would forgive and forget if he ever became the Democratic nominee. The first part of that wager had not worked out: Attacking Biden boosted her campaign for a few fleeting weeks, and then it had slowly crumbled. But as July turned to August in 2020 and the vice-presidential search continued to drag, it was not clear whether Biden would decide to put the whole experience in the past.

When Garcetti presented the search team's conclusions on Harris, the Los Angeles mayor put a fine point on just what a personal decision was at hand.

He told Biden: Only you can decide if you trust her.

* * *

On the first weekend in August, a private plane departed Lansing, Michigan, and touched down at an airfield near the Delaware coast. The VIP on board was whisked to the resort town of Rehoboth Beach and into a squat, blue-and-white-painted mansion a short walk from the beach. Waiting for her there were Joe and Jill Biden.

Gretchen Whitmer, the first-term governor of Michigan, was not an eager participant in the vice-presidential search. Like other state and city executives in the search, she had found it a time-consuming diversion from a harrowing day job. And Whitmer's job was more taxing than most: In Lansing, she was fighting a multi-front war against the coronavirus pandemic, an intransigent Republican legislature, and Donald Trump, who had continued leveling venomous criticism at Whitmer's health policies and stoking anti-lockdown sentiments in her state.

Among Biden's allies, there was a vocal, persistent contingent that argued Whitmer, more than any other vice-presidential contender, could be counted on to finish off Trump. Their reasoning was narrow and unsentimental. Biden's quickest path to victory was to reclaim the three Great Lakes states Trump had wrested away from the Democrats in 2016. Whitmer had carried one of those states by a near-landslide margin in her 2018 campaign, running up a huge advantage with a constituency that could easily tip the other two: suburban white women.

Only one other white woman had stayed in contention well into the process. Since ending her own presidential campaign, Elizabeth Warren had become a trusted adviser to the Biden campaign and maintained a muscular following on the left. Despite their ideological differences, Biden had been impressed for years by her powerful intellect and had contemplated her as a running mate in the 2016 campaign he never ran. She had also gained another influential admirer during her presidential bid: Barack Obama, who had clashed with Warren as president but later became a sincere admirer, swayed in part by his daughters' respect for the Massachusetts progressive.

In her interviews with the search team, Warren had pledged loyalty to Biden's still-developing agenda, and had suggested her own days of seeking the presidency were behind her—a sign, Dodd and others believed, that she would be an accommodating partner for Biden in government rather than a thorn in his left side. The Hoffman-backed polling project found that of all the candidates under review, voters found Warren both the most presidential and the most polarizing.

Yet Warren had turned seventy-one in June, in the midst of the search, and the idea of an all-white ticket of candidates past Social Security age did not seem to match the political moment. While Biden's advisers saw Warren as a fundamentally pragmatic politician, her reputation as a staunch liberal might turn off the upscale swing voters Biden was hoping to peel away from the GOP.

Whitmer, a moderate governor who was not yet fifty, was a different story.

Biden's chief pollster, John Anzalone, saw Whitmer as a sure thing to seal the general election in Biden's favor. Anzalone was largely locked out of the vice-presidential process because Whitmer was also his client, but another influential Biden ally was lobbying for the Michigan governor: Rahm Emanuel, the former Chicago mayor and White House chief of staff, who stressed to Biden that Whitmer would lock down the Midwest. Emanuel argued that Whitmer's race should not count against her—and besides, picking her for the vice presidency meant her lieutenant governor, Garlin Gilchrist, would become the first-ever Black governor in the Midwest.

If the goal of the vice-presidential search was to cement a political coalition capable of defeating Trump, Emanuel stressed, what more could Biden want than a partner who would secure Michigan, and perhaps Pennsylvania and Wisconsin, too? In the Hoffman polling, Whitmer also looked like a safe choice: She was largely unknown to the country, and the negative attacks on her had roughly the same middling effect as the ones tested against Harris.

Whitmer, recounting about eleven months later her meeting with the Bidens, says it had seemed to be a "gut check" moment for the couple—a last sizing-up of a vice-presidential finalist before Joe Biden had to make his choice. Biden had held precious few meetings in person since the onset of the pandemic, and for the most part the vice-presidential search had been conducted through a series of long-distance, virtual conversations that made it difficult for a self-described "tactile" politician to connect with some of the contenders. Now he was face-to-face with Whitmer—albeit behind masks—and taking her measure in a new way.

When Biden asked her why she wanted to be vice president, Whitmer gave the same answer her colleague from New Mexico had given many weeks earlier: "I'm here because you asked me to be here."

"If you think I'm the person you want to run with, I will be a great partner to you," she promised Biden, by her own account. "If it's someone else, I will be thrilled for you and I will keep the job that I love."

Whitmer returned to Michigan the same day, unsure of where she stood in the process. It was not clear to her at the time that she was likely the strongest candidate remaining other than Kamala Harris. Privately, Whitmer harbored reservations about whether she was the right choice for the moment.

Five months earlier, shortly before the Michigan primary and well before the summer of racial-justice protests, Whitmer had predicted in private that Biden would choose a Black woman as his running mate.

* * *

Biden had reached the same conclusion himself. Keenly aware of the thirst in his party for generational change, and of his own profound political debt to Black voters, he decided to embrace Harris as a partner who could help him win. He was prepared to put the Miami debate in the past and trusted his family and aides to do the same. After all, he reminded them, Kamala had been friends with Beau.

Before making his decision public, Biden called the runners-up one by one, telling them he had decided to go in another direction but insisting he would need their support in the campaign and as president. Two would join him in his administration: Raimondo as commerce secretary and Rice as domestic policy adviser. Others would wind up thwarted in their bids to win appointments to higher office.

For Harris, it was a moment of redemption and triumph—proof, it seemed, that she had been right to run an aggressive race in her own campaign, and that her opponents had been wrong to see her defeat in the Democratic primaries as a thoroughgoing repudiation.

For Biden, it was a moment of truth that summed up the blend of political caution and grand ambition that would come to define the early months of his presidency. He had done something no other presidential candidate had ever done, naming a woman of color as his running mate. And he had done it in large part through a process of elimination, striking from consideration every candidate who could divide the Democratic Party or sabotage him in a swing state, or even invite frivolous litigation—and finally concluding that the Oakland-born daughter of Jamaican and Indian immigrants was his most useful political partner at a desperate hour.

In the reckoning of one close adviser to Biden, Harris was "in many ways the safest, most obvious choice." But to call her merely a Goldilocks pick, this person says, would be to underrate the gumption Biden showed in putting her on the ticket. Harris had scored best in the campaign polling among all the Black women considered for the job, but the data had not suggested she would be a risk-free choice.

"You know, white women are incredibly racist, as are white men," this adviser says. "None of it was safe. It was a risky thing to do. But it was the safest of the choices that we had."

The rollout was as smooth as they come, and while Republicans used Harris's primary-season support for left-wing policies as fodder for their attacks, they did not seem to do much damage at the outset. Determined to cast her as an ideological radical, Republicans all but totally overlooked the most damaging arguments Hoffman's pollsters had tried out against Harris: that far from being a committed radical, she was a political chameleon who had changed her positions on a range of issues and had guffawed on the radio about smoking pot after spending years prosecuting drug crimes.

In the rollout, Biden hailed his partner as an inspiration to women and a "proven fighter." As she tore into Donald Trump in her early days as a running mate, Harris seemed to prove him right, cutting up the president's record of mismanaging the coronavirus and bungling the essential functions of government.

"Let me tell you as somebody who has presented my fair share of arguments in court," Harris said in her first speech as Biden's running mate, "the case against Donald Trump and Mike Pence is open-and-shut."

With an eye toward the difficult job of governing, Harris asked voters to give her and Biden not just a bare victory but an imposing electoral "mandate that proves that the past few years do not represent who we are or who we aspire to be."

In their first joint interview as a Democratic ticket—a gentle sit-down packed with mutual praise—Biden and Harris did not dwell on what they would both come to see as the worst-case scenario for America's democracy. Asked by the ABC anchor David Muir what he would do if Trump refused to leave the White House, even after being defeated, Biden allowed that was a real possibility but predicted the country would not stand for it.

"The American people will not let that happen," Biden said, adding for emphasis: "No one's going to allow that to happen."

*   *   *

Hidden behind the celebration of the vice-presidential choice, however, was a ruthless political maneuver by Biden's palace guard—senior advisers who believed Harris was the right choice for practical reasons, but who were simply incapable of forgetting either the pain she had inflicted on Biden in the primaries or the shambolic disorder of her own campaign. Harris would be the running mate, but she would not be allowed to bring along the dysfunctional entourage that had defined her candidacy.

Her California-based advisers were not going to come with her. Neither, Biden's advisers agreed, would her sister. The Biden campaign appointed Harris's staff for her in the general election, naming them before she was announced as the vice-presidential nominee. Should they win, Harris was told, her personnel choices would run through the same process Biden had endured as vice president: Her hiring would be subject to approval by the West Wing.

But Harris, too, would prove soon enough that she was capable of maneuvering—quietly, deliberately, and to crushing effect—to protect her personal political interests. She would show in her own way that she could hold a grudge as readily as the Biden team.

Months later, after winning election to the vice presidency, Harris spoke on the phone with her home-state governor, Gavin Newsom, about the matter of filling her Senate seat. It was up to Newsom to name someone who could serve out the final two years of Harris's unexpired term, and Newsom was being lobbied by a throng of ambitious politicians. (He ultimately chose Alex Padilla, California's secretary of state, to become its first Latino senator.)

Harris was too careful a politician to endorse someone for the job. She had too many friends vying to succeed her. But when the call was over, Newsom had the distinct impression there was one applicant Harris did not want to see in the upper chamber.

That candidate, the governor told people, was Karen Bass.

Chapter 3

Trump Determined to Strike

THE TIDE OF the election was running in Nancy Pelosi's favor by midsummer of 2020. President Trump was sagging in the polls, seemingly unable to recover his footing after the onset of the coronavirus pandemic and the weeks of racial-justice protests. His stomping photo op in Lafayette Square had backfired, and so had his not-so-triumphant return to the campaign trail in Tulsa.

Pelosi was hopeful that Trump's decline would infect the rest of his party, giving House Democrats a chance to expand their majority in November. They had gained forty seats in the previous election, harnessing public disgust with the Trump administration and wreaking devastation on Republicans in suburban areas from Miami to Orange County. Now, with Trump reeling and Republicans in disarray, Pelosi and her lieutenants aimed to press their advantage into redder parts of Florida, Kansas, Arizona, and even Texas.

Such an ambitious campaign of conquest was an expensive undertaking, and Pelosi knew her caucus was counting on her to secure the funding. She was a prodigious fundraiser thanks to the network of wealthy allies she had nurtured since her tenure as chair of the California Democratic Party four decades earlier.

One member of that network was Reid Hoffman. The California venture capitalist had become a cherished benefactor of the Democratic Party, the kind of funder who could expect long, respectful audiences with his party's most powerful legislator. And when Hoffman dialed into a video call with Pelosi over the summer, he had a lot on his mind.

Since Trump's election in 2016, Hoffman had bankrolled a series of studies aimed at decoding the president's victory and devising plans for a Democratic comeback. But like many wealthy Democrats, he was concerned that beating Trump at the ballot box might not be enough. He and an adviser, Dmitri Mehlhorn, presented Pelosi with a scenario they had studied in depth: one in which Trump was cleanly defeated on November 3, but then refused to give up power and instructed his party to thwart the transfer of power by any means necessary—up to the January 6 date when Congress would certify the results of the 2020 race.

It was not a science-fiction scenario. In July, Trump had already floated the idea of delaying the election before immediately backtracking on the dead-end idea. He had no power to postpone a vote set on the calendar by statute, but there was no reason to think he would not try a variety of other far-fetched gambits to undermine democracy.

If Trump really took the country down that path, Hoffman and his adviser warned, Pelosi needed to be prepared to strike back hard. It was within her power, they told her, to refuse to seat Republican lawmakers who were collaborating with Trump, and if Republicans seemed determined to use the January 6 convening of the new Congress to sabotage Biden's victory, Pelosi could simply decline to bring the House into session.

The Speaker listened carefully to their suggestions, without committing to any particular course of action. Deploying a favorite line—one she used regularly to convey her own authority, and to infantilize her opponents—she reminded Hoffman that she was a grandmother of nine. She knew how to handle tantrums and childish mischief.

If a child reaches for the cookie jar, she said, you've got to slam the lid shut.

At eighty, Pelosi was close to the end of her career and did not want to conclude it with a president she found singularly appalling still in office. In Biden she had found a political kinsman: a fellow East Coast–raised Catholic

Democrat with the same mix of liberal politics and traditional personal values. Though his father had been an auto salesman and Realtor and hers had been mayor of Baltimore, Biden was known during his vice-presidential years to call Pelosi his "Catholic sister." Both were sensitive to suggestions that they had lost touch with the left: Biden would invariably snap that he had been an early author or cosponsor of some progressive piece of legislation, back in the day, while Pelosi liked to cite the protest signs she once hoisted.

In truth, they were both politicians at their most comfortable working within the established system, and on tactics and policy alike both were ill at ease with the far left. Pelosi demonstrated as much when she belittled the Green New Deal, the utopian climate agenda advanced by the left wing of her caucus, as "the Green Dream."

For all Pelosi's discomfort with the quasi-socialist flank of her party, during the summer of 2020 she was fixated on how to expand her majority and defeat Trump.

To Pelosi and her aides, the scenario Hoffman described was a remote one, but still worthy of consideration. In fact, she had been approached separately that summer by a close ally in the House, Adam Schiff, a fellow Californian and the chairman of the House Intelligence Committee, with a similar set of concerns. There were too many pressure points in the electoral process that a rogue actor like Trump could exploit, Schiff believed, and he urged Pelosi to appoint a task force to study the most dangerous contingencies. What if the Electoral College count were tied? What if Mike Pence, in his role as president of the Senate, objected to a set of electors from one state or another?

Pelosi trusted Schiff implicitly, and she gave him her blessing to start assembling a secret committee to study where things could go wrong after November 3.

In the long, slow days of summer, it was not only fretful Democrats who were starting to consider the possibility that the fight to oust Donald Trump might extend beyond Election Day. At least one person who had worked intimately with Trump was privately expressing concern that the angry man in the Oval Office could put the bedrock ritual of American democracy—the peaceful transfer of power—to the test.

Mick Mulvaney, the former hard-line House member who became Trump's budget director and third chief of staff, confided as much to a colleague in Washington. Mulvaney was still nominally a member of the Trump administration, having been nudged out of his White House job and into a largely ornamental position as special envoy for Northern Ireland. Regarded by many of his former colleagues as a brittle know-it-all, Mulvaney was not known for his displays of humility or real reflectiveness about his role in an administration gone haywire.

But as Trump geared up for his final push to win reelection, Mulvaney let his public persona as a proud loyalist slip a bit in a conversation with the head of an influential Washington business lobby. Speaking with Josh Bolten, the former White House chief of staff to George W. Bush and now chief of the Business Roundtable, Mulvaney said he was worried that people were underestimating what the man he served was capable of.

"If Trump loses," Mulvaney said, "I'm not sure he'll leave office willingly."

Like most people close to Trump, Mulvaney would keep his fears private until it was far too late.

* * *

From his failed return to the campaign trail in Tulsa on June 20 until the eve of Election Day, President Trump waged a desperately aggressive campaign against Joe Biden and his party. Unwilling to adapt to the new realities of pandemic-era life, he dismissed pleas from within his own party to promote safety measures like mask-wearing and to speak in a nuanced but optimistic way about how the country could escape the ravages of the virus. Determined to deny the pain and suffering all around him, Trump staked his candidacy not on a plan for national recovery but on a total-war strategy of dividing the country and demonizing the Democratic opposition.

"Can you believe this shit?" Trump lamented repeatedly of the pandemic. "What have I done to deserve it?"

The absence of a forward-looking vision, long apparent to people around Trump, became unmistakable in late June. When the Fox host Sean Hannity asked Trump to define his second-term agenda at the end of the month, the president spoke in vague language about how he would start a new term with more experience and better staff.

Soon after, on the way to a weekend round of golf outside Washington, Trump found himself sitting in his presidential limousine for a remedial tutoring session on how to run for reelection.

Senator Lindsey Graham of South Carolina, perhaps Trump's best-known critic-turned-ally, spent the trip to the links playing teacher, even helping Trump sound out his answer on a second-term agenda. "I want to finish the job I started in the first term," Graham said, articulating the response he hoped Trump would adopt. "I want to close the deal on a broken immigration system and fix it forever, I want to be energy independent not just now but for future generations, more judges—the list can be a mile long."

"Here's what I predict," Graham said after coaching Trump, "the next time he's asked, 'What do you want to do in a second term?' he's gonna have a really good answer."

But in a second interview, with the conservative media personality Eric Bolling, he delivered a longer but no more articulate answer, complaining about the pandemic and speaking in indecipherable generalities about trade deals and prescription drugs.

"At the end of the second term, it's going to be at a level that nobody will have ever seen," Trump said. "We're doing it—whether it's trade, whether it's military, all made in the USA. So important."

As June turned to July, people close to Trump had effectively given up on convincing him to take the coronavirus seriously and tailor his comments and conduct accordingly. The virus was spiking again, especially in large states with Republican governors who had resisted strict lockdowns. With cases soaring in politically vital states like Arizona, Texas, and Georgia, several Republican governors went public with their frustrations. On a large conference call with the vice president, Gary Herbert of Utah pleaded with Pence to promote mask-wearing.

Asa Hutchinson, the Arkansas governor, went further, declaring he would require masking at any Trump rallies in his state and issuing a broad masking mandate of the kind the president had resisted. On a Sunday show interview on July 19, 2020, he called for "national leadership" to set an example by wearing masks.

Trump was uninterested. When his campaign pollster, Tony Fabrizio, presented him in July with data showing widespread public support for masking and other basic safety measures, the president shrugged it off. He had seen Joe Biden wearing a mask, Trump said, and everyone told him Biden looked weak.

That meeting became a rout for public health: Mark Meadows, the chief of staff, weighed in repeatedly to back the president's cavalier instincts. As Fabrizio made the political case for masking, Meadows interjected to say Trump could not afford to move in that direction.

Meadows warned: He'll lose his base.

Fabrizio, a gruff Long Islander not known for suffering fools well, shot back that Trump would never lose his base. But Meadows and other aides were insistent: Trump could not be perceived by conservative voters as impinging on their freedoms.

"With all due respect, we take away people's freedoms all the time for public health," Fabrizio said, according to his memory. "We make people wear seatbelts. They can't text in cars. They can't smoke indoors."

But the debate was over before it started, and masking had no chance. As the meeting wound down, Jared Kushner spoke up to call the idea of promoting masks an easy political win—"a no-brainer." It was something of a token endorsement, however: Kushner did not risk angering his father-in-law by pressing the matter.

Kushner was one of a few people in Trump's inner circle with the license to challenge the president, not that he used it often. In July, Trump removed his campaign manager, Brad Parscale, a flamboyant Kushner ally who had scant experience in or even basic familiarity with electoral politics, and replaced him with Bill Stepien, a far more seasoned but relatively obscure strategist, perhaps best known for his involvement in Chris Christie's "Bridgegate" scandal. Kushner appeared untarnished, in his father-in-law's eyes, by Parscale's bumbling leadership. Jared, Trump told a friend at his Virginia golf course, was "the smartest guy I've ever seen in my life.

"Can't throw a football ten yards, and Ivanka coulda married Tom Brady," Trump said, according to the friend. "But he's a great kid, he's got my back."

The president's refusal to treat the virus as a grave and persistent threat had a chilling effect throughout his administration, discouraging senior officials from doing what they knew to be the right thing when it came to public health. When Pence, still heading the federal coronavirus task force, visited Arizona in early July for a meeting with the state's Republican governor, Doug Ducey, the vice president's staff reached out in advance with a sensitive question. Ducey, a politically careful former ice cream company executive, had resisted the strictest lockdown measures in his state, but as cases rocketed upward he was moving in a sterner direction and thus tempting backlash from the right.

When Ducey greeted the vice president at the airport, Pence's aides wanted to know, would he be wearing a mask?

The subtext was plain: Pence was trying to reconcile his duties as a public health leader with the political pressure he was facing from his boss, and he needed a signal from Ducey about what to do. The vice president had invariably buckled to Trump's preferences, even authoring a column in the *Wall Street Journal* in June denying the very existence of a "second wave" in the pandemic. Governors were grateful to Pence for his work shipping ventilators and protective equipment to their states, but how far would he go in his rhetoric and conduct to appease an unreasonable president?

"Boy," Ducey responded, "the vice president could really help me if he got off Air Force Two wearing a mask."

Sure enough, when Pence disembarked in the scorching Phoenix sun his face was concealed in a black mask matching Ducey's own.

"You just took the heat down," Ducey told him, "at least for a little bit."

Trump was not interested in taking the heat down. He was not only refusing to wear a mask himself—dismissing an opportunity to model good behavior for his supporters—but also mocking those hoping to avoid illness.

On Air Force One, he would nudge reporters to remove their masks and insist he couldn't hear their question when they had face covers, even if they were hollering. At times, he would end question-and-answer sessions when the reporters didn't take off their masks.

Flying to Miami in early July, Trump teased a veteran White House correspondent who asked if he worried about Covid's spread.

"Not with you I don't," the president said, pointing to the reporter. "Always with the mask on."

In the same off-the-record session, Trump continued quite openly to focus on the political impact of the virus rather than the human toll, downplaying a lethal disease. Alluding to a conversation with his ally Ron DeSantis, the Florida governor, Trump lamented that coronavirus testing was driving public fear by yielding high case numbers.

Many cases, he said, "are kids that have the sniffles. Or somebody else who has gotten better already. Actually, they are very inaccurate. Now, it shows you location, but outside of that all it does is give the news fodder."

By the time Trump and Pence addressed the Republican convention in late August, even the vice president was no longer making an attempt to model good behavior. When Pence strode out into the dark night to address an unmasked crowd at Fort McHenry in Baltimore, he sported a thin smile unobstructed by a face covering. In a half-hour speech, the man ostensibly tasked with leading the federal response to the pandemic mentioned the word "coronavirus" only three times.

The president had spoken, and as far as his campaign was concerned the virus was not a threat. As the Republican nominating convention began, the recorded American death toll from the virus was nearing 180,000.

* * *

Yet Donald Trump was not a spent force, and even his most determined adversaries knew it. Mitt Romney had spent the summer telling reporters he expected Trump to win another term, and in an interview early in August he explained why. The president, Romney predicted, would launch some form of "October surprise"—a final stunt to upend the course of the election—and he would not hesitate to use the presidential debates to attack Joe Biden in an underhanded way.

Trump did not wait until the debates to begin the onslaught Romney anticipated. The president had lost a great deal, politically: His core argument, that he was a surefooted guarantor of economic prosperity and that the alternative was socialism, had been shattered by the virus and the nomination of a mainstream Democrat. His campaign and administration were in disarray.

But when he took the stage on the night of August 27—a stage erected on the White House lawn in defiance of yet another basic political norm against using the presidential residence for electioneering—Trump breathed fire back into his campaign.

"This election will decide if we save the American dream or whether we allow a socialist agenda to demolish our cherished destiny," Trump intoned, reciting language far more coherent but no less pugilistic than his most bilious tweets.

"Your vote," he told Americans, "will decide whether we protect law-abiding Americans or whether we give free rein to violent anarchists and agitators and criminals who threaten our citizens."

The speech was a brutish diatribe against Biden and his party: The congenial former vice president was, in Trump's telling, a property-seizing, job-killing, cop-hating, border-erasing, far-left extremist who would turn the quiet streets of the United States into lawless war zones. It was a thoroughgoing smear.

And Democrats had reason to worry it would work.

Trump had already signaled he was preparing to finish the 2020 campaign with a strategy of open race-baiting. He had greeted Kamala Harris's nomination for the vice presidency by floating a "birther"-style conspiracy theory about her, suggesting falsely that she might not be eligible for the office because of her parents' immigration status at the time of her birth. In early August, Trump tweeted that the "suburban housewife" constituency should vote for him, because if they did not, then Cory Booker, the New Jersey Democrat, would be empowered to destroy the suburbs.

Like the smear against Harris, it was a baseless claim that made no sense except as an appeal to racism. Booker—a Stanford-, Yale-, and Oxford-educated vegan with a vaguely New Age manner and strong suburban roots—was the only Black man in the Senate Democratic caucus.

Yet Trump had seen events on the ground move in a useful direction for him—as the first long wave of peaceful demonstrations had given way to spasms of violence and rioting in American cities, and as the inclusive watchwords "Black Lives Matter" drew competition from a harder-edged slogan: "Defund the Police." Trump and his advisers had spent the early summer watching keenly for signs of the backlash and looking to exploit it.

Trump's campaign was already spending heavily on television commercials branding Democrats as soft-on-crime socialists when a twenty-nine-year-old Black man, Jacob Blake, was shot in the back by police in Kenosha on August 23. Scenes of looting and arson erupted in the southern Wisconsin city, and Trump's advisers believed they had been handed a political weapon.

As Trump purged the coronavirus from his campaign's messaging, he replaced it with the language of law and order. His advisers staged the Republican convention not with an eye toward changing the voters' minds about Trump and the pandemic, but toward shifting their attention away from the disease entirely. The speaking lineup featured an eclectic array of pro-Trump testimonials, ideological stemwinders, and screwball stunts that abused the resources of the federal government. In one case, an official naturalization ceremony featuring Trump was staged for the camera and played for the national television audience.

Most consistently, it was a pageant of dystopian imagery about the havoc Democrats might unleash upon the country, featuring the widow of a slain police captain, the heads of multiple police unions, and a New Mexico man whose wife had been killed by an illegal immigrant. The political strategy was not subtle.

"The more chaos and anarchy and vandalism and violence reigns, the better it is for the very clear choice on who's best on public safety and law and order," Kellyanne Conway, Trump's longtime adviser, said on Fox News that week.

As the convention unfolded, leaders in both parties believed—or feared—that she might be right.

With national television networks showing storefronts alight in downtown Kenosha, Barack Obama told associates in private that it was the kind of event that could give Trump an opening for a comeback. For Obama, that was more than casual punditry: Only a week earlier, at Biden's largely virtual convention, the former president had warned that nothing less than the survival of American democracy was at stake in the 2020 election. Now, it seemed, social disorder in a crucial swing state was putting Biden's rescue mission at risk.

Among the most ebullient voices in the Trump camp was Jared Kushner. The president's son-in-law possessed limited campaign experience but Tom Brady–like confidence in his political intuition. He had spent some time early in the summer helping goad the rapper Kanye West into an improbable independent run for the presidency. Kushner had personally worked to recruit a campaign manager for West, in a far-fetched scheme he appeared to believe would help siphon Black voters away from Biden. (West ultimately won about seventy-one thousand votes nationwide.)

During the week of the convention, Kushner gushed about the president's prospects for a roaring political revival. He briefed a series of Republican dignitaries about the campaign at the White House, and in one meeting with two protégés of Mitch McConnell he virtually guaranteed victory. Huddled in his small office with Daniel Cameron, the attorney general of Kentucky, and Scott Jennings, a Kentucky-based Republican strategist, Kushner hauled out a set of maps of swing states to outline his thinking. In one battleground after another, he assured them: "There's no possible way that Donald Trump could lose this state." (In a sign of how unserious the White House remained about the coronavirus, Kushner asked Jennings why he was wearing a face mask during their meeting.)

Biden's campaign knew that Democrats had furnished Trump with ample fodder for damaging attacks. In some of the country's largest metro areas, the summer headlines had been dominated not only by Black Lives Matter protests but also by local officials scrambling to keep up with the demands of the most strident activists on the left. Moving hastily to match what they saw as local political imperatives, Democrats in New York City announced plans to cut $1 billion from the NYPD—a promise they would find hard to keep in practice—while Los Angeles officials voted to reduce police spending by $150 million. In Austin, Texas, the city council voted unanimously to reallocate about a third of the police budget into other programs and eliminate 150 vacant slots for police officers.

In Minneapolis, the site of George Floyd's murder, a group of local lawmakers had pledged to strip funding from the police department, before slowly retreating from that aim over the summer. They would eventually settle on a modest shifting of $8 million in police funds into other programs.

In Chicago, Lori Lightfoot, a centrist Black woman who had spent much of her tenure as mayor warring with labor unions and activist groups, grew so frustrated with the pressure to slash police spending that she told fellow mayors she had threatened to pull the cops entirely out of two aldermanic districts where lawmakers were hectoring her administration with demands to defund the police.

"I said, 'Okay, if you are literally saying you do not want police in your ward, send me an email to that effect and I will make sure that happens immediately,'" Lightfoot says, adding, "When you say this, literally, I'm going to take you at your word that you don't want any police in your ward."

In her telling, the left-wing officials backed down quickly.

Confronting the stresses of the pandemic and protests more directly than any other officials, the mayors turned to one another in group text chats and by the end of the summer even held a joint Zoom session to numb their pain with virtual companionship and stiff drinks.

"Mayor feels like the best job in the world, just not right now," says Eric Garcetti, the Los Angeles mayor, summing up the feeling among city executives at the time. "Our homes get painted at two in the morning. You know, folks throw rocks. It's brutal."

Joe Biden had never endorsed slashing police budgets. He had never made excuses for rioting. On the contrary, as a presidential candidate he had proposed adding $300 million in federal funds for community policing. Few people in either party could match Biden's pro-cop record, dating to the drug wars of the 1980s and the iron-fisted federal anti-crime laws of the 1990s. But the mood in Biden's party was volatile, and the last thing he wanted at the outset of the general election was a new conflict with the activist left.

On the night of August 25, the second night of Trump's convention, Biden phoned a trusted friend and asked: "What should I do? What should I say?"

Wracked with anxiety and indecisive by nature, the former vice president turned to the national traumas of his youth, an earlier age of civil strife and political killings. He had entered politics in the wake of the 1968 riots that tore through Wilmington, Delaware, after the assassination of Martin Luther King Jr. That period shaped Biden's conciliatory instincts and tough-on-crime policy preferences: He knew how ugly and violent things could get when social order broke down, and how quickly such events could trigger bitter political backlash.

Fifty-two years later, Biden asked a friend: When King was killed, what did Bobby Kennedy say?

Robert F. Kennedy's speech in Indianapolis on the night of April 4, 1968, was regarded as a masterful act of oratorical peacemaking—and his remarks on the assassination were entirely extemporaneous. Biden knew he was no Bobby Kennedy, but he was looking for some way to accomplish the same feat.

Even before Biden could settle on a suitable plan, Donald Trump vindicated the Democratic nominee's 1960s-era worldview in another sense. For much of his presidential campaign, Biden had been fond of saying that Trump was more like George Wallace, the segregationist governor of Alabama, than George Washington.

Now, as Biden reeled from Trump's law-and-order onslaught, the president proved Biden right by embracing racial demagoguery in the same spirit as Wallace and others who stoked racist backlash for political purposes.

* * *

On the last day of August, a Monday soon after his gloomy acceptance speech on the White House lawn, Trump appeared in the briefing room ahead of a planned visit to Kenosha. Reveling in the attention to a subject other than the coronavirus, Trump intended to keep up his offensive against Biden on the ground in a crucial swing state.

Then, on the eve of the trip, a reporter asked him about Kyle Rittenhouse.

A white Illinois teenager, Rittenhouse had made the short trip to Kenosha a few nights into the unrest there. By his own account, the seventeen-year-old was in the suburban town with the aim of protecting local businesses, assault-style rifle in hand. He ended up shooting three people and killing two of them. On social media he had expressed admiration for law enforcement, and for Donald Trump. (Rittenhouse would later be charged with multiple counts of homicide and then acquitted by a jury in 2021 after arguing that he had acted in self-defense.)

In the briefing room, the president responded with sympathy for Rittenhouse. From what he had seen, Trump said, it looked like the adolescent gunman had been "violently attacked" by protesters.

"He probably would have been killed," Trump said.

Rittenhouse was not the only apparent vigilante to receive an impromptu presidential defense. Portland had again become a scene of violence over the weekend, with clashes between left-wing demonstrators and a motorized caravan of pro-Trump activists leaving one person dead. Trump had responded on Sunday morning by praising the right-wing contingent as "GREAT PATRIOTS" on Twitter.

Just as in the previous four years, he was making no attempt to unify the country, or even present himself as a stern guarantor of public order. He was, yet again, playing the part of a factional brawler stoking conflict. But his rhetoric resonated with a wider swath of the country than most Democrats, and even some Republicans, wanted to accept.

His appearance in the briefing room was the most open display to date of a trend Trump's aides and allies had been observing behind closed doors. The president was not just waging a public campaign of fearmongering on crime and immigration. In private, he was increasingly embracing extremist elements and at least contemplating political messages that would have matched his 2016 campaign in their raw xenophobia and racism.

At the National Republican Congressional Committee, the House GOP's campaign arm, Trump's sympathy for extremists tripped an alarm bell in the middle of the summer. There was a House runoff election in progress in Georgia's rural north, where two Republicans were battling for the party's nomination. The underdog in the race was a mainline conservative, John Cowan— a physician who had been endorsed by the second-ranking House Republican, Steve Scalise of Louisiana.

The front-runner was a wealthy gadfly, Marjorie Taylor Greene, who had moved to the district from metropolitan Atlanta and rocketed to local prominence by campaigning as a fanatical Trump loyalist. Though Trump's base was often depicted as an army of working-class nativists, Greene was emblematic of a different kind of Trump Republican with equal claim on the president's movement: affluent but socially alienated whites who had been radicalized on social media and embraced extreme and paranoid views on subjects that ranged from vaccine science to race and education.

Greene had a history of embracing the QAnon conspiracy-theory movement, a far-right online community that the FBI called a domestic terror threat. After the first round of voting in Georgia, when Greene emerged as the leading Republican, *Politico* reported that she had a history of making grotesquely racist and anti-Semitic comments.

Aides at the House GOP committee convened to discuss an intervention. Greene was the favorite to claim the Republican nomination, and if she won the primary there was no chance she would lose the general election in the deep-red district. It was a long shot to stop her, but should the party try?

Kevin McCarthy quashed the idea. Ever focused on pleasing the president, the House Republican leader told campaign officials that he had checked with the White House about the Georgia race and the message back had been an emphatic instruction to back off. Trump did not want his party even to attempt to block Greene's advance. She might be a paranoid extremist, but she was a paranoid extremist who *loved* Donald Trump.

McCarthy had condemned Greene's offensive commentary, but he had no interest in tangling with Trump over a nomination fight in a safe Republican seat. Relaying the White House's stand-down order to the NRCC, McCarthy made it clear to committee officials that he expected them to oblige.

Greene won her primary easily, putting someone who was an embarrassment to mainstream Republicans and a surefire nuisance to McCarthy on an unobstructed path to Congress. Where Trump expressed obvious but measured sympathy for the Kenosha gunman, Greene embraced him wholeheartedly, calling him "an innocent child" who "acted in self-defense against anarchist criminal thugs."

Within Trump's campaign, too, there was an assertive cohort of formal and informal advisers pushing him to take up a demagogic cause similar to his 2015 proposal to ban all Muslim immigration to the United States.

They did not know precisely what that demagogic cause should be, but they were casting about for an inflammatory idea that would rile up their base and divide the country. The group included an eclectic set of people who fancied themselves in touch with the country's latent populist majority, including Newt Gingrich, the former House Speaker and would-be Trump whisperer, and Stephen Miller, Trump's senior adviser and chief speechwriter.

Joining them quietly was a notorious political survivor: Dick Morris, an Olympic-level political shapeshifter who had made his name as an adviser to conservative Republicans, like the North Carolina lawmaker Jesse Helms, before insinuating himself into Bill Clinton's inner circle at the White House. Felled by a lurid sex scandal, Morris had reemerged as a commentator on right-wing media, where he inevitably drew the attention of President Trump.

Morris, Gingrich, Miller, and others began forwarding provocative, even outlandish, polling questions to the Trump pollster John McLaughlin, lobbying him to see whether one issue or another might turn out to be a political silver bullet. McLaughlin in turn assembled them into documents that he forwarded to Tony Fabrizio: ideas like giving private citizens the right to sue

China and sending in the National Guard to battle social unrest were compiled in a collage of irregular fonts.

"John would send me these emails that went on for pages with these crazy fucking questions," Fabrizio says. "I'd say to him: 'Where are you getting these questions from?'"

Several ideas pushed by some of these advisers might have ignited an international uproar at the height of the presidential campaign, stoking anti-Asian racism while deliberately escalating tensions with China. In some cases, such as Trump's original Muslim ban, these proposals were more akin to the tenets of a white nationalist group than the platform of a modern American political party.

A round of polling in April 2020 tested several of those ideas, gauging how Americans would react to the mass expulsion of Chinese scientists and technicians who were working for American universities, companies, and the government. Casting these people as potential spies, the poll asked whether Americans would "favor or oppose requiring all scientists, researchers, and technicians that are Chinese citizens to leave the U.S."

Another poll question asked whether Americans would support strict limits on the number of Chinese nationals studying in American institutions of higher learning. Certain Trump advisers, most notably Stephen Miller, had long criticized the large number of Chinese nationals in the U.S. on student visas, attacking it as an invasion of American education. In the midst of a pandemic and a presidential campaign, Trump's pollsters were pushed to see how Americans would react to strictly limiting Chinese students' access to American universities.

If ideas like those had proven popular enough for Trump to act on them, they could have triggered a dangerous international incident—and a new wave of hostility against Asian Americans—in the middle of the campaign.

As it turned out, those proposals were something of a dud with voters: In the April polling, a majority of likely swing-state voters opposed cracking down on Chinese students and researchers. But, through the spring and summer, the far-out proposals only kept coming from Trump's fluid circle of formal and informal advisers.

There were certain dangerous ideas, however, that Trump floated or proposed without poll-testing them first or even talking them through with his close advisers. From the diet of conservative media he wolfed down daily, the president absorbed and regurgitated elements of a conspiratorial worldview that harked back to the fringe ideas of the John Birch Society. Before the end of the campaign, he would defend QAnon, calling it a good-government group, and come close to embracing the Proud Boys, a violent white-supremacist group, on the presidential debate stage.

And he began the final stretch of the campaign by embracing a teenage killer, only days after casting himself in the evening glow of the White House as an unbending champion of public safety.

* * *

That was the moment Biden struck back.

On August 31, already on his way to Pittsburgh to deliver a speech on public safety, the former vice president brandished Trump's comments against him. They were proof positive, he argued, that Trump had no problem with violence and thuggery as long as it was right-wing thuggery.

"Does anyone believe there'll be less violence in America if Donald Trump is reelected?" Biden asked.

In his most emphatic language to date, Biden denounced the destruction in cities like Kenosha and distanced himself from the far left. "Do I look to you like a radical socialist with a soft spot for rioters?" he asked.

"Rioting is not protesting. Looting is not protesting. Setting fires is not protesting," Biden said. "None of this is protesting. It's lawlessness, plain and simple. And those who do it should be prosecuted."

In a sign of how concerned his campaign was about Trump's attacks, Biden's slow-moving, spending-averse political operation immediately clipped a compelling segment of the former vice president's speech—showing the devout Catholic quoting Pope John Paul II—and adapted it for a television ad that blanketed the swing states. It was a textbook commercial aimed at reassuring restive moderates and anxious whites.

In public and private polling, Trump's uptick slowed in September as the president veered away from the teleprompter-ready version of his message and returned to his impulsive bomb-throwing. But the Biden campaign recognized it had endured a brush with real political peril, and both the former vice president and his political advisers knew that far-left elements of his own party had put him at risk.

Biden still hoped to avoid a direct clash with left-wing Democrats before November 3. He had steered his candidacy leftward the previous spring, and he had every intention of governing as an ambitious liberal president. To all outward appearances, his political bonds with figures like Bernie Sanders and Elizabeth Warren remained intact and his campaign advisers had reached out to other leading figures on the left. Yet Biden had shied away from personally engaging the confrontational young progressives in his party, like Alexandria Ocasio-Cortez. Behind closed doors, his advisers were open about their desire to deny those lawmakers additional prominence—and about their fear that Biden could make a small error in a private conversation that could get blown out of proportion.

Frustrated with the left but deeply averse to protracted conflict, Biden seemed to be hoping that the insurgency rattling his party would taper off on its own. Sure, there had been a few more left-wing victories in House races: The chairman of the House Foreign Affairs Committee, Eliot Engel, had been felled in a primary that summer, as had the longtime St. Louis lawmaker William Lacy Clay. But so far those upsets were largely confined to a few dense urban districts where older congressmen had grown soft and lazy.

Or so the Biden team wanted to believe.

The day after his speech in Pittsburgh, Biden seized on what he saw as a hopeful sign that perhaps the activist left was not so ascendant after all. In western Massachusetts, his old friend Richie Neal, the chairman of the powerful House Ways and Means Committee, crushed a progressive primary challenger in a hard-fought race.

Biden called Neal with fulsome congratulations.

This will calm the storm, Biden told him.

Trump's barrage of attacks around Labor Day had another effect on Biden, too: It jostled him and Harris from their zero-risk approach to campaigning during the coronavirus and prompted them to resume in-person campaign events. Both of them had been impatient to return to the campaign trail, and Harris in particular had been deluged with concerns from Democratic allies about the campaign's bunkered approach.

The Democratic ticket returned to the road again, albeit with the sparsest of public schedules. The candidates' health remained a prime concern, as did the imperative of modeling responsible behaviors like masking and social distancing. To the end of the campaign, down-ballot Democrats would be concerned—with good reason, it turned out—that their presidential ticket was behaving too cautiously while Trump and Pence stormed through the country revving up conservative turnout.

Susan Wild, a first-term House member from Pennsylvania's Lehigh Valley, said she pestered her colleague Cedric Richmond, a key Biden adviser, five or six times to plead for a visit to her district—a highly competitive area of a highly competitive state, within driving distance of Biden's Delaware home. Harris stopped there toward the very end of the campaign, but Wild says she was "livid at times" about the Democratic ticket's extreme restraint.

"I knew that he had to win my district in order to carry Pennsylvania. There was just literally no other way for him to carry Pennsylvania," Wild says, adding of Biden's aloof approach: "It boggles my mind."

Toward the end of the campaign, a group of Florida Democrats demanded a phone call with Biden campaign officials to deliver the same complaint: The campaign was too passive, and it was not doing nearly enough to contest the state or to rebut Trump's socialism-themed attacks. Stephanie Murphy, a centrist member of Congress from Orlando who participated in the call, says she was among the lawmakers ringing the alarm with national Democrats about the impact of the Republican onslaught.

"I was standing on a table, screaming through the election about socialism, to anybody who would listen," Murphy says. The Biden campaign, she believes, simply did not do enough to fight back.

Trump Determined to Strike

*　*　*

As the presidential race approached its final stretch, the Trump operation's polling had daunting news for the president. Biden was crushing him on the issue of the coronavirus pandemic, and Trump's advisers had given up on persuading the president to change his happy-talk message on the subject. Trump had managed to consolidate support on the right and with some conservative-leaning swing voters, a result of relentless law-and-order and anti-socialist messaging. But he had not caught up with the Democratic nominee in crucial states like Michigan and Wisconsin, and his advisers did not have a next trick up their sleeves.

Trump was still fixated on the unrest in Democratic cities, impatient to bring down the fist of the federal enforcement agencies in blue America. On September 4, he called his old adversary Kate Brown, the governor of Oregon, to push her to carry out her own crackdown on lawlessness in Portland.

"I'm calling as your friend," the president insisted. "It just makes the country look so bad, like we don't know what we're doing."

"Politically," he added, "for you, you'd look incredible if you put it out."

Brown was not in the habit of taking advice on politics or policy from Donald Trump. But the president's thirst for confrontation inspired her aides in another way. With the election approaching, they believed Trump was capable of abusing his power in an egregious way if he believed it would help him politically. Chris Pair, a senior adviser to Brown, approached the governor's lawyers with a delicate question: What could be done to obstruct Trump from taking over the Oregon National Guard around Election Day, if such a step became necessary?

The answer was: Not much.

Oregon was not the only state bracing for a potential showdown with Trump around the election, and the president further accelerated contingency planning in the nation's capital and state capitals around the country with a late-September outburst in which he declined to commit to a peaceful transfer of power. On September 23, the commander in chief bristled at a question about whether he would make sure there was a smooth transfer of the presidency despite the ongoing outbreaks of rioting and street clashes between the extreme right and left.

"I've been complaining very strongly about the ballots, and the ballots are a disaster," Trump told reporters at the White House, adding, "There won't be a transfer, frankly—there'll be a continuation."

Trump's attack on absentee and mail-in balloting was no surprise. His longstanding opposition to pandemic-driven changes to election procedure, aimed at making it easier for people to avoid voting in person, had hardened and grown increasingly paranoid over the summer. His rants also baffled some incredulous Republican allies, like Rick Scott, the Florida senator who wondered to advisers why Trump was criticizing mail-in ballots when Republicans in his state had relied on them for years to provide the margin of victory. But now Trump seemed to be ratcheting up his claims with intimations that he might not give up power willingly.

To people inclined to view him less as a despot than as a buffoon, those remarks sounded like pro wrestling–style bravado from a man who intended to win the election. Biden and other Democratic leaders did not respond with hysteria to the comment, opting instead to stay focused on driving their own closing argument in the election.

But some Democrats saw something far more sinister in Trump's attacks on a legitimate method of voting. In a hearing of the Senate Commerce Committee in October, Brian Schatz, the Hawaii Democrat, issued a prophetic warning about how the president might try to exploit confusion about the voting process and cast doubt on the legitimacy of the election.

"The data shows that Donald Trump is going to be ahead in same-day voting and deeply behind in mail voting—both legitimate ways to vote," Schatz declared. "So on election night, Donald Trump will declare victory and declare that the continued counting of lawful votes is a coup."

Behind the scenes, a range of actors—Biden campaign strategists, governors, congressional leaders, and even a cohort of alarmed Republicans—began preparing for the possibility of a contested election.

In Washington, Adam Schiff was meeting with colleagues about the possibility of disruptions to the electoral process after November 3, putting together the bones of what would soon become a more formal task force.

A different set of Democratic lawmakers gathered around Hakeem Jeffries, the Brooklyn lawmaker who was a key member of the Democratic leadership team. Their concern was the prospect of a deadlock in the Electoral College—a scenario in which neither candidate achieved the 270 Electoral College votes needed to win, either because of a legitimately tied vote or because Trump henchmen in the states managed to obstruct the appointment of Biden electors.

Should that happen, these lawmakers feared, then it would fall to the House to resolve the outcome of the election. It would do so through an obscure constitutional procedure whereby each state's congressional delegation would cast a single vote in favor of either Biden or Trump. This was a problem for Democrats, because while they held the majority in the House, Republicans controlled twenty-six of the fifty state delegations.

Jeffries and a few other colleagues, including Joe Neguse of Colorado and Mikie Sherrill of New Jersey, scoured the electoral map for places where they could flip one or two delegations as a way of closing that backdoor path for Trump to keep power. Their findings were not encouraging. The best targets were still long shots, in states like Kansas and Florida. If something went wrong with the Electoral College count, then a Republican heist in the House was a real possibility.

At the state level, Democratic leaders were concerned about a different extreme scenario: one in which a Republican state legislature went rogue and sought to nullify the popular vote in a state that Biden carried. In Michigan, Gretchen Whitmer was worried enough about her own state's legislature that she began conferring with other Democratic governors of swing states that had pro-Trump state legislatures.

Consulting with her state's attorney general, Dana Nessel, the Michigan governor concluded that if her Republican legislature attempted to override the popular vote and send a slate of pro-Trump electors to Washington, then Whitmer could act on her own to name a slate of electors that matched the popular vote. Congress would sort out the competing slates, and it seemed highly likely that Democrats would be in charge there after Election Day.

Separately, several Democratic and good-government advocacy groups had convened their own task forces on threats to the election, assembling huge reams of legal research about how elections are certified on the state and local level, how presidential electors are chosen by the states, how the Electoral College actually votes, and how the results of that vote are then transmitted to Washington and certified by the Congress.

Within the Trump administration, too, a handful of officials were eyeing the transition period with concern.

In the White House, Chris Liddell, a deputy chief of staff, had become the point man on preparing for a possible handover of power—a subject he took pains to avoid bringing up with Trump. A native New Zealander who previously worked at Microsoft and General Motors, Liddell had reached out quietly over the summer to some veteran Washington hands who knew about planning for the defeat and departure of an incumbent president. Among them were Bolten, the former Bush chief of staff, and David Marchick, a former Clinton administration official who went on to become a private-equity executive at the Carlyle Group.

Besides his day job, Marchick was head of the nonpartisan Center for Presidential Transition, a kind of think tank that studied and sought to assist the turnover of the presidency. Over steaks at Marchick's home in Washington's Cleveland Park neighborhood, he and Liddell and Bolten discussed how to plan for a transition with a sitting president who would not contemplate the possibility of defeat, much less prepare for that eventuality.

The three men reached a consensus on one point: Unless Trump lost in a landslide, he would not concede to Biden or facilitate the transition. If Trump were to lose by only a relatively modest margin, they believed it was likely that he would stonewall Biden for as long as he could. The trio dubbed this "the nightmare scenario" that evening.

In every analysis of the post-election period of danger, two dates loomed large.

The first was December 14, when the Electoral College would formally vote and designate one candidate as the legal winner. The second was January 6, when Congress would accept that determination. Under normal circumstances, both events were dry and bureaucratic processes, with little room for context or controversy.

But Trump was already injecting controversy into every step of the electoral process, and there was no reason to expect that to change.

One person at the center of the only serious disputed election in recent history felt compelled to come up with a contingency plan of his own.

Not long before Election Day, George W. Bush gathered several of his intimate White House advisers to decide how he might handle a post-election standoff. The former president, who had endured a brutal court battle over the Florida vote count in 2000, knew well that a delayed transition from one administration to the next could have grim consequences for the country. Huddling with Karl Rove and Karen Hughes, his top political advisers, and Bolten, Bush asked them to walk him through the likeliest outcomes of the election and how he might respond to them.

Bush had played a spectral role in national politics during the Trump era, offering very occasional criticism of the sitting president but mostly staying on the sidelines. He fancied himself retired from politics, and told associates that he worried that Trump could turn any former-presidential rebuke to his own political advantage. After all, Bush had seen what Trump had done to his younger brother in 2016.

But Bush harbored an intensely negative view of Trump, and in the rare moments when he shared it he sounded troubled and disappointed. He confided in Colin Allred, a Democratic member of Congress who represented Bush's home district in Dallas, that he believed Trump fundamentally did not understand the character of the United States. On a more personal level, Bush said, he had been upset by Trump's behavior at the funeral of his own father, George H. W. Bush: Trump had sat there with his arms folded, failing to muster the praise for a deceased former president that is customary at such moments.

Bush had kept such feelings almost entirely confidential for years. But when it came to enforcing the results of a democratic election, Bush told his advisers there was no room for such ambivalence. If Biden won, he would speak out to recognize his victory immediately and phone Biden to congratulate him and recognize him as president-elect.

* * *

It was still not certain that Biden would achieve that title. His campaign was confident of his standing in two of the big Northern swing states—Pennsylvania and Michigan—and solidly optimistic about Wisconsin, as well as the emerging Sun Belt battleground of Arizona. But two Southeastern swing states, Florida and North Carolina, were looking tougher, and Biden had not been able to grab a lead in either of those red-tinted states. His pollster John Anzalone told him in October he would be better off focusing on neighboring Georgia—a suggestion Chuck Schumer echoed eagerly, urging Biden to campaign on the ground and help a pair of long-shot Senate candidates there.

If Democrats didn't manage to take control of the Senate, Schumer told Biden, "you're not going to have a happy time as president."

Biden and Trump were supposed to meet for three debates in the last five weeks of the campaign, but as it turned out they would only meet twice, and only one debate would really matter.

Biden had real vulnerabilities heading into the debate: The law-and-order themes of the summer had not disappeared, nor had the ongoing Republican ad campaign branding all Democrats as socialists. As the summer surge in coronavirus cases slowed down, some Democrats feared that Biden's eat-your-vegetables message about abiding by public-health strictures was not quite connecting with swing voters who were losing patience with the spartan lifestyle the disease demanded.

A vacancy had suddenly opened up on the Supreme Court because of the September death of Ruth Bader Ginsburg, and Biden was struggling to evade demands from his own party that he pledge to expand the Supreme Court as president by appointing several new liberal justices. He ultimately ducked the issue by proposing a blue-ribbon commission on court reform.

Through no great feat of his own, Biden escaped any damage at the first head-to-head with Trump, in Cleveland.

The debate was a fiasco, as Trump badgered and blustered and interrupted his way through an hour and a half, hectoring Biden at every turn and jousting with the moderator, Chris Wallace of Fox News. Biden's political vulnerabilities were swallowed up in a fog of presidential bile. Trump had failed entirely to defend his management of the coronavirus; he'd belittled Biden's younger son and his battles with drug addiction; and in two inflammatory answers he had declined again to commit to accepting the results of the election and refused to condemn a far-right group known as the Proud Boys.

When Trump left the stage, he told one ally with undisguised pride: "I won."

Biden's campaign was delighted by Trump's self-destructive behavior, but unsettled by another aspect of the president's comportment: He had been sweaty and red-faced on stage, perhaps beyond what one might expect for a demagogue in high dudgeon. Members of the Trump family in the debate audience also flouted the rules of the event by declining to wear face masks, even after an executive at the Cleveland Clinic, the medical center cohosting the debate, asked them to comply.

It was the candidates' first in-person encounter of the campaign, and Biden's advisers could not help wondering if they had put their elderly candidate on stage with a coronavirus patient.

On Friday, October 2, Trump confirmed that was exactly what had happened. As his oxygen levels plunged, he was hospitalized at Walter Reed and dosed with multiple experimental treatments for the disease that had shattered the country and his campaign. Mark Meadows would later reveal in a book that Trump had tested positive for the coronavirus at least once before the debate but had proceeded to appear beside Biden anyway.

For Republicans who had long ago given up pleading with Trump to take the virus seriously, the window of opportunity seemed briefly to reopen. While he was in the hospital, an influential Republican strategist in Iowa took it upon himself to draft a speech for the stricken president.

David Kochel had a combination of high-minded and more practical aims. He was dismayed by the president's dismissive attitude toward the pandemic. And he was concerned that if his campaign crumbled in the final month, it would doom Iowa Republicans up and down the ballot.

In a document he forwarded to the White House, Kochel, with help from fellow Republican operative Bob Haus, drafted a speech that blended triumphalism with straight talk. The administration, Trump would say in their proposal, "has done a lot more than we'll ever get credit for" to master the pandemic.

"But you know what? It's not enough for the government to have done all that we have done. The virus doesn't care about any of that," the draft continued. "It's more important what YOU do. WE can't beat this virus until the American people decide to beat it.

"If the president can't hide from this virus with all of our testing and controls, everyone needs to do more to protect themselves," it went on. "What does that mean? Wear a mask. Keep your distance from others. Stay home when you can. Wash your hands and be responsible, especially around people with higher risk. And once we have a safe vaccine, strongly consider getting vaccinated."

Kochel, a happy-warrior former Jeb Bush adviser who personally detested Trump, believed such a speech could have effected a sea change in attitudes about public health among the president's fans.

"All his supporters would have come with him," Kochel says.

The proposal—a long shot at best, and perhaps an utter fantasy from start to finish—was not adopted. To the end of the campaign, Trump never made a concerted effort to shape how his most passionate supporters viewed their own options for staying safe. He seemed forever to be hearing the voice of Mark Meadows in that July meeting, warning that if he did the responsible thing he would lose his base—never mind that those voters had shown, again and again, that they would follow Trump into fire.

When Trump returned from the hospital to the White House, the grand gesture he chose instead of a hard-pivoting speech was climbing the steps to the Truman Balcony and removing his mask—the sort of move he knew *would* please his core voters.

"Don't be afraid of Covid," he tweeted the same day. "Don't let it dominate your life."

* * *

The next day, seemingly secure in his advantage over Trump, Biden traveled to Gettysburg, Pennsylvania, to deliver a plea for national unity. At the Civil War battlefield where Abraham Lincoln delivered his most famous speech, Biden called for an end to the country's relentless partisan warfare. It was a closing message that did not ask the country to validate a specific agenda—let alone one of sweeping and comprehensive progressive change—but rather one that offered a more traditional version of the presidency and American values that was likely to resonate with voters depleted by the tumult and division of the Trump era.

"Instead of treating each other's party as the opposition, we treat them as the enemy," Biden said. "This must end."

Later in the month Biden would issue a similar plea from Warm Springs, the town in southwest Georgia where Franklin Roosevelt recovered from polio. Speaking afterward with the historian Jon Meacham, who had become something of an intellectual guide for Biden, the Democratic presidential nominee expressed some misgivings about inviting comparisons twice in a month to the greatest American leaders of the past.

"I'm not one of these guys," Biden fretted.

Meacham replied, smoothly: "Neither were they, until they were. You just do your best."

* * *

There was one other last-minute appeal to the White House, from a genuine friend of Trump, that offered the president the chance to shift on an important matter of policy. Jim Justice, the wealthy governor of West Virginia, had switched parties to become a Republican after Trump's election. A hulking hotelier who had taken a far more hawkish approach to battling the pandemic, Justice pleaded with Trump to cut a last-minute deal with Democrats on a new economic relief package that he could trumpet at the end of the campaign.

The administration was in a standoff with Congress about new stimulus legislation—the first new aid package since the spring—with hundreds of billions of dollars separating Democratic and Republican negotiators. Trump had publicly terminated talks only to reverse course almost immediately and demand that Congress "go big," but he had done nothing behind the scenes to goad congressional Republicans in that direction.

Justice lobbied Trump repeatedly to spurn pressure from the small-government right and close the election with a big-spending bang. Show voters you're on their side, he told Trump, and if Democrats can't take yes for an answer then "blame them every day."

"I told him, hell, give Pelosi whatever she wants and pass your stimulus package," Justice says, "because you got small businesses shut down and all kinds of people really hurt."

Trump, who took the hard work of crafting legislation about as seriously as he took viral respiratory illness, did nothing of the kind.

*   *   *

No event may have captured the precarious state of the country better in the last weeks of the presidential race than the announcement by the FBI on October 8 that thirteen men had been arrested for plotting to kidnap Gretchen Whitmer. The alleged plotters were a ragged group of far-right activists, militia members, and would-be domestic terrorists, including several men who had attended anti-lockdown rallies at the state capitol earlier in the year.

It was the most visible manifestation of the mood of incipient violence that had settled in across much of the land. Trump's admiring rhetoric about domestic extremists and his peddling of conspiracy theories about the coronavirus and election fraud had blended into a toxic stew.

Governors, mayors, public health officials, and some election administrators around the country were experiencing death threats on an unprecedented scale. In battleground Pennsylvania, Tom Wolf, the Democratic governor, moved the state's election overseer, Kathy Boockvar, into the unused governor's mansion under watchful guard around the election because of the volume of threats against her, and deployed a security detail to protect his secretary of health.

In New Hampshire, Chris Sununu, the Republican governor, had boosted security at his private residence amid rowdy anti-masking protests there, including someone showing up with a gun. In New Mexico, Michelle Lujan Grisham was under heavier guard at the governor's residence as a "direct result of people getting way too close to the house with automatic weapons," she says.

It had been decades since outright violence was so close to the surface of American political culture, threatening to turn the end of an election into something much darker.

When Whitmer blamed Trump for inciting hatred against her, the president retaliated with a new barrage of denunciations. He again savaged Whitmer's public-health policies, accusing her of seeking to become "a dictator" and mocking her at a campaign rally in her state two weeks before the election. "You gotta get your governor to open up your state," Trump told a roaring crowd in Muskegon.

As a chant of "Lock Her Up" rose from the audience, Trump chuckled: "Lock 'em all up."

In that moment, Whitmer recalls, the extent of Trump's lethal irresponsibility became blazingly clear.

"After everything was revealed and they were still egging it on, did I feel like they're trying to get someone killed—get me killed?" she says. "Yeah, of course that dawned on me."

The governor was worried for more traditional political reasons, too. Trump kept coming back to her state with only days left in the campaign. She thought Michigan was a solid bet for Biden, but the state had been a heartbreaker for her party in 2016. Did Trump know something she didn't know?

She texted John Anzalone, the pollster she shared with Biden, and asked: Do we have a problem?

Chapter 4

The Blue Shift

ON THE NIGHT of November 3, the results of the election were rolling in and John Kasich was in a state of panic.

The sixty-eight-year-old former governor of Ohio had taken up a lonely position in the 2020 campaign. He was one of the few prominent Republicans to break with his party and endorse Joe Biden for president. A cantankerous former congressional budget-writer, Kasich had grown estranged from the GOP after Donald Trump's nomination in 2016. He had drifted toward the political center, scolding his former compatriots with a heavy-handed sanctimony that led some Republicans to joke that Kasich was a Democrat's idea of a good Republican.

In 2020, Kasich had given his support to Biden, and the Democrat's campaign had found him useful enough. He was a well-known name from a key state, and the Ohioan addressed the Democrats' virtual convention in a video message that exhorted swing voters to reject the Trump administration. There was some talk of a cabinet post for Kasich, or perhaps an ambassadorship—something to reward him for becoming one of the few Republicans of stature who aligned themselves actively with Biden.

As the first returns came in, Kasich feared he was about to be left out in the cold again.

Trump was leading nearly everywhere. In Florida, the country's largest swing state, Trump had seized a convincing advantage, cutting into the Demo-crats' traditional stronghold of Miami-Dade County.

In a tone approaching hysteria, Kasich placed a phone call to a Demo-cratic strategist who had worked with him during the 2020 campaign. Sput-tering profanities, he demanded to know what was going on. Had Democrats once again managed to lose to Donald Trump?

If Kasich had a particularly caustic way of asking the question, he was not the only one in the Biden camp looking for answers. Jill Biden was call-ing around early in the evening, unnerved by the first returns. Steve Ricchetti, Biden's normally relaxed confidant, placed a jittery call to the former governor of Virginia, Terry McAuliffe: Trump was leading the first returns in the state. Those votes were from rural areas, and the heavily Democratic population centers in suburban Virginia would come in strong for Biden soon enough. But even a nominal lead for the president was enough to send Ricchetti into a state of agitation.

Not for the first time, the coolest-headed figure in the Biden campaign was the candidate himself. When Jim Clyburn heard from the former vice president before midnight, Biden spoke with what sounded like well-informed trust that the election was going to turn his way. Clyburn was watching the returns in Columbia, South Carolina, where his youngest daughter was on her way to winning an election for the local school board. Like other close Biden allies, he was monitoring the national results on television and found them discouraging.

Biden's phone call was a gesture of thanks: He was reaching out to express appreciation for Clyburn's vital support. When Clyburn told his friend he was "holding out hope" for a turnaround, Biden's response surprised him. The former vice president sounded like a man on his way to victory.

"The tone in which he was talking was that we've got this," Clyburn says.

To Biden's party, the memory of the last presidential election was still a searing, immediate trauma. Democratic professionals could all recite in som-ber tones where they were late in the evening of November 8, 2016, when it became clear they had lost the presidency to the former host of *The Apprentice*.

His first victory had been so unthinkable, so damaging, so *wrong*, that some Democrats could not shake the feeling that it was destined to happen again, no matter how bumbling or self-destructive Trump might be.

Robby Mook, Hillary Clinton's 2016 campaign manager, was sending nervous texts midway through the evening. Trump was exceeding his polling numbers the same way he had four years earlier, Mook said. The emerging picture felt entirely too familiar.

By dawn, that picture would look different, with the tide of the election turning in Biden's direction in ways that were, for the most part, entirely predictable. Even in those harrowing early hours, Democrats who were reviewing the presidential results with a dispassionate eye had found relatively little to dismay them.

Trump's apparent strength in the early going was mostly a mirage, a function of the uncoordinated mishmash of voting and vote-counting procedures that had been carried out at the state level during the pandemic. Absentee and mail-in voting had surged among voters concerned about the potential health risks of voting in person on Election Day—a group mainly made up of Biden supporters. But in big states like Wisconsin and Pennsylvania, the results of the votes cast in person on Election Day were reported first, giving a false impression of Trump's strength.

Yet there was also a thread of political truth in the early returns. While they did not portend a victory for President Trump, they offered the first indication that the election was not going to yield a landslide victory for Democrats. Biden would ultimately win by a strong margin in the popular vote, but the Electoral College would be fairly close by historical standards and the down-ballot results in House and Senate races would be a disappointment for his party.

The divisions that had given Trump the White House in the first place—the widening cultural chasm between urban and rural areas, between college graduates and voters who lacked advanced degrees, between white voters and voters of color—had scarcely weakened even in the midst of a once-in-a-generation economic and public-health calamity.

One of the Democrats who maintained a certain detachment about the initial wave of the results was Michael Podhorzer, a soft-spoken veteran of the labor movement who had helped corral together a loose coalition of progressive groups to prepare for any attempts by Trump and his party to challenge the results of the election. In late October, Podhorzer, a professorial data analyst who tended toward a kind of matter-of-fact political pessimism, had assembled a PowerPoint presentation with a detailed prognosis of how the week of the election would unfold. It was unambiguous in its forecast that Trump would seize an illusory head start on election night.

"At 9:00 Trump will likely lead in votes reported even if Biden eventually wins by 10 points because of Democrats' big lead in mail and in person early voting," the presentation stated. But, the document said, there would be a "dramatic Blue Shift" by Wednesday morning, starting a trend that would lift Biden to victory over the course of the week.

"Ballots counted each day after that will very substantially favor Biden, most controversially in pivotal states where Trump has been attacking Democratic governors since COVID," Podhorzer's document projected.

That forecast proved prescient, tracking closely with the pattern of the results as they came in on the night of November 3 and the days that followed.

Podhorzer's document was clear-eyed in another sense, too. In the October 23 presentation, the strategist warned that winning the vote count on the week of the election might not be enough to make Biden the president. Democrats, he warned, would have to carry out a weeks-long—maybe months-long—campaign to neutralize any efforts by Republican state legislators, Republican-appointed judges, or Republican members of Congress to thwart the procedures that would make Biden's victory official. The fight, he warned, might not be over until Congress certified the election results in early January.

And on the night of November 3, while the John Kasichs of the world were inflicting their frayed nerves on helpless aides, Podhorzer was already looking to the next phase of the battle. With unaccustomed optimism, he said he was "supremely confident" Biden would defeat Trump that week.

The scary part, he added, was what the Republicans would try to do next.

*   *   *

At the White House, Donald Trump was more preoccupied with reversing a Fox News projection than with overturning the results of a democratic election. In his comparatively unstudied eyes, it was not the looming tide of absentee and early ballots that was hindering him that night, but a wrongheaded decision by the election desk of a channel that he could usually trust to act as an arm of his administration.

The call came forty minutes before midnight: Fox anointed Joe Biden as the winner in Arizona. It appeared to be a severe blow to Trump's path to 270 Electoral College votes, and a major breakthrough for Biden. No Democrat had carried Arizona since the turn of the century. If Biden was victorious there, then it was a dark omen for Trump in other Sun Belt states, like Nevada, Georgia, and perhaps even Texas.

Trump was irate. About three-quarters of the vote had been tabulated in Arizona and Biden was well ahead. But Doug Ducey, the Republican governor, had his own projection models that showed Trump was still in the game to carry the state and its eleven Electoral College votes.

Summoning advisers from their encampment in the Map Room to the presidential residence, Trump instructed them to push back on network leadership. The president, more familiar with the management personalities of cable news than the intricacies of the electoral map, was convinced that Bill Sammon, Fox's managing editor in Washington, was one of several important people at the network aligned against him. Jason Miller, one of the summoned Trump advisers, says he attempted to contact Sammon to plead his case, but never heard back.

Trump was not content to be ignored by middle management and instructed his son-in-law, Jared Kushner, to call Rupert Murdoch directly. But Fox was standing by the call.

Fox was nearly alone in doing so: The other television networks were holding back, recognizing that the count in Arizona was still tightening. The state was a mirror image of the Northern battlegrounds where the disjointed vote-counting procedures inflated Trump's early lead. In Arizona, state law allowed election authorities to tabulate ballots cast in the early-voting period well before Election Day, meaning that the first tranche of vote totals favored Biden supporters, who mostly voted before November 3. Biden's lead was substantial, but it was shrinking.

Indeed, Biden's lead was so narrow that when the Associated Press joined Fox in calling Arizona for the Democrat in the small hours of the morning, news organizations that traditionally followed the wire service—including CNN, NBC, and the *New York Times*—held back.

Even still, the call was a deflating blow to Trump. The president had been determined to declare victory as a propaganda stunt midway through election night, and he remained insistent on doing so. But the Arizona call was a setback to his attempt to project an aura of triumph. Trump would not be deterred from trying to deceive the electorate and muddle the actual results of the presidential race with a cloud of confusing lies.

One Republican watching the returns with some trepidation was Roger Wicker, the senior senator from Mississippi. Wicker had been listening attentively in October when his Senate colleague Brian Schatz had predicted in a hearing that Trump would try to contest the election results based on the early returns. As the initially favorable ballot counts came in, Wicker thought back to Schatz's warning: Perhaps the Hawaii Democrat had been on to something.

When Trump went before the cameras in the East Room after 2 a.m. on the morning of November 4, his claims were every bit as audacious and misleading as his allies and adversaries had expected going into Election Day. The president said he had clearly won the election and that any change in the electoral scoreboard would represent fraud.

"As far as I'm concerned, we already have won it," he said.

Mike Pence followed him to the microphone, holding back from echoing Trump's most outrageous claims but still delivering the yes-man conduct his boss had come to expect.

"I truly do believe, as you do," he said, "that we are on the road to victory, and we will make America great again—again."

* * *

Between midnight and dawn on November 4, the mood in the Biden campaign turned from anxiety to optimism, and then finally to confidence as the "Blue Shift" forecast by Podhorzer and others came to pass.

But when Trump faced the cameras at the White House, midway through that long night, the Biden team was still processing a weaker-than-expected set of results. The public polls had always shown the former vice president with a far more dominant lead than private Democratic polling: Outlets like the *New York Times* had churned out reams of data showing Biden on track for decisive victories in states like Wisconsin, Pennsylvania, and Arizona. Even the partial results on the first night of counting showed that was not where the race would end up.

On election night, Biden's data team, led by the strategist Becca Siegel, was initially heartened by Biden's performance in a House district in Omaha, Nebraska, which under an unusual local system could earn the former vice president a single Electoral College vote. Biden's team saw it as a harbinger of his strength in the suburbs.

But as the night went on, they saw some of their fears become reality.

They recorded their anxiety in real time, keeping a running log of the results and their analysis in a shared document. An entry at 2 a.m. on November 4 captured the cooling of Democratic optimism as rural areas of the Midwest reported their ballot counts.

"We continue to underperform in rural areas," the team wrote of Pennsylvania's election returns. The verdict was not much better in Wisconsin: "We are underperforming in rural areas, race looks like it will be close."

In Michigan, the team saw a "large deficit" of 290,000 votes, but noted there was still much counting to be done in Democratic strongholds. Even in states where Biden was faring better, like Arizona and Georgia, the campaign number crunchers were wary. Despite the Fox call, Arizona was bound to "get much closer before this is over."

For Biden, the size of the electoral map worked to his advantage. He only needed a few of the contested battlegrounds—Pennsylvania and Michigan, plus either Arizona or Wisconsin—to break in his direction in order to win the presidency. If his lead in Arizona held up, that meant that late-reporting results from the Detroit, Philadelphia, and Pittsburgh metro areas could secure his triumph over Trump. To win the presidency, he did not need to end the divide between the country's diverse metropolitan areas and its heavily white hinterlands. He just needed to navigate that divide slightly better than Hillary Clinton had four years earlier.

For other Democrats on the ballot, there were not many reasons to be hopeful that the election would turn into a resounding victory. Because of congressional gerrymandering and the outsize importance of rural states in the Senate, Democrats needed to make inroads into Trump country in order to take full control of Congress. And there were few signs that night that they had succeeded.

Nowhere was that truer than in the fight for control of the Senate. Republicans held fifty-three seats in the chamber, and Democrats had recruited a large and well-funded slate of candidates in red and purple states to challenge their grip on the chamber. They had pushed into states like Kansas and South Carolina, and Chuck Schumer had wooed Montana's popular Democratic governor, Steve Bullock, to challenge his state's junior senator, the Republican Steve Daines.

Montana's senior senator, Jon Tester, a Democrat, expected the race to be close. Montana was always a tough state for Democrats, and Trump was bound to win there easily. But voters there also had an independent streak and by all accounts they loved Steve Bullock.

Tester went to bed early on election night, around 10 p.m., anticipating it would be a long time before the outcome was clear in his state. Rising three hours later for a trip to the bathroom, he checked the vote count and got a rude shock. The race had already been called for Daines.

"I could not believe it—it was done," Tester says. "I didn't think Bullock was gonna win by a landslide. I thought it'd be close."

That story repeated itself in one contested Senate race after another.

Trump was crushing Biden in rural states, and Democratic Senate candidates were faring only a little better.

In Alabama, Doug Jones, the Democrat who won a Deep South Senate seat in a 2017 upset, was buried at the polls by Tommy Tuberville, the former Auburn football coach. In Iowa, where Schumer was so hopeful of an upset win that he'd persuaded Biden to campaign there in late October, the Democratic nominee, Theresa Greenfield, lost by more than 6 percentage points. Mitch McConnell won reelection by nearly 20 percentage points in Kentucky, while Jaime Harrison, a protégé of Clyburn who became a national Democratic folk hero running against Lindsey Graham in South Carolina, lost by 10.

Most humiliating may have been the lopsided outcome in Maine, where Biden was beating Trump by a double-digit margin but Susan Collins, the moderate Republican loathed equally by Schumer and Trump, was on track to defeat her Democratic challenger by nearly 9 percentage points.

Democrats looked like they were going to pick up two Senate seats in Arizona and Colorado, but despite all their recruitment efforts, and after hundreds of millions of dollars in campaign spending, they had failed to break through in even one Republican-leaning state. The Senate majority looked like it was out of grasp.

In the House, Biden's party was bleeding. Private polling in both parties had convinced Democratic and Republican leaders that the GOP was headed for another painful set of losses, with the Democratic majority growing by at least half a dozen seats and perhaps many more. But in areas where Trump was strong, Democratic lawmakers were losing—even young, promising lawmakers who had prevailed in conservative areas two years earlier. Democratic heroes of the 2018 midterms who were expected to win reelection easily saw their congressional careers evaporate.

Republicans would ultimately gain fourteen House seats, including a dozen that Biden's party had captured only two years earlier. It was a wrenching reversal for Democrats, and a sign that a national electorate that repudiated Trump still harbored serious misgivings about the liberal opposition party.

It was not only in white, rural areas that House Democrats lost ground in 2020. Their efforts to pick up additional seats in the suburbs of Texas and Florida came to naught. In South Florida, two first-term Democrats—Debbie Mucarsel-Powell and Donna Shalala—lost reelection as Hispanic voters there turned against a party that Republicans had relentlessly branded as an auxiliary of the left-wing regimes many of their families had fled.

In the eyes of Trump's party, it was a validation of Trump-style campaign tactics, even as the president himself was on his way to an electoral repudiation.

Steve Scalise, the second-ranking House Republican, said that when the Miami-area races were called in favor of GOP challengers it became clear that his party was in for an unexpectedly good night.

"That was, like, the big shock," Scalise says, recounting how he quickly called the two Republican candidates, Miami-Dade mayor Carlos Gimenez and Maria Elvira Salazar, a former television reporter, to congratulate them.

Those races, Scalise says, were proof that the strategy of demonizing Democrats as cop-hating communists had worked.

"That's why they still, to this day, cringe when you call their agenda socialist," he boasts.

*　*　*

By 7 a.m. on November 4, the Biden campaign saw its path to victory opening wider. A massive tranche of votes from Milwaukee had made Biden the clear favorite in Wisconsin. "We have it," the data team wrote in its log, "though waiting on Green Bay City and Kenosha."

Trump was still leading in next-door Michigan and in Pennsylvania, but in both states the Biden campaign now assessed their candidate as the likely winner. Podhorzer and his progressive war council concurred. Gathering hundreds of labor officials, liberal organizers, Democratic strategists, and election lawyers on a morning video call, the AFL strategist delivered a presentation that contained a definitive judgment on the election results.

"Every hour that passes, we are gaining ground," the PowerPoint document stated, projecting that Biden would carry Arizona, Wisconsin, and Michigan, with a national popular-vote lead exceeding 6 million votes.

Podhorzer called the election that morning: "Joe Biden will be the next president."

In the same document, however, Podhorzer and his close collaborator, the liberal messaging guru Anat Shenker-Osorio, acknowledged that the outcome was short of the electoral rout many Democrats had been expecting. They urged allied groups to "project calm, determined confidence" even as Republicans began to criticize the slow and seemingly disjointed vote-counting process. The apparent result, Podhorzer and Shenker-Osorio said, was "short of our highest hopes, but way better than in 2016."

"Turns out we still live in the country that elected Donald Trump," the presentation conceded.

To the liberal groups convened on the morning call—and to the Biden campaign, too—that dry observation had potentially dangerous implications. The country that elected Trump in 2016 was a cultural and political tinderbox, and there was no telling what an embattled demagogue in the White House might do in that environment once he felt cornered. If there was even a hint of public disorder, or disruption at vote-counting places, the groups feared that Trump would use it as a pretext to initiate a police crackdown on demonstrators or even on election administrators.

"Within the first twenty-four hours, it was really contentious to figure out: Should we be mobilizing, and when?" says Rahna Epting, the head of the activist group MoveOn. "We were ready, as a coalition, to mobilize as early as the next morning, but we weren't sure that was strategic or needed."

Capturing the mood of extreme fear on the left, Epting says her group and its partners were convinced that Trump was "looking for an excuse to issue martial law." The organizations abruptly canceled plans for mass demonstrations on Wednesday, insisting on a surfeit of caution and angering grassroots activists who were eager to mount a public display of pushback.

Within the Biden campaign, there were more measured concerns about what Trump might do during a protracted vote count. The president had threatened to go to court to stop the counting of ballots, but the counts were proceeding unimpeded, and Biden was gaining ground in nearly every important state. Both Michigan and Wisconsin were called for Biden on Wednesday, leaving him within striking distance of victory.

But the Biden campaign recognized that Trump was not likely to concede defeat anytime soon, even though it was more and more apparent that the election was headed for a definitive result: At half past nine on the evening of November 4, Biden's data team had enough information to project not just a win in a third big state, Pennsylvania, but a margin of victory there that would clinch the presidency for him.

For the first time, the team also assessed that Biden was likely to add a second Sun Belt breakthrough on top of Arizona. The Democratic ticket was trailing by 2,497 votes in Georgia, and as the Biden analysts mined the outstanding vote data they came away with a conclusion that had wide-ranging implications.

"We need 60.9% of the outstanding ballots to win and are projecting to receive 70.0% of outstanding ballots," they wrote in bolded text. "We project the final margin will be 3-5k votes in favor of the VP."

On the ballot with Biden in Georgia were two underdog Democratic Senate candidates, Jon Ossoff and Raphael Warnock, whose political fates were closely intertwined with his. If Biden's team was right and the last wave of ballots in the state broke for Democrats, it could keep two Senate seats up for grabs until a runoff election on January 5—giving Biden's party at least a thin wisp of hope that they could still take power in the upper chamber.

But Biden's advisers were anticipating a divided government and trying to find a bright side to a Republican Senate. Anita Dunn said then that with a split Congress at least Biden would not have to "go super-left on everything." Biden, she said, would have "a lot more space" to make decisions than in an all-Democratic Washington.

It was not a line of reasoning most Democrats found persuasive.

By the afternoon of Thursday, November 5, there was no reasonable doubt remaining about the outcome of the presidential race. Biden was ahead in three big states Trump had carried in 2016—Michigan, Wisconsin, and Arizona—and the outstanding votes in Pennsylvania were certainly going to move him ahead of the president. The race in Georgia, too, was close enough that Biden could still overtake Trump in an evolving state that had not voted for a Democrat since 1992.

Overseas, world leaders who had become fast friends of Trump were starting to see the writing on the wall. A senior aide to Benjamin Netanyahu, the embattled Israeli prime minister who had made a political calling card of his partnership with Trump, reached out to an adviser to the American president with a delicate inquiry. That Netanyahu aide, Aaron Klein, wanted to know if Tony Fabrizio believed his boss could still survive.

He asked Fabrizio: What do you think? Do you think it's going to turn? Are they going to find more votes?

The pollster recalls giving an unvarnished view. Biden was ahead in too many states for Trump to suddenly overtake him everywhere.

"I don't think it's going to turn," Fabrizio told Klein, by his own recollection. "Maybe one switches, but I don't see all three switching."

In the American media, something of a collective-action problem had taken hold. None of the people and institutions that could declare Biden the winner was ready to do so. The Associated Press had called Michigan, Wisconsin, and Arizona for Biden, but the Arizona call remained contested even among news networks, and the wire service was hesitating to call the election altogether for Biden. Accustomed to deferring to the wire service, the *New York Times* and the *Washington Post* were holding back from stating the obvious: Biden was almost certainly going to be the next president.

Despite mounting frustration in the Biden camp, the president-elect-in-all-but-name was also adamant in his refusal to claim victory before the traditional call by the news media. If he was going to turn the page on the Trump era and restore faith in the American democratic system, Biden reasoned, he could not lower himself to Trump's level and risk making the outcome of the 2020 election a he-said, he-said dispute between two rival candidates.

But in his public remarks day after day, Biden was running out of ways to express strong confidence without calling himself a winner.

The delay was costing more than time: Trump and a loose confederation of right-wing provocateurs were sowing misinformation about the election results with a vigorous enthusiasm that grew over the course of the week.

Several camera-hungry Republican lawyers, including Rudy Giuliani and Pam Bondi, the former attorney general of Florida, had begun hosting news conferences outside a vote-counting facility in Philadelphia to make baseless claims of Democratic chicanery. On that Thursday afternoon, Trump addressed reporters from a lectern in the White House briefing room to deliver a conspiratorial tirade, castigating media organizations for their flawed polling and promising to fight on for his base of "police officers, farmers, everyday citizens."

Intensifying his rhetoric from the night of the election, Trump described his vanishing leads in states like Pennsylvania and Georgia as self-evident proof of tampering in heavily Black cities. Those false claims played unsubtly to the racial panic of the president's hard-core base.

"They are trying to rig an election and we can't let that happen," he said. "Detroit and Philadelphia, known as two of the most corrupt political places anywhere in our country, easily, cannot be responsible for engineering the outcome of a presidential race."

While many Republican lawmakers held back from echoing his most overheated statements, only a few repudiated them. And some went further than just nodding along as Trump began his assault on the election. Kevin McCarthy was among them, going on Fox News to take up the battle cry of election fraud in the absence of any evidence to substantiate such claims.

"President Trump won this election, so everyone who's listening: do not be quiet," McCarthy said on television. "Do not be silent about this. We cannot allow this to happen before our very eyes."

Looming behind McCarthy in the camera frame, as he delivered talking points that helped fuel months of anger and insurrection, was the Capitol dome.

McCarthy's counterpart in the Senate was taking a different and quieter approach. Mitch McConnell was under no illusion that Trump had won the election, and he did not intend to pretend otherwise on television. It did not take a political tactician of McConnell's caliber to see that the race was trending in Biden's direction. In fact, the 2020 election appeared to be yielding an outcome that delighted the dour Kentuckian: the simultaneous ejection of Donald Trump and preservation of the Republican Senate majority.

McConnell could not show his elation in public, but he wanted to take covert steps to smooth the pathway to the post-Trump era in American government. In a maneuver more reminiscent of Cold War–era diplomacy than conventional American politics, McConnell on Thursday phoned a trusted deputy, John Cornyn of Texas, and asked him to establish a back channel of communication with the man he viewed as the incoming president. McConnell knew it would be politically toxic in his own party to treat Biden as the victor before Trump had conceded the election, but he did not want to slight his former colleague who was going to be the next president of the United States.

He assigned Cornyn a mission: Speak with Chris Coons, the Delaware senator, and give him a message to pass on to Biden. Cornyn was to make it clear to Coons, a moderate eager to foster bipartisan good feeling, that McConnell would recognize Biden as the winner of the presidential election, just not quite yet.

He was to convey another request, too: Biden should not call McConnell too soon, because the Republican senator wanted neither to enrage his party by embracing Biden in public, nor to slight the president-elect by ignoring his call.

While McConnell opened a covert line of communication to Biden, some Democrats were working that week to identify Republicans who would publicly recognize his clear victory as soon as possible. Nancy Pelosi was among them. After dining with her husband, Paul, and some friends of the Bush family, the House Speaker wondered if George W. Bush could be persuaded to speak up and acknowledge Biden's win.

Instead of calling the former president directly, Pelosi contacted another mutual friend of theirs. She understood that Bush had his own "equities" in the situation, this friend recalls—an apparent reference to the political ambitions of his family members, including his nephew George P. Bush, in a Trump-led Republican Party. But, she asked, would the forty-third president consider issuing a statement about Biden?

Pelosi did not know that Bush had resolved even before Election Day to speak out when the moment came. Within days, he would publicly congratulate Biden and call him "a good man."

* * *

Jeff Zucker knew on Friday, November 6, that his network was going to call the election for Biden. The only question was when.

The president of CNN understood by then that only a few news organizations were going to be in a position to call the election and his was one of them. The AP appeared frozen because of its premature Arizona call. So was Fox, and the pro-Trump channel was unlikely to further enrage its conservative viewers by being the first network to call the time of death for the president's campaign. The country's major newspapers seemed unwilling to get ahead of television.

At CNN, the network's decision desk had zeroed in on the metric it would use to issue a call. Biden needed to win Pennsylvania, which along with Wisconsin and Michigan would put him well over the top even without a final call in Arizona or Georgia. But to determine Biden had won Pennsylvania, beyond any plausible doubt, CNN's election-data team decided it wanted to see him establish a lead exceeding 30,000 votes.

And at 9 p.m. on November 6, Biden's lead was stuck at 21,118 votes.

The outstanding ballots were expected to favor the Democrats by a significant margin: Biden's data team estimated nearly a quarter-million votes yet to be counted, with almost half that number coming from mail-in votes and uncounted Philadelphia ballots. Both categories would lean heavily toward Biden.

The Biden campaign had planned a victory rally for Friday night in Wilmington, and members of the Democrat's team were lobbying news organizations to call the race already. But in an age of improbable political outcomes—none more seemingly improbable than Trump's first victory in 2016—a more timid approach prevailed. No news organization called the race, and Biden's campaign pulled down its celebratory event.

By Saturday morning the margin was tantalizingly close to CNN's desired threshold. At Biden headquarters, the data team recorded at nine o'clock that there was a 29,133-vote gap in the former vice president's favor, thanks to newly counted ballots in Pittsburgh's Allegheny County and the Philadelphia suburbs. With one more dump of votes in Pennsylvania, Biden crossed the 30,000 mark just after eleven o'clock. Zucker green-lighted the call.

"After four long tense days, we've reached a historic moment," the anchor Wolf Blitzer declared. The other television networks stampeded to join the call, with newspapers following soon after.

Americans have long taken to the streets to celebrate presidential election results, yet what took place on Saturday, November 7, went beyond the festivities of a normal election year. The cheering and chanting, the joyous honking of car horns and spontaneous dancing in the streets, the mixture of elation and relief—it was the kind of giddy scene Americans had previously seen in foreign countries after the ouster of a dictator.

"The Wicked Witch is dead," exclaimed one reveler in Washington.

On an unusually warm late fall day, thousands massed near the White House to savor Trump's humiliation. There was a woman in the passenger seat of a top-down Jeep holding a white sign with blue letters: "Get Out of Our House Loser." Nearby, a man was wearing an American flag as a cape with Trump's image and Biden's memorable words from the first debate: "Will You Shut Up, Man."

Even closer to the White House, near the site where protesters had been tear-gassed before Trump's Bible-hoisting photo op, one person held an over-size "Eviction Notice" for Trump from 1600 Pennsylvania Avenue. Others strolled on the street rechristened Black Lives Matter Plaza with cans of beer, bottles of champagne, and fragrant joints. Some took turns posing before a massive "YOU'RE FIRED" poster that had been affixed to the black fencing that had ringed Lafayette Square since the aftermath of George Floyd's murder. Hanging there, too, were black-and-white images of John Lewis, the civil rights champion and congressman, and Ruth Bader Ginsburg—two heroes to American liberals who had died in the last few months.

The enthusiasm in the diverse crowd seemed to have little to do with Joe Biden. They were jubilant about Trump's defeat, and in some cases about Biden's history-making running mate, Kamala Harris.

"It makes me so proud. It gives me hope. It is inspiring," Katrel Angry, a Black educator, said of Harris, her voice barely audible above chants of "Na, Na, Na, Na, Hey, Hey, Hey, Goodbye!"

Angry's fiancé, Jerry McGaughy, was humming a favorite tune of his own: "Hit the Road, Jack."

"I'm just so happy just to get our country back to normal," said McGaughy, a real estate investment executive.

Others in the mostly masked crowd could only exhale. "We're a country in crisis, but we've got to keep struggling through it," said Steve Brescia, who runs an environmental nonprofit.

Asked if he was excited about a President Biden, Brescia hesitated: "I admire the man, but I'm not . . ."

"I'm excited about democracy," he finished.

There was good reason to interpret Biden's win with caution. But with a message of restoring dignity to the presidency and hauling the country out of overlapping economic and public-health crises, Biden had made inroads into once-red suburbs and turned out Democratic-leaning constituencies in big cities. He had wrenched into the Democratic column five states that had voted for Donald Trump in 2016, restoring his party's historic strength in the Great Lakes region and summoning enough support from the suburbs of Atlanta and Phoenix to achieve breakthroughs in the Sun Belt.

The white, rural areas up North that had once regarded Democrats as the party of the little guy were lost even to a moderate like Biden. But in key places he chipped away at Trump's margins, merely losing badly in rural parts of Northern Michigan and Central Pennsylvania where Hillary Clinton had been utterly annihilated.

The Democrats' down-ballot defeats briefly seemed to recede into the background in a long-awaited moment of triumph. There would be ample opportunities, soon enough, for Democrats to ponder what it would mean for Biden to govern with a Republican Senate; to probe why, even as a multiracial coalition in the country's big metro areas propelled him to victory, Biden had markedly lost ground with working-class Hispanic voters in Florida and Texas; and to process the unsettling reality that in defeat Trump had still collected about 12 million more votes than he had in 2016.

But those questions could wait.

Biden finally declared victory in an outdoor address from Wilmington that evening. Introduced by Harris, the first woman ever elected to national office, Biden said "a time to heal" was at hand. His opponent was refusing to concede and the electoral map itself was a diagram of the country's most intractable social fissures. But Biden spoke of a country that could be united in a spirit of cooperation, capable of confronting climate change and racial inequity and overcoming a devastating pandemic.

"Let this grim era of demonization in America begin to end," Biden said, "here and now."

Using considerably less elevated language, the Biden data-analysis team made a final update to their normally dispassionate catalog of election returns.

"WE FUCKING WON."

*   *   *

Trump was not watching television when the networks declared him the big loser of the 2020 campaign. Nor did he seem especially upset when a close political ally spoke to him minutes later. The country's erratic chief executive, who for much of the week was delivering slashing attacks on the electoral process, was on the links at the Trump National Golf Club in Northern Virginia. Trump had invited Lindsey Graham, the newly reelected South Carolina senator, to join his party that day. But Graham, usually an eager partner for Trump on the links, had been otherwise occupied, and so Trump called him from the course.

The president had spent part of the morning angrily tweeting allegations of election tampering. But when he spoke to Graham, rather than dwelling on his ouster from the world's most powerful office, Trump held forth about a new golf club he was using and went on at some length about how eager he was to play a round with Bryson DeChambeau, the winner of the 2020 U.S. Open two months earlier. Graham proposed that Trump post a tweet that implicitly conceded the election, but with a touch of the Terminator: "I'll be back."

Graham, who had reinvented himself as a kind of ambassador-at-large facilitating the president's relationship with the Senate, says he encouraged Trump to explore his legal options for challenging the election without veering into tinfoil-hat territory.

"Let's fight hard," Graham told him, by his own account. "Let's make every credible challenge we can, let's not do bullshit stuff but credible stuff. And it may not flip the outcome."

Trump heard him out. But once the president left the golf course he owned and returned to the presidential residence he was borrowing, a hard and predictable stubbornness set in. He was not ready to concede or to limit his legal options merely to the plausible and responsible. At the White House, a mood of gloom and anger was taking hold.

Still, for the moment, the visible consequences of Trump's obstinacy were tending more in the direction of farce than tragedy.

The central event of the day for his die-hard supporters had been a screwball news conference in Philadelphia, organized by Giuliani and Corey Lewandowski, Trump's on-and-off-political adviser, to level wild claims of election fraud without furnishing a hint of evidence. Neither man came off as terribly menacing, speaking as they were outside a run-down lawn care business, Four Seasons Total Landscaping, adjacent to a smut shop and a crematorium. (A briefing Podhorzer prepared for liberal groups put it drily: "No serious threat starts at Four Seasons Total Landscaping.")

Mindful of Trump's volcanic temper, Graham was urging his Republican colleagues to give the president space to come to terms with the election results. Trump would have a few weeks to rage and rail, but the votes would all be counted soon enough and the outcome would be incontestable. He called his Democratic colleague Cory Booker and argued that Democrats should not try too hard to humiliate Trump or force him to concede defeat. Let the man exhaust his options, Graham advised.

Even if Trump persisted in a dead-end litigation campaign against the election results, there was a date certain, December 14, when the states would approve their slates of electors and a standoff would be over.

Other Republicans were not so sure. Chris Christie, too, spoke with Trump that day and found him in an unreasonable frame of mind. The former New Jersey governor called his friend the president and urged him to concede gracefully—or as gracefully as any person named Trump could manage.

Losing hurts more than winning feels good, Christie told him. The only way to do this was to pull off the Band-Aid.

Trump brushed aside the idea.

"Chris, I'm never going to concede," he said. "So, what else have you got?"

Christie had no other ideas for the defeated president. And within the White House's minuscule transition operation, there was a sense of dismay about what the president was likely to do next.

Chris Liddell, the deputy chief of staff furtively preparing for the transfer of power, called his new friend David Marchick. Alluding to their concerned conversation over steak a few months earlier, Liddell said the election results were about as troubling for the transition effort as they could be. The possibility that Trump would obstruct the transfer of power now looked all too likely.

"Remember that dinner we had in your garage?" Liddell asked him. "The nightmare scenario is about to happen."

Chapter 5

The Dark Winter

THE QUEEN THEATER in downtown Wilmington was an unlikely focal point for negotiations that would bring a new presidential administration to life. A restored nineteenth-century structure in a lively strip of the blandly corporate downtown, the Queen had been adopted by the Biden campaign as a flexible venue for all manner of set-piece events: speeches, video tapings, the occasional virtual summit.

On November 20, it was to the Queen that Nancy Pelosi and Chuck Schumer trekked for their first face-to-face meeting with the president-elect.

The full impact of the election results had by then sunk in with party leaders. Their elation at Donald Trump's defeat had cooled into a recognition that the job of governing would be immensely difficult. The tiny House margin would present a difficult challenge for Pelosi, but her personal dominance of the lower chamber gave Biden and his advisers reason for hope. A Republican-held Senate, on the other hand, had the potential to be a killing field for Biden and his party's agenda.

"It wasn't really clear how much he'd be able to get done as president with forty-eight senators, narrow House majority," says Ron Klain.

At that point, Klain says, Biden believed his legacy was less likely to be monumental policy change than: "I'm the guy that beat Donald Trump."

Biden himself outwardly maintained an attitude of dogged optimism, insisting to a number of allies and outside luminaries that an era of great change was on the way. In a virtual meeting with CEOs and labor officials in mid-November, days before his summit with congressional leaders, Biden insisted that he intended to carry out a major rebalancing of the economy. He told a group including the chief executives of Microsoft, General Motors, and Target that he was dead serious about making the economy fairer.

But neither Biden nor the people closest to him had articulated how they thought they could do that in a divided government. And as the president-elect met with Schumer and Pelosi on that Friday in November, it was not clear that the three of them had an answer to that question.

The legislative leaders were effusive in congratulating Biden, but the substance of the meeting was sobering. Schumer and Pelosi were locked in tense negotiations over pandemic relief funding with the Trump administration, which was inclined to spend heavily, and Republican leaders on the Hill, who were not. For months, Schumer and Pelosi had approached the talks with a high degree of confidence that they would emerge from the election with greater leverage.

Now it seemed they had miscalculated. Trump was on his way out, and congressional Republicans had little interest in passing a huge spending bill that would set up Biden for a smooth first few months. Still, for just a few more weeks, Republicans had to be mindful of the Senate runoffs in Georgia. With two seats in play, they might not want to take the risk of handing Democrats a prime campaign issue by obstructing a new relief package.

Pelosi and Schumer needed to know if Biden understood that. They both believed they had to reach a short-term deal with the Republicans just to keep the country afloat. But they expected that deal to be relatively limited, in the hundreds of billions but not trillions of dollars, and they believed the country would need a lot more spending in the new year. Unless something miraculous happened in Georgia, that meant Biden and his party would have to somehow wrangle huge new sums of money out of a Republican Senate.

During that meeting in Delaware, Schumer urged Biden to take a confrontational approach once he was in the Oval Office: As president, Schumer said, Biden should go big, however daunting the Senate math might be. Only by seeking a huge new relief package that would stir mass public support, Schumer believed, could Biden hope to get anything remotely adequate from the Hill.

The congressional leaders found Biden's response reassuring enough. He was under no illusion that a winter relief bill signed by his predecessor would be enough to carry the country forward, or that a Republican Senate would be easy to work with. He would later describe a short-term deal, struck between the parties in late December, as a "down payment" on legislation that would truly meet the country's needs.

But unclear after the meeting was whether any of the principal participants had a real theory for how to move major new spending—or any large-scale legislation—through a Senate that seemed all but certain to stay in Republican hands.

If they could not devise such a plan, then the great mission of the Biden administration could be over before it even began. There would be no bringing the country together, no showing that Washington could be made to work, if the new president could not speedily confirm a cabinet and deliver a relief bill capable of reviving a listing economy and heading off cataclysmic budget cuts at the state and local level.

Should Democrats fail to accomplish even the basics of steadying a plague-stricken nation, then there was not much hope for the larger vision Biden had laid out in his campaign. From climate and health-care legislation to policing and immigration reform, the Democratic agenda was frozen at the start of a dark winter.

*　*　*

Without an obvious path forward for their governing plans, Pelosi and Schumer were already seeing divisions emerge among Capitol Hill Democrats—fissures that challenged them as leaders and that flummoxed the president-elect and his advisers. The strains of political polarization gripping the country—racial, regional, generational, and ideological—were now shaking the Democratic Party's leaders.

For Nancy Pelosi, aiming to stay as Speaker of the House, the election results had turned an expected coronation into a political obstacle course.

The election had left Democrats in charge of the House, but it had cut down their majority to a minute margin. A few seats were still undecided, but Pelosi knew Democrats were likely to remain in power by half a dozen votes at best. There would be no room for error on any matter of important legislative business, from the most consequential bill to the most perfunctory procedural votes, for two years.

That began with the vote to reinstall her as Speaker of the House.

To keep her job, Pelosi would have to win a vote of the chamber's full membership, with all the Republicans voting against her and only a few Democratic votes to spare. In 2019, the last time Pelosi had claimed the Speakership, fifteen Democrats had declined to support her, many of them having promised uneasy constituents back home that they would not give their support to a liberal leader unpopular in swing districts. But those dissenting Democrats had known full well that Pelosi would win the vote to become Speaker anyway. Back then, voting against her was a highly symbolic act.

This time, Pelosi's margin of control was a fraction of what it had been in 2019. Any breakaway Democratic votes could be far more dangerous.

Her caucus, from the furthest-left member of the Progressive Caucus to the most outspoken moderate, along with every one of Pelosi's personal critics and rivals in the chamber, would have to hang together. The Speaker vote would reveal whether the party could manage to do that. And then lawmakers would have to do it again and again and again, for two years.

In November, the prospect of such lockstep unity seemed highly uncertain. House Democrats had not waited even until the election was called for Joe Biden to begin issuing complaints and recriminations. On November 5, as Democrats were still waiting for the news networks to declare Biden the winner, the Democratic caucus had held an hours-long conference call that laid bare the anger and confusion coursing through the caucus, and the ideological rifts dividing the party.

Pelosi attempted to set a valedictory tone, announcing that Democrats had received "a mandate" in the election because of Biden's enormous popular-vote total. She was not about to share her own private assessment of the party's missteps. But her members had no use for the wishful-thinking spin the Speaker offered them.

Where Senate Democrats had faced annihilation in red America, House Democrats had bled seats even in diverse metropolitan districts that had revolted against Trump two years earlier. Rural America had been unkind to House Democrats, too, but salting the wound were losses in big cities and prosperous suburbs: two seats in Miami; two more in Southern California; one each in Oklahoma City, Salt Lake City, and Charleston, South Carolina.

Lawmakers from conservative districts instantly diagnosed the force that felled them.

"We need to not ever use the word 'socialist' or 'socialism' again," decreed Abigail Spanberger of Virginia, the former CIA officer who had barely hung on to her seat in a conservative-leaning district.

Jim Clyburn pointed a finger at his party's left wing in diplomatic but unmistakable terms. Still seen by many in his party as a Biden proxy, Clyburn was smarting from the landslide loss of his protégé Jaime Harrison in his state's Senate race. Democrats had suffered, Clyburn said, from "racialized voting" across much of the country, with white voters swinging hard toward the Republican Party. That could happen again in the looming Georgia runoffs, Clyburn warned, particularly since one of the Democratic nominees, Raphael Warnock, was Black.

In the November election, Clyburn argued, Democrats had not made things easier for themselves by allowing the party to be depicted as a boldly progressive organization in all time zones. He said lawmakers should be able to decide for themselves "whether or not you are going to run on Medicare for All or defunded police or socialized medicine or whatever.

"I would hope that we would sit down," Clyburn said, "and have some serious discussions about how to approach these campaigns."

The left pushed back fiercely. Rashida Tlaib, the outspoken progressive from Detroit, took umbrage at the criticism centrist Democrats were leveling at her faction of the party, equating it to silencing voters of color—a grave charge that implicated senior Black and Hispanic moderates.

"When I hear this from my colleagues," she said, "what I hear is stop pushing for what Black folks want, people of color folks that are living in poverty, and that we need to appeal to a certain number of people, suburban people, and to shut up. That's how I feel—like I am being asked to be quiet."

The tense meeting could have erupted in full-scale internal warfare, but both progressive and moderate leaders intervened at key moments to lower the temperature. Pramila Jayapal of Washington, the head of the Progressive Caucus, reminded her colleagues that the party could not win without turnout from young people and other liberal-leaning constituencies and pleaded for a shift in tone.

"Let's try to find a way to have a conversation that doesn't scapegoat, particularly progressives who are often the scapegoat of the other side," she said.

But the gap between rank-and-file professions of support for unity, and the hard work of actually forging consensus on politics and policy, was enormous. As Pelosi began counting the votes she would need to secure the Speakership, the practical obstacles to bringing her caucus together came into focus.

The threat of the coronavirus posed a challenge, particularly for members in ill health. Unlike other votes, which could be offered via proxy during the pandemic, the roll call for the Speakership required in-person attendance. Pelosi's team was concerned enough that they were prepared to fly in Alcee Hastings, the Florida congressman who was suffering from an advanced cancer that would claim his life in a matter of months.

More broadly, Pelosi would have to quell dissent from lawmakers who had opposed her in the past. She would have to ensure that no new renegades emerged to demand her ouster. And looking past the Speaker vote, she would have to stop too many members from quitting the chamber to take jobs in the Biden administration, thereby leaving temporary vacancies where she needed reliable Democrats.

That last part was the most straightforward for Pelosi, and perhaps the most aggravating for her members. Dozens of House members coveted jobs in the executive branch. There were well-known contenders, like New Mexico's Deb Haaland and Ohio's Marcia Fudge, who were effectively campaigning for cabinet jobs, and California's Karen Bass, who hoped to become ambassador to the United Nations. But a far larger group had aspirations to leave the Hill to fill out subcabinet jobs and embassies.

The voting math of the House dictated that most of those hopes had to be thwarted. In public, Pelosi evinced no concern about the appointments, chiding reporters for asking about the implications for her tissue-thin majority. But in private conversations, Pelosi and her deputy, Majority Leader Steny Hoyer, told the Biden team that they simply could not take more than a small few from the caucus. To do more than that, they said, would be to sabotage the Democratic House from the start.

"If you're taking the House members out for your cabinet, that's going to hurt your objective and our objective of passing policy," Hoyer told Steve Ricchetti, the incoming White House adviser.

Yet the delicacy of the moment meant Pelosi and Hoyer could not afford to be seen as publicly sabotaging the professional dreams of their own members in a way that would anger their friends and allies. When Hoyer said on the way into the House chamber one day that taking even two members from the House was "too many," he faced swift anger from liberal lawmakers who were promoting Haaland's bid to become the first Native American interior secretary. To calm the anger, Pelosi and Hoyer both lurched in the other direction, endorsing Haaland for the job and effectively ensuring her nomination.

Winning over her longtime opponents in the caucus had the potential to be harder than fending off job offers from the administration. Pelosi's first efforts at a charm offensive met with resistance. She enlisted Filemon Vela of Texas, himself a former critic of her leadership, to circulate a letter of support for her with other sometime renegades. The circumstances had changed since 2019, and the consequences of voting against Pelosi could be rather more severe. Lawmakers who had cast protest votes against her two years earlier, knowing she would win anyway, might be coaxed now into lending her their support.

Vela reported back that two lawmakers who had opposed Pelosi in the past, Tim Ryan of Ohio and Seth Moulton of Massachusetts, rebuffed his request to sign the letter. It was an unsettling omen.

At least one dissenter used Pelosi's obvious distress to their advantage. Ruben Gallego of Arizona, an ambitious Marine veteran who had been pressured out of running for the Senate the previous year, told Pelosi that he wanted to move on from the House and pursue a job in the Biden administration when the time was right. When that moment came, he said, he wanted Pelosi's support. She agreed, and he pledged to back her for Speaker.

Some in the caucus were immovable, defying pressure and pleading, threats and enticements. Mikie Sherrill of New Jersey was one of them, telling Pelosi that she had made a promise to her constituents not to support Pelosi for Speaker and that she intended to keep it.

"I told her, quite frankly, that I thought that her legislative agenda had been good, but that I do think we need to see new leadership in the caucus," Sherrill says.

Yet Pelosi saw other centrist Democrats move in her direction for a surprising reason: They saw her as a bulwark against the far left. Long caricatured by Republicans as a San Francisco radical, Pelosi was in fact a political realist through and through—a woman of progressive values but above all an old-school legislative power broker. She was no activist who saw honor in fighting for lost causes.

After the election, Pelosi was careful not to split her caucus by blaming one wing or another for the party's losses, but in a few strictly confidential conversations she pointed a finger leftward. Pelosi told one senior lawmaker that Democrats had alienated Asian and Hispanic immigrants with loose talk of socialism. In some of the same communities, the Italian Catholic Speaker said, Democrats had not been careful enough about the way they spoke about abortion among new Americans who were devout people of faith.

In a breakthrough for Pelosi, Kurt Schrader, a leader of the Democrats' centrist faction, shed his history of opposing her and backed Pelosi for Speaker because he trusted her to keep the ultra-left in check.

"There's no other person that could control the progressives in this Congress besides her," Schrader explains.

Indeed Pelosi was working the left-wing activists in her caucus as intensively as she was courting the cranky moderates. They, too, could block her path to the Speakership if they wanted to. The Speaker gathered a group of six of the most outspoken young progressives in the House—including Alexandria Ocasio-Cortez and the newly elected lawmakers Jamaal Bowman and Cori Bush—for a meeting in her office to hear out their priorities for the new Congress. Bowman and Bush had both defeated incumbent Democrats in primary elections the previous summer, and both had been quiet about their intentions toward the Speaker.

The progressives left impressed. All of them ended up supporting Pelosi for Speaker. Bowman, an educator by training, was taken with her commanding style: "Speaker Pelosi is a gangster," he says admiringly.

By the time she went to meet with Biden, Pelosi was confident she would maintain her position, albeit in part because no other Democrat had stepped forward to run against her. On November 18, the caucus voted without dissent to approve Pelosi as their candidate for Speaker. She still had to minimize defections on January 3, when the full House voted on the post. But without an open challenge to Pelosi's leadership it was unlikely that a meaningful number of Democrats would take that risk.

The November 18 vote was a significant victory for Pelosi, but to those around her it seemed like a joyless one. One ally recalls Pelosi expressing her fatigue and frustration with unusual vehemence that day, discussing her political future in a way she rarely did around colleagues.

"You couldn't pay me a billion dollars to run for Speaker again," she said, according to this person.

Speaking to another friend days later, Pelosi still sounded discouraged. The experience of begging for support to stay on as Speaker was wearing on her. The precarious margin of control and her party's ideological divisions in the House demanded an experienced, authoritative hand. Pelosi was the only Democrat in the chamber—the one Democrat *alive*—who had already served as Speaker, who had shown she could do the legislative arithmetic and twist the necessary arms to get things done.

And yet they were making her grovel.

"At this point in my life, I don't need this," she said, according to this friend.

That point in her life, after all, was eight months past her eightieth birthday. She had promised her party in 2018, as she prepared to reclaim the Speakership, that she would serve at most two more terms. Now, at the start of the second one, she was confronting a Democratic caucus that was hazing her and a Republican-controlled Senate that threatened to suffocate every consequential piece of legislation she wrangled out of her own chamber.

In their assessment of Senate Republicans, Pelosi and Schumer were of one mind. Both believed the Republican Party that was open to negotiation and reason was a thing of the past, displaced by Trump's cult of personality and McConnell's relentless obstruction. The party of Bush and McCain was gone.

Pelosi said as much to a lawmaker who visited her in her office in November. Reflecting on the grim implications of divided government, Pelosi turned to a photo of herself with President George Herbert Walker Bush and Barbara Bush, the first lady, who died within months of each other in 2018.

"I miss them both so much," she said.

* * *

The mood was even more mournful in the Senate. The party's wipeout in rural America had once again denied Democrats the majority they craved, and for some long-suffering lawmakers it was too much to bear.

A generation's worth of ambitious Democrats had languished in the Senate since 2010, the last time their party had enjoyed full control of the federal government. Up-and-coming Democrats—a spritely-for-the-Senate cohort of legislators under sixty—had long since tired of watching their policy dreams wither against the opposition of McConnell's Republican Conference. These Democrats had anticipated the 2020 election as their best chance to take power and, for the first time in their Senate careers, to actually govern.

Just as aggravated was a grayer-haired, or not-very-haired-at-all, group of senators who had more actuarial reasons to be impatient. For lawmakers nearing the end of their time in public life, the prospect of reclaiming a chairman's gavel had dangled as a golden enticement. Now that reward seemed out of reach.

The Senate math seemed immovable: Ninety-eight Senate seats had been allocated to one party or the other, with fifty of them going to Republicans and forty-eight to Democrats and independents aligned with them. Two seats held by Republicans were still up for grabs in Georgia, but Democrats had little hope for a sweep there. Before Thanksgiving, Schumer predicted to a friend that both Democratic nominees there, Jon Ossoff and Raphael Warnock, would lose on January 5.

The 2020 election was not the first time in his four-year tenure as Democratic leader that the party's hopes for Senate control had fallen to pieces, with races that seemed eminently winnable slipping away from Democratic candidates in their final weeks. In almost every case—from surprise defeats in Pennsylvania and Wisconsin in 2016, to agonizing losses in Maine and North Carolina in 2020—the shattered Democratic candidates had been personally recruited, coached, funded, and supervised by Schumer, often via direct calls from his ever-present and antiquated flip phone.

Since taking over as minority leader, Schumer had managed his caucus mainly through conciliation and compromise, working to appease an eclectic group that ranged from staunch progressives like Sanders and Warren to stubborn centrists like Joe Manchin of West Virginia and Kyrsten Sinema of Arizona, and a whole cohort of idiosyncratic Senate elders mostly unknown to the public. Schumer had adopted a strategy of placation and patience, urging Democrats to hang together against Trump, focus on winning reelection, and wait for the moment when power would return to them.

On the eve of the 2020 election, Schumer had believed that moment was at hand. In late October, he spoke by phone with a longtime friend and political ally who told the Brooklyn Democrat he believed the Senate majority was a pure toss-up—a fifty-fifty shot at best. The irritation Schumer flashed in response underscored just how badly he needed to win.

No, he fired back, it was a better shot than that.

After November 3, as Schumer struggled to process his own failure to read the odds, he tried to deal with his colleagues' disappointment mainly by evading it. In private, he was scorching in his assessment of how the far left had hurt his party: The "defund" movement, Schumer told allies, had simply devastated his candidates. But he never tempted the wrath of the left by saying so in the press.

Senate Democrats convened shortly after Election Day in the Dirksen Building, a normally buzzing office complex abutting the Capitol. The imposing marble edifice had been largely emptied during the pandemic, giving it a strange and hollow atmosphere, less like a locus of government than a vacant temple or even a tomb.

The Democratic meeting was an awkward hybrid affair, with some lawmakers attending in person and others beaming in virtually. Their agenda was to vote on their leadership team: Schumer and his deputies, Dick Durbin of Illinois and Patty Murray of Washington State. There was no question that they would stay in their roles, but some in the room expected an open discussion of the disappointing election results.

Schumer sought instead to make it a pro forma session, asking his colleagues to reinstall him in his job without discussion.

It was no trouble-making firebrand who objected, but Jeanne Shaheen of New Hampshire, a seventy-three-year-old moderate who had just won a third term. A former governor who had shepherded her once-red state's transformation from a cranky libertarian enclave into a low-tax magnet for socially liberal professionals, Shaheen was frustrated at the Democratic Party's implosion in rural America.

"When are we going to talk about what happened?" she asked, according to several people in the room.

Schumer's response amounted to pleading for time. Using the fractured

146

nature of the sessions as a shield, he promised Shaheen that they would have the conversation she wanted soon enough. But, he said, it would be unfair to have such an important debate with so many senators unable or unwilling to participate in person. It was not an entirely contrived excuse: Several senators, including Sinema, the mercurial Arizonan, had complained that there was even talk of holding in-person meetings during a pandemic.

But if Schumer hoped that pushing off the confrontation would allow the vexed mood to dissipate, it did not work out that way. In the chamber, Democratic frustration only continued to mount.

In another late-autumn meeting of Senate Democrats, Michael Bennet of Colorado, a cerebral moderate in his mid-fifties, said that the Democratic leadership team had let down the caucus. Without attacking Schumer himself, Bennet said it was obvious that the party's approach to winning elections was badly broken. Despite his prep-school manner and gentle voice, Bennet's comments fell with the force of a hammer.

He asked his colleagues to imagine the implications for a business that had appealed to its investors for round after round of new funding: What if you asked the board three times for an extra $100 million and promised each time to double the size of the business, and you failed and you failed and you failed?

The comparison to the back-to-back-to-back failures of Schumer's campaign committee was unmistakable. "Only here is there no accountability, no transparency, no discussion, and no potential change," Bennet said, according to two people present.

Schumer responded with blandishments and vows to do better next time. He promised colleagues they would "fight like hell" to take back the majority in 2022.

But Schumer's critics were not reassured. In a succession of meetings, some virtual and some in Schumer's Capitol office, a set of Democrats from politically forbidding states offered the equivalent of a private vote of no-confidence in the party's political strategy. A self-appointed task force that included Shaheen, Bennet, Chris Murphy of Connecticut, and Sherrod Brown of Ohio drafted an outline of proposed changes, reflecting what they saw as an urgent need to update the campaign machinery Democrats used to contact and turn out voters. They feared too much money was being burned on one-size-fits-all advertising strategies from another age.

Moderate Senate Democrats had another reason to worry about Schumer. The Democratic Senate leader was up for reelection in 2022 in a state where the activist left was on the march. New York's most prominent left-wing lawmaker, Alexandria Ocasio-Cortez, had not ruled out a campaign against Schumer, and the Democratic leader was seen by his colleagues as racing leftward to head off a primary. They worried that put him in an exceptionally bad position to resurrect the Democratic Party's brand in middle America.

In one meeting of the Democratic caucus, Tom Carper of Delaware nudged Schumer on precisely that subject. A seventy-three-year-old Vietnam veteran who had thrashed a more liberal primary challenger in 2018, Carper urged Schumer not to overestimate the threat from the left. "We ought to just have the damn fight," he said, according to a colleague. Carper promised Schumer his colleagues would fight at his side against AOC if she ran against him.

Things came to a head in early December, when a small group that included Bennet, Brown, and Jon Tester, the Montana farmer who had done a stint atop the Senate campaign committee, met with Schumer in his office. They had some gentle but firm demands.

The Democratic Senatorial Campaign Committee, which recruits and funds Democratic Senate campaigns, was the chief instrument of Schumer's rise to power. He had helmed the body during the breakthrough victories of 2006 and 2008, when Democrats gained fourteen Senate seats on a wave of backlash against the Bush administration. Schumer had maintained functional control of the body ever since.

His colleagues told him it was time for that to change.

"We basically said that Chuck was trying to do too much," Brown says, alluding to Schumer's joint roles as legislative chieftain and political field marshal.

According to Brown, Schumer responded with palpable relief, acknowledging freely that his visitors were right. He was stretched too thin. After a decade and a half as the de facto boss of the Senate campaign committee, Schumer promised to cede authority to other lawmakers. It marked a concession, of a kind, that the electoral Midas touch of Chuck Schumer might have expired sometime after the 2008 election when Democrats built a filibuster-proof majority.

Yet to the extent that stepping back from electoral maneuvering was supposed to free Schumer to devise a legislative agenda, it was not clear to anyone how much he would be able to deliver on that front. Even as he prodded Biden to "go big" and seek to force McConnell's hand, Schumer privately told friends that a miserly relief bill might be all they could get from Senate Republicans. At times, Biden's relative optimism seemed to grate on the downcast Senate leader.

Schumer told one former Senate colleague it was frustrating that Biden was so much more optimistic about working with McConnell than anyone who had dealt with the Republican leader recently.

* * *

Before Biden could even devise a strategy for confronting McConnell and a Republican Senate, he had to master the volatile currents within his own party. Democrats had held together through the general election, bonded together in large part through fear of Donald Trump. But the varied Democratic factions that had locked arms with Biden had done so anticipating that they would be rewarded richly in victory.

Now it was time to collect. Biden had promised an administration of historic diversity, a White House defined by smooth competence, a policy agenda of extraordinary breadth and boldness, and a cultural transformation that would heal the country and make Washington work again. In the weeks after winning the election, he found that keeping just the first of those promises would be a tall order.

The most urgent business of the presidential transition was assembling the people who would keep the essential functions of government running. Biden advisers had been engaged for months in readying a massive slate of appointees to fill those jobs, efforts that were now complicated by Trump's refusal to concede defeat. So far, Biden's operation was taking a patient approach with the outgoing administration: If they had to wait until late November for the General Services Administration, a federal agency involved in transition mechanics, to start working with Biden's chosen team, then so be it. For the moment, Trump's behavior seemed more petulant than scary.

In the weeks immediately following the election, some of the Biden team's greatest headaches involved their fellow Democrats.

The battle over executive appointments was always bound to be intense and even bitter. Many of the party's most impressive professionals had seen their careers derailed in 2016 by Trump's surprise victory, and were now eager to elbow their way into top jobs. A whole new cohort of fast-rising elected officials, policy thinkers, lawyers, and strategists had emerged since then, surging to prominence as leaders of anti-Trump movements and big brains of the 2020 campaign.

But the tug-of-war for administration jobs became more ferocious with the Democrats' failure to take the Senate. The Democrats' deficit in the Senate all but ensured that Biden would not pluck anyone from the chamber for his administration. The two leading progressive presidential candidates of 2020, Bernie Sanders and Elizabeth Warren, had both been eyeing cabinet jobs, but they hailed from states where Republican governors would have the authority to fill any vacant Senate seats. A third Democrat, Patty Murray, was being eyed for a cabinet job, but that prospect ended as well when the Biden team decided to adopt a semi-official no-senators policy.

The growing assumption in the party that Biden's policies would wither on the Hill meant that the great engine of change over the next four years would be the executive branch. That made many Democrats even more determined to make the Biden White House and cabinet a human reflection of the multicultural, progressive future they desired.

Biden described that goal somewhat apologetically to one eventual appointee, using a dated political euphemism. "I've got a lot of constituency politics," he confided.

But Biden also had his own interests and preferences to consider. He intended to bring his inner circle of advisers with him into the White House, and that tight-knit group was almost uniformly white. His first choice for the cabinet, secretary of state, was telling: From a very short list that included Chris Coons, the Delaware senator, and Susan Rice, Biden picked Tony Blinken, the veteran diplomat, Biden aide, and personal friend. "Tony wanted secretary," Biden told one of the runners-up, giving all the explanation necessary.

The first set of personnel announcements in the middle of the month came as a shock to Black, Hispanic, and Asian American Democrats. The names themselves were not so surprising, but the cumulative effect was unsettling: Ron Klain as chief of staff, with Jennifer O'Malley Dillon as his deputy; Steve Ricchetti as counselor to the president; Mike Donilon as senior adviser; Dana Remus as White House counsel. All had been at Biden's right hand throughout the campaign. Some had been there for decades.

All were white.

Joining them in the West Wing, to be sure, were Cedric Richmond, the former head of the Congressional Black Caucus, and Julie Chavez Rodriguez, a former Obama White House official. But the main takeaway appeared to be that the Biden White House would be run chiefly by white people. It did not help that the people tasked most visibly with running the transition, Jeff Zients and Ted Kaufman, were a pair of white men. Despite the sprawling apparatus set up to oversee the transition, the crucial decisions on cabinet jobs were made by an exceedingly small group that included those two men, Klain, and the incoming commander in chief.

In mid-November, Governor Michelle Lujan Grisham of New Mexico, the former head of the Congressional Hispanic Caucus who had been named a co-chair of the transition, called a friend on Capitol Hill to vent about the insularity of the inner Biden circle. Despite her co-chair role, Lujan Grisham told this friend: "I don't know shit."

The Biden team quickly recognized that they had made a mistake with their rollout of the senior staff. But it was not an easy error to correct, because the impression they had given to their friends was fundamentally an accurate one. While Biden had many people of color in his political orbit, his most intimate and trusted aides were white. It was a reality that they had managed to obscure for much of the 2020 campaign. Thrust into public view, it became a defining political challenge of the transition.

And Biden was not finished installing his longtime counselors and friends from the Obama administration—a heavily white group—in super-staffer positions with close proximity to the Oval Office.

"The people around him were defensive," says Al Sharpton, describing their response to criticism of the staff announcement. "They were like: We're going to make everybody understand that they're represented, don't jump the gun."

But that response wasn't good enough: "My position was, I'm not talking about what you're going to do, I'm talking about what you did," Sharpton says. "We are in the middle of what we consider a racist administration. We don't need subtlety coming out of it."

Biden and his aides hastened to unveil additional appointments that would ease the mood of alarm, picking Alejandro Mayorkas, a top official in the Obama-era Department of Homeland Security, to become its first Latino secretary, and Linda Thomas-Greenfield, a highly respected career diplomat, as the second-ever Black woman to serve as ambassador to the United Nations. The transition team pleaded for time in private, promising that they really would assemble the most diverse administration in history. It would just take a little while.

In late November, Donna Brazile, the former Democratic National Committee chair, called Klain to complain about the lack of Black appointees. Klain said they were making progress and reminded her that Barack Obama had not named a Black cabinet member until December. That was not a reassuring point of comparison for Brazile, who remembered well how the administration of the first Black president had been dominated by white men.

On matters of diversity, Brazile shot back, "Obama wasn't exactly the gold standard for Black folks."

One cabinet selection after another turned into a charged standoff. Biden angered his friends in the Congressional Black Caucus with his determination to bring back Tom Vilsack, the former Iowa governor who held the job of secretary of agriculture for eight years in the Obama administration. Clyburn preferred Marcia Fudge, the Ohio lawmaker, for the job, and pressed Biden to make her the first Black woman to lead the department, while Bennie Thompson of Mississippi, a senior House Democrat, circulated a memo outlining Black leaders' reservations about Vilsack's record.

And Fudge lobbied publicly for the job, declaring in an interview with *Politico* that it would be a meaningful breakthrough for Black leaders. She said she was tired of Black appointees being steered toward a few arms of the federal bureaucracy, like the Department of Housing and Urban Development.

"As this country becomes more and more diverse, we're going to have to stop looking at only certain agencies as those that people like me fit in," she said. "You know, it's always 'we want to put the Black person in labor or HUD.'"

But Biden wanted Vilsack for the job—wanted him more, in fact, than Vilsack wanted the post himself. A devoted supporter of Biden's primary campaign during its bleakest days, Vilsack told associates he hoped for a new and different gig in government that would give him a hand in myriad policy areas—he wanted to oversee the Office of Management and Budget. Still, he allowed himself to be persuaded by the president-elect. Biden offered Fudge a different cabinet job, as housing secretary, and she accepted.

The position of health secretary was even more fraught, setting off a chain reaction of hurt feelings and grievance among Hispanic and Asian American lawmakers. One leading candidate, Gina Raimondo, the Rhode Island governor, saw her prospects fade as labor unions with whom she clashed at the state level mobilized against her, and concern mounted about diversity in Biden's appointments. She withdrew from consideration, expressing disillusionment with the process and questioning whether the HHS secretary would even be an influential person in the administration. She texted a political ally: "I've always hated D.C."

A second leading candidate seemed to be Lujan Grisham, whose background as a former state health secretary and pandemic-management record seemed to make her a natural fit. However, she was also a take-charge executive who had little patience for being told what to do: One of her favorite stories from her time in Congress was about being denied an invitation to a meeting at the Trump White House, and showing up anyway after smuggling her way through the gates in a colleague's car.

It soon became clear to both Lujan Grisham and transition officials that she was not prepared to approach the job with the self-effacing deference Biden officials desired. She wanted an expansive policymaking role. The transition wanted a functionary who would happily take orders from the West Wing, including the super-staffer Biden planned to put in charge of pandemic response—Jeff Zients.

In an interview months later, Lujan Grisham expressed neither bitterness about the outcome of the process nor regret about having conveyed to the Biden team exactly how she would have hoped to do the job. But as she sat in the living room of the governor's mansion in Santa Fe, which is filled with Native American art and includes a chicken coop outside, she made clear her pull-no-punches style may not have been a good fit for an administration that micromanages policy from the White House.

"I get shit done, but I do it the way that it needs to be," Lujan Grisham says, adding: "I am well known for that. And if that was an issue, I get it."

The transition sought to nudge her instead into a different position: interior secretary, a slot often reserved for a Western governor. She said she did not want the job. After declining a post that three other New Mexico Democrats were actually interested in, her reluctance was leaked to *Politico*. The Congressional Hispanic Caucus saw it as a breach of Lujan Grisham's privacy, an insulting attempt by transition officials to embarrass her for declining a job she did not want. They demanded a meeting with Klain and Zients to address the incident, as well as their concerns about a lack of senior Hispanic appointees besides Mayorkas.

Another caucus of minority lawmakers was also demanding a meeting with the same white men: the Congressional Asian Pacific American Caucus, which was similarly dismayed by the absence of Asian American appointees so far. They, too, were annoyed about the process of choosing a health secretary. Vivek Murthy, the Indian American former surgeon general, had been one of Biden's closest health advisers during the 2020 campaign, and if he was not getting the job of health secretary then these lawmakers felt he should be granted another cabinet-level post.

Both meetings went poorly, reinforcing the sense among lawmakers of color that the people assembling the new government were too white, too male, and too comfortable telling the cornerstone constituencies of the Democratic Party to bide their time.

Klain attempted a conciliatory approach in the meeting with Hispanic lawmakers on December 3, telling them he was sorry about the leaks and that he did not know where they had come from. The anger among Lujan Grisham's former colleagues was palpable, with Ben Ray Luján, the newly elected senator from New Mexico, speaking forcefully in defense of his home-state governor.

The wounded lawmakers urged Klain and the other Biden aides to speed up the appointment of more Hispanic cabinet members. The contents of the tense meeting leaked to reporters immediately, irritating Klain and panicking transition officials who feared that a public narrative about spurned lawmakers of color could spiral out of control.

Desperate to calm the situation, Biden and Klain made a hasty choice from their remaining candidates for health secretary. The day after the CHC meeting, transition officials reached out to Xavier Becerra, the congressman-turned-California attorney general who was hoping to lead the Department of Justice, to ask if he'd consider taking a different cabinet job—perhaps health secretary. When Becerra said he would, Biden quickly called him to offer him the job, and on December 6, three days after the meeting with Hispanic lawmakers, transition officials confirmed to reporters that Becerra had been chosen.

It may have been a sign of the harried selection process that when Biden formally announced Becerra as his nominee, he referred to him as "Xavier Baqueria."

To some Democrats, Becerra was a baffling choice. He was not a public-health expert, and he was certain to face a tough confirmation fight if Republicans held the Senate. Among the flummoxed Democrats was perhaps the most significant political partner for the incoming administration: Nancy Pelosi. The Speaker had worked closely with Becerra in the House and saw him as untrustworthy.

Pelosi seldom strayed from party-line talking points in public, and when she openly expressed dissent from other Democrats it was almost always in coded or passive-aggressive language. But her colleagues knew she could be far blunter in private about other Democrats, particularly those who had crossed her in the past. Becerra had done so during his time in the House, and Pelosi was annoyed that the Biden team had not checked with her before nominating him.

"You should know who you're hiring," she chided Ricchetti, according to a person briefed on the conversation. Noting that she was a former colleague of Becerra, and a fellow Californian, she added archly: "I may have some valuable information."

The Biden advisers' meeting with Asian American lawmakers was just as tense. Klain, fuming at the leaks from their meeting with the CHC, declined even to show up for this session, leaving the job to Zients, Ricchetti, and Kaufman. They, too, attempted a conciliatory approach, acknowledging that there was frustration at the limited representation of Asian Americans in nominations so far. Only one cabinet-level position, the Office of Management and Budget, had been slated for an Asian American—Neera Tanden, the head of the Center for American Progress—and Senate Republicans who viewed her as a noxious partisan were calling the nomination dead on arrival.

Judy Chu, the California congresswoman, told the Biden aides that it was not good enough for the incoming administration to nominate Asian Americans in the name of diversity if they did not ultimately make it through the confirmation process.

"We want to make sure they are not just token nominees to make it look like you're trying to achieve diversity, but who are all ultimately not successful," Chu said.

Pramila Jayapal, the progressive lawmaker from Washington, pressed the men to double that number by making Murthy, nominated for his old job as surgeon general, a cabinet-level official. She pointed out that Becerra had less management experience than him.

Zients deflated the idea. Murthy was not likely to be elevated, he said. Invoking his own days as head of the National Economic Council in the Obama administration, Zients said he regularly attended cabinet meetings without being a full-fledged member of the group. Some participants found his manner condescending, and Chu said bluntly that his response was disappointing.

The group presented the three white men with a list of Asian Americans they hoped to see in the cabinet, including Katherine Tai, who would eventually be nominated for trade representative. But the Biden officials made no commitments in the meeting. Grace Meng, the New York Democrat, told them there was a lot of pain in the Asian American community about feeling overlooked by the new administration.

"As a caucus, I think we do feel slighted," Mark Takano, the California congressman, said in a January interview. "We've always had this struggle with presidential candidates and their teams. I think AAPIs are just sort of looked at as kind of an afterthought in a lot of ways, and frankly now."

By the end of the transition, the Biden team eventually managed to assemble a cabinet of striking diversity, including the first woman to helm the Treasury, Janet Yellen; the first Black defense secretary, Lloyd Austin; and Haaland, the first Native American to oversee America's public lands. Tai and Becerra were part of the group, as was Raimondo, who was plucked from Providence to serve as commerce secretary. Fearful of backlash against white nominees, the Biden team made sure to roll out some of the most prominent white cabinet selections with deputies who were people of color, or as part of a slate of nominees who represented diversity.

Biden also lifted one of his former Democratic primary rivals into the cabinet, boosting an ambitious young moderate widely expected to run for president again. Pete Buttigieg, the former mayor of South Bend, Indiana, had considered a number of next steps after his presidential campaign ended. Buttigieg had unsuccessfully pursued the jobs of United Nations ambassador and commerce secretary, and had discussed the possibility of becoming a university president.

A few of Buttigieg's political advisers floated an inventive idea to some of the former mayor's big donors, suggesting that perhaps the young Hoosier could move to New York City and run for mayor there. Buttigieg was not interested, and when Biden finally called with a job offer, the decision became easy: Buttigieg would be the transportation secretary, and the first openly gay person ever confirmed to a president's cabinet.

Yet even as the immense diversity of the cabinet drew celebratory headlines and Democratic applause, the president continued to install white veterans of the Obama administration at the uppermost levels of the White House, some of them with policy portfolios that overlapped heavily with the mandates of historic cabinet appointees. Would it be Deb Haaland and Michael Regan, the first Black administrator of the Environmental Protection Agency, who would spearhead the environmental agenda, or John Kerry and Gina McCarthy, the Obama cabinet officials granted climate-czar status by Biden? Would it be Lloyd Austin, the first Black defense secretary, who would have Biden's ear on matters of national security, or Jake Sullivan, the forty-three-year-old policy wonder boy Biden had put atop the National Security Council?

The insularity and whiteness of Biden's brain trust, and the president's apparent preference for veterans of the Obama administration, wounded at least one trusted loyalist from the earliest days of his campaign. Symone Sanders, who joined Biden early and became one of his most important surrogates through months of attacks on his record on race and criminal justice, had coveted the job of White House press secretary. She was offered neither that job nor the deputy slot, and instead took a senior position in the vice president's office. It was a stinging disappointment.

In a text message to a friend, Sanders alluded to a memorable episode from the campaign when she physically blocked a protester from getting near then-candidate Biden. That friend paraphrased her message in these words: "What is the point of tackling people for white folks if they want to tackle nobody for you?"

In an unguarded moment around New Year's, Klain told a political ally that he had already grown weary of managing the various identity-based interests of the Democratic coalition. He sighed that the Biden team had itself to blame, at least in part, for treating the cabinet as an identity-politics Rubik's Cube, and he believed that they had wound up choosing at least two nominees—Tanden and Becerra—who might never get confirmed by a Republican Senate.

Once they panicked about the Lujan Grisham spat and scrambled to elevate Becerra, Klain acknowledged, it had become "open season."

*　*　*

While the frustrated factions of the Democratic Party were rattling Biden, Schumer, and Pelosi, remarkably patient during the dark winter were the leaders of the ideological left in Washington. Figures like Bernie Sanders, Elizabeth Warren, and Alexandria Ocasio-Cortez, who could have detonated Biden cabinet appointments or demanded a change in leadership at the congressional level, were playing a longer game, lobbying the Biden team quietly or biding their time for the new Congress to take power and begin the great legislative maneuvering of the new term.

All had reasons to show restraint. As the year came to an end, Sanders was still pursuing a cabinet position: He wanted to be a kind of super-labor secretary, with a mandate not just to lead one executive department but to direct policy on workers throughout the administration. It was a long shot and Biden's staff was unenthused, but Biden himself had not entirely ruled out the idea.

Warren, meanwhile, had a close relationship with Klain, and the two were consulting on economic and regulatory nominations. She had endorsed Yellen privately for treasury secretary before her selection, telling Klain: "I'm my first choice, but if not me, I think Janet Yellen is the right person." She had given Klain a list of her favorite names to take over the agency she founded, the Consumer Financial Protection Bureau, and from that list Klain and Biden had picked a former aide to Warren, Rohit Chopra, for the job. Her list of personnel preferences was long and stretched deep into various cabinet departments and agencies.

But for all the forbearance the left showed in November and December, a different kind of test was not far off for Biden and his congressional allies. For Schumer and Pelosi, quelling Democrat anger in the Senate and division in the House had been difficult enough. For Biden, putting together a cabinet had been similarly trying. The party was in a fragile state and it had not yet begun to govern.

At least a few advisers to Biden were already on guard for a revolt from the left, venting preemptively about progressives lacking political sense or misreading the results of the 2020 campaign. Most heated had been Cedric Richmond, who had phoned a close ally in Louisiana after his White House appointment was announced. Richmond had drawn some fire from the left, including the Sunrise Movement, an activist group with close ties to House progressives, because of his ties to fossil-fuel interests. He was angry in return at the group of left-wing House women, including Ocasio-Cortez and Tlaib, sometimes known as "the Squad."

Those lawmakers, Richmond told this friend, were "fucking idiots."

Less venomous was the language Steve Ricchetti used in early January with a Biden ally on Capitol Hill. Congressional progressives had begun to voice criticism of the coronavirus relief deal Democratic and Republican moderates had struck with the Trump administration, viewing the stimulus checks as stingy and the lack of aid to state government as a devastating omission. In the eyes of some Democrats, it looked like a dress rehearsal for how progressives might seek to pressure Biden in a complex legislative negotiation.

"The problem with the left," Ricchetti said, "is they don't understand that they lost."

There was no telling whether Biden's political coalition would hang together when it encountered real adversity. Unless an almost unimaginable stroke of good luck awaited Democrats in Georgia—unless Republicans somehow managed to lose not one but two Senate runoffs there—Biden was facing a dreary future. To avoid that fate Democrats needed the political equivalent of a miracle, and they needed two of them.

As it turned out, what they needed was Donald Trump.

Chapter 6

The Last Line

By early December, President Trump's frustration at losing the election had curdled into a paranoid conviction that Joe Biden had somehow stolen his victory. Though his lawyers had been unable to identify any serious grounds for challenging the election in court, and Trump himself could not articulate a clear theory of how, exactly, the Democrats had snatched away the race from him, the president was immovable on the subject. He had not been defeated.

From that passionate and baseless belief emerged a dangerous plan. As usual with Trump, it was less a considered strategy than a series of aggressive impulses, carried out with a certain crude determination and often yielding unintended consequences. In this case, that meant badgering Republican leaders in Washington and in the states, strong-arming ostensible allies, and even hectoring municipal-level election officials, with a demand that they do the impossible: overturn a fair election simply because he wanted them to.

The consequences of Trump's conduct would have a tidal-wave effect on the American political system—destabilizing his own party, demolishing the Republican Senate majority, obstructing the transfer of power to Biden, and sowing suspicion and anger about the legitimacy of the 2020 election among his core supporters. By convincing his own voters the election was rigged, Trump paved the way for Democrats to take full control of the federal government and for his most extreme supporters to mount an attack on the Capitol.

With millions still unemployed, coronavirus infections and death rates soaring, and the vaccine not yet widely available, the end of 2020 marked one of the grimmest holiday seasons in the peacetime history of the country. It was also a winter of despair for American democracy.

Nowhere did Trump do more to attack the foundations of democracy than in Georgia.

Not long before the Electoral College was set to vote on December 14, the president called in to a meeting of Republican Senate leaders on Capitol Hill. He had just been to Georgia to campaign for the two Republican senators facing runoff elections there, David Perdue and Kelly Loeffler. Trump had some observations about the voters down South.

They love their president, he told the Republican leaders. But they don't like their senators.

Trump believed he knew why conservative voters lacked enthusiasm for Perdue and Loeffler, and he explained as much to Mitch McConnell. Brian Kemp, the governor, had defended the election as safe and secure even though Biden won his state by a small margin. Voters would not stand for this, Trump believed, and neither should Perdue and Loeffler.

Mitch, he said, these guys are going to lose if they don't get Kemp to change his position on the election.

But the president had more on his mind. Switching the outcome in Georgia—even if such a thing were possible—would only shift sixteen Electoral College votes into Trump's column, and Biden would need to shed more than twice as many to tip the election back into Trump's hands. The president was convinced that he could engineer a reversal on that scale.

I won by four hundred or five hundred thousand votes in Georgia, Trump told McConnell. If we can get the governor to recertify, we can then move on to Michigan and Pennsylvania. I've been calling folks in those states and they're with us.

Trump was emphatic: We can win this thing.

When the call was over, McConnell removed his glasses, rubbed his forehead, and shook his head.

"We've got to stay focused on Georgia," the leader said.

He made no other comment to the astonished senators who had listened in on the conversation.

* * *

The Republican Senate leader had been worried about Georgia for some time. It had not taken a deranged phone call from Trump to show McConnell that the president was thrashing around and looking for other people to blame for problems of his own making.

On December 3, several weeks after he had established a back-channel line of communication with Biden, McConnell held a press conference in the Capitol and avoided any criticism of the outgoing president. He was worried that if Trump grew angry at him, the president would take it out on the Republican Senate as a whole by doing something to sabotage Perdue and Loeffler. For that very reason, McConnell had not yet publicly recognized Biden as the winner of the election.

But away from the cameras that day, McConnell did not mince words about the president's fixation on disputing his obvious defeat in the presidential race and his apparent desire to scapegoat state officials in places like Georgia.

"What it looks to me like he's doing is setting this up so he can blame the governor and the secretary of state if we lose," McConnell said in an interview outside his office in the Capitol. "He's always setting up somebody to blame it on."

McConnell said he had tried to nudge Trump toward conceding defeat. "Everybody around him except for clowns like Sidney Powell and Lin Wood are trying to get him to do the right thing," he said, referring to two pro-Trump attorneys who'd become infamous in the post-election period for their preposterous claims.

Could nobody get through to the president? "Not yet," McConnell said.

In private, the Senate leader had begun to complain that Trump was increasingly listening not to the handful of serious people around him, but to "the clowns." McConnell's wife, Elaine Chao, the transportation secretary, had begun telling their friends more openly of her household's shared discontent with Trump: "Every day the leader and I wake up saying, 'How do we manage the president?'" Chao told one friend, according to this person's recollection.

McConnell had his eye on Trump's planned trip to South Georgia that coming Saturday, December 5. He was trying to control what Trump would say there, keeping him focused on pro-Republican talking points rather than bizarre conspiracy theories. "We wrote the script for him, which I believe will be in the prompter and I believe he will say it," McConnell said, speaking about the president as if Trump were a kind of windup toy.

But, McConnell added: "What we don't know is what else he'll say."

A few hours later, and about 640 miles to the south, Brian Kemp was at his wits' end over what Trump had already been saying for most of a month. The state had already certified Biden's victory after conducting a recount that affirmed Trump had lost. But the president would not stop berating Kemp and Georgia's Republican secretary of state, Brad Raffensperger, about concocting some way to change the outcome.

A former real estate developer who had slowly climbed the ranks of Georgia politics, Kemp was not one to clash with party leaders. But he had become a whipping boy for Trump, first because he had appointed Kelly Loeffler to the Senate over Trump's preferred candidate, and then because Kemp would not seek to overturn Biden's legitimate victory.

As McConnell was predicting that Trump would set up Kemp as a fall guy in Georgia, the unhappy governor was convening a meeting in the suburban stadium of the Atlanta Braves to vent about the president's unrelenting attacks on him. He summoned Perdue, Loeffler, and a handful of aides to a suite in the Delta Club there before a fundraiser for the two senators in Truist Park.

Kemp told the senators he was getting his "ass kicked" by Trump, a Republican present recalls. The president was wrong on just about everything relating to the state's election results and what Kemp could and could not do about the outcome. The governor appealed to the group: Can you help me calm the situation down?

When the senators balked, the meeting grew tense. Perdue emphasized that it was he and Loeffler whose careers were on the line in a month. And really, he said, it was the governor who should be helping them out. Perdue said it would give them political cover with Trump's riled-up base if the governor called a special session of the legislature, nominally to look into election irregularities. Without that kind of sop to the White House, Perdue said, Georgia's Trump-loving conservatives might simply sit out the runoff—and, he added, they might not show up for Kemp's reelection in 2022.

It was a shameless and cynical demand that reflected Perdue's desperate need for Trump's help. A wealthy businessman and perhaps the best-tailored member of the Senate, the former Reebok and Dollar General executive was a textbook country-club Republican. He made his home in Sea Island, where the golf courses were as picturesque as the houses were pricey, and spent plenty of time on the links.

Elected to the Senate in 2014, he had attempted to forge a bond with his party's working-class base by becoming one of Donald Trump's best friends in the Senate and bonding over their shared love of golf.

"He's nobody's choirboy, but neither were people like Winston Churchill, for example," Perdue said in a 2017 interview.

Perdue's junior colleague had made an even less subtle version of the same bet. An Illinois farmgirl who rose in the world of finance and married the future chairman of the New York Stock Exchange, Loeffler and her husband, Jeffrey Sprecher, were pillars of the Atlanta business and philanthropic community. They hosted receptions at a Buckhead mansion with nine antique fireplaces, co-owned the city's WNBA franchise, and contributed generously to the Republican establishment. Loeffler even toted her phone in a case bearing the logo of the party's 2012 ticket: "Romney-Ryan."

Regular Trump rally-goers they were not.

But Kemp had appointed Loeffler to join the Senate in 2020 after a long-serving Republican, Johnny Isakson, resigned midway through his term for health reasons. The governor had chosen Loeffler in the hope of stemming the exodus of Atlanta-area women from the Republican Party. Yet within months Loeffler had reinvented herself on the campaign trail as a hard-line Trump supporter, donning a baseball cap and branding herself as "more conservative than Attila the Hun" in an effort to head off a challenge from the right.

Now both senators had a real political problem on their hands.

Perdue and Loeffler had tethered themselves unbreakably to Trump in a state that was changing fast—so fast that a Democratic presidential candidate had carried it for the first time in the twenty-first century. The city of Atlanta had exploded into a sprawling metropolis: an affordably priced, temperate magnet for a diverse community of transplants from all over the country.

Long identified with Coca-Cola and Delta Air Lines, the Atlanta area had also become a corporate behemoth, home to companies like CNN, UPS, and Home Depot, and the American headquarters of the carmakers Mercedes and Porsche. These companies came to Georgia for a business-friendly climate, and brought with them an educated, multicultural workforce. With its civil rights–era history, renowned historically Black colleges, and New South brand, Atlanta was an especially strong magnet for Black professionals and their families from around the country.

Taken together, these changes did not bode well for Trumpism, and David Perdue knew it.

In a November presentation for donors the senator had laid out the state's political trend lines with a PowerPoint precision that showed him for the business executive he was.

"I won by eight points in 2014," the senator recalled. "Trump won by five points in '16, and our governor won by less than half a point in '18, and it's not because we had declining candidates."

The state, Perdue said, had added 2.5 million new voters in the last six years, and 5 million people had voted on November 3. "You can kind of do the math," he said.

He and Loeffler were not facing terribly fearsome Democratic challengers.

The party had attempted to recruit Stacey Abrams, the former gubernatorial candidate, to run for the Senate, and after she declined the party had to settle for a pair of more obscure candidates. Perdue was running against Jon Ossoff, a young documentary filmmaker who had lost a high-profile special election for the House in 2017 before setting his sights even higher. To challenge Loeffler, Democrats had backed Raphael Warnock, the senior pastor of Atlanta's storied Ebenezer Baptist Church, who had a stirring up-from-poverty personal story but no political experience to speak of.

But on November 3, neither Republican had won an outright majority of the vote, and in Georgia that meant the races would get pushed to a second round of voting on January 5, with only the top two finishers in each contest on the ballot. Perdue had come tantalizingly close to the necessary threshold to win outright: Only the presence of a Libertarian candidate on the ballot had kept him at 49.7 percent.

As a result, control of the U.S. Senate was at stake in Georgia. Perdue and Loeffler calculated that the outcome would depend on whether Donald Trump's base turned out to vote on January 5 with greater enthusiasm than the millions of new Georgians who had never before voted in a runoff election for the Senate.

And so Perdue and Loeffler would not help Brian Kemp, or even recognize Joe Biden as the winner of the presidential race in their state. They believed they needed to stay on the right side of a president who was increasingly choosing to live in an alternative reality in which hundreds of thousands of illegal votes had been cast in Georgia. To a great extent, the two senators followed him into that alternative reality.

The wealthy duo were so afraid of angering the president that they discarded perhaps the strongest argument they might have made to swing voters: that Democrats were sure to control the White House and half of Congress in 2021, so voters should keep Republicans in charge of the Senate for balance. Making that case would mean acknowledging Trump had lost.

Only a week after the election, both Perdue and Loeffler attempted to wriggle out of acknowledging Biden's narrow but clear advantage in their state.

On a joint conference call with donors, Loeffler hemmed and hawed, saying that she had "concerns about the election."

"We voiced that, um, and we're going to make sure that we have an election process that folks can trust in January," she said.

Perdue was more expansive in his comments, and in the privacy of a donor call he acknowledged that Trump's political prognosis was not strong. His hope for his own race, Perdue said, was that there would be some voters "who voted in an anti-Trump way, voted for Biden and then voted down the list, that we think may come back to us in this plea for split government."

Yet even as he spoke to wealthy contributors he needed to rouse, Perdue was reluctant to flatly state that the president had lost, even three days after every network had called the race. He had to talk around the fact of Trump's certain defeat or risk enraging the president and his supporters.

"President Trump, it looks like now may not be able to hold out, we don't know that, but there are four states that they're contesting and we'll just have to see how that plays out," Perdue said.

But Karl Rove, the former George W. Bush adviser who was helping the senators raise money, made it clear enough that he expected Biden to become the president. Republicans needed to win the Senate races in Georgia if they wanted to control any elected arm of the federal government.

"This," he said, "is the last line of defense for conservatives."

People close to Donald Trump had a different set of priorities in Georgia. At the Georgia Republican Party headquarters, a four-story concrete building in a commercial part of Buckhead, party strategists convened on an upper floor throughout November to plot a two-month runoff campaign that would cost hundreds of millions of dollars. But days after the November election, the president's son paid a visit to the party to push his own agenda.

Presiding over a meeting of Senate-oriented strategists and local Trump loyalists, Donald Trump Jr. said his party had to put first things first.

No one should focus on the Senate races until they fight for Trump, Don Jr. said.

When Georgia's recount ended in late November, ratifying Biden's victory, the Trump lawyers Sidney Powell and Rudy Giuliani held a rambling news conference at the Republican National Committee in Washington. The November 19 session resembled an elaborate prank more than a credible litigation announcement: Powell, introduced as a member of Trump's elite legal team, uncorked a bizarre theory about how software devised by the long-deceased Venezuelan despot Hugo Chávez had rigged elections in the United States through a specific voting machine company.

Giuliani's most memorable contribution to the session, meanwhile, was to perspire so heavily that some sort of hair product went streaking down his face.

For a few Republicans, it was a breaking point.

"The conduct of the president's legal team has been a national embarrassment," Chris Christie intoned on ABC's *This Week*.

Trump responded angrily to the criticism, and phoned Christie to complain. The former New Jersey governor repeated his televised remarks and went further: He urged Trump to concede and warned that his behavior was going to overshadow his accomplishments in office. But the president wasn't swayed. He insisted the election had been stolen and he would not give up his crusade against the results.

Christie continued to press. If Trump had evidence of wrongdoing, he should present it. But he hadn't provided any so far, likely because there wasn't any. Then Christie asked Trump: "You're not embarrassed by Sidney Powell? Because if you're not, you should be."

That night, Giuliani and another Trump attorney, Jenna Ellis, issued a statement cutting ties with Powell. But if Christie had shamed Trump about one of his lawyers, he had done nothing to deter the president from pressing forward with his campaign of fruitless litigation and public slander against the electoral process.

Neither Loeffler nor Perdue wanted to attempt even a faint version of Christie's come-on-man conversation with the president. To them, holding the line meant indulging Trump's attacks on the integrity of the election without reservation.

Before the middle of November, the two senators called for the resignation of Georgia's chief election official, Secretary of State Brad Raffensperger, for unspecified "failures" in election administration; Perdue and Loeffler did nothing to push back on the increasingly unhinged presidential rhetoric, including tweets deriding Kemp and Raffensperger by name and claiming they were ignoring a "goldmine" of voter fraud.

So, in early December, an official in Raffensperger's office, Gabriel Sterling, walked before a bank of television cameras in Georgia's state capitol, ripped off his mask, and standing between a pair of Christmas trees, issued a prophetic warning.

"Stop inspiring people to commit potential acts of violence," Sterling said, speaking to Trump. His voice filled with anger and urgency, Sterling continued: "Someone's going to get hurt, someone's going to get shot, someone's going to get killed, and it's not right."

* * *

It was not only in Georgia that Trump was testing the mettle of Republican officials with demands that they engage in a version of election tampering. He may not have been a sophisticated political strategist, but the president recognized he needed to flip several states to win the election, all of which Biden had carried by far more than his 11,779-vote margin in Georgia.

The absurdity of that task did not deter Trump from attempting it. On November 20, he summoned the Republican leaders of the Michigan legislature to the White House. The president wanted to speak with them in the Oval Office about the outcome of the presidential race there and apply pressure on them to block Michigan's sixteen Electoral College votes from going to Biden.

It was precisely the scenario that Gretchen Whitmer and other Michigan Democrats had anticipated the previous fall, before Biden carried the state by more than 150,000 votes. Should the state legislators attempt to appoint a separate slate of pro-Trump electors, in defiance of the popular vote, Whitmer was prepared to name another slate consistent with the will of the people.

But neither the state House Speaker, Lee Chatfield, nor the Senate Republican leader, Mike Shirkey, took Trump's bait. After leaving the White House, they issued a statement saying they were not "aware of any information that would change the outcome of the election in Michigan." They said they had used their visit to press Trump to deliver more federal relief funds for Michigan in the pandemic.

After the meeting, Chatfield told Ronna McDaniel, the Michigander at the helm of the Republican National Committee, that he had done his best to disabuse Trump of one particular conspiracy. No, he had told the president, there was no mass fraud with the voting machines in rural Antrim County, a Northern Michigan locale that became a fixation for baseless MAGA speculation.

The Michigan House Speaker also called the state attorney general, Dana Nessel, a day after the White House visit. Nessel, a Democrat, had indicated that her office would scrutinize the White House meeting if there was any indication that the lawmakers had been offered some kind of unlawful inducement in exchange for doing Trump's bidding on the election.

"He was basically trying to let me know that he was not going to do anything that was illegal," Nessel says, noting that Chatfield did not use those precise words.

In Arizona, Trump was hunting after the governor, Doug Ducey, to demand his help overturning the election as well. The low-key former ice cream executive aspired to other offices—perhaps even the presidency—and he had made a point of keeping a cordial relationship with Trump.

Ducey had spoken to Trump a handful of times since the election, and he had done a better job than Kemp of keeping him at bay. But a far-right faction in the Arizona GOP that had been present for many years had grown in size and stridency during the Trump years, and they had been stoking the president's anger. When Ducey certified Biden's victory at the end of November, his cell phone went off in the middle of the event with a specialized ring tone, "Hail to the Chief," that alerted him of calls coming in from the White House.

The governor had returned the call to Trump later, pacifying the president by telling him that since the election was certified he was now free to bring forward a legal challenge. But as the president and his circle plunged deeper into conspiracy theorizing, Ducey kept his distance.

Yet his quiet remove was not enough to shield Ducey from Trump's attacks. On December 5, the president unleashed a double-barreled attack on Ducey and Kemp, faulting them for not doing more to help his hopeless quest.

"They fight harder against us than do the Radical Left Dems," Trump said of two men who were his allies. "If they were with us, we would have already won both Arizona and Georgia."

The next evening, Ducey called a friend in a state of despondency.

"If I do anything in the future, he's going to primary me," the governor said of Trump, according to his friend.

Trump's inner circle would keep up their pressure on Ducey for another month, almost to the eve of Biden's inauguration. The weekend before the Democrat's swearing-in, Ducey would find himself standing over the stove cooking his mother's red-sauce recipe along with some sausages when his phone rang. It was Rudy Giuliani, and not for the first time. Ducey sent the call to voicemail. And unlike when Trump telephoned in November, Ducey did not call back.

* * *

In Georgia, Kemp did not have the luxury of screening calls from Trump-world.

When the president headed to Valdosta on December 5, he called the governor before he even touched down. The fig-leaf pretext for the call was for Trump to offer his sympathies about the death of a young man who was a close friend of the Kemp family and had perished in a car crash.

But Trump spent much of the call bullying Kemp to call a special session of the legislature and pursue Trump's latest cure-all. Trump was convinced that if Kemp demanded a rigorous standard of signature verification and reviewed all of the absentee ballots cast in the state, it would result in the overturning of the election.

On the call, the president invoked L. Lin Wood, a Georgia litigator making extraordinarily outlandish claims on his behalf, as well as Sidney Powell, whom he had supposedly dismissed from his circle.

Kemp told the president that those two attorneys were making things up. You should discount their claims, the grieving governor said.

Well, Trump replied, a lot of people are talking about their accusations and many people believe them.

That clunky rhetorical trick was one of Trump's favorite escape hatches when pressed to defend a baseless claim, and it was all Kemp could do to maintain his composure.

But the president's bogus message was catching on in a way Kemp could not ignore: When a Republican group involved in the Senate race took a poll of Georgia voters in mid-December, it found that nearly half of Republican-leaning voters agreed with the statement that Kemp and Raffensperger were allowing Democrats to steal the presidential election in their state.

Kemp knew that was no small problem for him. What the governor did not know was that on the same flight to Valdosta, Trump used part of his time in the air to try to recruit a primary opponent for the governor in his next reelection campaign. Doug Collins, the Republican congressman Trump had hoped to see appointed to the Senate, was on board the plane, and the president inquired about his interest in the governorship.

Collins stalled. He wasn't sure, he told Trump. After all, he had just run for the Senate, mounting an unsuccessful challenge to Loeffler.

But Trump was on a mission.

"I think you'd actually probably enjoy being governor more than the Senate," the president told him, according to Trump's aide Jason Miller.

After Trump relocated to another cabin, Miller turned to Collins and said: "You realize he's going to say that at the rally, right?"

Sure enough, Trump used a rally dedicated to the January 5 Senate runoff to suggest Collins challenge the state's incumbent Republican governor in a primary in 2022. And he proved Mitch McConnell right in his concern about the scripted remarks: Trump brought Perdue and Loeffler on stage, mostly reading from the script when he was talking about their campaigns, but he was far more focused on the race he had just run.

"You know we won Georgia, just so you understand," Trump said upon taking the stage.

He claimed "they cheated and rigged our presidential election but we'll still win," prompting the red-hatted faithful on Valdosta's airport tarmac to chant: "Stop the Steal!"

Trump's performance—the bitterness, the faulting of others, the need for affirmation—was entirely predictable to anybody following his presidency. What was more striking and worrisome was what his supporters said after the event as they waited for buses to take them back to their cars. A month after it had become clear Biden had won the election, not a single attendee interviewed said they thought Biden would be inaugurated in January.

The Trump supporters had come from Georgia, nearby Florida, and well beyond to show their support for the president. They repeated all the claims he had been making on television and on Twitter, naming all the same bad guys.

Michael Pons, a retiree who trekked from the Atlanta suburbs, said it was "a distinct possibility" there would be no president in office on January 20 because the election would not yet be adjudicated. Julie Okins, who came with her husband to Valdosta from their home near Memphis, refused to contemplate what was next for the GOP.

"He'll win the election, I'm not even going to think about that," she said.

These were the voters on whom the Republican Senate majority depended.

And Trump was not finished with his rampage—not even close. He was adding names to his Georgia enemies list, it seemed, by the day.

"Who the fuck is Chris Carr?" the president asked Perdue in a phone call the second week of December.

Carr was Georgia's Republican attorney general, and Trump had heard that he was unenthusiastic about the latest no-hope lawsuit filed on the president's behalf. The Texas attorney general, Ken Paxton, had filed a flimsy lawsuit challenging the election results. It was a hopeless stunt that skeptics viewed as a bid by Paxton, who was under indictment, to score himself a presidential pardon, but a number of other Republican state attorneys general had signed on. Trump said he had heard from some unnamed source that Carr was discouraging his fellow attorneys general from signing on.

Perdue scrambled to calm the president, promising he'd call Carr to smooth things over. The attorney general assured Perdue that Trump had bad information.

"You're going to call the president and tell him that," Perdue said, effectively serving as Trump's in-state enforcer in what he knew was a fruitless campaign against the election results.

On the Democratic side, there was still not much optimism that Trump's thrashing around in Georgia might somehow work out to their benefit. One senior aide to Biden believed the party's best chance was to prevail in one of the two races, but feared the two Democratic candidates and the party organization on the ground were too weak for a sweep that would flip the Senate majority. Ossoff was micromanaging his own campaign and Warnock was just still very green, this person believed.

"I am aghast at what we are putting forward," the pessimistic Biden adviser said of the Democratic ticket.

As it turned out, Democrats were underestimating just how much Trump might do to kneecap his own side.

*   *   *

On December 14, the Electoral College formally voted to anoint Joe Biden as the next president of the United States. There was no doubt about the outcome of the vote, but given Trump's obstinate refusal to concede defeat it was a more important formality than usual.

For McConnell, it was a decisive formality. The Senate leader had established contact with Biden through intermediaries in early November, but he had resolved that once the Electoral College voted he would seek out direct contact with the president-elect. He knew that he still needed Trump in his corner to win Georgia, but the Electoral College vote had indisputable constitutional force and he was not about to ignore it to maintain Trump's fantasy version of the election.

Before heading to the Senate floor on December 15, McConnell phoned the White House chief of staff to tell him what he planned to say. The president was free to call him, McConnell told Mark Meadows, but he would not be dissuaded from his plan.

"Today I want to congratulate President-elect Joe Biden," McConnell said in the chamber a short while later.

Trump called immediately. It was a tense conversation. McConnell said the Electoral College had spoken. And the president told McConnell he was making a mistake, reiterating his view that the election was rigged. One McConnell adviser called it "the Sidney Powell argument."

It was the last time Trump and McConnell spoke.

Biden and McConnell talked the same day, with the incoming president thanking his old colleague and political adversary for acknowledging the results of the election. Addressing a friend, McConnell joked drily about his conversations with the forty-fifth and forty-sixth presidents.

"Got one good phone call and one bad one," the laconic Kentuckian said.

McConnell's delayed recognition of Biden's victory marked a rupture with Trump, and not only on a personal level. For four years, Senate Republicans and the Trump White House had maintained a functional working relationship based on mutual self-interest. Neither side could govern or win elections without the other, and so despite considerable feelings of loathing in both directions they simply suppressed that distaste and made things work.

After December 15, Trump increasingly turned his ire on congressional Republicans.

As the president's enablers continued to press forward with theories for how to block Biden's accession, Trump lashed out at lawmakers who spoke up to question them. The latest last-ditch idea was to object to certifying the

Electoral College results on January 6, and John Thune, the second-ranking Senate Republican, told CNN's Manu Raju such a gambit would "go down like a shot dog."

"He will be primaried in 2022, political career over!!!" Trump said of Thune shortly before Christmas, deriding him as "Mitch's boy."

In private, McConnell offered Thune some terse words of solidarity.

"Welcome to the club," he told his deputy.

McConnell was still consumed with Georgia and preserving his majority. Yet he was also fielding calls from senior officials in Trump's White House, who were coming to him for reassurance. He urged several of Trump's close aides, including the White House counsel Pat Cipollone and Robert O'Brien, the national security adviser, to stay in their jobs because they could help head off a constitutional crisis. McConnell stayed in touch with Gina Haspel, the CIA director, for the same reason: Only a few days after the election, he had asked Haspel to make a highly visible appearance to his Capitol office, in full view of the news photographers staked out there, to offer the levelheaded intelligence chief a sort of vote of confidence in case Trump was tempted to fire her.

In deep denial about his loss in the election, Trump was not terribly discriminating about whom he turned to for sympathy. As he was trashing his fellow Republicans, he was also bending the ears of Democrats, going on about the unfairness of it all. A few days after the Electoral College vote, the president called up his pandemic-era friend-of-convenience Phil Murphy, the governor of New Jersey, supposedly to talk about a federal disaster declaration for the state. He talked instead about the election, as if it had been held the day before.

"Did you see what I did in Iowa?" Trump prodded the Democrat, according to Murphy and his chief of staff, George Helmy. "How about Texas?"

"Did you see how I blew it up in Florida?" the president asked, regaling his captive audience with tales of his red-state success.

Then he hit Wisconsin.

"Did you see all the votes that came in at the last minute?" Trump asked.

Murphy knew well that there had been nothing underhanded about the election, and that the late-counted votes in Wisconsin had been a function of the state's hybrid voting system.

But the president, Murphy says, was "going ape over the Wisconsin vote." As usual, there was not much for Murphy to do but wait him out.

*   *   *

Three days before Christmas, the president posted a video to Twitter that showed him speaking from the West Wing, an array of Christmas wreaths in the background. It was not a presentation of holiday cheer. Before releasing the message, Trump had given no warning to his erstwhile allies in the Capitol that he was about to detonate their painstaking talks on a new coronavirus relief package and a bill to fund the government.

Congress had been stalemated for months over how to deploy new federal aid for stricken families, businesses, and states. Senate Republicans had been resisting another multitrillion-dollar package that Democrats were demanding, and Democrats had been reluctant to pass a slimmed-down bill that lacked funds for states and cities with tax revenues obliterated by the pandemic.

But starting in late November, an ad-hoc group of moderates in the House and Senate had begun working to break the impasse, ultimately spurring congressional leaders to fashion an $892 billion compromise bill that would extend enhanced unemployment benefits, ship new aid to small businesses, fund vaccination programs, and send $600 stimulus checks to individual taxpayers. Some of the big-ticket items were left to the side, including aid to states, but to the negotiators it looked like a model for how a divided government might still manage to get things done.

In his video on December 22, Trump called the bill a "disgrace" and threatened not to sign it. His critique was typically slapdash: The president at once denounced the scale of spending in the government funding bill as excessive yet derided the stimulus payments as "ridiculously low." He did not want taxpayers getting $600 checks.

That number, Trump said, should be $2,000.

That surprise demand went off like a hand grenade in the Capitol and in the Georgia campaigns. In the House, Nancy Pelosi immediately called a vote on the more generous checks, forcing House Republicans to decide between Trump's stated preferences and their own opposition to additional aid spending.

Schumer, stuck in the Senate minority, could not call a vote. But he was just as delighted as Pelosi, sensing an opportunity to go on offense in Georgia. His candidates suddenly had a closing issue: Would Perdue and Loeffler stand with Trump and back generous cash payouts to the people of their state, or would they stand with Mitch McConnell and the stingier Senate majority?

"This," Schumer told an adviser, "is *great.*"

As grim as that Christmas was for many Americans, it was the moment that Democrats began to feel a sense of hope about Georgia. Winning both seats would still be difficult, but Trump seemed determined to help—by depressing voters on his own side, and by shifting the issue debate onto friendly ground for the party that believed in a robust social-welfare state.

Loeffler and Perdue were pinned. They had little choice but to endorse Trump's demand for more and bigger checks, but they badly wanted the president to go ahead and sign the existing relief bill and head off open warfare between the White House and Senate Republicans. The greater and the more obvious the divisions were between Trump and McConnell, the likelier it was that Georgia's many MAGA voters would decide the Senate majority was not really their concern.

Perdue was spending the holidays in Florida with David Dorman, a former AT&T executive who had a place near Mar-a-Lago, and the senator made it his mission to convince Trump he should sign the legislation. Over golf and a series of meals, Perdue told Trump that, yes, it would help his campaign in Georgia.

But there was more at stake, too, he reminded the president: People were counting on relief from the government. What better way to brighten Christmas spirits than with checks from President Trump?

Trump shot back: Republicans aren't fighting for me! Why the hell would I give them this?

Perdue told his advisers it was the most unreasonable he had seen the president. Trump was conflating everything together: his loss, the refusal of Republicans like Kemp to sabotage Biden's victory, and now the decision by McConnell and other lawmakers to recognize Biden.

Perdue and other Republicans eventually broke the impasse by appealing to Trump's vanity. Lindsey Graham lobbied him on the sunny fairways of South Florida and patched in Steven Mnuchin, the treasury secretary, to help. If Trump didn't sign the bill soon, Mnuchin told him, it would not be his name on the checks.

Trump finally relented and signed the measure on December 27.

National Republicans could feel they were losing ground in Georgia, and even McConnell was starting to speak about the races there with undisguised pessimism. Reviewing the early voting numbers, the Senate leader was struck by the enthusiasm on the Democratic side.

"We're not going to get there," he told advisers, acknowledging in the most direct terms yet that he might not remain majority leader.

Two days before the runoff, an explosive revelation about Trump's attempts at election tampering upended the Georgia races yet again. On Saturday, January 2, Trump had called Georgia's top election official, the long-suffering Brad Raffensperger, and told him in no uncertain terms that he wanted Raffensperger to come up with the votes he needed to claim victory.

"I just want to find 11,780 votes, which is one more than we have," Trump said, deploying barely veiled threats to pressure the astonished secretary of state.

"You know what they did and you're not reporting it," Trump said. "You know, that's a criminal—that's a criminal offense. And you can't let that happen."

It wasn't the first time Trump had leaned on the secretary of state's office, nor the first time Raffensperger's aides had recorded the conversation. But this time, the hour-long call leaked within a day, erupting into public view in the *Washington Post* on Sunday, January 3.

Graham was in the Capitol basement grabbing a quick lunch when the news broke. Ever searching for a silver lining, the South Carolina senator was predicting to a reporter that the upcoming January 6 vote to certify the Electoral College results would "clear the air" and help the country get past the recent unpleasantness.

Rick Allen, a Republican House backbencher from Georgia, ambled into the café and found himself hailed down by Graham for intelligence on the Georgia races. Allen, a former construction executive, said he expected Perdue to survive but had less hope for Loeffler.

"I think because of what the president is doing to Brian Kemp—I mean, everybody knows he appointed her," Allen said, his voice trailing off.

As the two men discussed Trump's call to Raffensperger, they could barely contain their laughter at the president's cartoonish intimidation tactics. Allen, though, took umbrage at one element of the story: Raffensperger's recording of the call.

"All I can tell you is, he's going to have to move out of the state of Georgia," the congressman said of his state's top elected official.

The next day, January 4, the United States attorney in Atlanta, BJay Pak, quit his post. He later testified that he resigned because he understood Trump was considering firing him amid concerns about voter fraud in Georgia. It was the most visible sign at that point of the deep turmoil at the Department of Justice, where a clique of Trump diehards were lobbying to issue false statements calling into question the results of the election.

Trump's final speech in Georgia was only hours away.

*　　*　　*

At this point, Republicans were unraveling and Democrats knew it. Shortly after New Year's, on a call with Biden and senior transition officials, Jennifer O'Malley Dillon, Biden's savvy former campaign manager and now his top political adviser, told the president-elect she believed they could win both seats.

Anita Dunn, one of Biden's top strategists, was floored. She was close with O'Malley Dillon and knew well that she had been a real skeptic about Georgia.

"Oh my God," Dunn recalls thinking—this could actually happen.

On the eve of the election, Karl Rove held a final conference call with donors who had poured millions of dollars into the runoff effort. He projected a kind of optimism for the crowd, but conceded that Republicans would "need to have a big election day" to overcome the advantage Democrats had run up in early voting. At the end of the call, Anthony Gioia, a former CEO of the National Pasta Association who was George W. Bush's ambassador to Malta, raised what he described as a "controversial" question.

"Do you think that Donald Trump's appearance," he began, "is going to be beneficial to us?"

Rove acknowledged that the president would vent about his loss, and that such ranting had taken a toll on Republican turnout.

"Those people have taken it to heart, what the president has said about the whole electoral system," Rove said. "And so, Ambassador, they need to hear from him tonight that it's critical to him, that they go out and vote tomorrow."

The president was headed to Dalton, the so-called carpet capital of the world, in the deep-red part of northwest Georgia where Republicans saw turnout lagging. The trip had spooked some White House lawyers, who were worried after the Raffensperger call that Trump could create new legal exposure for himself with yet another stemwinder laden with grievances and threats.

Perdue, concerned that the White House might pull back from his race, worked the phones nervously. Mark Meadows assured him the trip would go ahead.

To the surprise of no one with a realistic view of Trump, the president used the Dalton rally to insist he had won the 2020 election by "a landslide" and vowed to "fight like hell" to reverse the results. Two days before Congress was slated to certify the election results in a formal vote, Trump publicly targeted his own vice president with the unheard-of demand that he lead an effort to object to the signed-and-sealed Electoral College ballots.

"He's a great guy," Trump said of Pence. "Of course, if he doesn't come through, I won't like him quite as much."

At the same rally, Loeffler committed a final act of public fealty to the president: She announced she would object to the results of the 2020 election in the Senate two days later, aligning herself with the most extreme members of the GOP Conference over the Senate leaders pleading with lawmakers not to go down that path.

Biden also appeared in Georgia the day before the election, rallying support for Ossoff and Warnock at a drive-in rally near downtown Atlanta. Now excited about the prospect of an all-Democratic government in Washington, Biden tore into Georgia's "two senators who think they've sworn an oath to Donald Trump, not to the United States Constitution."

"One state can chart the course, not just for the next four years but for the next generation," he said.

* * *

By January 5, the date of the Georgia election, Democrats in Washington understood that they were facing a serious threat of disruption in the certification vote the following day. What had begun as a stunt by pro-Trump House Republicans had metastasized into a bigger effort by Republicans to undermine the speedy affirmation of the election results.

First one Republican senator, Josh Hawley, had said he would join the House objection—guaranteeing a debate on the floor—and then a larger pack of senators, including Ted Cruz, had come up with reasons for following suit. The number of election objectors in the Senate now appeared certain to climb into the double digits.

Three of the four party leaders in Congress wanted the certification vote to proceed without event. In the Senate, McConnell had pleaded with lawmakers not to object, calling the vote to certify Biden's election—and ensure legitimacy for the transfer of power to the opposing party—the most important vote of his own career. In private, he had encouraged Tom Cotton, the Arkansas conservative, to come out quickly against Hawley and Cruz's efforts. McConnell knew well that the young pro-Trump lawmaker could change minds that were closed to his own appeals.

In the House, Pelosi had assigned a team of trusted lawmakers to prepare to argue the case for certification, assuming that Republicans followed through with triggering a floor debate. She turned to Adam Schiff and a few other lawmakers he had gathered around him as he studied possible threats to the election, including Jamie Raskin of Maryland, a constitutional law professor, and Joe Neguse of Colorado, a thoughtful junior member of the Democratic leadership team.

This group and their aides generated a collection of memos gaming out ways Republicans could attempt to sabotage the final certification of the election, raising possibilities such as an effort by the vice president to block the acceptance of Biden electors in the Senate. The documents they prepared anticipated extensively the very same far-fetched strategies that Trump's most extreme advisers were proposing, as the right-wing law professor John C. Eastman did in an infamous missive. Without knowing precisely what Trump's cadre might be up to, Schiff's team thoroughly mapped out tactics and legal arguments for thwarting them.

"Vice President Pence might improperly attempt to influence the election results in favor of the Trump/Pence ticket by invoking his status as presiding officer at the joint session," one memo warned, detailing potential avenues for Pence-led sabotage such as unilaterally refusing to count Electoral College votes for Biden on one pretext or another.

"Pence lacks the authority to take any of these actions," the memo concluded—but, it warned, that did not mean the vice president would not try.

Pelosi understood that there was no majority in either chamber for objecting to the election results, and she had followed McConnell's criticism of the far-right effort. But she distrusted the GOP on a gut level and did not want to see her lieutenants caught off guard.

She told one of them in private: "Never trust Mitch McConnell to do the right thing."

On the day of the vote in Georgia—with his own fate as a Senate leader hanging in the balance—Schumer used a call with Senate Democrats not to review the runoffs but to go over the certification process they would all participate in the next day. There was nothing about the procedure itself that needed to be especially complicated, but if Republicans were determined to make trouble, then Schumer wanted his people to be ready.

The one congressional leader who was not actively working to suppress potential sabotage on January 6 was Kevin McCarthy. The House minority leader was not willing to draw the same line as McConnell and say flatly that the election was legitimate or that opposing certification was out of bounds. In the White House, there was no thought that McCarthy might act independently of Trump's wishes: A few days before Christmas, Trump's adviser Jason Miller described McCarthy as "the de facto political director" for the outgoing president, casting him in the role of a dutiful staffer rather than an independent political force.

During a January 5 meeting with the House Republican Conference, McCarthy kept his own position on certification vague but offered to assemble a task force on "voter fraud and integrity," in an obvious sop to the Trump view that the election had been tainted.

One lawmaker, Larry Bucshon of Indiana, was entirely forthright about his motivations in objecting to the election. Trump's popularity with Republicans in his district, he said, was 95 percent.

"Right now, almost all of those people believe that the election was stolen," said Bucshon, a physician by training. "Do I believe it was stolen? I don't know. Maybe it was, maybe it wasn't. I agree it comes down to the states. But the reality is this is a political vote for many of us."

Some Republican lawmakers were fed up with the head-patting toleration of baseless election conspiracies, and with the party's determination not to call Trump's defeat what it was. Anthony Gonzalez, the former professional football player from Ohio, said the law was "unbelievably clear" about the role Congress was supposed to play, and urged his colleagues not to threaten 245 years of American political tradition by undermining the handover of power.

"This is not a political vote. This strikes at the very heart of who we are as a country," he said, adding a stark warning: "If you're on the fence on this, and you want to make it a political vote, I beg you to find your courage because I am convinced that this day, what we do tomorrow, the precedent we set will be used in every single election going forward."

Another Republican voice of dismay was Don Bacon, a former air force general who represented a Nebraska district Biden had carried. It was obvious, he said, that the Congress was supposed to have a "minimal" role in certifying the election results, and the party shouldn't pretend otherwise.

"I got 11 percent more votes than the president did," Bacon said on the call. "Why? Because people couldn't tolerate the first debate, the name calling, the Twitter. He lost suburban America. That's what happened in Atlanta. It's what happened in the suburbs of Philadelphia, in the suburbs of Detroit."

Bacon put an exclamation point on his comments by addressing McCarthy directly. The lawmakers from the most competitive districts, he said, were in an untenable position on certification.

"Mr. Leader, this is a lose-lose. Purple districts are going to get their ass kicked because of this," he said. "If you vote against your base, they're not coming back; I'm pretty sure of it. I've heard them. If you vote with the base on this, you're going to lose the middle. We should be winning big in two years and four years. We are shooting ourselves in the foot right now."

McCarthy responded in his customary mode of chipper conciliation. He knew that many of the loudest voices on the call were Trump loyalists determined to obstruct Biden's election, and that many others were in a position like Bucshon from Indiana of trying to placate the MAGA diehards back home. McCarthy had no desire to alienate either of those groups of lawmakers by taking a principled stand.

"It's a tough issue, but it doesn't have to be a lose-lose," McCarthy said in response to Bacon. "This is just the beginning of this Congress."

* * *

Early in the evening on January 5, Josh Holmes, McConnell's close adviser, saw signs of trouble in Georgia. Republican areas were not coming in with the massive force the party needed to catch up with Democrats' lead in the early vote. The party, Holmes lamented, had chosen not to use the message that might have won the elections—that a Republican Senate would be an important check on President Biden—and now they were paying a price.

One of McConnell's trusted strategists, Ward Baker, who had been dispatched to Georgia, called the Senate leader late in the evening. A blunt-speaking former Marine who hated to lose about as much as anything in the world, Baker shared his unhappy read on the incomplete election results in a matter-of-fact fashion.

Perdue and Loeffler were both on track to lose, Baker told McConnell. The Senate leader did not seem surprised and thanked the operative for his effort.

The result in Georgia was a repudiation of Donald Trump and a humiliation for his party. The state's two senators, Perdue and Loeffler, had decided to indulge a campaign of lies and election sabotage rather than risk angering a president who had lost touch with reality. A huge number of lawmakers within and beyond Georgia had opted to cower rather than tell conservative voters the truth: that Joe Biden had been elected fair and square, and Trump had lost because he had alienated a majority of the country.

The party's reward for its acquiescence had been defeat in Georgia and the loss of the Senate majority. Democrats would control both chambers of Congress by the smallest of margins, with an even split in the Senate tipped their way by Kamala Harris's tie-breaking vote. Joe Biden would have a real chance to govern—not entirely on his own terms, but without McConnell holding veto power over his entire agenda.

The Democrats' victory in Georgia was an affirmation for the party in another way, too: After Biden's win there in November, the two Senate races ratified the strength of a new political coalition that was transforming the electoral map and reopening the New South to Democrats. It was a complicated coalition, one that might be tough to maintain: an alliance of Black voters who turned out strongly across the state, educated whites who reviled Trump, and

Asian Americans, all of whom showed up in record-breaking numbers in the Atlanta suburbs.

Together, they had overwhelmed Trump's heavily white voting base, a chunk of which had stayed home in response to the president's relentless message of discouragement and personal grievance. The biggest drop-off in turnout between November 3 and January 5 was in the rural North and South Georgia communities where Trump's support was deepest, and where he had campaigned in person.

Much like the narrowly divided country, Georgia had long been tugged between its past and its promise. It was a state where the eighteenth-century colonial leader James Oglethorpe defied his fellow founders and welcomed the migrants who organized the South's first Jewish congregation, but also where Leo Frank was lynched near Atlanta in 1915. It was the home of Lester Maddox and Richard Russell, the notorious segregationists, but also of John Lewis and Martin Luther King Jr., heroes of the civil rights movement.

It was a state that rejoiced when it hosted the 1996 Olympics, viewing it as a chance to demonstrate that it was a cosmopolitan state with a world-class city. But it's also a state that did not strip the Confederate banner out of its state flag until half a decade after the games ended.

Now Georgia, after voting for a Democratic presidential candidate for the first time since 1992, had made history again. In one swoop, it elected to the Senate a preacher from King's pulpit, making him the first Black Democratic senator from the South, and sent to serve beside him the first Jewish senator from the Deep South since the nineteenth century.

And it had dealt a stinging blow to Trump and Trumpism—the most potent distillation of white grievance, xenophobia, and raw racism to strike American politics since the end of segregation.

It is an irony of history that the state managed all that with help from Donald Trump himself.

* * *

As January 6 dawned, Democrats awoke to a world transformed. Biden knew now that he would be able to confirm his cabinet more or less freely. He knew, and so did Pelosi and Schumer, that the possible scope and price tag of their legislative agenda had just grown by orders of magnitude.

In state capitals and big cities, a mood of jubilation and relief took hold as the biggest obstacle to federal aid fell away. In Chicago, Anne Caprara, the chief of staff to Governor JB Pritzker, found herself in tears watching the Georgia returns, knowing that the Democrats' electoral success would translate into a new relief bill with desperately needed funds for her stricken state.

When House Democrats dialed in to a meeting on the morning of January 6, many of them had only begun to process the multiplicity of paths that had suddenly opened for them in government.

As the virtual session began, they heard the strains of "Georgia on My Mind," a celebratory tune queued up by Steny Hoyer, the delighted majority leader.

Then Pelosi came on.

"Good morning," she said. "And it *is* a good morning."

Before the Speaker said much more about Georgia or the party's agenda, there was another matter close at hand. The Congress still had to vote to certify the results of the 2020 election. The Speaker told her members to maintain their decorum and dignity on a historic day, and not to dive into a gutter with Donald Trump and his minions. January 6 was about something greater than Trump.

"It's about the Constitution," Pelosi said.

Chapter 7

Defeat and Dishonor

ANTHONY GONZALEZ WAS worried about the traffic on the morning of January 6.

The Ohio Republican had grown accustomed to a commute from Northwest Washington during the pandemic. With relatively few cars on the road, it usually took him about twelve minutes to reach the Capitol. But Gonzalez had expected the city to be busier that day. After all, he had spent the night before arguing with his fellow Republicans and beseeching them not to do more than they already had to stoke the anger of the Trump supporters converging on Washington.

Gonzalez left home before dawn to beat the crowds, and even at that early hour he was struck by the number of buses crawling around Washington. There were already packs of people moving around the city, some with banners and signs.

"Wow," Gonzalez thought to himself. "If it's already like this, and it's five in the morning, I can only imagine what it's going to be like at noon."

As Gonzalez was starting his day, a number of his colleagues were only just falling asleep. They had stayed up late, riveted by the returns in Georgia and eager to see whether Democrats would capture the Senate and take full control of government. Since the election, it had been the previous day— January 5, the date of the Georgia runoff—that lawmakers, party strategists, and the incoming administration had been eyeing most anxiously.

But the first months of the Biden administration, and the fate of both political parties, would be shaped even more drastically by the events of January 6.

More than a few lawmakers had premonitions of the violence that day: young Democratic lawmakers like Abigail Spanberger and Andy Kim, whose national security training had triggered a sense of imminent danger, as well as long-serving committee chairs like Maxine Waters and Adam Smith, who had spent enough decades in Washington to recognize that the atmosphere in the capital was not just tense but explosive.

Jason Crow, the Colorado Democrat who'd sent his family home in advance of the vote out of concern for their safety, may not have awakened quite as early as Gonzalez. But in the members-only gym that morning, the former Army Ranger had barely worked up a sweat when he got into a heated exchange with a Republican friend who was equally committed to fitness: Markwayne Mullin of Oklahoma, a former mixed martial arts fighter.

"People are going to get hurt today," Crow told Mullin. "Mark my words."

The sense of foreboding was pervasive: Anna Eshoo, a California Democrat and a close friend of Nancy Pelosi, rode to the Capitol and was surprised looking at its east side to see how few police officers were stationed there. Like other lawmakers, Eshoo had received an email two days earlier from the House sergeant at arms, urging members to arrive early and to use the tunnels under the Capitol rather than walking outdoors. An aide in the car with Eshoo wondered if the police presence was light because the officers were changing shifts.

"No, they're not changing shifts at a quarter to nine in the morning," Eshoo remembers replying.

Eshoo did not share her next thought aloud, but in her head she was contemplating a more ominous image: the scene from *The Godfather* in which Sonny Corleone, the crown prince of his father's mafia empire, drives up to a seemingly sleepy tollbooth only to find himself in a fatal machine-gun ambush.

"I had a bad feeling," Eshoo says. "I had a bad feeling about that day."

There was not a universal mood of gloom. In some corners of the government, there was a sense of optimism that the Trump era, and the post-election standoff instigated by the president, would soon be over. The certification vote would be an unsightly chore, and then that would be the end.

In Northwest Washington, Chris Liddell, the transition-focused Trump aide, woke up and told his wife how relieved he was that a resolution was at hand. To Liddell, January 6 represented the possibility of closure—the full and final end to navigating around the president's obstinacy and delusional thinking. After Congress certified the results, he thought, there would be a glide path to the inauguration.

Also in a cheery mood that morning was the senior senator from West Virginia. Joe Manchin, the centrist Democrat, was abuzz with optimism about what that day might bring, and about the role he was poised to play in the new Congress as one of fifty crucial votes in the new Senate majority. Manchin, seventy-three, had an extra reason to be enthused: He was on his way to get vaccinated against the coronavirus before that day's session got under way.

Beyond his shot in the arm, Manchin was excited because Washington could get on with the transition to the work of a Congress that was about as evenly divided as it had ever been. That, he believed, was an ideal atmosphere for the dealmaking he relished, and that the incoming Biden administration seemed eager to support.

"We got a chance to bring bipartisanship back to the country," Manchin crowed.

To the optimists in the nation's capital, it seemed the peaceful transfer of power was at hand.

President Trump had other plans.

Only a few hours later, the defeated president mounted a stage on the Ellipse, between the Mall and the White House. The smooth transition to a Biden administration was the farthest thing from Trump's mind. Even the advent of the first coronavirus vaccines, a lightning-fast achievement that his advisers were pleading with him to embrace as a high note for his exit, was irrelevant to the president. Having spent two months attacking the integrity of the election results, Trump was not about to stop now.

"We will never give up, we will never concede," he told all those people who had poured off the buses Gonzalez observed. "You don't concede when there's theft involved."

Firing up the crowd with Trump were a few of his political footmen, including Mo Brooks, the Alabama congressman who told the crowd to start "taking down names and kicking ass," and Rudy Giuliani, who called for "trial by combat" over the election results. Making the Trump family's message crystal clear, the president's eldest son, Don Jr., aired a video of himself backstage at the rally, praising the White House aide Mark Meadows as "an actual fighter, one of the few," before spinning his camera around to face his girlfriend, Kimberly Guilfoyle.

"Have the courage to do the right thing," she said. "Fight!"

True to form, Trump reveled in the size of his crowd and demanded the news cameras capture how many of his supporters he had summoned to Washington on the day Congress was to certify his defeat. The president also wanted his devotees to know who was to blame for his defeat, criticizing GOP leaders in Congress who "led you down the tubes" and repeatedly hectoring Mike Pence to use his ceremonial role in the Senate to overturn the election.

Republican voters, Trump said, should take revenge in 2022 on those who did not join his crusade to overturn Biden's election. He singled out one in particular.

"We got to get rid of the weak Congress people, the ones that aren't any good—the Liz Cheneys of the world," he said, feeding the crowd the name of a highly recognizable Republican dissenter sure to be at work that day in the building down the Mall.

In the halls of Congress, lawmakers were still going about the business of the day without interruption. But the law enforcement officials at Trump's rally recognized a security threat when they saw it.

"POTUS is encouraging the protesters to march to capitol grounds and continue protesting there," an officer wrote.

The country was perched on the edge of a political trauma—an act of mob violence that would mark an end-of-innocence moment for American democracy. Two decades earlier, the Capitol had been spared from attack by foreign terrorists on the worst day in the country's modern history, September 11, 2001. Now, it was on the verge of being defiled by American citizens whipped into a frenzy by their president.

In some respects, the story of January 6 is of a near miss with catastrophe. The riot at the Capitol was a national disgrace, but there was no massacre of lawmakers, no assassination of the vice president or the House Speaker, no revolt in the armed forces—and no attempt by President Trump, with rank-and-file lawmakers locked down in office buildings and congressional leaders sequestered on a military base, to seize and hold power by brute force.

But as a raw political trauma, it exceeded any other event in the history of the modern Congress.

To many Americans and admirers of America, the implications of the insurrection were devastating. The images of lawmakers crouching in hiding or running in fear, of smashed glass and ransacked offices, of the Confederate flag unfurled in the Capitol more than a century and a half after Appomattox—taken together, they evoked Lyndon Johnson's description of another act of homegrown violence as "the foulest deed of our time."

On January 6, all the most malevolent currents of the 2020 election and much of the poison of Trump's four-year term converged on a single place, at a single time. The result was an inflection point in the history of the Congress, the two parties, the not-yet-born Biden administration, and the country. It was a moment that clarified the true scale of the threat Trump posed to the country and exposed the degree to which America's divisions had come to imperil a rite of democracy long taken for granted: the peaceful transfer of power.

The attack of January 6 would wound lawmakers and change their outlook on their colleagues, their own roles, and on Congress as an institution. For Democrats, it would imbue them, at least briefly, with a sense of solidarity and mission—a burning desire to wield their new power to maximum effect and, for many of them, to deposit Trump's congressional allies on the ash heap of history. They could not, and would not, forget the right-wing lawmakers who had enabled the insurrection, whether they did so by parroting Trump's lies on television, joining him at the Ellipse, or voting later that day to block certification of the vote.

Among Republicans, January 6 seemed at first to be equally clarifying. In the harrowing hours of the Capitol siege, people at the highest levels of the party believed they would no longer have to defend, excuse, or dodge the actions of a man many of them saw as something between clownish and cancerous. Yet it would become apparent soon enough that the GOP was at the start of a longer process of internal reckoning—a "Which Side Are You On?" moment that would throw Republicans into turmoil for months—or perhaps years—to come.

As Trump concluded his midday remarks on January 6, some lawmakers watched them live while others learned about them from reporters. For Republicans who were already poised to certify Biden's victory—defying Trump, his political entourage, and his mob—the president's line-crossing rhetoric steeled their spines to finish the job.

"Our allegiance and our oath is to the Constitution and laws of the United States, they're not to any one person," said John Cornyn, the Texas senator, as he made his way through the Capitol before the rioters arrived.

Asked if it was time for the Republican Party to move beyond Trump, Cornyn was circumspect about his party's relationship with a president exhorting a horde to violence.

"This is the beginning of a long process of reevaluation and reassessment," he said. "I think that's going to take a while."

He could not have known in that moment how right he was.

* * *

When pro-Trump rioters breached the Capitol, most senators were in their seats in the Senate chamber. But because of social-distancing measures put in place during the pandemic, the 435 members of the House were far more scattered. Some were in their offices, some on the floor of the chamber, and a small number were seated above the floor as spectators in the House gallery. A select group had applied specially for the privilege.

Val Demings was among those in the last group; the former Orlando police chief and vice-presidential hopeful was excited to witness democracy in action. She had only just been sworn in to her third term as a member of the House, and she was thrilled to be among the members seated in the House gallery as the proceedings got under way.

Though she was aware of the crowd outside the Capitol, Demings was not one of the lawmakers who sensed incipient violence. After all, she reflected, there are usually protesters at the Capitol, though on most days they numbered in the single and double digits.

The members beside Demings in the gallery made up a cross-section of the Democratic caucus, including Jason Crow; the Biden confidant Lisa Blunt Rochester; straight-talking Pennsylvania lawyer Susan Wild; the suburban centrists Josh Gottheimer and Lizzie Fletcher; Pramila Jayapal, the chair of the Congressional Progressive Caucus; Raul Ruiz, the chair of the Congressional Hispanic Caucus. They were all watching intently as the Republican challenge to the election began, with Republican members of the House speaking in Trump's name to make wild claims of election fraud.

It was as Paul Gosar, a far-right Arizonan, claimed without evidence that his state's mail-in ballots had been doctored, that Nancy Pelosi's security detail swiftly took her from the dais where she had been presiding. At first Pelosi was unsure why she was being yanked from the chamber: Sometimes her aides ushered her out as a political choice, to avoid having the Speaker on the floor as Republicans engaged in some political stunt or another.

Pelosi's two deputies, Steny Hoyer and Jim Clyburn, quickly exited the chamber behind her, with Hoyer's security detail escorting him out. When Gosar complained that the House was out of order, it was clear something was seriously amiss, and a voice rang out from the gallery.

"This is because of you!" shouted Dean Phillips, a normally mild-mannered Minnesota Democrat.

Jim McGovern, the Democratic chairman of the Rules Committee, replaced Pelosi on the dais, while some staffers on the floor urged security officials in the gallery to lock the doors. McGovern soon gaveled the House into a recess, bringing an abrupt end—at least for the moment—to the Republicans' oratorical attack on the election results.

In the gallery, members had realized that something dangerous was afoot. Demings immediately thought of her law enforcement training.

"There's an outer perimeter, there's an inner perimeter, and sometimes bad people get past the outer perimeter," Demings says, thinking back on that moment. "But they never get past the inner perimeter."

"What I knew then," she says, "was that all hell had broken loose and we were in trouble."

Near Demings in the gallery was Lizzie Fletcher, a Texas Democrat elected in the 2018 anti-Trump backlash to represent a district once held by George Herbert Walker Bush. Fletcher had chosen to wear a pair of Cole Haan flats that day because she knew it would be a long one. There was no telling how long the Republicans could drag out their quixotic objections.

What Fletcher had not planned on was being told to wear a gas mask.

"We have tear gas in the Rotunda," a Capitol Police officer yelled out, referring to the cavernous hall beneath the building's great dome. "Please be advised there are masks under your seats."

On the floor, Ruben Gallego, the Marine veteran from Arizona, removed his suit jacket and mounted a table usually reserved for speech scripts. He began instructing his colleagues on how to put on the masks. Most of them had not even known the gear was stowed there. Rank-and-file lawmakers had never been taught how to use them.

In the gallery, Crow used his own military training, coaching his colleagues on how to don their masks. Ruiz, a former emergency room physician, helped out, too. Another Democrat in the gallery, Diana DeGette of Colorado, was worried that security officials were so focused on securing the House floor that they had forgotten the group in the mezzanine seats.

"What about us?" she called down to the floor.

A mood of panic was setting in. Blunt Rochester, the Delaware Democrat, shared DeGette's concern that the group there had been forgotten. When someone dropped their phone and it clattered down the steps, Blunt

Rochester remembers someone telling her not to pick it up because it could be a bomb.

Squeezed on her knees between the first row of balcony-style seats and the railing, Blunt Rochester recited a prayer. She noticed some of her colleagues on the phone to family members or aides, but her own view was that the moment required divine intervention. ("I said, 'You call your aunt, you call your mom—I'm calling Jesus,'" she says, citing the gospel standard "Jesus on the Mainline.")

"Father God, you have all the power," Blunt Rochester said in the gallery, asking the Almighty to "protect all of our brothers and sisters in this Congress."

Crow did call his wife. He told her that he and his colleagues might either have to make a stand in the House gallery or fight their way out, and that he loved her and their children. The young congressman scanned the vicinity for any sort of weapon he could use but found only a ballpoint pen. He contemplated whether he might ask a Capitol Police officer to give him a sidearm and decided it would be an inappropriate request.

On the phone, his wife, Deserai, reminded Crow he was a father with obligations to his family.

"Don't be a hero," she said.

The doors to the gallery were now sealed and the members were inside. The lawmakers could hear yelling and a gunshot—the bullet that felled the insurrectionist Ashli Babbitt as she tried to break into the House—and then someone began jostling the gallery doors from the outside. For those trapped within, it was a moment of cold terror.

"I thought, 'Who's on the other side of the door?'" Fletcher says. "It turned out to be Capitol Police and they showed us the way out."

As they were fleeing the chamber, Crow looked back to the nearly abandoned House floor, where the burly colleague he had argued with that morning, Markwayne Mullin, was one of only a handful of people left there.

"Markwayne," Crow called down to him, "you have to leave, too!"

Mullin was loath to retreat from the floor, but the Capitol Police could not reposition themselves as long as they had members to defend there. Crow's pleas connected with Mullin and he agreed to leave.

On the way to the elevators, the lawmakers from the gallery passed a scene that Fletcher would later describe as burned into her memory: Capitol Police officers with automatic weapons drawn and pointed down at a group of rioters spread-eagled on the floor of the Capitol.

The gallery was only one scene of the siege. While the highest-ranking leaders of the Congress were taken to Fort McNair in Southwest Washington, the waterfront site of the National Defense University, other senior lawmakers and junior backbenchers were virtual prisoners in their offices and conference rooms.

Richie Neal, the Irish American chairman of the powerful Ways and Means Committee and a kind of unofficial ambassador from Congress to the Emerald Isle, was on the phone with Brandon Lewis, Britain's secretary of state for Northern Ireland, when his aides barked at him to end the conversation: "They're out there," his staffers told him. Neal cut off the call and turned out the lights in his committee office, just off the House floor, so that rioters would not know there was anyone inside.

Neal and a few aides pushed the twenty-five-foot-long conference table against the door as a makeshift barricade. As the screaming grew closer, a deputy sergeant at arms with Neal asked him and his aides: "Could I ask you all to write down your names and your addresses in case this goes off the rails?"

One floor down at the Capitol, Tom Cole, the Oklahoma Republican, was in his Capitol hideaway—one of the cozy, tucked-away offices that a number of lawmakers keep in the building as a perk of their seniority. It was a small suite of rooms stocked with cigars, bourbon, and salted nuts and ornamented with a buffalo statue, a nod to Cole's Chickasaw heritage. Cole was puffing away at a cigar and watching the proceedings on television with his chief of staff, Josh Grogis, when they heard noise in the hall. They, too, built a makeshift barricade.

Before long there was pounding on the door. The rioters likely did not know much about Oklahoma's Fourth Congressional District, which Cole represented, or about the House Rules Committee, on which Cole was the senior Republican. But they could read his name on the door, and when they did they bellowed it loudly.

"Cole!" the lawmaker could hear them shouting. "Come out! Come out!"

When the Capitol Police showed up a short while later to escort Cole out of his office, they burst through the door with guns drawn, yelling "Blue! Blue!" to identify themselves. The first person they saw was Grogis, a broad-shouldered and bearded man, dressed casually that day—not all that differently from some of the rioters. The aide quickly explained who he was, and that he had a congressman inside who needed to be evacuated.

Anthony Gonzalez was locked down in his own office. The Ohio Republican had gone to the House gallery earlier in the day to watch the preliminary proceedings, but he left in disgust after a short while.

It was a fateful choice.

He returned to his office just as his aides were glued to the television, watching Mike Pence get hauled out of the Senate by the Secret Service. They turned out the lights, closed the blinds, and barricaded the door, and Gonzalez changed out of his suit into jeans, tennis shoes, a T-shirt, and a baseball cap.

"If they come in," Gonzalez thought, "basically, they can jump over this barricade, I can go out a different door, and just outrun them, probably."

"As long as they don't have a gun," he thought, "I should be fine."

He placed a call to the Capitol Police to notify them of unsettling noises in the hall. The woman on the other end of the line did not sugarcoat the situation for the congressman. "If somebody shows up, call us," she said, according to Gonzalez. "But, you know, it's gonna be tough to get to you."

As the congressman settled into a waiting game, he took one other precaution. He wrote a letter to his wife and put it in his desk—just in case.

"I just thought, well, I don't know what's going to happen," Gonzalez recalls. "I think I'll be fine, but just in case I'm not I want to at least get my final thoughts down for her."

New Jersey congressman Andy Kim, a former State Department official who had worked in Afghanistan, was still in the Rayburn Building when he got an alert on his phone telling him to shelter in place. The wording of the bulletin was chilling to him: The police said they no longer had control of the building, and that lawmakers should stay in their offices if possible.

In his office, he called home, trying to beat the news to his wife and children. She had already heard from her coworkers that something was going on at the Capitol, and Kim tried to reassure her that he was all right. It occurred to Kim that there was only one other time when he had called home from work to try to communicate with Kammy before the news networks did that job for him.

That was years before he became a member of Congress, in 2011, when he was working in Kabul and the American embassy and NATO headquarters came under heavy attack and a siege that lasted nearly a full day.

*　*　*

In the Hart Senate Office Building, on the northern side of the Capitol known as "the Senate side," the senators sequestered in a sprawling hearing room were placing calls of their own to make sure family members knew they were safe. One lawmaker was making a different kind of call: Mitt Romney knew he was safe, but he was worried that his family might not be.

After he entered the room with an eruption of hot anger about President Trump, Romney called Utah's newly inaugurated governor, Spencer Cox, on his personal cell phone with an urgent request: Please, Romney asked him, could you dispatch the state police to my home outside Salt Lake City?

It was hardly an overheated or panicked entreaty. The most immediate audience for Trump's incitement was his crowd in Washington, but MAGA activists all over the country had heard and seen his remarks on television that day and they had been bombarded with his venomous tirades on social media for months. There was no more recognizable Republican dissident in the country than Mitt Romney. Even before the riot, he had already been berated on airplanes by seething Trump fans.

"There were some reports that there were protesters heading to the Romney home—their personal home," Cox says. "I immediately got the highway patrol there and we got the family out of there."

Congress is full of leakers: Some secret meetings and conference calls don't even end before the leaks begin. But this moment required total secrecy so as to not tip off the rioters about their location.

"Nobody announce your location to your staff!" yelled Ben Sasse, a Nebraska Republican.

Somebody else then hollered: "Or your family!"

Hoping to assuage the lawmakers' concerns, and perhaps buy some time, a Capitol Police captain addressed the group and stated what was obvious to the senators looking at their phones.

"Right now, the Capitol is breached," the captain said, explaining that the plan was to move all one hundred senators to buses that they were bringing in behind the Hart Building. "We need you to be patient and then we'll move you in orderly fashion."

One senator, however, was growing impatient. Having spent the previous two months soothing and stroking the unhinged president, Lindsey Graham now vented anger at the mob Trump had unleashed. When another police officer stood up to speak, the South Carolina senator did not let him do so for long.

"Our evacuation plan," the officer began, "is to come here in SH-216, hold until we determine what the next step is going to be—"

At this, Graham, who was situated close to the officer in the front of the room, loudly interjected.

"The next step is to get 'em out!" he said. "Whatever force you need to do. You're here to protect us. This is the center of democracy. You let people breach the Capitol."

But some of Graham's colleagues recoiled from his outburst, viewing it as so much grandstanding from a politician who loved attention.

"Shut up, Lindsey!" called out Sherrod Brown, the Ohio Democrat.

Another person could be heard calling out: "There are no cameras—come on!"

The officer tried to pick up where he had left off. Their plan, he said, was to secure the Capitol.

"I don't know how long that's going to take," he acknowledged. "It could take a while, so just hold on, try to get some water, and we'll keep you abreast of what's going on here as we try to make a determination of the next step here."

Another officer spoke up to impress upon the captive senators just how dire the situation was.

"We're securing the Capitol, and it's taking time because we have a lot of injured officers and a lot of injured civilians inside the Capitol that we're getting out right now," he said, exhorting the lawmakers to stay put. "The worst thing you can do is walk away, and then if we make a decision to leave here, we don't want to lose you."

Graham didn't leave, but the South Carolinian could barely stand still. He was a ball of nervous energy, and in an interview his inner monologue poured forth. An air force reservist who had repeatedly traveled to combat zones as a senator, he suggested the rioters should be dealt with like Islamist insurgents.

"Look, this will work out," he said. "I was on a base in Iraq when they breached the gate. Suicide vest on. We all hunkered down. You could hear the . . ." He imitated the cadence of machine-gun fire.

Graham did not, however, mask his disappointment with Trump, the president to whom he had been a fiercely supportive political partner. Trump, he said, "plays the TV game and he went too far here." His mind flitting from one subject to the next, Graham expressed optimism that the riot could become a turning point.

"People will say, 'I don't want to be associated with *that*.' There will be a rallying effect for a while, the country says we're better than this," Graham said, adding that perhaps the incoming president was the right man at the right time. "I mean, how mad can you get at Joe Biden?"

For all his effort to put on an upbeat face, however, Graham was stewing. As he saw that Trump was declining to forcefully condemn the attack, Graham leveled a threat at the White House. Telephoning the White House counsel, Pat Cipollone, the senator told him that if Trump did not act more aggressively to denounce the mob "we'll be asking you for the Twenty-Fifth Amendment" to remove Trump from office.

Nearly every senator was present and accounted for by this point, either because they were in the Hart Building or because they were among the very few locked down at Fort McNair. But one member of the Senate leadership was still stranded in the Capitol as rioters ransacked the building.

During the certification debate, Patty Murray of Washington State had gone to her hideaway in the Capitol. Murray, the third-ranking Senate Democrat, did not evacuate along with the rest of her colleagues because from her hideaway she did not know what was happening.

Roy Blunt, the senior Missouri Republican who was close with the Capitol Police, got on the phone with Murray and told her he was dispatching officers to hustle her away. Blunt told his Democratic colleague the name of the officer who was coming for her, and that he would identify himself when he arrived at the hideaway. Murray was nervous, and with good reason: She had been hearing people outside her door—one had barked something like, "I saw one of them in there!"—and she was hesitant about opening the door. The police eventually spirited her away.

As the hours went by in Hart, Blunt and the other senators, across the political spectrum, grew angrier.

"I've been here a long time," said Blunt, who first came to Congress in 1997. "And this is the day I have the most concern about what America projected to the rest of the world."

Bernie Sanders also alluded to the images of the United States being beamed across the globe.

"This is a nation that has been a model for the world in terms of democracy," he said, "and we have a president who is encouraging insurrection against that very democracy that he took an oath of office to defend."

* * *

Away from the main hearing room, in a much smaller room across the hall, a self-selected group of Republican senators were plotting their next steps. The group included Ted Cruz, who had been planning to oppose certification of the election. But now there was uncertainty in their ranks.

Could they still go forward with their objections, given the attack?

In that meeting, some senators argued for dropping their opposition to the certification in light of the violence that day. But Cruz pushed back hard: He says that he made the case that they should not "let a violent mob dictate how we do our jobs."

McConnell was more eager than ever to quash the objection effort. And before he was taken to Fort McNair, the Republican leader had flashed a rare kind of emotion to one of his colleagues.

Tim Kaine of Virginia, the Democrat who had been Hillary Clinton's running mate in 2016, had quietly formed a sort of friendship with McConnell. Approaching McConnell in the Hart Building after the insurrection began, Kaine told him that he knew it had to be a painful day for the Senate Republican leader, given his devotion to the institution that was under attack and his loss of the Senate majority he had fought so hard to claim.

"Neither of those things would have happened had it not been for Donald Trump," Kaine told McConnell, according to his memory.

McConnell said nothing in response. "But the anger I saw in his eyes," Kaine says, "was unlike anything I have ever seen. And he was not mad at me."

Soon enough, McConnell had been taken to Fort McNair along with the other congressional leaders. Surrounded by their Capitol Police details and uniformed soldiers, the lawmakers at McNair were at first separated by party.

John Thune, McConnell's deputy, was working his cell phone, trying to reach the senators who had been planning to challenge the certification. Given what was going on, he asked the ones he could reach, would they consider backing off their objections whenever the Senate reconvenes?

The same push was taking place at the staff level. Steve Daines, the Montana Republican who had developed a warm relationship with Trump, had been planning to join Cruz and a number of other senators to object to the certification. But Daines changed his mind after the attack began, and his top aide, Jason Thielman, drafted a statement that he hoped the dozen-strong group of Senate objectors would sign together.

"We now need the entire Congress to come together to vote unanimously to certify the election results," Thielman wrote, supplying the senators with the language to explain a pullback. "We must rise above the violence. We must stand together as Americans. We must defend our Constitution and the rule of law."

Thielman sent the proposed statement to other chiefs of staff of senators in the Cruz-led group. He got no immediate pushback, but the staffers were in spotty contact with their evacuated bosses and unable to reach consensus on their own.

At McNair, as the congressional leaders began to mingle across party lines, McConnell muttered a brief congratulations to Schumer on capturing the Senate majority—the development that had, up until a few hours earlier, been the most important political news of the day. But now both McConnell and Schumer were mostly focused on reconvening the Senate and bringing order back to Capitol Hill.

McConnell felt that returning to the Capitol was an overwhelming imperative, and the country had to see that the attack had failed and the Senate could carry out the business of democracy.

On a call with Pence and top Pentagon officials, the Republican leader said: "The thugs won't win."

Hoyer remembers McConnell using other heated language, demanding the Trump administration had to "damn well get this thing under control."

Schumer was just as frustrated. With Trump having pushed out his attorney general and defense secretary, there were only acting officials at two departments critical to the continuity of government: Jeffrey Rosen at Justice and Christopher Miller at the Pentagon. Schumer got both men on the phone and pressed them to promise that they would urge Trump to call off the rioters.

Schumer and Pelosi pressed Rosen hard: "Can you tell us now," they demanded, "that you will tell Trump to publicly call off the rioters?"

Rosen would not promise.

"Disgraceful," Schumer told Pelosi.

The two Democratic leaders then took matters into their own hands, issuing a joint statement: "We are calling on President Trump to demand that all protestors leave the U.S. Capitol and Capitol Grounds immediately."

With Trump still invisible, the leaders at McNair saw Biden address the unfolding situation from his home base in Wilmington. He had been slated to make remarks about the economy but events had overtaken things.

"At this hour, our democracy is under an unprecedented assault," Biden began, speaking in a level tone. Branding the riot the work of "a small number of extremists," the president-elect called on the mob to "pull back" and demanded that Trump bring an end to the siege.

So far, there was no sign Trump was working toward that end.

Kevin McCarthy was as determined as the rest of the lawmakers to return to the Capitol, and by this point he was the only one of the four congressional leaders on speaking terms with the president. In a direct call to Trump, he implored the president to tell his supporters to go home.

But when Trump released a video addressing the mob, it was hardly a stern denunciation. He repeated, once again, that a "landslide" victory had been "stolen from us," before adding that everyone should disperse and go home for the sake of "peace."

As the hours went by and afternoon turned to evening, McConnell spoke repeatedly with another House Republican who was back in the Capitol complex, and who shared his anger about Trump far more fully than McCarthy.

Liz Cheney had come to Congress the same month Trump arrived in the White House. A national security hawk like her father, she had parted ways with Trump on foreign policy but largely muted her concerns about his conduct. After his defeat, she stood out among the otherwise pliant House Republican leaders in her refusal to abet Trump's effort to undermine the election.

"Are they going to stop their objections?" Cheney asked McConnell of the pro-Trump senators who had concocted an elaborate pretext for challenging the election.

McConnell and his deputies were pushing all of the senators who had been planning to oppose certification, but it was not clear how many of them would relent.

They would find out in a few hours.

Cheney, however, was already thinking past that day.

* * *

As the Wyoming Republican was being evacuated from the Capitol to the Longworth Building a short while earlier, she had crossed paths with Hakeem Jeffries, the Brooklyn Democrat regarded by much of his party as a future Speaker of the House. Cheney and Jeffries were the chairs of their respective caucuses, and they had developed a cordial if not close relationship dealing with joint logistical matters.

Encountering Jeffries, Cheney said they had to take action against Trump. Jeffries said they should discuss the matter further once they got to a secure location.

While the senators were hustled over to the massive and modern Hart hearing room, House members were taken to the older and slightly more gilded confines of the Ways and Means Committee's hearing room. Filled with oil portraits of previous chairs of the prestigious tax-writing committee, the room was now a refuge for panicked lawmakers and the site of the first strategy session over Trump's second impeachment.

Tom Malinowski, a former diplomat turned New Jersey congressman who had been in the House gallery, approached Cheney once he saw her in the room. The two did not have much in common, but both had served in the State Department and Malinowski suspected Cheney might share part of his perspective on the events of that day.

"Liz, I hope you'll agree with us, but the moment we get the all clear, the moment it is safe to go back, we've got to get back in that chamber," Malinowski said, according to his recollection.

"Yeah," she said, "and impeach the son of a bitch."

Malinowski was taken aback because Cheney was ahead of him—he was a Democrat, and he was not even thinking about impeachment yet—but he quickly agreed to discuss the idea.

Jeffries, too, was struck by Cheney's determination to confront Trump. Once they got to Longworth, she told him that she was going to talk to McConnell about impeachment because he, too, felt something had to be done to punish Trump for the riot. To Jeffries, that was the signal that she was serious about taking action and not just venting about Trump in the midst of an evacuation.

But first the unlikely duo—a conservative white woman from Jackson Hole whose parents were vice president and second lady, and a progressive Black man from Brooklyn whose parents were a social worker and a substance-abuse counselor—had to calm their members. Once they had been in the Ways and Means room for a little while, members realized the higher-ranking House leaders had been taken elsewhere. It was up to Cheney and Jeffries to take charge.

That was no easy task. Fear and anger were rippling through the room, triggered not only by the riot but also by the refusal of some Republican lawmakers to wear face masks in the confined and crowded space.

When Bill Johnson, a pro-Trump Republican from Appalachian Ohio, tried to lead the room in a prayer, he was all but shouted down by Democrats who blamed him and his ilk for the attack that led to their predicament.

"A bunch of us were like, 'Fuck you, right now,' right? 'No, you don't get to do that,'" one moderate Democrat says.

Other Democrats grew even angrier when Lisa Blunt Rochester tried to distribute masks and was rebuffed by Republican lawmakers who insisted on being bare-faced despite being bunched together.

The fear of physical violence was still present. Lauren Underwood, the young Illinois Democrat, remembers that Colin Allred, a Texas Democrat and former NFL linebacker, was carrying a long metal pole of the kind used to hang velvet rope lines. "I'm going to keep Colin in my sight," Underwood thought to herself, "because if something happens right behind him, he's got a weapon and he's a big guy."

Malinowski was still making his way around the room, talking to his colleagues about the symbolic importance of returning to the House floor that evening. But he did not always find a receptive audience for the message that they had to show the world American democracy was safe. Katie Porter, a California progressive, shot back: "What I learned today is that we're *not* safe."

Among Democrats, there was also tension flaring about the role of the Capitol Police and whether the force had done its best to protect them.

When Cheri Bustos, the Illinois Democrat, told a group of colleagues in the room that she hoped the day would be a lesson to lawmakers about the importance of police—"They just saved our lives," she said—multiple colleagues were taken aback. The police, other Democrats believed, had failed, perhaps deliberately. One Democrat showed Bustos a video, already rocketing across social media, that appeared to show the police allowing rioters to pass by unimpeded.

"Look at this video—you still want to defend police?" the Democrat, whom Bustos declined to name, asked her. She could not deny the video was troubling.

Bustos texted the clip to her husband, a county sheriff back in Rock Island, to ask for an explanation.

"They're overrun," he responded. "Their own lives are in danger."

Recognizing the ugly environment at hand, Cheney and Jeffries determined that they had to speak with one voice to the huddled members. They had to impress upon them the importance of keeping their location secret and, eventually, returning to the Capitol to finish certifying Biden's victory. The duo spoke twice to the members, the second time to a round of applause after the announcement that they would soon return to the chamber.

Cheney and Jeffries were addressing the room a third time that night when Pelosi and Hoyer returned from Fort McNair to join them. Pelosi entered as Jeffries was speaking, and the younger Democrat immediately yielded to the Speaker, who thanked him for holding things down in her stead. Anna Eshoo remembers coming up behind her dear friend, the Speaker of the House, and kissing her on the shoulder.

When Pelosi neglected to mention Cheney, Jeffries spoke up to thank his Republican counterpart, noting they had worked as partners throughout the day. It was an illustration of the respect Democrats had come to have for Cheney in the months after the election and in those hours of crisis on January 6. It also showed why a staunch conservative would soon come to be more admired by liberals than by her fellow Republicans.

For the moment, there was a pervasive mood of relief. The Capitol, it seemed, was secure. The work of the Congress would go on.

* * *

Yet the chaos of the day had spread beyond Capitol Hill. There had been pro-Trump protests in state capitals around the country, and some of them had yielded spasms of political violence. At the Oregon capitol in Salem, demonstrators had burned an effigy of Governor Kate Brown. In Phoenix, protesters had broken windows at the Arizona capitol and assembled a guillotine there.

In New Hampshire, Chris Sununu, the Republican governor, was watching the insurrection on television in his office and wondered if there would be copycats in his state. He called the state police right away.

"Give me another bunch of cruisers here at the statehouse," he said, according to his account.

In Minnesota, Tim Walz was working in the state capitol, but his fourteen-year-old son was back at home when protesters marched on the governor's mansion. The state patrol swooped in to evacuate Walz's son to a secure location. Hundreds of demonstrators menaced the nearby state capitol, with audible chants about civil war.

In Washington State, a MAGA mob breached the security perimeter around the governor's residence. Jay Inslee, a former presidential candidate best known as a champion of fighting climate change, was on a Zoom call and trying to ignore the chanting he heard outside when a state trooper burst into the room.

"You need to go right now," the trooper said, according to the governor's memory. "You need to go to the safe room."

A large group of insurrectionists, some of them armed, had broken through the gates around the residence, though none of them made it inside.

As with the riot in Congress, there was no telling what might have happened had the mob reached Inslee before the troopers.

* * *

Unbeknownst to most members of Congress, the work of punishing Donald Trump had already begun.

While most of their colleagues were in the Ways and Means room, a pair of House Democrats on the Judiciary Committee, Ted Lieu of California and David Cicilline of Rhode Island, were in Cicilline's office in the Rayburn House Office Building crafting what would eventually become the impeachment article against Trump.

The Rhode Islander, an attorney and former Providence mayor, had watched Trump's speech that morning. When Cicilline then saw the Capitol being attacked, he immediately recognized it was no accident. It was obvious to him that a great crime had been committed, and that Congress would have to act.

"This is all connected," he thought.

Because he was not on the House floor when the building was breached, Cicilline remained in his office throughout the ordeal and used the time to strategize with Lieu, who had fled his own office, and Judiciary Committee staff about what the language of the impeachment should say.

As the House members returned to the chamber, they did so under a dark cloud: They still had to vote on the Republicans' objection to the election results, and there was no sign that the GOP would relent after the horrors of the day. As the certification debate dragged on, Andy Kim remembers that for the first time a colleague approached him around 2 a.m. and asked him for his thoughts on impeaching Trump.

"I'm not in the right state of mind right now to make determinations," Kim recalls saying. "I need to sleep on this and try to gain a little perspective."

Then he asked his colleague: "How fast is this moving?"

The answer, it would soon become clear, was: extremely fast.

House Republicans only sped things up further with a vote that showed the unbending loyalty to Trump in the lower chamber. A group of 147 members, the overwhelming majority of the GOP Conference, voted to object to the election results from one or more states.

Kevin McCarthy, just back from Fort McNair, was among them.

*　　*　　*

When the senators returned to their chamber, it was still unclear what Trump's bitter-enders would do. As they walked, the senators who had been planning to object ignored reporters' questions about their intentions.

It was just after 8 p.m. when Mike Pence, back on the Senate dais, declared a "dark day in the history of the United States Capitol."

The always stern vice president spoke the words Trump refused to utter: "We condemn the violence that took place here in the strongest possible terms." He also took care to note that the Congress had reconvened within hours of the attack "to support and defend the Constitution."

"Let's get back to work," he said, prompting a lengthy standing ovation.

McConnell took the floor first and said he had a message for the American people.

"The United States Senate will not be intimidated," he declared. "We will not be kept out of this chamber by thugs, mobs, or threats."

Barely suppressing his anger, he called the attack a "failed insurrection."

McConnell did not mention Trump's name, but the man who would soon supplant him as majority leader did. When he rose with his own remarks for the nation, Schumer called the attack "the final, terrible, indelible legacy of the forty-fifth president of the United States—undoubtedly our worst."

Few senators who spoke that night were more animated than Graham, who belittled the complex election-objection rationale engineered by Ted Cruz and rattled off Trump's false claims of fraud and his unbroken record of courtroom defeats.

"Count me out," Graham said. "Enough is enough."

It seemed like a breaking point for a senator who had relinquished his maverick reputation to become a volunteer Trump adviser. And to put an exclamation mark on his comments, Graham offered a word of encouragement to the beleaguered vice president, telling Mike Pence: "Just hang in there."

Graham's renunciation of Trump would prove fleeting. But when Romney stood that night to say he had been "shaken to the core," there could be no question of his sincerity. His face was flushed, his eyes were red, and his voice was nearly breaking.

The Utah senator invoked the people he met abroad "who yearn for freedom" and "look to this building and these shores as a place of hope." Then he unloaded.

"We gather due to a selfish man's injured pride," Romney said of Trump.

No, Romney said, the fact that Trump's supporters were angry about the election was not sufficient reason to obstruct democracy. Bringing senators on both sides of the aisle to their feet, he declared: "The best way we can show respect for the voters who are upset is by telling them the truth!"

Standing just inches away was Josh Hawley, the first Republican senator to announce his plans to object. Romney warned his colleagues that anyone who followed through with that scheme would go down in history as "being complicit in an unprecedented attack against our democracy."

"That will be their legacy," Romney said, with Hawley sitting stone-faced below him.

Yet in a sign of Trump's persistent grip on the GOP—and the intransigence of Republican senators who were loath to backtrack in full on an ill-conceived, ill-intentioned plan—only about half of the Republican senators who announced their intent to contest the election abandoned that plan. One of them was Kelly Loeffler, who only days earlier had endorsed the objection scheme in a last-ditch bid to pander to Trump's base in Georgia.

Eight other Republicans, including Hawley and Cruz, objected to the votes from one or more states, even as the Capitol was still stained with the mud and blood of insurrectionists.

That night, the strategist David Kochel, who had been a Mitt Romney adviser in Iowa since well before his first presidential bid in 2008, emailed the senator to tell him how proud he was of his conduct that day.

Romney replied by paraphrasing Winston Churchill.

"The G.O.P. was given a choice between dishonor and defeat," Romney wrote. "They chose dishonor. They will have defeat."

*　*　*

As Wednesday turned to Thursday and the Senate finished its business, the anger of the lawmakers seemed to continue mounting. The Capitol was filthy. There was trash strewn about, shattered glass on floors throughout the building, and grime smeared the floor of the Rotunda. Here and there, smears of blood were visible, including on a bust of Zachary Taylor, the little-remembered twelfth president.

A few members helped the custodial staff, but it was difficult to clean up thoroughly with soldiers and police in seemingly every corner of the building. Because of all the broken glass, the bomb-sniffing German shepherds deployed in the complex had to be outfitted with black booties on their paws to avoid injury.

It was already easy to detect some of the Republican votes for impeachment.

Fred Upton, a Michigan Republican and one of the longest-serving members of the House, stood in the defiled Rotunda and said Trump would be marked forever by the events of that day.

"This is his legacy," Upton said.

Walking outside the Senate, Lisa Murkowski, the Alaska maverick, said flatly the GOP should break with Trump and January 6 showed why.

"I think today was a pretty good example," she said.

And Cheney's determination had not faded. Encountering Pence in the Rotunda just after midnight, she stopped him to offer her gratitude for his comportment that day, calling him a patriot and telling him she admired his courage.

"Thank you so much," Pence replied.

As she headed to the Lindy Boggs Room, the cloakroom reserved for female members, Cheney told reporters the day had been a "tremendous tragedy" and "an insurrection." She stopped short of saying in public what she had already said in private about impeachment. Yet even as an aide tried to usher her away from reporters, Cheney signaled her break with Trump and the party he'd continue to dominate.

"A president who refuses to leave office and concede after he's lost the vote in the Electoral College is something completely unprecedented and very serious and can't be tolerated," she said.

Another Republican congressional leader from the West said in no uncertain terms that it was time for the party to move on from Trump. As John Thune was leaving the Capitol in the early morning hours of January 7, he reflected that the Republican Party had to have a reckoning about its identity "pretty soon."

"Our identity for the past several years was built around an individual," he said. "We've got to get back to where it's built on a set of principles and ideas and policies."

Thune expected that in the struggle to liberate his party from Trump, he could count on the Republican Senate leader as a crucial ally.

Mitch McConnell had been uneasy about Trump since he entered the 2016 primary. The Kentucky conservative had hoped his fellow senator Marco Rubio would win the nomination, and when Trump emerged as the dominant candidate McConnell told his Senate colleagues that if Trump was hurting their own reelection campaigns then they could "drop him like a hot rock."

But Trump had won in 2016, and for most of the last four years McConnell had made an uneasy but productive peace with a president he came to see as a means to the end of cutting taxes and appointing conservative judges. McConnell never grew close to Trump, like Kevin McCarthy, but viewing Trump as something of a useful idiot, he had routinely enabled or ignored his norm-breaking ways and flagrant corruption.

The first time Democrats had impeached Trump, for pressuring a foreign government to smear Joe Biden, McConnell backed the president to the hilt.

And when Trump started down the path that led to his second impeachment—spreading pernicious lies about the legitimacy of the 2020 election—McConnell largely held his tongue, putting his electoral interests in Georgia first.

By the early hours of January 7, McConnell had had enough. His majority was broken, the Capitol was desecrated, and the country was humiliated in the eyes of the world. The Senate Republican leader summoned his staff into his chief of staff's office and delivered an impromptu speech that was one part pick-me-up for downcast aides and one part jeremiad against the president whose followers had put the Congress under siege.

Donald Trump, McConnell said, was a "despicable human being."

We all knew he was unqualified but some thought he'd grow into the job, McConnell said. We quickly learned he wouldn't grow into the office, so we tried to make the best of it, he went on. They had done good work for the country, McConnell assured his staff, and they had constrained the president in important ways.

Now, McConnell said, we will have to fight him politically.

Not long after, McConnell prepared to leave the Capitol after perhaps the worst day of his career. Seeing one of the authors of this book on the ground floor, McConnell made clear he wanted a word and stepped inside a doorway opposite the Senate Dining Room.

"What do you hear about the Twenty-Fifth Amendment?" he asked, eager for intelligence about whether his fellow Republicans were discussing removing Trump from office. Then McConnell said he had talked to Schumer and Pelosi at Fort McNair about the possibility of issuing a joint statement urging Trump to stay away from Biden's inauguration on January 20.

Strikingly, after all the trauma of the day, the seventy-eight-year-old senator seemed almost buoyant. It soon became clear why.

Trump, McConnell said, "was pretty thoroughly discredited by this.

"He put a gun to his head and pulled the trigger," he said. "Couldn't have happened at a better time."

But would rank-and-file Republicans walk away from Trump?

McConnell entertained the question by invoking one of his proudest political triumphs: his sustained campaign in the 2014 elections to clobber insurgent candidates on the far right. He had run the tables that year during primary season, and his reward in November had been capturing the Senate majority. He had taken on the extremists and he had won.

"We crushed the sons of bitches," he said, "and that's what we're going to do in the primary in '22."

Beyond that promise of payback, McConnell remained focused on Trump personally and the havoc he had inflicted on the Capitol. His treatment of Pence had been disgraceful but unsurprising to McConnell: "There are no permanent allies with this guy," he said of the president.

But what was his larger reaction to the day? How did Mitch McConnell feel as he absorbed the images of the rioters in his beloved Senate?

Mitch McConnell seldom discusses his feelings at any articulate length, even in private.

"You asked me how I feel?" he replied. "I feel exhilarated by the fact that this fellow finally, totally discredited himself."

As McConnell left the Capitol in what he hoped was a new day, he might not have known how immediately Trump's fate—and the fate of the Republican Party—would rest in his hands.

Chapter 8

Do the Right Thing

MITCH MCCONNELL'S PRIVATE declaration of war in the small hours of January 7 would remain that way—as a confidential oath of vengeance against the man who had brought mayhem to the Capitol. But in the weeks after the mob attack, the Republican Party as a whole faced a highly public choice: What would it do about President Trump?

Trump still had two weeks left in his term, meaning all the powers of the presidency were still within reach of someone many in his own party had concluded was a madman. And even beyond Inauguration Day, when Trump would presumably surrender his office, Republicans were contemplating the possibility that they could be defined for a generation as the party of riot and rebellion.

For the country, the aftermath of January 6 represented another test of the political system: Could it deliver justice and punishment for a politically motivated attack on the national legislature? Or would the Republican Party's loyalty to Trump, and fear of its own radicalized voters, prevail again?

For a fleeting moment, a large number of officeholders believed it was time to make a sharp break with Trump and his increasingly extreme circle of loyalists.

Three Republican governors, all independent-minded centrists from the Northeast, called on Trump to resign. Several members of the Cabinet, including Betsy DeVos, the education secretary, and Elaine Chao, the transportation secretary married to McConnell, quit their posts. Several others came close to resigning but were persuaded to stay to assist the transition.

And in the House, Kevin McCarthy gathered his leadership team and told them the time to confront Donald Trump was at hand.

The House minority leader recognized at once that the January 6 attack could be politically devastating to his party. In private, he issued a harsh moral judgment on Trump's behavior that day: "What the president did is atrocious and totally wrong," McCarthy said on a call with House Republican leaders on January 8.

"Internally, we've got severe problems as a party," McCarthy said. He faulted Trump for "inciting people" and reiterated that "what the president said was not right by any shape or any form."

On that call, McCarthy's deputy, Steve Scalise, said it was time for the Republican Party to think about how to define itself without Trump.

"We're going to have a lot of introspection to do," Scalise said. "You know, what does the post-Trump Republican House look like?"

Still, McCarthy was not sure what to do in response to the Capitol attack. After all, he noted, the transfer of power was only twelve days away. The obvious ways of punishing Trump—such as impeaching him or demanding his resignation—might just add "fuel on the fire," McCarthy said. He told his colleagues on the leadership team that he was trying to reach Biden to see if he could come to an understanding on how to proceed with the president-elect.

Yet as the outcry against Trump continued mounting, McCarthy seemed to change his mind. For a few days, at least, Trump's eager footman in the House decided he would have to do something more drastic than merely wait out the outgoing president's dwindling term.

On January 10, McCarthy convened a smaller group of House Republican leaders to share his thinking. Speaking with just three other top Republicans on a private call, McCarthy said he might call on Trump to resign. He conferred for more than forty-five minutes with Scalise, Liz Cheney, and Tom Emmer, the Minnesota lawmaker who led the House Republicans' campaign committee. The usually upbeat McCarthy was audibly anguished. The gravity of the attack was still sinking in, and it seemed increasingly clear to him that he had to break with Trump.

It was finally time to end their alliance.

His plan, McCarthy said on the January 10 call, was to approach the president and tell him it was inevitable that Congress would impeach him and it was time for him to go.

He envisioned telling Trump of an impeachment resolution: "I think this will pass, and it would be my recommendation you should resign."

"I've had it with this guy," McCarthy said near the end of the call. "What he did was unacceptable. Nobody can defend that and nobody should defend it."

McCarthy's fellow leaders were split on how to proceed, though they all recognized Trump had crossed a dreadful line. Cheney spoke up to say Republicans had to be "very clear-eyed about what happened Wednesday and what the president did." It was already clear, she said, that Trump had "unleashed a mob that came up to the Capitol, that attempted to kill a number of us, probably any of us they could have found." Even more disturbing facts could still emerge, Cheney added.

Emmer, by contrast, wondered if there was a way out of taking on Trump directly, asking McCarthy if there was "any other way to hold the president accountable instead of impeachment." Betraying his own misgivings about a head-on clash with Trump, McCarthy floated the idea of a censure resolution— a largely symbolic punitive measure without the teeth of impeachment. But it would still be the most significant Republican rebuke of a president to whom they had spent four years in near-total obeisance.

McCarthy said Democrats would not view censure as a sufficient sanction. He had already checked in with a member of Democratic leadership, Steny Hoyer, who had told him as much.

"What if we offer it?" Emmer asked of a censure resolution.

"Well, that's what I'm throwing out right there," McCarthy shot back.

Emmer was not ready to let go of the idea—or of his own instinct to placate Trump. He suggested that McCarthy go to Trump and effectively ask the president's permission to punish him: Perhaps, he suggested, McCarthy could ask Trump to sign off on a censure resolution. Emmer wondered if the president could be made to understand that allowing Republicans to censure him might help head off impeachment.

"I don't really want to talk to the guy," McCarthy replied, perhaps recognizing how fruitless such an approach would be.

More than that, though, McCarthy seemed to be genuinely shocked about the events of January 6. He had defended Trump to the hilt the last time Democrats had impeached him, for abuse of power and obstruction of justice after it was revealed that he had pressured the Ukrainian government to smear Joe Biden. But this time was different, McCarthy said, and he wondered aloud if Democrats had a point about censure.

Given Trump's role in what happened, McCarthy asked, "is that letting him off on something?"

"I'm just throwing ideas out," he insisted. "I'm just brainstorming with everybody, getting feedback from everyone."

Trump was not the only Republican McCarthy sounded willing to punish in the immediate aftermath of January 6. He and his leadership team had to grapple with the most extreme members of the GOP Conference: far-right lawmakers, like Matt Gaetz, Marjorie Taylor Greene, and Lauren Boebert, who had stoked Trump voters' paranoid rage about the election and made reckless comments about the riot. Now, some of them were attacking Republicans who spoke out to criticize Trump.

"We can't put up with that type of shit," McCarthy said. The big social-media companies had stripped Trump of his accounts after January 6, and now McCarthy jokingly pondered whether the most problematic House Republicans might meet the same fate: "Can't they take their Twitter accounts away, too?"

Most troubling to the House minority leader seemed to be Mo Brooks, the Alabama Republican who had joined Trump in riling up the mob on January 6. McCarthy was not initially familiar with what Brooks had said that day, and an aide spoke up on the call to read Brooks's comments about "taking down names and kicking ass." The top House Republican reacted with horror.

"You think the president deserves to be impeached for his comments—that almost goes further than what the president said," McCarthy said.

Scalise told him there was already talk among House Republicans about stripping Brooks of his committee assignments. McCarthy sounded intrigued, asking what committees Brooks served on. An aide told him Brooks was on Armed Services, the powerful panel overseeing the American military.

McCarthy ended the call with no certain plan. He told his colleagues he wanted to lay out the facts, as he knew them, to the Republican Conference. But when he hung up, he had not committed to do anything concrete—whether it was urging Trump to resign or backing a censure motion.

Outside the House leadership team, there were indeed conversations spreading through the GOP Conference about taking action against the extremists in their midst. Steve Womack of Arkansas, a retired National Guard colonel with a sober mien, believed Mo Brooks was the worst of the worst. He told colleagues he was determined to strip Brooks of his seat on Armed Services. As a member of his party's steering committee—the influential panel that hands out committee assignments to members—Womack might just have the clout he needed to make that happen.

Other House conservatives who had long aligned themselves with Trump agreed that the president and his most extreme allies had finally gone too far. One lawmaker, Dan Crenshaw of Texas, a former Navy SEAL who wore an eyepatch because of injuries sustained in Afghanistan, knew exactly which of his House colleagues were to blame. In public, Crenshaw broadly denounced lawmakers who had recklessly stoked conspiracy theories and anger about the election. In private, he went further: Speaking with a Democratic colleague, he named specific names of House members he saw as complicit in the riot.

These people need to be held accountable, Crenshaw said—though he did not say what exactly that meant, or whether he would do anything to mete out punishment himself.

It was still uncertain whether anyone in the GOP would take the risk of publicly demanding accountability for these lawmakers or the president they served. But in the days after January 6, it truly seemed to some House

Republicans like even their malleable leader might be prepared to stiffen his spine.

Like most everyone else in his party, McCarthy had spent four years trying to keep the president happy, even accepting a nickname more suited to a golden retriever than a leader of an independent branch of government: "My Kevin." A fifty-five-year-old political climber, McCarthy had approached his time in the House with one overriding goal—to become Speaker—and he had calculated for years that an alliance with Trump was his best shot at the job.

Now the Capitol had been defiled, his caucus was deeply divided, his counterpart in the Senate was vowing retribution, and the business community was threatening to cut off contributions to lawmakers who had refused to certify the election. Democrats were marshaling their strength for another impeachment trial—one that could end with Trump being barred from holding office ever again.

It was the kind of moment that forces a leader to show his mettle.

But McCarthy was simply not sure what to do. Outside the strict confidentiality of the leadership call, he was even foggier with fellow Republicans about his plans for dealing with Trump. He told House colleagues he hoped Trump would "do the right thing," without quite saying what that was.

The one thing McCarthy was clear about—even as he wrestled with impeachment, censure, resignation, and more—was that the country needed to know the truth of what happened on January 6. And the way to make sure that happened, he believed, was through a bipartisan commission.

"We need to have all the facts, especially for all of us," he told a gathering of House Republicans several days after the attack. "And we should do it in a bipartisan manner."

Before the end of the month, McCarthy's appetite for punishing Trump would disappear completely. He would be photographed on January 28 posing happily beside the ousted president at Mar-a-Lago. By the spring, McCarthy's interest in a bipartisan inquiry would vanish, too. At Trump's encouragement, McCarthy and his leadership team whipped votes against legislation to enact the very idea he had proposed in the wake of the attack on the Capitol.

In the end, McCarthy chose not to lead his party into conflict with Donald Trump. Instead, bereft of obvious and easy options, he chose the path he thought would secure his own political future: surrender.

* * *

When House Republicans convened for a virtual meeting on January 11, McCarthy still had not settled on a plan. Over a two-and-a-half-hour session with his colleagues McCarthy attempted to convey a stern attitude toward Trump without endorsing any course of action that could divide his conference. He alluded to speaking with Trump, but made no mention of a possible call for resignation, as he had done with his leadership team the previous day.

"Let me be very clear to all of you, and I've been very clear to the president: He bears responsibilities for his words and actions, no ifs, ands, or buts," McCarthy said at the start of the January 11 session. "I asked him personally today, Does he hold responsibility for what happened? Does he feel bad about what happened?"

"He told me he does have some responsibility for what happened," McCarthy continued. "And he needs to acknowledge that."

Several Republicans spoke up to express well-founded skepticism that Trump would take any such responsibility. Peter Meijer, a newly elected army veteran from a powerful Michigan business family, said Republican voters were being misled by party leaders. He voiced concern that using the phrase "election integrity" was "a dog whistle" for Trump's claims of a stolen election. McCarthy sought to placate him without quite agreeing.

Many rank-and-file lawmakers were neither determined to punish Trump nor eager to defend him, but were instead desperately seeking a way out of what they saw as a political jam. One Florida Republican, the war veteran Brian Mast, suggested that the entire GOP Conference could stand together on the Capitol steps and urge the rioters to turn themselves in. Another, the Arkansas banker French Hill, said that if Trump would concede and meet with Biden then it would "save us a lot of pain and misery."

But nearly a week went by and Trump had not yet responded to such entreaties. One of McCarthy's fellow GOP leaders believed it was time for tougher action. Echoing language she had used on her January 10 call with McCarthy—and with Democrats on January 6—Cheney signaled that she believed impeachment should be on the table. The upcoming vote, she said, was "not one that I believe that we ought to be in a position where we're telling people how to vote based on partisanship.

"If this is an attack against the Congress by the president, you know, that is a high crime and misdemeanor," Cheney said.

Two Republicans from Washington State who would soon vote for impeachment suggested equally drastic actions. Dan Newhouse noted that no one on the video call had yet raised "invoking the Twenty-Fifth Amendment," which allows the cabinet to remove a president from office—an extreme step that no one in the executive branch appeared to be contemplating. His colleague Jaime Herrera Beutler proposed a more direct approach.

"I think another way out that we should consider as a conference," she said, "is asking our own leadership to join with the Republican leadership in the Senate and asking this president to resign."

As the conversation progressed, it was obvious to lawmakers that McCarthy did not intend to outline a game plan. Tom Cole, the canny Oklahoman who had barricaded himself in his hideaway, noted the same lack of direction from the top. There were "widely divergent views" on impeachment in the conference, Cole said, and he was hearing rumors that some 30 or 40 percent of Republicans might ultimately vote against Trump.

"Any guidance you could give us about where members are at or whether or not we'll have an opportunity, collectively, to deliberate on that before we sort of stumble on to the floor?" he asked the party leaders.

McCarthy was silent.

The reason for his paralysis was plain as day, for even as one set of Republicans was articulating their frustration with Trump, another was still crusading for the president's lost cause. On the same long call, the far-right flamethrowers of the House, including Greene and Boebert, were laboring to shift attention away from their beloved president. Boebert, a pistol-packing Coloradan, railed against the Black mayor of Washington, D.C., Muriel Bowser, for not sending Metropolitan Police to rescue the Capitol.

Herrera Beutler cut in angrily, reminding Boebert that she had tweeted the location of lawmakers during the insurrection. "Don't ask us about security if you're telling the attackers where we're at," said Herrera Beutler.

McCarthy did not want to take on the far-right members of his conference in such a blunt way.

The most telling comment of the session may have come from Bill Johnson, the little-known Ohioan who had tried feebly to recite a prayer in the Ways and Means room during the siege. On January 11, he gave voice to his Appalachian district that had just handed Trump 72 percent of the vote.

Johnson said he did not think the president was blameless for the Capitol attack.

"I'm not saying he didn't do anything wrong, don't get me wrong on that at all," he said. "Because I do think that he could have handled it very, very differently. And accountability is certainly in order."

But Republican voters, Johnson continued, didn't want to hear it.

"The seventy-four-plus million people that voted for him, including the over two hundred and fifty some thousand in my district, when I practice various avenues to suggest to them that there's some accountability to be shared here, man—they go ballistic right away," Johnson said. Voters, he said, were asking, "Where in the hell is the accountability, starting with Hillary Clinton."

He rattled off a few more names and institutions that conservative media had fixated on, including the FBI and Hunter Biden, the president-elect's troubled son.

"I'm just telling you that that's the kind of thing that we're dealing with, with our base," Johnson finished. "I'm not asking a question about it. I'm just telling you that's some of the raging fire that's going on out there."

* * *

If McCarthy was deflated and indecisive after January 6, McConnell was angry and determined. Here, he believed, was his opening to purge Trump from the party. His Senate majority was gone. The Capitol had been desecrated. But there was now a chance to send the president he despised into exile.

A man of few words and fewer passions, McConnell spent the weekend after the attack in a lather, using profanity to refer to Trump and telling donors he would never speak to the president again. Other Senate elders expressed a feeling that the attack would make it easier to cut ties with Trump. Rob Portman of Ohio, a member in good standing of the GOP establishment, predicted to a group he spoke with that weekend that a censure of Trump would get more than eighty votes in the Senate.

"As bad as last week was, it may be what allows us to move on more quickly," Roy Blunt, the Missouri senator who was co-chairing the upcoming presidential inauguration, told an associate.

To these establishment Republicans, the attack of January 6 seemed to represent the party's best chance to break with Trump since the *Access Hollywood* video in the fall of 2016. Then, Trump had been exposed as a proud assaulter of women, and his party had lurched away from him before re-embracing him. The insurrection was another such opening.

McConnell believed a more lasting break was now possible.

On Monday, January 11—the same day McCarthy meandered his way through the House conference call—McConnell shared a Chick-fil-A takeout lunch with a pair of longtime advisers, Terry Carmack and Scott Jennings. In Jennings's Louisville office, McConnell outlined what he saw as Trump's imminent demise.

"The Democrats are going to take care of the son of a bitch for us," he said, referring to Pelosi's determination to bring impeachment charges that very week.

The Senate leader had been in touch with Liz Cheney and understood that they were of like mind on the subject of Trump's culpability. The House had the votes to impeach Trump, likely with a meaningful stamp of bipartisanship. And during that lunch, McConnell told his advisers there would be at least seventeen Senate Republicans ready to affirm Trump's impeachment, supplying the two-thirds vote needed to convict. Trump would already be out of office by the time the vote took place, but a conviction would mean he could be barred from running for office ever again.

Trump's role on January 6, McConnell said, was clearly impeachable. He suggested that he would be among the Republicans who would vote for conviction.

"If this isn't impeachable, I don't know what is," he said.

The two aides responded in different ways. Jennings, a public-relations consultant, egged McConnell on, telling him Trump would never be weaker than he was at that moment. If McConnell was going to war with him, the strategist said, waiting was not an option.

Carmack was more circumspect. The top aide in McConnell's personal office, which manages his affairs in Kentucky, he asked if the leader was concerned about blowback from the thoroughly Trumpified Kentucky grass roots.

Sometimes, McConnell said, you have the luxury of sticking your finger in the wind and sometimes you don't.

It was a loose paraphrase of an axiom handed down to McConnell by his political mentor, John Sherman Cooper, a liberal Kentucky Republican who defied immense political pressure at home to back the Voting Rights Act and the Civil Rights Act. McConnell was fond of citing comments Cooper made to him, explaining those votes: "There are times when you are supposed to lead, and other times to reflect the views of your state, and I think it is time to lead."

On that Monday, McConnell seemed to believe it was time to lead.

The lunch was interrupted by the ringing of McConnell's cell phone. It was the president-elect.

"Hey, pal, how're you doing?" Biden asked him, expressing concern about his former colleague's safety.

Alluding to the Capitol rioters, Biden added, "These guys are crazy."

McConnell assured Biden he was fine, and the two got down to talking business. The incoming president did not ask the Republican leader for his views on impeachment, and McConnell did not offer them. But Biden wanted to know whether the Senate could juggle two things at once: an impeachment trial and confirmation hearings for Biden's cabinet. McConnell said he would get back to Biden with an answer.

The senator also wanted to offer a bit of good news for his old colleague: McConnell told Biden that he would vote to confirm Merrick Garland as attorney general. That endorsement may have come as a surprise to Biden, since McConnell had been the architect of a Senate blockade against Garland's earlier nomination to the Supreme Court in 2016. But on the phone, McConnell assured the new president he would have his chosen man at the Justice Department as the FBI was launching a nationwide manhunt for the perpetrators of the Capitol attack.

At least in private, McConnell was talking like someone who wanted to see swift and certain justice meted out to Trump and the horde that did his bidding.

* * *

However, another party gathering around the same time captured the ambivalence of the Republican Party's traditional establishment, and the enduring loyalty to Trump of the hard-core conservative base. By coincidence, the Republican National Committee had previously scheduled its winter conference in Amelia Island, Florida, for the weekend after January 6.

The party's central committee had been transformed over the previous generation from an army of political operatives and lobbyists into a hive of right-wing activists, evangelical organizers, and more recently, MAGA devotees. Under the direction of Trump's eventual campaign manager, Bill Stepien, the committee had worked to purge dissenters and install Trump loyalists in most all of the RNC's 168 seats. In the wake of January 6, it showed.

On Trump's watch, Republicans had lost the House, Senate, and White House—the first time a sitting president had lost all three in one term since

Herbert Hoover. And that was before a mob inspired by the president ransacked the country's seat of government.

None of it mattered to the great majority of committee members. There was little in the way of reflection about the election results, no demands for a campaign autopsy, and ample support to reelect the national party chair and co-chair Trump had selected. Most members were unwilling to even fault Trump for the Capitol attack, let alone to consider cutting ties with him.

"I surely embrace President Trump," declared Michele Fiore, the committeewoman from Nevada, that weekend. Sporting a Trump-emblazoned vest, Fiore said the president was "absolutely" a positive force in the party.

Two would-be Republican presidential candidates illustrated the party's divided brain. Nikki Haley, the former United Nations ambassador and until that moment a devoted Trump ally, intoned that the president's "actions since Election Day will be judged harshly by history."

Governor Kristi Noem of South Dakota, an even more energetic MAGA performer, suggested to an attendee that Haley would come to regret those comments. "I don't think that's very wise," she said, according to this person. In her own remarks, Noem avoided rebuking Trump for the events of January 6 or anything else.

When a committee member took an informal survey on whose closed-door speech the other Republican members had liked better, the response was clear. The party officials preferred Noem because she had not criticized Trump.

Still, even at the RNC retreat, there were scattered signs that Trump's grip on the party might, indeed, be weakening. One of his fiercest state-level allies for half a decade offered a privately harsh assessment of the man now seemingly doomed to leave office in disgrace.

Jane Timken, the chair of the Ohio Republican Party, owed her position to Trump. A Harvard-educated attorney who married into a prominent family, Timken had become party chair four years earlier when the new Republican president personally whipped votes in the chairman's race to exact vengeance on her anti-Trump predecessor.

At the RNC retreat, Timken said her days as a loyalist were over. "I'm done with Trump," she told one Republican.

*   *   *

On January 11, House Democrats introduced a single article of impeachment, accusing Trump of "inciting violence against the government of the United States."

The next day, the *New York Times* reported that McCarthy and McConnell were angry at Trump and that McConnell believed the president's actions were impeachable. The Senate leader's office declined to comment for the story, other than referring back to McConnell's censorious remarks on the night of January 6.

The story sent a wave of anxiety through the Senate Republican Conference. If McConnell was seriously considering a vote to convict Trump, he had not told any of them. Many of them were eager to know McConnell's intentions and worried about divisions in their ranks. A few had been rattled the previous weekend by Trump supporters who hectored them in airports. (A crowd at Washington's National Airport had berated Lindsey Graham: "Traitor! Traitor! Traitor!")

John Thune was out to dinner with his wife that evening when his phone began lighting up with calls and texts from his colleagues. Another concerned senator called one of the authors of this book to ask why McConnell had not challenged the accuracy of the story: Surely he was not actually going to vote for conviction—was he?

McConnell did nothing to attack the story, since he knew it to be accurate. But neither did he immediately issue a clarifying comment. When Thune relayed the concerns of the conference to its leader, McConnell said he appreciated the feedback, but not much more. Thune urged the leader to put out a statement saying, well, something about his present thinking.

McConnell stalled. Despite his private talk, casting that week as a moment for leadership, he was seemingly unready to go public with his enthusiasm for impeachment. Nor was he willing to shoot down the idea outright and give his senators an easy way out of a tough decision.

With McConnell keeping his own counsel, someone else stepped forward to supply his Senate colleagues with political armor.

J. Michael Luttig was a longtime federal appeals court judge who had spent the George W. Bush administration waiting for a Supreme Court nomination that never came. He had stepped down from the bench for a lucrative job at Boeing, but the former clerk to Supreme Court justice Antonin Scalia was still active in the close-knit conservative legal world. On the night before the House voted to impeach Trump, he published an opinion piece in the *Washington Post* arguing that the Senate could not convict the president after he left office.

"Trump would no longer be incumbent in the Office of the President at the time of the delayed Senate proceeding and would no longer be subject to 'impeachment conviction' by the Senate, under the Constitution's Impeachment Clauses," Luttig wrote.

It was a hotly disputed argument, with significant legal and historical evidence lined up against it. But Trump's Senate allies lunged at the column like a drowning man at a life preserver. Here, it seemed, was a pretext for not convicting Trump that would skirt the issue of his evident culpability.

Tom Cotton, the Arkansas senator who was close to McConnell, was also friends with Luttig and spoke with him after the *Post* piece ran. "The Senate lacks constitutional authority to conduct impeachment proceedings against a former president," Cotton said, echoing the column.

McConnell told Cotton he believed that was a smart position for him to take and predicted many other Senate Republicans would follow suit. McConnell did not mention Cotton's well-known presidential ambitions, or the incentives not to cross Trump ahead of a contested 2024 primary. But then, he did not have to.

Still, McConnell did not betray his own position on impeachment to the senator he had taken under his wing.

* * *

On the eve of the January 13 impeachment vote, hours before the brief House debate was to begin, President Trump met with his counsel, Cipollone, and some outside attorneys. The question of resignation came up.

Trump was dead set against it. "What fucking good did that do Nixon?" he asked.

The lawyers reminded Trump that Nixon could have run for president again after quitting, since he had never been convicted at trial. They knew Trump wanted to keep open the possibility of a 2024 campaign, and there could be no big, beautiful Trump comeback if he was found guilty.

That night, the possibility of mounting bipartisan support for impeachment did not seem so far-fetched. The Senate and House conferences may have been divided and fearful, their leaders uncertain, quiet, or both. But one member of the Republican leadership detonated the party's internal deliberations with an emphatic, unyielding statement that evening that some anti-Trump Republicans hoped would trigger a stampede.

"The President of the United States summoned this mob, assembled the mob, and lit the flame of this attack," Liz Cheney declared in a press release. "Everything that followed was his doing. None of this would have happened without the President."

"There has never been a greater betrayal by a President of the United States of his office and his oath to the Constitution," she said.

The third-ranking House Republican was voting for impeachment.

*　*　*

When the House gathered on January 13 to impeach President Trump for the second time, the grounds of the Capitol appeared more like a military encampment than a government complex. Thousands of uniformed National Guardsmen stood watch, many having donned helmets and hoisted machine guns, and black fencing had been hastily constructed to form an extended perimeter around the Capitol.

There were still reminders of the attack throughout the building: broken panes of glass, makeshift memorials, and signature books for some of the police officers who had been killed or had taken their own lives. Disturbing information about the nature of the violence on that day had continued to trickle out, including details about unexploded pipe bombs placed outside the Democratic and Republican Party headquarters in Washington by an unidentified perpetrator.

In conference calls and virtual meetings of the Democratic caucus, lawmakers were sharing feelings of betrayal and symptoms of trauma, and trading stories about being bullied in airports by Trump supporters. Raul Ruiz, the former emergency room doctor who had been evacuated from the gallery, disclosed that he had been experiencing arrhythmia in his heartbeat and shortness of breath, and urged his colleagues to seek professional help.

Joyce Beatty, the new head of the Congressional Black Caucus, spoke for many Democrats when on one video call she argued that the police would have moved faster to protect the Capitol if the violent demonstrators had been Black.

In a sign of the deep mistrust even between House colleagues, there were now metal detectors at the entrance to the House floor, installed at the instructions of Speaker Pelosi out of concern that Republicans would bring firearms into the chamber.

The Speaker had been on war footing since the January 6 attack. The day after the riot, Pelosi held a video call with members of her leadership team and vowed that there would be consequences for the Republicans' "disgraceful" behavior. On a phone call with political donors a few days later, she described Trump as an outright monster: "an unhinged freak of nature," she said, according to a person on the call.

It was only in private that Pelosi confided to a friend that she was in a state of deep grief about what had happened, expressing a sense of devastating loss that she likened to losing a child.

"If I slow down for a second, I start crying," she said, according to her friend.

Far from slowing down, she had thrown a lightning-fast impeachment process into action.

As the proceedings began, Pelosi implored her colleagues to repudiate the president in irreversible terms, putting him in the same category as a foreign enemy of the United States.

"He is a clear and present danger to the nation that we all love," Pelosi said.

But it was Cheney, rather than Pelosi, whose words echoed loudest in the floor debate. One Democrat after another invoked her statement denouncing Trump, forcing their Republican colleagues to confront a momentous vote with the words of one of their own leaders ringing in their ears.

Though subsequent events would quickly minimize this moment in public memory—and for good reason—the mood of the Republican Conference that day was hardly one of enthusiastic loyalty to Trump and his shattered presidency. The rumors Tom Cole mentioned on the GOP call two days earlier, of mass Republican defections on impeachment, had been well founded. At least two dozen members seriously considered breaking with their party to support impeachment, and dozens more acknowledged in private that Democrats were in the right.

Emblematic of the tortured deliberations on the Republican side were two lawmakers who met for lunch that day: Don Bacon of Nebraska and Tom Rice of South Carolina, a pair of center-right lawmakers who had shown neither particular personal affection for Trump nor any enthusiasm for seeking out confrontation with him. Rice, from a deeply conservative district, surprised his colleague by confiding that he planned to vote for impeachment. It was a vote that could doom Rice back home.

Bacon, a scholarly former air force general, acknowledges he had been tempted to do the same. But he would not follow Rice in making the ultimate break with Trump. The president's behavior was "shameful," he says, but the rushed impeachment process made him uncomfortable.

"I have to admit," Bacon says, "I was torn."

Such sentiments were widely in evidence on the day of the vote, with lawmakers who had seldom or never taken on Trump in four years openly saying they hoped his conduct on January 6 would marginalize him. Their comments were a variation on an old congressional saw—"vote no, hope yes"—that explains what members do when they cast their own vote a certain way based on political considerations, but hope that their stated position does not carry the day.

In this case, some were willing to say in so many words that they were voting no on impeachment and hoping yes—that Trump would be sidelined as a political force.

Patrick McHenry, a Republican from a conservative part of western North Carolina, had never antagonized Trump in four years. And he did not vote for Trump's impeachment on that day in January.

But as the forty-five-year-old lawmaker stood outside the House chamber speaking to a small group of reporters after the impeachment vote, he let the anger he had been feeling since November come to the surface. There had to be "deep soul-searching about who we are as Republicans," he said.

McHenry was not sure what would happen to Trump. But he felt confident that once his constituents saw the footage from January 6, then they, too, would see the need for a Republican reckoning. People who condone violence or who refuse to condemn it, he said, "should be put out of our political debate and put back in the dark recesses of the abyss.

"I've watched every piece of fucking social media," McHenry said. "I'm as upset as you are."

In the run-up to the vote, as Kevin McCarthy was agonizing over how to address his colleagues that night, his sphinxlike Senate counterpart delivered two more unexpected surprises—conflicting signals about his own intentions in the upcoming Senate trial.

In a letter to Senate colleagues, McConnell finally addressed the *Times* story: He confirmed that his vote was in play for conviction, though he stopped well short of repeating his private comments about Trump's obvious guilt.

"I have not made a final decision on how I will vote and I intend to listen to the legal arguments when they are presented to the Senate," McConnell said.

At the same time, McConnell issued a separate statement that opened the way for even more of his Senate colleagues to embrace the Luttig defense. He announced that he would not move to hold a Senate trial before Biden's inauguration the following Wednesday, explaining in a statement that there was "no chance that a fair or serious trial could conclude before President-elect Biden is sworn in next week."

The tone of the statement was defensive, suggesting McConnell was already sensitive to the charge that he was doing Trump's bidding by deferring a trial. His assessment of the timetable, McConnell insisted, "is not a decision I am making; it is a fact."

Was the Senate leader quietly steeling himself to convict the outgoing president, or paving the way for an easy acquittal on procedural grounds? His own friends and confidants were unsure, but two senior Republicans, Thune and Portman, privately assessed that week that McConnell was indeed serious about a potential conviction. There was another senior senator who also thought McConnell might vote to convict: Chuck Schumer, who told Democrats privately he believed his Republican counterpart was angry enough to move on Trump.

"I don't trust him, and I would not count on it, but you never know," Schumer told a group of progressive leaders in a late January conversation. "He is mad. He does believe that Trump is the reason he's the minority leader, not the majority leader—because he thinks Trump screwed up in Georgia for them."

There was never any question about how Kevin McCarthy would vote on impeachment. The House minority leader knew the great majority of his conference would be against impeachment, and that the party's voters would not likely accept a future Speaker of the House who joined with Pelosi to punish Trump. When he took the floor on the day of the impeachment vote, McCarthy was consumed with keeping all factions of his party happy, and merely voting against impeachment would not accomplish that.

Feeling pressure from colleagues and donors to condemn Trump's behavior, McCarthy rebuked him more harshly than ever before—and perhaps than he ever would again.

"The president bears responsibility for Wednesday's attack on Congress by mob rioters," McCarthy said, laying blame squarely at Trump's feet. "He should have immediately denounced the mob when he saw what was unfolding."

Rather than impeaching Trump, McCarthy offered: "I think a fact-finding commission and a censure resolution would be prudent."

When the roll was called, Democrats were unanimous in their support for impeachment.

Ten Republicans voted to impeach Trump, risking electoral challenges from the hard right in order to cast a vote of conscience against the instigator of the Capitol riot. The president's conduct, Tom Rice explained later, had been "completely despicable" and demanded the sternest response.

"I will vote that way every single time," he said.

Several of the ten had signaled their intentions in advance, including Cheney, as well as Meijer and Herrera Beutler, whose comments on the January 11 conference call made their inclinations clear enough. Others had been quieter before casting their votes, wrestling with the conflicting pressures of political expediency and, as they saw it, the moral demands on their eternal souls.

Anthony Gonzalez, the Ohio athlete who had written a farewell letter to his wife during the January 6 siege, was one of those who took the plunge. In an interview several weeks later, he put the decision in nonpolitical terms, acknowledging that the cost back in his district could be significant.

"When I think of my kids, and what I want them to know and think about their father's service during this tumultuous time in their country, when I think about the oath I took, when I think about being able to look myself in the mirror and be proud of this work for the rest of my life," he says, "it's a no-brainer."

After the vote, Cheney assured Gonzalez that his support for impeachment would stand the test of time. Both lawmakers believed that the Republican vote for impeachment would have been considerably higher had members not been intimidated or downright fearful about their own safety. Others were getting pressure from within their own families, with radicalized parents or siblings berating them for even contemplating a break with Trump.

"There were and are a handful of members who I've spoken to since, who have said things like 'You know, I agree with you, but, you know, I don't want to put my family through this, or I don't want to put my staff through this,'" Gonzalez says.

That concern was real enough. A number of lawmakers had been assigned security details due to credible threats, and some of those details grew in size after January 6. That group of lawmakers included Cheney and the House impeachment managers as well as Ilhan Omar, the left-wing Democrat from Minnesota and Somali-American immigrant who had been a frequent target of Trump's race-baiting tirades. Mitt Romney had taken matters into his own hands and hired private protection.

Drawing cheers from Democrats and a combination of open resentment and quiet respect from fellow Republicans, the ten impeachment voters would become something of a close-knit fellowship, bonded by a common political predicament and a text-message chain on which they discussed it. While they drew little applause from their own party leaders, they earned the approval of some other Republicans with a long view of history. In private, Mark Esper, the former defense secretary whom Trump fired days after the 2020 election, described Cheney and Adam Kinzinger, another Republican who voted for impeachment, as "superheroes."

Among the elder statesmen proudest of Liz Cheney was her father, the former vice president, who made it clear to friends that he looked on his daughter's vote with admiration and assent.

Trump, Dick Cheney said, was "a maniac."

* * *

As the impeachment process moved to the Senate, McCarthy was consumed with tamping down tensions in his conference. Yet there was still unfinished business from January 6. Trump, after all, had not been the only Republican implicated in inciting a riot.

Steve Womack, the Arkansas military veteran, was determined to see Mo Brooks punished for inciting the mob. Womack served on the influential

Republican Steering Committee, which assigns lawmakers to serve on standing committees of the House that govern areas from banking to the military to taxes to education. Brooks's acts of incitement were "unforgivable," Womack believed, and the Alabaman needed to be stripped of his seat on the Armed Services Committee.

At the first meeting of the steering committee after January 6, Womack said as much. He asked his Republican colleagues if they had seen Brooks's speech, and most raised their hands to indicate they had not. Womack had anticipated as much. He had the video of Brooks's remarks ready to roll.

"I took the microphone, and I put my phone to it and they listened," he recalls. "And I saw jaws drop."

Republicans needed to be the "adults in the room," Womack said, and do something about the far-right member acting as an arsonist in their midst.

But McCarthy cut things off there. The Republican leader said the group's task for the day was to make appointments to the Foreign Affairs Committee and that they could consider Brooks's status on Armed Services when they met again later in the month. Womack agreed to wait, though it was not really clear why the delay was necessary. He heard nothing from McCarthy on the subject before the next steering meeting.

When the committee reconvened later in the month, Womack says, "I was prepared to raise my hand and proceed on with my initiative."

Before he could do so, however, McCarthy said at the start of the meeting they would not consider any effort to strip Brooks of his committee membership. Womack said he felt as if McCarthy was effectively saying it was time to move on.

"I cannot tell you how angry I was," he says.

Womack got to say his piece in the meeting.

"This Republican Congress is going to regret not taking the actions I thought we would be able to take here today," he warned, by his account.

At noon the same day, Womack sent McCarthy a letter resigning from the steering committee. The minority leader never even responded. His refusal even to have a direct conversation on the subject, Womack says, "demonstrated a lack of leadership."

McCarthy's row-back to Trump was only getting started.

* * *

The week of Biden's swearing-in, McCarthy was frantically trying to head off a civil war between the most stridently pro- and anti-Trump members in his conference. Mitch McConnell, supplying another possible clue as to his intentions in the upcoming impeachment trial, said on the Senate floor that Trump had "provoked" the attack on the Capitol—an affirmation of the central charge in the Democrats' case. When reporters asked McCarthy about his Senate counterpart's comment, he recoiled.

"I don't believe he provoked if you listened to what he said at the rally," McCarthy said. It was an abrupt retreat from his own remarks on the House floor the previous week.

Then he took another question, regarding what role Trump should have in the Republican Party going forward. The minority leader spoke of Trump like any other elder statesman—the way a Democrat might have spoken about Barack Obama in January of 2017.

"This president brought a lot of great success within—he brought people to the party that hadn't been involved before, and he should continue to engage in that way," McCarthy said.

In his eagerness to calm the waters in his own party, McCarthy had essentially resolved that there would be no further action or discussion related to January 6. Punishing Mo Brooks could only divide his party. Reiterating criticism of Trump would do the same. To McCarthy, even letting bad blood linger with the former president was starting to feel like an intolerable risk.

Trump had spent much of January in an uncommonly quiet state, finally stripped of his office and, perhaps more painful for him, banned from social media platforms. Behind closed doors, Trump had menaced Republicans by chewing over the idea of starting his own party—a "Patriot Party"—and continuing to trash a long list of Republicans he saw as insufficiently committed to him. One of them was McCarthy, whom Trump had taken to calling a "pussy."

Another officeholder might have been so enraged by the crude slur as to turn away from Trump permanently. But like many men Trump belittled,

McCarthy responded not by defying the former president but by more or less setting out to prove him right.

The weekend after Biden's inauguration, in an interview with the journalist Greta Van Susteren, the Republican leader said "everybody across this country has some responsibility" for the events of January 6—yet another effort to dilute Trump's direct culpability. In the same interview, McCarthy said he had "concerns" about Liz Cheney's role in leadership. While he said he supported her, McCarthy said there were "a lot of questions" Cheney had to address after voting for impeachment.

Then, on January 28, McCarthy stood beaming with the former president at Mar-a-Lago.

In the minority leader's telling, he just happened to be in the neighborhood, raising money in South Florida, when Trump invited him over for a casual lunch.

The visit blindsided his colleagues and the excuse was laughable on its face. To the surprise of no one, Trump had insisted McCarthy pose for a photo, then released it with a triumphant statement declaring that his own "popularity has never been stronger than it is today."

It was a head-snapping reversal for McCarthy, only weeks after he had talked in private about urging Trump to resign. Now he was grinning beside Trump at his personal club. After ten of his own members had voted for impeachment, the leader capped his visit to Mar-a-Lago with a statement scorning Democrats for "impeaching a president who is now a private citizen."

When Republicans confronted McCarthy for once again seemingly giving his blessing to Trump and all his antics, the leader hemmed and hawed and, as usual, sought to placate his immediate audience. Adam Kinzinger recalls lawmakers calling McCarthy to ask him: "What the hell's going on?"

McCarthy insisted that he just happened to be in the vicinity of Mar-a-Lago and got an invitation from Trump that he could not rightly turn down. According to Kinzinger, McCarthy told Republicans that he was trying to get Trump to lay off his internal critics—"or at least most of you."

"I didn't know they were going to take a picture," McCarthy insisted to one upset lawmaker.

In that moment, Kinzinger says, McCarthy "resuscitated Trump—Trump was on life support. He resuscitated him."

Cheney saw McCarthy's trip as something worse: an abdication of leadership.

"That's following, it isn't leading," she says. "There was a moment where Kevin could have said, 'Absolutely not, if you provoke an attack on the Capitol, you're finished,' which would seem to be like the common-sense approach."

Instead, Cheney says, "He's trying to kind of ride the wave of the crazy. And I think that's really dangerous."

* * *

McCarthy's haphazard management of the Republican Conference came to a head on February 3 in another long meeting of the House minority. Liz Cheney's vote for impeachment had triggered a crusade against her by her far-right colleagues, including several of the lawmakers involved in spreading election-related conspiracy theories before January 6. That evening, the House Republicans gathered to decide if Cheney could keep her job as chair of the conference despite having spurned Trump.

A separate storm was building in the conference at the same time, this one around Marjorie Taylor Greene, the extremist freshman from Georgia whose open embrace of bizarre anti-Semitic conspiracy theories and fringe ideas about school shootings was drawing more and more attention in the media. Lawmakers were tired of getting pelted with questions about someone who had just barely arrived in Washington, and whose major role so far had been as an energetic participant in Trump's attacks on the election.

Under pressure from traditional Republicans to repudiate Greene, and from hard-right lawmakers to punish Cheney, McCarthy again sought to keep the peace by doing as little of either as possible. He pleaded with Cheney in private to consider expressing regret for her impeachment vote, or at least for the manner in which she announced it. Cheney rebuffed him every time, including in the hours before her own confidence vote.

Striding into McCarthy's office on the afternoon of February 3, Cheney said with a smile that she was "steeled for battle."

Her fate would be sealed—for the moment—in a three-and-a-half-hour meeting that exposed how fractured the Republican Party remained over Cheney and the president she had imperiled her career to condemn.

The session would also reveal how singularly fixated McCarthy was on trying to keep everyone happy. The GOP's challenge, as he saw it, was not its link to a disgraced, twice-impeached former president who had just fomented a bloody riot in the Capitol. The issue at hand was that Republicans appeared to be in turmoil and that was creating bad press.

"We're not where we need to be, no one needs to tell you that," McCarthy said at the outset of the meeting. "We're sitting in here, and the press is writing about Republican-upon-Republican battle."

For the sake of tranquility, McCarthy made clear he wanted his members to keep Cheney in place. "I want this leadership team to stay together," he said.

But far from standing boldly with a mainstream Republican leader against the far right, McCarthy sought in the same session to placate the most far-out members of his conference by offering a foursquare defense of Greene, describing her repeatedly as a successful businesswoman who had "disavowed" her most bizarre comments.

Greene, he stressed, "says she's changed.

"Marjorie, correct me if I'm wrong, you sat there and said you don't believe in QAnon, what they're trying to tag us all with," McCarthy said.

Democrats were preparing to strip Greene of her committee assignments, and McCarthy depicted that as a threat to every single member of the Republican Conference. The Democrats, he warned, "won't stop with her—they'll go to the next and the next."

His contorted defense of Greene did not escape notice.

"This party has lost its damn mind," said Kinzinger, a pro-impeachment Republican, when it was his turn at the microphone.

He then spoke directly to McCarthy, faulting him for spending "more time defending Marjorie Taylor Greene than saying a word about Liz Cheney."

Herrera Beutler's comments were even tougher.

"Marjorie Taylor Greene is not the moral equivalent of Liz Cheney," she said, adding, "Liz is standing up here, standing up to the most powerful man in the world and her entire leadership team, and you assholes are making her the same as Marjorie Taylor Greene."

McCarthy at first said nothing to defend himself.

But it was Tom Rice, the quiet South Carolinian, who unloaded most fiercely on him. The former president, he said, "threw a two-month temper tantrum after the election" that resulted in a deadly riot on January 6. Even some Republican voters were reassessing their allegiance to the former president, Rice said, citing a poll.

"And yet, Kevin went to Mar-a-Lago this weekend, shook his hand, took a picture, and set up Trump majority dot com," Rice said, referring to a McCarthy-backed fundraising site. "Personally, I find that offensive."

McCarthy insisted the website was old—"I have, like, forty different sites"—and supplied a new rationale for his meeting with Trump.

"I go to lunch with Biden, too," he said. "I think a big problem we have in this country is we don't talk to one another, and I think one of the things as well, I want to make sure everybody works together."

When it came time for Greene and Cheney to speak, it was clear enough which woman had the easier sales job to make. Greene conceded that she had "said some stupid things on Facebook," but stressed that Republican leaders in her district still supported her and, not incidentally, had written a letter to McCarthy saying as much. When she was finished speaking, a number of lawmakers gave her a standing ovation.

Cheney received a far more mixed reception, and she made no effort to appease Greene or other far-right members. The Republican Party, she said, cannot become the party of QAnon, of Holocaust denial, or of white supremacy.

Republicans, she said, "have to decide who we are as a party. And the choice for us is a clear one. And it's a choice that history is going to watch."

Cheney never directly mentioned Trump's name in her appeal but concluded her pitch by reminding Republicans of the leader she hoped would remind them of the better angels of their nature.

"We have to be worthy of the mantle of Abraham Lincoln," Cheney said.

The debate over Cheney's fate was as long as it was predictable. Few sought to defend Trump, let alone his conduct on January 6. Cheney's offense was that, in a time of maximum polarization, she was siding with the other tribe.

Andy Biggs, a far-right Arizonan, accused her of giving "aid and comfort" to Democrats. Capturing the mind-set of apocalyptic battle on the right, Biggs argued that Democrats "are not just an opponent. They're an adversary that's trying to wipe this country out and change it forever."

Mike Kelly, a Pennsylvania car dealer before his election to Congress, said watching Cheney's response to the Capitol attack was akin to playing a difficult opponent in sports "and you look up in the stands and see your girlfriend on the opposition's side."

A female lawmaker interjected: "She's not your girlfriend!"

"Yeah," Cheney said. "I'm not your girlfriend."

Her ally, Peter Meijer, warned his colleagues that if Cheney "is the person who suffers most for what happened on January 6, we're in a dark, dark place." But capturing the increasingly glum mood among anti-Trump Republicans, Meijer added in an aside, "I probably won't be back here in two years."

The vote on Cheney was not close: One hundred forty-five House Republicans voted in favor of Cheney remaining as the third-ranking House Republican and only sixty-one voted to oust her. McCarthy sought to take credit for Cheney's victory, though Cheney herself was quick to remind people that McCarthy had tried to stop the vote from even happening.

Two days later, as Cheney walked out of the Capitol, she was in a triumphant mood, beaming as a reporter called her "Landslide Liz."

She was also still thinking about January 6—and how many of her Republican colleagues shared her view about Trump's conduct but couldn't bring themselves to publicly break with a president who had charmed, hectored, and intimidated them for four years.

"I think that if the vote, the impeachment vote, had been secret, it would've looked more like the vote two nights ago on me," she said.

* * *

The team of House Democrats that would argue the impeachment case to the Senate had been handpicked by Nancy Pelosi, and it overlapped heavily with the group she had appointed before January 6 to argue against Republican efforts to block certification of the election.

In anticipation of a quick Senate trial, the Democratic impeachment managers drew up a rough whip list of the Republican jurors, breaking them up into several tiers based on how persuadable they appeared to be. In one tier were Republicans certainly open to voting for conviction, like Mitt Romney, who had already voted to convict Trump in the previous year's impeachment trial. On the other extreme of the caucus were lawmakers like Josh Hawley and Rick Scott who were thoroughgoing Trump loyalists who had voted against certifying one or more states.

In between was the bulk of the conference, including McConnell.

Democrats wanted to move swiftly on Trump's impeachment, in part because Biden was mostly focused on filling out his government and pushing through his economic relief bill at a time when coronavirus infections were soaring. This meant they had little appetite for protracted court battles over subpoenas of potential witnesses. House Democrats were effectively pursuing the maximum sentence and expecting the jury to rebuff them.

The Democratic managers understood that their chances of securing a conviction rested heavily on the Republican leader. If he was truly determined to banish Trump—if he followed through on what he had said over that Chick-fil-A lunch in early January—then Democrats believed McConnell could bring a substantial bloc of other senior Republicans along with him.

"I held out hope that he would lead," says Madeleine Dean of Pennsylvania, one of the Democratic impeachment managers.

It came as a blow to Democrats on January 26 when McConnell voted with forty-four other Republicans in favor of a resolution challenging the constitutionality of the trial. Introduced by his Kentucky colleague, the gadfly physician Rand Paul, the resolution echoed Luttig's argument that the Senate simply could not try a former president who was a private citizen.

McConnell was still insisting in public that he wanted to hear the arguments before making a final decision, but by that last week in January it seemed that he had reached more or less the same political conclusions about his party that McCarthy had followed in the House. That week, he tipped his hand again by suggesting the law professor Jonathan Turley address the Senate Republicans' weekly lunch. A media-hungry academic at George Washington University Law School, Turley had become a vocal proponent of the Luttig view on impeachment.

In the lead-up to the Senate trial, McConnell's office and group of outside advisers were divided, with some urging him to convict and others urging restraint. He also heard from another constituency that largely wanted him to convict: his closest friends outside of politics and family, his University of Louisville classmates and decades-long football tailgate posse. They mostly reviled Trump, and they saw an opportunity for McConnell to cement his place in history as a man of courage.

But those were only a fraction of the Kentuckians he was hearing from. The emails and phone calls into his office were running at approximately ten to one in favor of acquitting Trump. This was a state, after all, that had just handed Trump a twenty-six-point win a few months earlier.

With friends, McConnell was somewhat sheepish about his vote in favor of Rand Paul's motion, and to one he acknowledged that his vote was about self-preservation in a pro-Trump party.

"I didn't get to be leader by voting with five people in the conference," McConnell said.

Would that reasoning carry the day with his final vote in the impeachment trial? Was McConnell starting to worry about a revolt in his own conference, the way McCarthy lived in terror of the rifts in his?

When it came time for House Democrats to make their case to the Senate, they treated McConnell as a central focus of their argument. Joe Neguse, the young Coloradan, researched the Republican leader's political history, watching old C-SPAN clips late into the night.

"Our thought process was, 'We're at the end, why not make this a Hail Mary?'" Neguse says. "If he voted to convict, there were somewhere between three to five senators that would also vote to convict, which would get you awfully close to sixty-seven."

The Democratic prosecutors were so speedy in preparing their case that in the last days of arguments they discovered they had overlooked a significant piece of evidence already in the public record. Jaime Herrera Beutler had been going around her home state for days telling a story about McCarthy confronting Trump on the phone during the January 6 riot. In her account, McCarthy had said that Trump had effectively sided with the rioters and had faulted the Republican minority leader for not being angrier about the election results.

Herrera Beutler's account burst into the East Coast media on February 12, with a report on CNN, but her remarks had been reported out West several days earlier. Democrats briefly contemplated subpoenaing Herrera Beutler to testify, perhaps along with McCarthy. But with conviction looking like a long shot and pressure building to move on with the business of Biden's agenda, they opted for what was a mostly ornamental measure: admitting a written statement from Herrera Beutler into the record.

In a public statement, Herrera Beutler implored other witnesses to come forward, addressing herself to "the patriots who were standing next to the former president as these conversations were happening, or even to the former vice president."

No one answered the call.

In his final appeal on the Senate floor, Neguse laid it on thick with McConnell. He quoted the Kentucky statesman Henry Clay and invoked John Sherman Cooper's support for civil rights—the very model McConnell himself seemed to have in mind when he considered voting for conviction only weeks earlier. In a paean to rising above party divisions, Neguse alluded to McConnell without mentioning his name, as he recounted the senator's boldest vote as a freshman.

"In 1986, this body considered a bill to override President Reagan's veto of legislation imposing sanctions on South Africa during apartheid," Neguse said to the lawmakers. "Two senators who sit in this room, one Democrat, and one Republican, voted to override that veto."

There are, he continued, "moments that transcend party politics and that require us to put country above our party because the consequences of not doing so are just too great."

McConnell told associates that Neguse had "done some homework."

Yet the leader, in the end, could not bring himself to lead. Months later, McConnell would explain that he had given no instructions to his colleagues or even an indication of how he would cast his own vote.

"I've never tried to persuade them one way or the other," McConnell says. "I called it a vote of conscience from the beginning, and I didn't give anybody sort of a heads-up of what I was gonna do."

On February 13, he joined the vast majority of his caucus in voting to acquit Trump.

McConnell was not finished with the former president. Before heading to the well of the Senate, he told a colleague: "I'm going to light him up."

Immediately after the vote, McConnell took the microphone and, as if to atone for his vote or at least convey his true feelings for posterity, denounced Trump in unsparing language.

He called Trump's conduct "a disgraceful dereliction of duty" and held him "practically and morally responsible" for the Capitol attack.

That mob violence, he said, arose from an "intensifying crescendo of conspiracy theories, orchestrated by an outgoing president who seemed determined to either overturn the voters' decision or else torch our institutions on the way out," McConnell said.

However, he said that after "intense reflection," he had concluded the Senate did not have the "power to convict and disqualify a former officeholder who is now a private citizen."

One of McConnell's longtime advisers said McConnell "saw it wasn't going to happen—he wasn't going to be a leader who stood with 15 percent of the caucus," but he wanted to deliver the speech "to make sure the country understood what he believed." It may have done something to salve McConnell's conscience, but his vote marked a dramatic abandonment of his post–January 6 vow to bring ruin to the House of Trump.

And even McConnell's half measure—denouncing Trump but voting to acquit him—angered some of his pro-Trump colleagues. Ted Cruz, the Texas conservative and sometime political adversary of McConnell, says there was significant frustration with the leader's speech after the impeachment vote. It simply did not make political sense, the senator says, "for the Republican leader in the Senate to be openly at war with the outgoing Republican president.

"I think a lot of members of the conference thought that was a mistake and thought that was ill advised," Cruz says. "My sense is that there was pretty significant pushback from folks in the conference and across the country."

Democrats had managed to generate the biggest bipartisan impeachment vote in history, with seven Republicans voting for conviction. Among their number were not only well-known mavericks like Romney, Susan Collins, and Lisa Murkowski, but a number of others, including the Louisiana physician Bill Cassidy and Richard Burr, the former chairman of the Senate Intelligence Committee who was retiring from public life.

Murkowski, one of the few Senate Republicans to challenge Trump while he was in office, had feared on the day of the Rand Paul–forced test vote that there wasn't the will in her caucus to purge Trump. She suggested she knew why they had drifted back to Trump: Republican voters had demanded it.

"To this day I'm still stunned by the number of Americans who just feel this election was stolen," she said outside her office in Hart, not far from where senators had taken refuge on January 6.

Murkowski was reluctant to criticize McConnell: She praised his strategic acumen but couldn't fully conceal her disappointment. Had the vote happened immediately after January 6, in a mood of fresh outrage and indignation, Murkowski said the outcome would certainly have been different.

"I don't know what his calculus was about," she said of McConnell. "I wish that it had been different."

An army of Republicans followed McConnell and McCarthy in their retreat from confrontation with Trump, though McCarthy was in a category by himself in the extent and range of his reversals. And McCarthy seemed to resent the way he was portrayed as submissive and craven, in contrast to Cheney and even McConnell.

In a February interview with the *New York Times* journalist Mark Leibovich, McCarthy gave yet another defense of his Mar-a-Lago trip, and perhaps this time a more honest one. He had been worried, McCarthy said, that Trump would break away from the GOP. The deep-freeze approach McConnell was taking, for which the Senate leader was drawing praise, had put a heavier burden on McCarthy's shoulders to avert a Trump-initiated schism.

"Look, I didn't want him to leave the party," McCarthy said of the former president. "Mitch had stopped talking to him a number of months before."

By the end of February, McCarthy saw much of his party follow his lead: Many of the other Republicans who had expressed sharp disapproval of Trump had either rescinded their criticism or headed for the exits of professional politics.

Nikki Haley, who had chastised Trump at the RNC meeting in early January, sought a makeup meeting with him in Mar-a-Lago only weeks later. Even after Trump rejected her overture, Haley privately counseled Cheney to try to make peace with the former president rather than continuing to antagonize him.

Several of the Republicans most openly uncomfortable with Trump, but who could not bring themselves to vote for impeachment, simply retired from Congress, including Steve Stivers and Rob Portman of Ohio. Jane Timken, the Republican chair in that state who had privately pronounced herself "done with Trump" in early January, launched a campaign to succeed Portman in the Senate the next month. In her announcement, she boasted that she had "stood next to President Trump and supported his America First agenda."

Dan Crenshaw, the Texas military veteran who had privately called for some of his far-right colleagues to face some kind of sanction, continued speaking out against people he called irresponsible "performance artists" in the party. But in a comment for this book, he fiercely denied ever having "serious discussions" with any Democrats about any "official punishment against specific members."

Meanwhile, Patrick McHenry, the North Carolina Republican, acknowledged later that he had been incorrect in his prediction that the Republican base would come to be as horrified by the events of January 6 as everyone in Washington, once they processed the footage from that day.

"I was wrong," he concedes.

* * *

One person unbowed by the experience of impeachment, humbled not even slightly by the scolding he endured on the floor of the House and Senate, was Donald Trump.

In an interview the authors conducted with Trump at Mar-a-Lago in the spring of 2021, the former president expressed utter confidence in his control of the Republican Party and waved away the criticism he had drawn from both the party's legislative leaders.

McConnell, he said matter-of-factly, "is bad news."

"Had Mitch stuck with many members of the party who knew the election was rigged, I think we wouldn't be at Mar-a-Lago," Trump said, clinging to the fantasy of a stolen election. "We would be at the White House having this conversation."

Yet in a sign that no amount of flattery can protect anyone from being humiliated by Trump, the former president was dismissive of McCarthy.

Trump waved aside McCarthy's claims of challenging the former president in private. According to Trump, the Republican leader's tough talk after January 6 was just that—talk.

No, Trump says, McCarthy had not clashed with him over the phone with the riot still in progress.

"He wouldn't say that," Trump said.

So why, then, did McCarthy go around claiming to other people that he's tougher with Trump in private than he really is?

The former president packed his two-word diagnosis with contempt.

"Inferiority complex," Trump said.

Chapter 9

"How Big Can We Go?"

AS JOE BIDEN prepared to take office, he could sense the fire in his party.

The incoming president had long struggled to ignite real passion among his fellow Democrats. They had embraced him as a leader for pragmatic reasons, not because of his raw charisma or his visionary policy ideas. It was no sure thing that Biden would be able to command the energetic support of his party for executing an agenda in office.

The events of early January changed things. Now, for the first time in a decade, Democrats had full control of the federal government, and they were determined to deliver monumental change to the country. The nation was in a state of crisis, still reeling from the January 6 attack and the ongoing scourge of the coronavirus. Days before the riot, the American death count from the pandemic had exceeded 350,000.

To the Democrats, this looked like a moment for daring action—action that would redeem American democracy and deal a crushing repudiation to the far-right party that had done so much to degrade it. Tiny though their congressional majorities were, Biden and his party intended to move fast and do big things.

It was not clear how long this moment of fire would last.

In the Senate, Chuck Schumer was readying his caucus for a legislative blitz. There was a huge backlog of Democratic priorities that had languished in the last few rounds of pandemic-relief negotiations, including the fate of enhanced unemployment-insurance programs and the hundreds of billions of dollars the party wanted to spend on aid to state and local governments. In both chambers, senior Democratic legislators were hoping to use the emergency bill as a vehicle for larger economic reform, including raising the federal minimum wage to $15 per hour and creating a greatly expanded tax credit for people with children.

Schumer knew it was highly unlikely that Republicans would go along with most of those policies. His party would likely have to enact a bill through the procedure known as reconciliation: a legislative tool that bypasses the Senate filibuster—with its sixty-vote threshold to bring legislation up for a vote—and requires only fifty votes to pass, so long as the contents of the bill in question concern spending and revenues.

Going down that path would require that Schumer keep his own caucus entirely united. It would also require Democrats to submit their legislation to the review of the Senate parliamentarian, an obscure official who would adjudicate whether certain items were eligible for inclusion in a reconciliation bill.

Pelosi had a minute majority to work with in the House, but Schumer had only a nominal majority in the Senate. With fifty votes on his side, he would have to keep every single Democrat in line so that Kamala Harris could break a tie in their favor as the newly inaugurated vice president.

At seventy, Schumer was the young man of the Democratic Party's leadership trifecta—a comparative adolescent next to the eighty-year-old Speaker and the seventy-eight-year-old president-elect. But he had spent a long time in public life, winning his first election to the New York State Assembly in 1974, just two years after Biden was elected to the Senate.

In his decades-long climb to the most important job in the Senate, Schumer had acquired a reputation as a reasonably self-aware political opportunist: a publicity hound who chased big headlines and big donors, a campaign tactician rather than a policy visionary, who spent far more time poring over polling data and advertisements in battleground states than the think-tank studies and academic papers some of his colleagues favored.

Biden himself was known to express wariness of Schumer. The two men had not clicked when Schumer arrived in the Senate in the late 1990s as a scrappy brawler fresh out of the House. Biden, already a Senate elder by then, had sized up Schumer as a man overly comfortable with the art of political spin—a person whose word he could not necessarily take to the bank. Schumer, in his eyes, had been a younger man in a hurry, and in some respects Biden still saw him that way as the Democratic leader entered his eighth decade.

Even Senate Democrats who liked Schumer were still uncertain of his capabilities as a *majority* leader. Centrists feared that Schumer would be excessively sensitive to left-wing activists back home in New York, while progressives still worried about his long history of catering to Wall Street and other big-money interests.

In an early meeting with Biden's advisers after the election, Schumer poked fun at one close presidential aide for his perceived ideological transformation over a decades-long career in Washington. Alluding to Ron Klain's emergence as a trusted ambassador to congressional progressives, Schumer joked: "I knew Ron before he was a big liberal." It was probably not lost on Schumer that Klain could have said the same about him.

Yet Schumer's colleagues also knew him as more than the camera-chasing hype artist of much-caricatured notoriety. He had shown real facility during the Trump years in managing the competing factions of an opposition party, regularly checking in with his caucus on their cell phone numbers he learned by heart and dialed from memory on the flip phone he refused to upgrade. He had also been an effective legislative negotiator and salesman in the past, helping drive major gun-control legislation through the House in the 1990s.

Now Schumer was in salesman mode again, goading his caucus to support the largest possible aid bill, all while preparing for an impeachment trial and confirming the Biden cabinet as quickly as they could. He enlisted the two unlikely heroes of the Georgia campaign, Raphael Warnock and Jon Ossoff, to help him make the case for going very, very big on relief aid, prodding them on a conference call to tell the other Democrats just how much help they had promised the voters of their state. They had promises to keep, and so did their party.

Beyond the forty-nine other members of his caucus, there was a fiftieth target of Schumer's salesmanship: the incoming president.

Joe Biden felt the same urgency as the congressional leaders about showing the country that help was on the way. He, too, was angry about the January 6 attack and the conduct of the Republican Party. But Biden had also talked throughout his campaign about bipartisanship and reaching across the aisle, and he still seemed to believe that he might be able to maneuver McConnell into being something less than a full-on obstructionist.

To Schumer, that was a dangerous way to think and he told Biden as much.

McConnell, he told the president-elect, will try to thwart you in any way possible.

He won't always act like it, Schumer acknowledged. But if you give him the opportunity to block your agenda, then block it he will.

As Biden prepared to take office, he was still not quite sure how he wanted to approach the Congress and how he should balance his promise to enact a bold progressive agenda with his aspiration to unite the country and reach across the aisle.

He had insisted from the start of the campaign that he believed it would be possible to work with Republicans for the good of the American people—and he had meant it.

Biden had also promised to remedy the greatest crises facing the country through bold federal action, from climate change to racial injustice—and he had meant that, too.

* * *

The period between January 6 and the passage of Biden's first major piece of legislation marked an early test of Biden's ability to juggle those goals and hold his party together as it began to govern. As united as Democrats were in the spirit of trying to get something done, there were still important gaps between what different wings of the party wanted to do and how they wanted to go about doing it.

As overjoyed as Democrats remained about capturing the Senate majority, they learned quickly in February and March that controlling the Senate with fifty votes and a vice-presidential tie breaker was not quite a license to govern without obstruction.

The last president had never bothered to learn the details of lawmaking: Trump did not study the details of the bills his own party crafted, and he had even less interest in holding good-faith negotiations with his Democratic opponents or winning over outspoken Republican dissidents. Those traits sank some of his central legislative initiatives, most importantly his effort to repeal the Affordable Care Act.

Biden would take the oath with nearly half a century of legislative experience and a firm conviction that he could unite the unwieldy Democratic coalition. But he had never before negotiated a major deal from the Oval Office, and the balancing act ahead of him was one of elaborate complexity. Like Trump, Biden had rogue lawmakers in his own party—on the far left and in the stubborn center—and any small combination of them could become a major problem for his agenda. And his majorities were smaller than Trump's had ever been.

In a conversation with his old friend Chris Dodd, the former Connecticut senator, before taking office, Biden said he was eager to get back into the thick of negotiations. Dodd warned him to proceed with caution.

As president, Dodd said, Biden could not simply dive into high-stakes talks without having a reasonable expectation that they would work out. He could not routinely take political risks like that.

"You could do it as Obama's vice president—you can't do it as president," Dodd recalls saying. "You don't want to go into the room not knowing the answer as president."

Biden heard him out but sounded undeterred.

"I'm good at it," he replied, according to Dodd. "I mean, I do this!"

Dodd said that was true—"You're better than all the people you're going to hire to do it"—but he pressed Biden to focus on recruiting skilled deputies and then letting them do the dirty work of making offers and counteroffers with unpredictable lawmakers.

Biden had done plenty of hiring already, and the people he had put in place at the highest levels of the White House largely aligned with Schumer and Pelosi in their view of congressional Republicans. Mostly veterans of the Obama administration, they were haunted by their party's last experience governing in an economic crisis, in 2009, when a newly inaugurated Democratic president and his top staff had spent months pleading and horse-trading for Republican support on various essential priorities and come away with little to show for it.

Ron Klain was among the Biden aides who was clear-eyed about the early missteps of the Obama administration.

An Indianapolis-raised son of a plumbing-supply business owner, Klain had worked beside Biden on and off for decades. He was in some respects the Platonic ideal of a Biden aide, with a middle-class Midwestern background that appealed to the Scranton-reared president and the elite credentials—degrees from Georgetown and Harvard, along with a Supreme Court clerkship—that Biden prized in his closest aides.

Not all Democrats shared Biden's admiration for Klain; some party leaders grumbled about his hard-charging manner and expansive intellectual confidence. The Speaker of the House was one of those Democrats. Late in the 2020 campaign, Pelosi grew openly annoyed when an adviser urged her to consult with Klain about health care legislation.

What, she asked, does Ron Klain know about *anything*?

In Biden's reckoning, Klain knew quite a lot about quite a lot of things. The loyal aide had served as Biden's counsel on the Senate Judiciary Committee and as his chief of staff in the vice presidency, and he had managed the Obama administration's response to the Ebola virus. Klain had left that administration with a view of its strengths and weaknesses that lined up closely with that of his longtime boss.

The Obama administration, Klain believed, had moved too slowly in its early days to address the recession, and it had done too little to explain to the public what it was doing. A few days after the Capitol riot, with Washington still in a daze, Klain was already fixated on the puzzle of putting together a relief package and then selling it to the country.

To a colleague who served with him in the Obama administration, Klain fretted that there was a risk Democrats would make the same mistakes again: allowing a drawn-out congressional negotiation over dollar figures and time-tables to overshadow the real benefits the administration wanted to give voters.

"Some of our friends have learned nothing from 2009," Klain said, according to this person.

* * *

A mood of deep fear shrouded the nation's capital in the days before Joe Biden's inauguration. Even before January 6, the event was shaping up as a somber and pared-back version of the traditionally grand ceremony. There would be social distancing and masking requirements in place, and rituals to mark the dreadful number of American fatalities would replace the black-tie balls.

The riot raised questions about whether even that version of the swearing-in could proceed. Washington already looked like an armed camp, with thousands of soldiers and guardsmen bearing heavy weaponry and black fencing installed around the Capitol. Even with those precautions, was it worth the security risk?

A handful of Democrats, including Dianne Feinstein, the longtime California senator, thought it was not.

But Biden would brook no talk of moving the event indoors. The world, he believed, had to see that the American system was stronger than Trump's lies and the violence of his supporters. His inauguration had to look like an inauguration.

In the days before his swearing-in, Biden already felt the awesome burden embodied in the event. It was a feeling Harry Truman described, after ascending to the presidency, as if "the moon, the stars and all the planets had fallen" on him.

On January 18, two days before he would take the oath, Biden told a friend: "The responsibility really hit me at dinner last night.

"I was around the table with the five grandkids—they're so brilliant, so conversant with the world," Biden said, according to this friend. "And I was thinking about what kind of world we're going to be leaving them—the kind of world they will be living in."

* * *

Among members of Biden's party, however, there was more earthbound anxiety about moving ahead with the event. During a pair of conference calls the week after the riot, a series of Democrats spoke up to raise concerns with party leaders and with security officials about the inauguration. Lawmakers feared the possibility of an attack from protesters or from guests at the inauguration, or even from rogue members of the military—or their Republican colleagues.

During a January 13 phone briefing with FBI and Secret Service officials, Marcy Kaptur of Ohio raised the possibility that the security forces themselves could be infiltrated by would-be terrorists or assassins. Could the security services guarantee, Kaptur asked, that there would not be Proud Boys or other domestic extremists among the National Guard forces called into Washington for the inauguration?

The security officials on the call told Kaptur that those troops were screened by their units, but they stopped short of a definitive statement that infiltration was an impossibility.

Abigail Spanberger, the former intelligence officer, raised another possible threat: Were people invited to attend the inauguration by members of Congress being subjected to security screenings? Spanberger herself had invited guests, and she said she had not been asked for any information about them.

The Speaker of the House raised the most sensitive subject of all. Channeling her caucus's fear of their own Republican colleagues, Nancy Pelosi asked the Secret Service to commit to ensuring that every member of Congress would pass through a magnetometer to enter restricted areas on Capitol Hill. Pelosi did not name the Republicans she and other Democrats were worried about, but she did not have to. Every member of her caucus knew the names of the lawmakers who had whipped up the mob. They knew, too, that Republicans like Lauren Boebert and Marjorie Taylor Greene made a practice of showing off their love of firearms.

The Secret Service punted the issue to the House sergeant at arms, to whom Pelosi gave the same edict. Every lawmaker had to be screened for guns and other weapons like any civilian in an airport. The Congress, Pelosi believed, could not afford to take a laxer approach.

Nor could Joe Biden. On two calls the week before the inauguration, Peter DeFazio, the seventy-three-year-old Oregon liberal who chaired the House Transportation Committee, spoke up with alarm about part of the president-elect's inaugural itinerary. Biden had long considered himself among the country's leading evangelists for rail travel, and he intended to journey from Delaware to his swearing-in on an Amtrak train.

DeFazio said that plan had to be abandoned. It would be far too easy for a domestic terrorist to strike his train in a remote area, or even to attempt to halt it and board it.

That view carried the day: Though Biden would not move his inauguration indoors, he would arrive at the Capitol by more discreet means than the Acela.

On January 20, the crowds lining Pennsylvania Avenue were considerably thinner than usual and the audience for the new president's inaugural address was deliberately sparse. And as Biden stepped to the lectern to deliver his speech, two Capitol Police officers stood guard behind him.

It was not only the pandemic that President Biden had in mind when he said the country had just come through "a crucible for the ages." Americans had learned anew, he said, "that democracy is precious, democracy is fragile.

"And at this hour, my friends, democracy has prevailed," Biden said.

Biden again extended a rhetorical hand to his political opposition. It was time, he said, to end the country's "uncivil war" and work together as Americans.

Arrayed on the platform around Biden was a bipartisan set of dignitaries who embodied the traditional political establishment, a group that included the woman who'd lost the presidency in 2016 to Donald Trump.

Hillary Clinton had never hidden her anger about what happened in 2016. But in this moment she offered a gesture of conciliation, quietly reaching out to the man who had loaned Donald Trump a veneer of Christian respectability in his campaign against her four years earlier. Approaching Pence, Clinton offered the outgoing vice president an earnest thank-you for his refusal to challenge the election results in the Senate. Pence, just as earnestly, expressed his appreciation for Clinton's overture.

Donald Trump did not attend. The departed president, then bracing for his imminent impeachment trial, left the White House on the morning of Inauguration Day, decamping to his South Florida estate hours before Biden's swearing-in. His absence was neither surprising nor disappointing to the event organizers. Trump had announced two days after the Capitol attack, in his very last tweet before the social-media site banned his account, that he would not join the ceremonies. His early escape made him the first president since Andrew Johnson, the failed and impeached successor to Abraham Lincoln, to skip his own successor's inauguration.

There was no final effort by Trump to sabotage the transfer of power, nor was there an outbreak of violence at the inauguration. The twenty-five thousand or so National Guard troops in Washington likely had something to do with that.

On the morning of January 21, Biden awoke in an optimistic mood. The country had been through a lot and it was still suffering badly. A towering mountain of work lay ahead. But the transfer of power was finally complete. The United States, he believed, had shown the world that it was a resilient and free nation.

In that hopeful spirit, Biden telephoned his old congressional colleague, Roy Blunt, the Missouri Republican who had helped oversee the inauguration from his perch on the Senate Rules Committee. Blunt, who had just turned seventy-one, also happened to be one of a few old-line Republicans left in the Senate who might—just might—be open to doing business with Biden.

According to Blunt, Biden told him repeatedly after the inauguration: "The way you conducted the day made a big difference in how the whole day looked to the whole world."

In foreign capitals, the inauguration was a reassuring ritual; in many of them

Trump's departure was more than welcome. But to some of America's most important allies, there were still alarming questions about the strength of American democracy and what Biden could do to restore it. Tony Blair, the former prime minister of the United Kingdom, says he phoned friends in America, including former Clinton administration officials, to commiserate over that concern.

It was already apparent in January, Blair says, that Trump's defeat had not cleansed America of its dangerous divisions.

"You take as a given that the sixth of January was a terrible event," Blair says. "The question is, what does it say about what you need to do to bring the country back together?"

* * *

It did not take long for President Biden and his party to remind Republicans that they were in charge of Washington.

On his first day in office, Biden signed a suite of executive orders that tore central elements of the Trump legacy into shreds: He rejoined the Paris climate pact that Trump had repudiated and ended Trump's travel ban targeting mainly Muslim countries. He imposed masking and distancing requirements for federal employees that Trump had resisted and stopped construction of Trump's beloved border wall. He terminated the major pipeline project known as Keystone XL and halted new oil and gas leases in the Arctic National Wildlife Refuge, among other measures.

On the Hill, Pelosi and Schumer were both moving with dispatch to advance the legislation Biden's team had branded the American Rescue Plan: a $1.9 trillion aid bill that borrowed extensively from proposals House Democrats had passed the previous year only to see them sputter in the Republican-controlled Senate.

There was still some debate among leaders of the Democratic Party about the right path for steering that package into law. One view, held by Pelosi and Schumer, was that the party should bundle everything up in one bill and pass it through the reconciliation process, sparing themselves the burden of a long and potentially costly negotiation with Senate Republicans.

Another view, entertained by Steny Hoyer, the House majority leader, and a cluster of moderates in the House and Senate, was that Democrats could take a two-track approach: split off the most popular measures and pass them quickly in a bipartisan bill, and then do the rest through reconciliation.

Pelosi dismissed that approach out of hand, telling one adviser it was a "dumb idea." Ron Klain was just as emphatic in private: Pelosi and Schumer did not want to take the two-track approach, he told associates, and so that was off the table. Besides, the legislation was popular as a full package—why break it up?

If moderates and Republicans wanted to vote for the most popular stuff, then they would also have to vote for the most expensive and progressive stuff, too.

Schumer exposed his own strategy for the rescue bill in a phone call with a set of progressive groups and labor unions on January 24. Four days after the inauguration, as Biden was still weighing how to handle his diplomacy with the Senate, Schumer all but told these groups that he expected any efforts at bipartisanship to fail.

The new president wanted to reach out to Republicans, Schumer acknowledged, and he believed Biden was doing that sincerely. But, Schumer said, the main objective was getting the relief bill into law by whatever means necessary. If that meant a party-line bill, then so be it.

"On Covid, as you know, Joe Biden's talking about bipartisan," Schumer said. "But number one, like on everything we do, our number-one goal is not the means to getting there but getting there. We need a big, bold package."

That sentiment was very much what Schumer's progressive audience wanted to hear. But the Democratic leader elaborated in ways that made clear he really meant it, naming several mainstream Republicans who had already criticized the cost of Biden's relief proposal and arguing that the path to compromise did not seem to exist. The chances of Biden's outreach working out, Schumer said, were "not very good."

"The bottom line is, if they won't come along with us, we're not going to make the mistake—at least *my* judgment, and I am arguing strongly internally—is we should not make the mistake of 2008 and let them whittle it down, and then it took ten years to recover," Schumer said, referring to the long slog back from the recession under the Obama administration.

In an Oval Office meeting, two of Schumer's colleagues spelled out for Biden just how challenging his path through the Senate might be. In the House, the president and his team were confident that Pelosi could deliver the votes they needed to pass just about anything. The Senate was a different beast. Chris Coons and Tom Carper, the two senators from Delaware, met with Biden in the early days of his presidency and stressed that the president would have to walk a legislative tightrope to enact the draft legislation now known as the American Recovery Plan.

Biden could pursue a bipartisan option by slimming down the bill and negotiating with Republicans, Coons told him. That would give him a chance of getting sixty votes for passage, avoiding reconciliation and overcoming a filibuster.

But Coons, a second-term Democrat who believed deeply in the value of bipartisanship, did not downplay the problems with that approach. If Biden steered the rescue bill to the middle in pursuit of Republican votes, he would lose votes on the left. If that happened, then Democrats could find themselves having burned time on negotiations and bargained away key priorities, only to come up short of the votes needed to break a filibuster anyway.

There was no guarantee that negotiating with Republicans could yield a deal at all. The Senate GOP was still in a scattered state, struggling to prepare for Trump's impeachment trial and to figure out how their own lives would work in the Senate minority. Republicans had given Biden mixed signals so far, and they had received mixed signals in return. A few, including Susan Collins of Maine and Lisa Murkowski of Alaska, had indicated to the White House they were open to working together. In a November call, Collins told Klain she wanted to do business.

But that was when Republicans expected to have a strong hand in negotiations, because they believed they would be in the Senate majority. Now, Democrats had the fifty-senators-plus-Kamala-Harris budget-reconciliation option at their disposal, and they seemed inclined to use it, so long as they could get their more conservative members to go along with the plan.

Still, Republicans knew the Democrats' margin of control was precarious—so precarious that Biden and his party might be willing to offer handsome rewards for even modest cooperation. A few Republicans had already engaged in political horse-trading in order to extract goodies from the Biden administration. Murkowski and her fellow Alaskan, Dan Sullivan, had been enraged by Biden's moratorium on new drilling leases—but not so enraged that they would not make a deal with Biden to back his progressive nominee for interior secretary, Deb Haaland. Both voted to confirm the New Mexico congresswoman to the important job governing public lands, in exchange for Biden replacing his existing nominee for the department's number-two job with a more business-friendly pick.

There had been a number of robust bipartisan votes for other Biden nominees, including all four of the cabinet's most prominent offices: State, Treasury, Justice, and Defense. Mitch McConnell himself had voted in favor of all four of Biden's nominees for those jobs. For administration officials inclined to seek out compromise, there were at least a few encouraging signs so far. At the very least, there was no full-on blockade attempt from the Republican side.

But Biden and his advisers were not naïve about the less-hospitable currents within the Senate Republican Conference. Schumer's observation about the harsh criticism of Biden's plan, even from traditional Republicans, was spot-on and the White House knew it.

And Biden himself had absorbed more personal reasons for distrusting the GOP.

For all Biden's insistence that he did not hold grudges, he was keenly sensitive to which Republicans had and had not acknowledged the legitimacy of the 2020 election. It rankled him when he had to deal with senior Republicans, like Kevin McCarthy, who had echoed Trump's most egregious lies about the vote that made Biden president. The Senate had more than a few of those.

Biden had seen, too, how the Trump years had exposed the most opportunistic impulses of people he used to respect. No one loomed larger in that category than Lindsey Graham, who had gone from being Biden's personal friend to joining Trump's attacks on Biden's troubled son Hunter. Graham had called up Biden after the election to try to patch things up and offered the president-elect some advice: Biden, Graham said, should reach out to Trump and invite him to play golf, as a way of lowering the political temperature.

It was an off-key suggestion. Biden was not interested in following Graham's footsteps onto the fairway with Trump. The first lady, Jill Biden, had told people during the campaign that Graham had crossed a line. And as much as the often malleable Graham was a potentially promising negotiating partner for his administration, Biden saw the South Carolina senator's decision to join forces with Trump against their family as a profound betrayal.

But White House aides knew that they had to make some form of an overture to the GOP. There were Republican senators who wanted to have that conversation, and Biden wanted to have it with them. There were also a few Senate Democrats who felt strongly that it was important at least to give bipartisanship a try.

After all, Republicans might no longer be in the Senate majority, but having a constructive relationship with a handful of them could make a big difference down the line—especially if Biden really was serious about wanting to show the country and the world that the two parties could work together.

What the White House did not know was that Susan Collins and a handful of other Republicans had not yet given up on reclaiming the Senate majority by attempting to flip a friendly Democrat. Even as they engaged in tentative talks with the new president about a possible legislative compromise, Senate Republicans were on a covert mission to win back control of the chamber they had lost at the ballot box, and their focus was on Joe Manchin.

And for a brief moment, it seemed that Vice President Harris might have given Republicans an unexpected opening.

*　*　*

Kamala Harris did not say anything particularly surprising in her January 28 interview with WSAZ, the NBC affiliate in Huntington, West Virginia. The country, she said, was confronting a "crisis of unbelievable proportion" and needed politicians to "step up and stand up for them." She did not mention Joe Manchin, the state's senior senator, by name.

But Manchin, the Senate's most conservative Democrat, knew political pressure when he saw it. Harris had done only two local television interviews on that day in late January. The other one had been with a station in Arizona, the home state of another centrist Democratic senator, Kyrsten Sinema, who needed some nudging to back Biden's plans.

It was not exactly brutal arm-twisting by a domineering White House. But Manchin did not appreciate it, and he made his displeasure known publicly.

"I couldn't believe it," he said, complaining that no one in the White House had given him a heads-up on the interview. In a brushback to Harris's implicit pitch for a fast-moving reconciliation bill, Manchin stressed: "We're going to try to find a bipartisan pathway forward."

That weekend, a plan took shape among Senate Republicans. Susan Collins initiated it. She shared a warm relationship with Manchin, and the West Virginia Democrat had crossed party lines to endorse her reelection in 2020. Collins knew Manchin well enough to understand that his identity as a Democrat meant something to him, as a seventy-three-year-old Italian Catholic who came up revering the Kennedys.

The view of Manchin, ubiquitous among progressives, that he was practically a Republican in sheep's clothing overlooked the depth of his relationship with the Democratic Party. He had been approached multiple times by Republicans about switching parties—Trump had even dangled a cabinet job in front of him—and Manchin had rebuffed them every time. The conservative Democrat had voted over and over to defend his party's core priorities, like the Affordable Care Act and opposing tax cuts for the wealthy, and he enjoyed close relationships with state and national labor leaders, including the powerful teachers-union president Randi Weingarten.

Manchin had a habit of calling the famed political consultant James Carville to complain that the left did not appreciate that he was a "real damn Democrat."

Susan Collins understood this about her friend.

But Collins also knew Manchin liked working with Republicans and cared about getting along with them. He had already doomed Biden's nominee to lead the Office of Management and Budget, Neera Tanden, because he was upset about her history of nasty tweets about his Republican colleagues. Besides, if Manchin wanted to run for another Senate term in 2024, it would be far easier as a Republican.

Collins called up John Thune, the number two Senate Republican. She wanted his help making the case for Manchin to defect. On Monday evening, February 1, they took Manchin to dinner in an upstairs room at Bistro Cacao, a French restaurant on Capitol Hill. Thune, Collins, and a third Republican, Rob Portman of Ohio, plied Manchin with entreaties to leave his party.

Manchin had rejected appeals to become a Republican in the past, so Thune pitched him on a middle option, one that would not involve formally embracing the GOP label.

You don't have to join our caucus, Thune told him. Just become an independent and caucus with us.

Thune suggested Manchin would likely be rewarded for taking such a step: You could write your own ticket, the South Dakotan told him. Chair a committee, we'll help you raise money for your campaign.

Manchin heard them out and gave Thune a politically deft response.

John, he said, if you were the leader I would do it.

It was not exactly a hard no, but Manchin was not about to put Mitch McConnell back in charge of the Senate.

The West Virginian conveyed something else to his Republican colleagues. Biden had quickly shown real contrition about his White House's misstep in deploying Harris that way. Before the Republicans could get to Manchin, Biden had already hosted him in the Oval Office to patch things up.

In Manchin's telling over dinner, Biden had been solicitous.

Biden had welcomed Manchin into the Oval for a joint meeting with him and the vice president, a gesture the White House intended to convey that Biden and Harris were a steadfast political team. But at one point, when Biden had wanted to talk candidly with Manchin about his views on the rescue bill, the president had asked everyone else to leave the room—including Harris.

In Manchin's recounting to those three Republicans, Biden had told him: Joe, you're my friend, I'll never ask you to vote against your conscience. I'll never ask you to do anything you are uncomfortable doing.

Manchin believed him. He was not going to become a Republican.

What it would take to get Manchin's vote on a rescue bill was still an open question. While the daily chaos of the Trump era was receding, Manchin's private meetings on that first day of February suggested that the equilibrium of Joe Biden's Washington was delicate indeed.

* * *

By the time Manchin sat down to dinner that evening, the bipartisan approach he favored seemed to be disintegrating. Also that day, Biden hosted a meeting with ten Republican senators—including Collins, Portman, Murkowski, and Mitt Romney—who said they were open to striking a deal on a rescue bill.

But the group brought Biden something *else* unpleasant: a proposed framework for bipartisan legislation that envisioned a much, much smaller relief bill than the one Biden had put together. Biden had asked Congress for $1.9 trillion in spending. The Republicans wanted the price tag to come down by about two thirds, they told the White House.

The two sides did not move much closer in the meeting with Biden. Republicans were willing to fund the basics of vaccine distribution, smaller stimulus checks aimed only at lower-income Americans, and less than a sixth of the school safety funding in Biden's plan. They offered no aid to state and local government. It was a spare offer that made it easy for Biden to say no.

Biden did no scolding or lecturing in the meeting, and neither did his guests. It was a respectful back-and-forth, but there was no easy path to a middle ground. At one point, the president echoed his tutorial from Coons, explaining almost apologetically that if he cut down the size of his legislation to placate Republicans, he would lose votes from his own party.

Both Biden and his advisers shared a skepticism about the basic political seriousness of the offer Republicans put on the table. Steve Ricchetti, one of Biden's most important emissaries to the GOP, said to one lawmaker before the meeting that they needed to know there was enough potential Republican support for a compromise before entering serious negotiations. "Until they've got ten signatures on a piece of paper, we've got nothing to talk about," he said, according to this person.

The meeting was not encouraging on that front. The White House told Senate Democrats after the meeting that it was not clear that all ten of the Republicans who met with Biden could be counted on to vote for a bill even in the $600 billion range they proposed.

If Republicans were not offering a guaranteed win for a smaller package, what was the point of even attempting to go small?

The White House released a statement shortly after the meeting that all but rejected the Republican offer. "The President also made clear that the American Rescue Plan was carefully designed to meet the stakes of this moment, and any changes in it cannot leave the nation short of its pressing needs," said the statement attributed to Jen Psaki, the press secretary.

The same week, Biden addressed a video call of House Democrats and did not sound like a president preparing to slash more than a trillion dollars out of his draft legislation. He told them his economic advisers, including Treasury Secretary Janet Yellen, had warned against doing just that.

The mistake would be going too small rather than going too big, Biden said.

His chief of staff was even blunter in his rejection of calls to trim things down. When Larry Summers, the former treasury secretary, wrote critically about Biden's plan, warning that it could spur inflation, Klain privately dismissed Summers by pointing to his role shaping the deficient Obama stimulus.

People should ask Summers, Klain sniped, how far he got on economic recovery legislation or anything else after the first stimulus was "a bust."

The Biden-Klain view was already the prevailing attitude in Nancy Pelosi's

House. On February 1, the Speaker and Schumer filed a joint budget resolution to start the process of turning Biden's $1.9 trillion rescue package into law. The legislative body language was not difficult for Republicans to interpret. They were welcome to have their talks with the White House, but the Democratic Congress was moving forward with or without them.

While some of the most intense trauma of January 6 had begun to subside, many Democrats could not forget how the most extreme members of the Republican Conference had behaved—and how so many others who considered themselves mainstream had gone along with an unconscionable plan to oppose certification of the election results.

Val Demings found after January 6 that she could not bring herself even to say hello to Republican lawmakers she had once considered her friends. She and the other House Democrats who had been trapped in the gallery were still in close touch, forming a text chain they called the "Gallery Group" to keep an open line in the aftermath of that searing experience. Within her congressional office, Demings responded to the attack with a stern instruction.

When a Republican comes to us with a proposal they want me to endorse, she told her aides, check to see if they voted to overturn the election. If they did, Demings felt it was going to be much tougher to work together.

Anna Eshoo, the senior California lawmaker close to Pelosi, had a painful conversation with her daughter about the experience of interacting with Republicans after the riot. To the seventy-eight-year-old Californian, after a quarter century in Congress, the physical space of the Capitol felt defiled. There was a pervasive sense of violation, she says: "I think it's with all of us—that they were there, what they did, what they said, how they desecrated the place and how close we came to the government being overthrown."

When her daughter asked how it felt to go to work with Republicans who were still denying the election results, Eshoo offered one of the most wrenching comparisons imaginable.

"It feels like being in the same room with your rapist," she recalls saying.

The House majority took action in early February against one of the Republicans most deeply implicated in Trump's attack on the election. Marjorie

Taylor Greene had long since been exposed as an extreme conspiracy theorist, and more recently years-old videos had surfaced of her hounding David Hogg, the Parkland school shooting survivor, and promoting threats against Pelosi. During her congressional race in 2020, Greene had posted a photo of herself holding a gun beside an image of Alexandria Ocasio-Cortez and two of the other progressive women of color sometimes known as "the Squad."

If there was one Republican who had shown she had no business serving in Congress, Democrats believed it was her.

Pelosi thought it would be pointless to try expelling Greene from the House. Even if an expulsion vote succeeded, the Speaker believed Greene would easily win a special election in her district and return to Congress in a matter of months. But Pelosi and other Democratic leaders agreed Greene could not be allowed to serve on policymaking committees. A person who harassed student gun-control activists had no place on the Education Committee, of which Greene was a member.

Kevin McCarthy, once again trying to avoid a hard choice, asked Steny Hoyer if they could cut a deal on Greene: Republicans would strip her of her spot on the Education Committee but leave her on the Budget Committee. Hoyer rejected the offer. Democrats were going to punish Greene in a floor vote and Republicans could be with them or against them.

A gentlemanly moderate who hailed from a more collegial era and sought out relationships with Republicans, Hoyer was in some respects an unlikely contender to lead the charge against Greene. But the majority leader, then eighty-one, was no factional leader of centrist Democrats. Having spent nearly two decades as Pelosi's deputy and on-and-off rival, Hoyer was keenly sensitive to the diverse currents of the Democratic caucus, and he understood how much the liberal women targeted by Greene needed to feel the support of their party.

In a small leadership meeting before the February 4 debate on Greene, Hoyer told Pelosi he needed fifteen minutes to make remarks on the floor. Pelosi was skeptical: Steny, she asked, who wants to hear from you for fifteen minutes?

On the floor, Hoyer brandished the image Greene had posted the previous year demonizing three progressive women of color. Challenging Republicans to look at her extremism and incitement for what it was, Hoyer pleaded with them to stand up for the decency of the House. Ocasio-Cortez and her allies, he said, deserved a basic human respect that Greene had refused to give them.

"They're not 'the Squad,'" he said, his voice rising. "They're Ilhan. They're Alexandria. They're Rashida. They are people. They are our colleagues." Ilhan Omar, the progressive Minnesota lawmaker whose face appeared in Greene's ad, was sitting directly behind Hoyer as he spoke. As he mimicked holding up an AR-15, the Democrat who'd left Somalia as a refugee said just loud enough to be picked up by the microphone: "Sounds like the guns I fled."

Hoyer's ferocious defense of the House and his liberal colleagues stirred Democrats, and the party voted unanimously to strip Greene of her committee assignments. But only eleven Republicans joined them in meting out the Democrats' chosen penalty—just one more than voted to impeach Trump for inciting the attack on the Capitol. Trump's party was not ready to punish or purge the extremists in their ranks, and certainly not at a time and in a fashion of Nancy Pelosi's choosing.

Remarkably, the poisonous atmosphere in the House did not generate an especially bitter front of Republican resistance to the American Rescue Plan.

As the Democrats moved the multitrillion-dollar piece of legislation through committees, House Republicans were not making much of an argument against it. Trump's free-spending ways and his December endorsement of distributing $2,000 checks had clouded the party's approach to pandemic relief and fiscal policy generally. Republicans were also too tangled in their own civil war—and a still-ongoing impeachment trial—to focus on the mammoth rescue package rolling through the chamber. Two days after Pelosi introduced the budget resolution with Schumer, the House GOP was debating whether to keep Liz Cheney in her leadership role.

Not that Republicans in the House could have stopped the American Rescue Plan, even if they had been better organized and more attentive. Unlike the Senate, the House offered no powerful legislative tools to the minority. To have any influence at all, they had to use their political megaphone to raise a cry of outrage from the voters.

But voters seemed to be on the Democrats' side, at least where pandemic relief was concerned. They liked what they knew about the basics of the bill—the huge sums of money for economic aid and public health—and Republicans were not really trying to change their minds.

As the House Ways and Means Committee began assembling the bill in committee meetings during the second week of February, Richie Neal, the chairman, called up Pelosi one evening with an astounded observation.

"Madam Speaker, there was no acrimony," Neal told her, according to his memory.

Pelosi was confused. "What do you mean?" she asked.

"They made some proposals," Neal said of the Republicans, "but they didn't challenge us on facts and need."

After fighting like mad to block the certification of a fair election, House Republicans were largely taking a pass on a debate over $1.9 trillion in relief spending that included a new social-welfare benefit in the greatly expanded child tax credit. The Republicans' passivity was a welcome gift for Democrats, in a way, but it also showed the degree to which Republicans were animated by Trumpian grievance and lacked a core set of guiding principles on policy.

* * *

The Republicans' passivity had only done so much to help the Democrats, who were wrestling with their own divisions. They had a bill to pass, and, once Trump's impeachment trial concluded on February 13, Democratic impatience to pass the rescue plan began spiking.

Biden had been in office nearly a month and the House was moving quickly toward passing a sweeping bill. But the Senate was still more of a question mark. Bipartisan talks had not ended, and Joe Manchin had still not quite indicated what he would and would not vote for.

In a virtual meeting on February 17, House Democrats began to flash annoyance with the legislative process and angst about the looming review of the rescue bill by the Senate parliamentarian. Some were especially focused on the minimum wage hike: The measure was a huge priority for the party as a whole and for labor unions in particular. But it was uncertain whether raising the federal requirement to $15 per hour would survive either the Senate parliamentarian or the centrist flank of the Senate Democratic caucus.

During the House video call, Bobby Scott, the chairman of the Education and Labor Committee, warned his colleagues that the fate of the minimum wage was very much in doubt in the Senate and said Democrats could not afford to back down easily.

"Activists are ready to go to bat and fight for this, and House Democrats cannot give up on this issue," Scott said, according to one account of the meeting. "We promised we would include it and we must deliver."

Pelosi, trying to keep spirits high, closed the call by reciting a quote from Tennyson—"For I dipt into the future, far as human eye could see / Saw the vision of the world, and all the wonder that would be"—and insisting to her caucus that a wondrous victory was at hand.

But in private, the Speaker was also starting to tire of the ambiguity on the Senate side. While Pelosi would never say so to a group of hundreds of House Democrats, she was puzzled by Biden's deference toward Manchin and the White House's seeming eagerness to cater to a tiny number of moderates in the Senate who did not yet seem to know precisely what their red lines were. One friend who spoke with Pelosi during this time says she expressed genuine confusion about the White House's handling of Manchin. In her own chamber, the Speaker had not made a habit of letting one recalcitrant lawmaker hold up her plans.

Pelosi was drawing plenty of red lines on her own, conveying to the White House and Schumer that if Manchin or anyone else tried to shave down the state and local aid in the bill then there would be hell to pay. She delivered the same message to Schumer on the generous tax credits included in the House legislation. If the Senate tried to limit the refundability of those benefits, restricting how many lower-income Americans could access them, she would consider it totally unacceptable.

Pelosi and Schumer had a trusting but not close relationship. One Pelosi adviser acknowledged that the Speaker felt she had to keep the senator close because if she didn't then he'd "veer into his own waters," as the adviser put it. The two leaders had to be in constant touch, this person said, for Pelosi to feel confident that they'd stay in political lockstep.

Schumer promised Pelosi his chamber would observe her red lines.

The White House was getting impatient, too. Biden and his aides had continued to stroke the most moderate members of the Senate Democratic caucus, and they had developed a sharper sense of how the legislation would need to change to get nearly fifty votes. Centrists in both the House and Senate did not like the idea of giving $1,400 stimulus checks even to wealthy people, and so the White House agreed to phase out eligibility for Americans making more than $75,000 per year.

Still, they were not quite at fifty votes, and Manchin was not the only one frustrating the president and his team. Biden confessed in private that he did not really understand Sinema, the aloof Arizona Democrat known on the Hill for her cryptic policy views and flamboyant attire. In December, she had attended the swearing in of her state's junior senator, Mark Kelly, in a purple wig and tiger-print coat. More recently, Sinema had joined Manchin in voicing a preference for bipartisanship and resistance to a $15 minimum wage.

One person close to the president likened Biden's perplexity at Sinema to his difficulty grasping his grandchildren's use of the viral-video app TikTok. He wanted to relate, but he just didn't quite get it.

Manchin was vexing to the White House for less generational reasons. The conservative Democrat hailed from a state with a long history of amassing congressional seniority and then extracting huge federal subsidies for parochial interests. But Manchin did not seem interested in claiming the crown from Robert C. Byrd, his venerable predecessor in the Senate, as the King of Pork. In fact, he told the White House he was concerned about the generous cash payments in the House bill because of the effect they might have on voters back home.

Too many people in West Virginia, Manchin said, would just use that free money to buy drugs.

Negotiation in the Senate simply was not the same beast it had been during Biden's heyday as a senator in the late twentieth century, or even during his two terms as vice president. A president could not often count on being able to sway wavering senators by directing money to their states, nor could he have any consistent expectation that the opposition party would give some deference to a new administration elected by a wide popular majority.

Biden was within striking distance of a major legislative victory, but he was not there yet—and his second goal, of showing the country that the two parties could get things done together, seemed exceedingly remote.

On February 20, Biden spent an afternoon with someone who understood just how much things had changed since the Senate of the last century. Taking a short ride from the White House to the Watergate apartment complex, the new president paid a visit to Bob Dole, the former Republican Senate majority leader who had recently been diagnosed with advanced lung cancer. The two men had served together for twenty-three years; both had run for president in 1988, during the last election before the fall of the Berlin Wall.

Dole was a proud Republican to the core, and he had supported Trump even in moments when other party elders declined to do so. But he had been deeply troubled by Trump's refusal to concede defeat in the 2020 election and even more so by the January 6 riot. The people who stormed the Capitol that day, he said in an interview for this book, "were not patriots—they were troublemakers."

By February, Dole, then ninety-seven, was ailing badly, and the visit from Biden meant something to the old World War II hero. The visit, Dole said afterward, was "mostly happy talk."

"It wasn't 'Mr. President,' it was Joe and Bob," Dole said. "We were back in the Senate, and we talked about the good old days.

"You know, that was a good time in our lives—in both our lives," Dole reflected. "When we seemed to work together, and worked across the aisle, and generally got things done."

In Dole's reckoning, that wasn't possible anymore for a pretty simple reason.

"Trust," he said. "They don't trust each other."

*　*　*

One week later, on February 27, the House passed the American Rescue Plan on a nearly party-line vote. Pelosi lost only two Democrats on the roll call: Kurt Schrader of Oregon and Jared Golden of Maine, both among the most conservative members of her caucus. Every Republican voted against the bill.

Speeding the bill toward passage in the Senate was a ruling from the Senate parliamentarian, Elizabeth MacDonough, on the eve of the House vote: The minimum wage did not belong in a reconciliation bill, she decided. It was a tough setback for progressives and unions, but on a tactical level it was something of a gift to Biden because the biggest sticking point for Manchin and Sinema was gone. Even if all fifty Democratic senators had wanted a $15 minimum wage, passing it in the rescue bill was not an option.

Far fewer than fifty Democratic senators did want to vote for a $15 minimum wage. In a largely symbolic vote on March 5, just forty-two members of the caucus voted in favor of the measure. Both Manchin and Sinema voted against it, and Sinema drew progressive rage online by communicating her vote with a theatrical thumbs-down gesture. But the tally of no votes included half a dozen others—including Coons and Carper, Jon Tester and Jeanne Shaheen—confirming that the avowedly moderate faction in Biden's party was more than just one or two habitual renegades.

But Manchin went out of his way one more time to earn his reputation as the chief Democratic stumbling block to Biden's agenda, insisting on one more last-minute concession on the day of the Senate vote. Some of his Republican friends, including Rob Portman, had been lobbying him to insist on phasing out the federal government's program of enhanced unemployment benefits as soon as July. That was a nonstarter for Manchin's party, but the West Virginian stalled a vote for hours as he negotiated a more modest paring-back of those benefits.

It was an exasperating final stretch for the White House and Senate Democrats, and in the heat of the back-and-forth with Manchin one of Biden's closest advisers wrote in a text message that the senator seemed more focused on the symbolism of supporting Republican-backed changes to the bill than on any matters of substance.

"What he really wants is to vote for Republican amendments," this adviser wrote, "because they are Republican."

It was a shrewd read: For Manchin, bipartisanship itself was the objective, more than the underlying issue. It was a lesson Democrats would learn again and again for the rest of the year.

But the final concessions to Manchin yielded a breakthrough: a party-line vote in the Senate to push a $1.9 trillion rescue plan into law. With fifty votes in the Senate, Democrats secured federal spending that saved state and local governments from fiscal disaster; poured money into vaccination efforts, school safety, and aid to businesses; and forged a fully refundable tax credit that would give up to $300 per month to parents of young children. The last of those was an expensive, short-term benefit, but one that Democrats said they fully intended to make permanent as a decisive blow against child poverty.

At a Rose Garden ceremony with Pelosi and Schumer on March 12, the proud new president said he had promised the American people that "help was on the way" and now Democrats had made good on that promise. Detailing the expansive benefits of the legislation, Biden lavished praise on both the congressional leaders. Klain had nudged Biden immediately after the bill was passed to make sure he praised Schumer—the Senate process had been messy, but it had ended with an enormous win for a majority leader who was still proving himself.

"I owe you, Chuck," Biden said. "You did an incredible job."

But the president had a larger message.

"We are showing it's possible to get big, important things done," Biden said, adding, "It's critical to demonstrate that government can function—can function and deliver prosperity, security, and opportunity for the people in this country."

The legislation was encouraging for the new administration on several levels. It guaranteed that they would not, like the Obama administration in 2009, wind up regretting that they went too small on economic relief. The American Rescue Plan ensured that Biden's first year was not dominated by mass layoffs in municipal school systems and police departments, or by mass grievance that a new Democratic government was providing far less generous government aid than Donald Trump's administration.

And it showed that, under certain dire circumstances, Biden's complicated party could close ranks around an immense work of government policy and ram it into law without a single Republican vote.

There were more bracing takeaways from the legislative process, too. There was no sign that Biden had made meaningful headway in working with Republicans, and Manchin and Sinema had made it clear enough that they could not be counted on to drive a sweeping liberal agenda into law. Even in victory, some progressives were fuming at their defeat on the minimum wage and frustrated at the extent to which Senate centrists had dominated the final negotiations.

In other words, if the American Rescue Plan was a political triumph, it was not certain that it provided Biden and his party with a blueprint for enacting the rest of their agenda.

But in the Rose Garden that day, thoughts were not yet fixed on the heavy lifting ahead.

In an interview that week, Schumer was elated. Congressional Democrats held their own celebration on the Capitol's West Front, ahead of the White House ceremony, on an early spring day that matched their bright mood. Striding back inside, Schumer said the new law was "one of the most important things we've done in decades."

Schumer's Republican counterpart sensed a potential sea change, too. Talking to a friend a few weeks after Biden signed the rescue bill into law, McConnell confided that he was deeply concerned that the Democratic legislation could have such far-reaching effects on the country that would make it hard for Republicans to undo benefits like the child tax credit even if they retook Congress in 2022. If Americans grew used to the benefits in the new law, he suggested, it would become politically untenable for Republicans to repeal its most popular measures. The country, McConnell lamented, might cross a point of no return toward becoming a European-style social welfare state—exactly the outcome he had spent his career arguing against.

And the Democrats were far from finished with their legislative agenda.

*   *   *

The success of the American Rescue Plan only reinforced President Biden's inclination to go big—to reach for a Rooseveltian place in American domestic policy, and to shed the incremental policy promises of his primary campaign in favor of a far more daring governing vision. He had still not abandoned his desire to work with Republicans, but if two great strains of ambition had been competing within Biden—his desire to foster national reconciliation and his aspiration to craft a presidency of grand and lasting impact—there was little doubt which was stronger as springtime approached.

In early March, he hosted a gathering at the White House with a group of historians, including the prominent biographers Doris Kearns Goodwin and Walter Isaacson, the Princeton historian Eddie Glaude Jr., and the Harvard historian Annette Gordon-Reed. The session stretched for three hours as Biden posed question after question to the group and soaked up the lessons of past presidential greatness.

Biden told the historians he wanted to turn America into a country where working people would know "we have your back." Glaude supplied him with another description for that agenda: What Biden was talking about, he said, was creating "a broad infrastructure of social care," according to one attendee.

Biden wanted to be known as a great champion of science, he said, and Isaacson offered him Dwight Eisenhower as a model to follow. Biden grilled Goodwin, who was seated directly across from him, about how Franklin Roosevelt governed.

The president wanted to know: Should he do fireside chats, as Roosevelt did? Should he find some more modern version of a direct conversation with the American people?

According to one person in the room, the president kept returning to one central question.

"How big can we go?" Biden asked them.

*   *   *

As Biden contemplated the great presidents of the past, one more recent occupant of his office was following the new administration's success with a mixture of respect and—well, some more complicated feelings.

Barack Obama had taken note of the way that Biden aides and even congressional Democrats like Schumer were criticizing his first year in office and his early handling of the Great Recession. The former president felt they were unfairly disparaging his record. Obama did not think he and his team had been played for fools by Republican senators, nor did he think the stimulus law he negotiated was such an obvious failure.

You know, he told one former administration official, it was a different world in 2009. The Democratic Party was different back then, with far more conservatives in the Senate than people remember. The country was different, too.

Some veterans of Obama's administration went much further in private than their old boss ever did, griping about how Biden had no business positioning himself as a bolder, braver president when back in the day he had been one of their administration's biggest proponents of bipartisanship and political caution.

Obama and Biden spoke by phone occasionally, but not often. Their conversations were friendly and supportive, but hardly the stuff of the tight brotherhood both men had sold to the country as a cheery political fable. A few people close to both men detected a certain tension, at least on one side of the relationship.

Nancy Pelosi, who spoke regularly with the former president, came away from her conversations with Obama during this period with a matter-of-fact diagnosis.

She told a friend: "Obama is jealous of Biden."

There was another prominent Democrat who shared that assessment: Joe Biden himself. Having finally shed his dutiful supporting role in the Obama show, the forty-sixth president echoed Pelosi's view in a conversation with an adviser several months into his tenure. His days of being looked down upon by the smart set in someone else's West Wing were over, and Biden knew it.

"I am confident that Barack is not happy with the coverage of this administration as more transformative than his," Biden said, according to this adviser.

Chapter 10

Flat-Ass Stalled

DEMOCRATS WERE STILL in a season of good feelings when Joe Biden took the stage at the Pabst Theater near the Milwaukee riverfront on February 16.

The president and his congressional allies were still grinding through the final details of the American Rescue Plan, but victory was close. The coronavirus pandemic was not over, but cases were falling rapidly. About 40 million Americans had been vaccinated, with more than a million people getting new shots every day.

The president was in Wisconsin for a town hall–style event moderated by the CNN anchor Anderson Cooper. It unfolded smoothly enough until Joycelyn Fish, a marketing director at a community theater, asked Biden about student debt. Telling him that education-related debt was "crushing" her family and friends, Fish urged Biden to consider canceling all student loan debt up to $50,000.

Biden rejected the idea. He had already endorsed debt cancellation up to $10,000, but he had been resisting pleas to go higher from liberals as mighty as Bernie Sanders, Elizabeth Warren, and Alexandria Ocasio-Cortez. Even Chuck Schumer, a more recent convert to the cause, had pressed Biden in private on the subject, arguing that relieving student debts would be an enormous blessing to working-class people of color—the core of his political base.

Biden had not been persuaded, and Joycelyn Fish was not about to change his mind.

"I will not make that happen," Biden told her.

He said he wanted to give people a measure of debt relief, but he was not about to "forgive the debt, the billions of dollars of debt for people who have gone to Harvard and Yale and Penn."

The unsupportive answer left no room for uncertainty or interpretation. It was a repudiation that seemed to come mainly from the president's gut. Student loan debt was a widespread American affliction that burdened more than 43 million borrowers, few of whom attended expensive Ivy League schools. But Biden plainly associated hefty debts with fancy universities and recoiled from the idea of bailing out the privileged.

"I went to a state school," he noted on CNN.

The comments sent a shudder through the progressive wing of Biden's party, drawing a thread of frustrated tweets from Ocasio-Cortez and a stern joint statement from Schumer and Warren. Biden's advisers had been urging the left to be patient, stressing that the administration had not finalized its policies on student debt. But Biden seemed to have demolished those claims in Milwaukee.

Or had he?

Within twenty-four hours, the White House press secretary, Jen Psaki, tempered Biden's remarks. The Justice Department would conduct a legal review of the debt-cancellation issue, she said, and that would shape how the president proceeded.

In private, Biden's chief of staff spoke with several congressional supporters of debt cancellation to assure them his boss had not intended to take such a firm position. One lawmaker who spoke with Ron Klain recalled him saying gently that sometimes Biden gets a little tangled up in his public statements.

When a group of House progressives raised the subject again with Klain in a meeting several weeks later, the trusted aide alluded to Biden's comments as an error.

"We corrected that the next day, right?" Klain said, according to one lawmaker's recollection.

The blunder blew over quickly, but the moment had exposed real disagreements within the Democratic Party even in a period of relative unity.

The party had closed ranks around Biden for nearly a year, first to drive Donald Trump from office and then to pass an urgent pandemic-relief bill into law. Yet Biden's political coalition remained complex, containing a great diversity of ideologies, identities, and political priorities.

Biden had made grand and sometimes contradictory promises to nearly every faction, pledging to transform the economy and social fabric of the United States while restoring a spirit of normalcy to Washington and reaching across the aisle to work with Republicans. Though he had passed the rescue package on a party-line vote, Biden remained serious about the last of those goals: He continued to tell advisers and lawmakers that the world needed to see that Americans could work together in order to restore the global reputation of American democracy.

Once he won the fight for the American Rescue Plan, Biden faced the tangled task of working through the rest of his stated agenda. The bulk of his party expected nothing less than an all-out push for Democratic priorities on taxes, climate, health care, infrastructure, voting rights, policing, immigration, gun violence, and so much more. The Democrats' centrist wing was eager to address many of these issues, too, but with more incremental legislation and ideally with Republican partners.

In this next phase of Biden's young presidency, he and his advisers would confront just how hard it would be to keep his promises and how quickly his party might fracture if he did not.

Facing mounting legislative adversity, Biden would eventually settle on a complex, two-pronged strategy for managing Congress and the two parties. On one side, he would hold talks with Republicans and centrist Democrats on infrastructure legislation, and on the other side he would work with his party's liberal majority to devise another multitrillion-dollar reconciliation bill containing many of the Democrats' larger spending priorities.

If Biden and his party's congressional leaders managed everything just right, they could satisfy the moderate wing of their party with an infrastructure bill and earn their cooperation on much larger legislation that would pass solely with Democratic votes.

Or so the theory went.

It was a difficult path, and in the spring and early summer of 2021, the first signs of dissension began to appear at every level of the Democratic Party—even within Biden's White House, in the office of his vice president.

* * *

Until the end of winter, Joe Biden's political honeymoon with his fellow Democrats was still very much in progress.

The White House had embarked early on the kind of congressional charm offensive that Democrats had never enjoyed during the Trump years, and that few had experienced even during Barack Obama's administration. To Obama, courting House committee chairs and midlevel senators had been a tedious chore—one that many of his young aides spoke about with an eye-rolling ennui that lawmakers could only experience as insulting.

Biden had a different attitude toward the Hill, and in the first months of his administration it showed. He and his aides showered congressional Democrats with attention, hosting dozens of lawmakers at the White House in the first month of his presidency and holding larger virtual meetings between the president and scores more. When he hosted a group of House committee chairs in the Oval Office in February, Biden welcomed them with lavish enthusiasm for the role he hoped they would play in shaping policy.

Biden wooed Republicans, too, with the trappings of his office. He had not managed to achieve a breakthrough with the GOP on pandemic relief, but in private meetings Biden insisted that he wanted bipartisan support for parts of his agenda. The new president seemed sensitive to complaints from Republicans that his more liberal staff was hostile to the idea of compromise.

In a mid-February meeting with a bipartisan group of mayors and governors, Biden drew an explicit distinction between himself and his aides, according to Francis Suarez, the Republican mayor of Miami who attended the meeting. The president wanted to pursue cooperation where possible, and so that is what his administration would do.

"I let them handle the fine points of policy," Biden said of his staff, according to Suarez. "But I handle the politics."

For the most part, the subjects of Biden's charm offensive were his fellow Democrats. He used many of the meetings to underline his respect for the different foundational constituencies of the Democratic Party. In his Oval Office meeting with House chairs, Biden made an emphatic statement of his support for the union movement, pointing his index finger into the seat cushion next to him and declaring that they were in "labor's house."

When he met with the executive committee of the Congressional Black Caucus in April, Biden was even more solicitous. After the group of lawmakers sat down with the president, Biden rose to acknowledge a deep political debt.

"I want you all to know, you're the reason I'm here," Biden said, according to one person's recollection.

The president told the group they could expect to spend more time in the Oval Office. "There's a lot of work for us to do," he said.

In one early virtual meeting with Senate moderates, Biden's long relationship with Congress showed in a vivid if unintentional way: He kept addressing Mark Warner, the centrist Democrat from Virginia, as "John"—as in John Warner, the Republican whom Mark Warner succeeded in the Senate, a man with whom Biden served for three decades. It was the kind of senior moment that Biden's colleagues took note of, though in this case they found it endearing.

At the end of February, *Politico* reported that Biden had already hosted almost fifty members of the House and Senate in the Oval Office, offering some of them their debut visits to the storied room. Jon Tester, the third-term Montana senator, startled even Biden's aides when he disclosed that an early visit with Biden in the Oval was the first time he had ever been in the room.

Biden was surprised, too. Getting shut out of the White House in the

Trump years was one thing, but Tester had been in Congress throughout the Obama presidency.

How, Biden wondered aloud, was it possible that he had never been in the Oval Office before?

During this period, Democrats had reasons to celebrate Biden besides their new access to the White House grounds. The American Rescue Plan was proving popular, sending aid checks to millions of families and generating a huge wave of local headlines about narrowly averted cuts to law enforcement, transit, and more.

The scale of funding going into distressed localities was staggering: multibillion-dollar packages for metropolises like New York and Chicago, but also giant sums for smaller cities like Akron, Ohio, which received more than $150 million, and Laredo, Texas, which got nearly $100 million. The relief money was so popular that even conservative Republican governors were finding themselves hard-pressed to complain.

"We'll put that money to work," acknowledged Pete Ricketts, the Republican governor of Nebraska whose wealthy family bankrolled the national GOP. In Mississippi, Tate Reeves, a conservative governor who thirsted for national media attention, scolded Democrats for the "ridiculous" size of the rescue plan but conceded he might try to use its funds to patch his state's shoddy water infrastructure.

Most telling might have been a rupture over relief funds between Florida's pro-Trump Republican governor, Ron DeSantis, and its equally ambitious Republican senator, Rick Scott. Scott, an eccentric former health-care executive with designs on the presidency, called for governors and mayors to reject rescue-plan money. DeSantis, who had a long-running rivalry with Scott, dismissed the idea.

"It doesn't make any sense," DeSantis countered, arguing that Florida deserved its fair share.

With rare exceptions like his trip to Milwaukee in February, Biden did not spend much time on the road hawking his accomplishments in the first few months of his presidency. His aides were hypervigilant about protecting the president from the coronavirus and limited his travel accordingly. But he had promised Democrats over and over that he was going to be an enthusiastic salesman when the time was right. It was one of the rare subjects on which Biden openly criticized the previous White House he served in: The Obama administration, he believed, did not do enough to explain its policies to the country.

In the glow of victory, Democrats expected Biden would soon begin to make the hard sell for his achievements. He would not, they believed, trust his administration's work to speak for itself. Biden, after all, had learned from the mistakes of his old boss.

"Obama thought salesmanship was beneath him," says Tim Kaine, the Virginia senator and close Obama ally, adding that he meant that in an "affectionate" way.

His prediction in May: "Biden and his team are not going to repeat that mistake."

At the time, it was easy to understand Kaine's confidence. After all, Biden spent much of 2010 campaigning for Democrats who lost badly in the midterm elections that year. Few understood better than Biden the price his party could pay if they did not define and defend their expansive agenda.

* * *

On March 22, two of Biden's senior advisers made the case to Senate Democrats that the new administration was on the right political track. During a virtual meeting, Biden's longtime political counselor Mike Donilon and his top political aide Jennifer O'Malley Dillon delivered a presentation arguing that the "Biden-Harris coalition" was a muscular and stable force. They walked Senate Democrats through an assessment of Biden's strength in 2020 with voters of color, women, independents, suburbanites, and young people, and said the party now had to sell its achievements to those voters and more.

"In 2020 we brought the right voters to the table and persuaded them to support us; we need to constantly talk to and deepen our support among key components of our coalition," the two said, according to a copy of their presentation.

For starters, Donilon and O'Malley Dillon said, that meant promoting the American Rescue Plan aggressively until the next election in 2022.

"In addition to the ARP," they said, "we need to stay on the offensive between now and November 2022 by highlighting this administration's efforts on popular issues (e.g., health care, infrastructure) and highlighting GOP obstruction of commonsense legislation."

It was the kind of broad-and-simple strategy that had sustained Biden through a tumultuous 2020 primary and general election. The Biden-era Democratic Party would do popular stuff, promote it tirelessly, and chastise Republicans for standing in the way. Democrats just had to stay in line and stick to the plan.

One Democrat was not in the mood to fall in line that evening.

Like many Asian American lawmakers, Tammy Duckworth remained frustrated that Biden and his team had not managed to put a single person of that background in charge of a cabinet department. She and other Asian Americans in Congress had given Biden's team so many names to consider, only to see all of them passed over, in many cases for white people with close ties to the president. With two of Biden's closest advisers on the line, Duckworth seized the chance to raise the issue again.

O'Malley Dillon tried to placate the former helicopter pilot by pointing to the most prominent person of Asian descent in the White House: Kamala Harris, whose mother was Indian American.

We are incredibly proud of the vice president, O'Malley Dillon told Duckworth.

It was a line Duckworth had heard from other white people in Biden's inner circle. She found it condescending. No one had told the Congressional Black Caucus that they should be satisfied with a Black vice president and nothing else. The Illinois senator laced into O'Malley Dillon and made her anger public the following day, telling reporters on the Hill that the Biden adviser's comments had been "incredibly insulting."

Then Duckworth offered the White House an abrupt reminder of what one angry senator could do to their agenda. She vowed she would not vote to confirm a single Biden nominee who did not represent diversity until Biden did something about the paucity of Asian American people in senior administration roles.

The White House was rattled by the threat. Duckworth's ultimatum itself was troubling, since they could not afford to lose any Democratic votes on contentious nominations. More concerning still was the precedent it might set if the administration allowed Democratic senators to hold the White House hostage one by one.

Steve Ricchetti called Duckworth with a firm but diplomatic message.

You've issued an ultimatum to the president, the Biden adviser told her. We don't like ultimatums.

The senator was undeterred.

You guys give in to Joe Manchin's ultimatums on a daily basis, Duckworth shot back. What's wrong with an Asian American issuing one?

Ricchetti could not help chuckling. Duckworth had a point. After the negotiations with Manchin around the American Rescue Plan, the administration could hardly claim it had a blanket policy of not rewarding senatorial brinksmanship.

In this case, Duckworth relented for a modest price. The White House quickly agreed to name a former aide of hers, Erika Moritsugu, to a senior role as a liaison to the Asian American community and set in motion a series of other conversations about naming Asian Americans to influential jobs. In private, the senator allowed that she had probably been too tough on O'Malley Dillon, who was not really responsible for the administration's defective relationships with Asian American leaders.

A few weeks after the clash between Duckworth and O'Malley Dillon, Biden hosted Duckworth and several other Asian American lawmakers, including Judy Chu, Grace Meng, and Mark Takano, in the Oval Office. He conceded that he needed to "do better" on personnel matters. Again invoking his lifetime in Washington, the president told the group that one of his most important mentors had been Asian American: Daniel Inouye, the Hawaiian senator and World War II hero of Japanese descent, who served in the Senate for nearly half a century before his death in 2012.

For him, Biden said, Inouye had been "a teacher." To the group before him, the president said he remained "willing to learn," one lawmaker recalls.

It was a gracious meeting, and when Biden alluded to Kamala Harris's presence he did so more gingerly than his aides. When he mentioned the significance of having an Asian American vice president, he quickly added: "I know that's not the only thing you want to hear," according to one attendee.

Yet as quickly as it receded, the brief standoff with Duckworth proved a larger point about Biden and his party. While there were plenty of important forces holding the Democratic Party together, there were also powerful interests that could strain party unity. With no room for dissension in the Senate and precious little in the House, that was a looming challenge to the rest of Biden's agenda.

And Tammy Duckworth was hardly the most dangerous hostage-taker in Congress.

*　　*　　*

The next phase of Biden's agenda was still coming into focus. The president and his party had an enormous to-do list, but many of the biggest items on it had no obvious path through the closely divided Senate. Even with Democrats in the majority in the chamber, they still faced a sixty-vote threshold for passing legislation because they would need to break a filibuster in order to end debate and hold a vote. There were not ten Republican votes available to advance legislation on most of the Democratic Party's governing priorities.

Much of the party still dreamed of abolishing the filibuster and turning the Senate into a majority-rule body like the House. But Schumer had canvassed his caucus countless times on the subject, and he knew the votes were not there to change the rules of the Senate. It was not just Manchin and Kyrsten Sinema who objected: As many as half a dozen other, quieter centrists saw the filibuster as a check on raw partisanship and wanted to keep it in place.

Besides, Joe Biden himself had never even called for doing away with the filibuster.

There were bipartisan talks under way on a few subjects where lawmakers were trying to forge filibuster-proof compromises. In the Senate, the Connecticut Democrat Chris Murphy and the Texas Republican John Cornyn were holding quiet negotiations on gun regulation. A small group of Black lawmakers were trying to find a middle ground on police reform. Democrats had empowered Karen Bass in the House and Cory Booker in the Senate to lead bipartisan talks on policing legislation. On the Republican side, Mitch McConnell had promised Tim Scott of South Carolina, the Senate's lone Black Republican, that if he could strike a deal, then the GOP leader would not obstruct passage.

But at the start of the spring none of those negotiations seemed on track for a quick breakthrough, and Democrats wanted to keep up the momentum they felt they'd achieved with the rescue plan.

Biden and his advisers did nothing to discourage Democrats' great expectations. When Klain met with House progressives on March 23 and soothed them on the subject of student loans, he renewed the White House's promises to the left on a number of other subjects. The administration was not done fighting for a $15 minimum wage, the chief of staff said, and it intended to push hard as well for a broad bill supporting labor unions, known as the PRO Act.

"Keep up the pressure on us," he told the progressives, according to a person in the room.

Biden, too, was vowing to fight hard for policies that had faint prospects on the Hill.

At the start of April, Biden announced a series of executive actions aimed at showing forward motion on liberal priorities, including gun control and restructuring the federal judiciary. He had little enthusiasm for the latter, but during the campaign he had promised to create a commission to study the composition of the courts to mollify progressives who saw them as hopelessly stacked in favor of the right. In April, Biden gave them that commission.

On other subjects, his passion for action was genuine. On April 8, after calling America's gun-violence problem an "international embarrassment," Biden huddled in the Oval Office with activists and victims' families and told them he was determined to see Congress enact an assault weapons ban. The cause felt as urgent as ever after recent massacres in Boulder, Colorado, and Atlanta, the second carried out by a white gunman targeting Asian massage parlors.

Standing beside the Resolute Desk, Biden told his guests that the gun issue was a test of American democracy in the eyes of the world. The United States could not lead other nations if it could not keep people safe at home.

By mid-April, Biden had also issued two major policy documents that conveyed the scope of his governing aspirations. On the last day of March, he proposed a $2 trillion infrastructure package; in a discretionary spending request to Congress he released on April 9, Biden laid out an ambitious blueprint for pumping trillions into education, health care, housing, and fighting climate change.

Yet while these announcements excited many Democrats, it was not clear whether they amounted to much more than simple political posturing. Biden still had not devised a fresh strategy for getting large-scale legislation through Congress, and the divisions that had afflicted his party through the winter had not simply vanished.

While he was getting pressure from the left to move fast and keep going big, Biden was also hearing signs of discomfort from the middle of his party—centrists in the House and Senate who were wary of plunging into another multitrillion-dollar spending fight and who wanted Biden to make good on his promise to reach across the aisle.

There were concerning signs among the moderates in the Senate. While moderate Democrats celebrated the rescue plan along with their more liberal colleagues, some had been annoyed by the way Schumer and the White House had managed the process, with what they saw as a constant determination to soothe the left. At one point, even the levelheaded Chris Coons had vented frustration at Schumer for his continued public pledge to pass a $15 minimum wage and his insistence on putting the measure to a vote, when everyone knew it simply could not pass.

No Democratic senator was more discomfiting to the White House in this period than Kyrsten Sinema. After the passage of the rescue plan, the aloof Arizonan had reached out to the White House with a jarring request. While the first-term senator had voted for the rescue plan, Sinema asked Biden's aides not to send the president to Arizona for his victory lap. She did not want to be associated with him too closely.

It was a puzzling demand, since Biden had carried Arizona and remained popular there in the early months of his term. White House aides were quickly approaching the conclusion that Sinema was simply a difficult person. The senator had been in Washington for eight years, six of them in the House, and the stories about her were already legion. A former Green Party activist who had reinvented herself as a Fortune 500–loving moderate, Sinema had bewildered her colleagues in Congress long before she flummoxed the Biden White House.

One House Democrat with ties to Biden still marveled about an early interaction with Sinema, after learning of the up-from-poverty personal story she unspooled on the campaign trail. When this lawmaker told her that he had heard a moving account of her biography on NPR, Sinema responded in a way that seemed to belittle voters for caring.

"Can you believe they go for all that bullshit?" she had replied, according to this Democrat.

(Later, during her 2018 Senate campaign, the *New York Times* and the *Washington Post* reported that Sinema appeared to have embellished her life story.)

Democrats knew, too, that Sinema had close relationships with Republicans on the Hill. Before her election to the Senate in 2018, she had enjoyed aisle-crossing friendships in the House and joked with Democrats about how easy it was for her to charm Republican men: Sinema, a fitness enthusiast who was thirty-six when she entered Congress, boasted knowingly to colleagues and aides that her cleavage had an extraordinary persuasive effect on the uptight men of the GOP. She told one House Republican that while she would never switch parties, her father would be delighted if she did.

After the 2020 election, Sinema became especially chummy with Republicans in the evenly split Senate, and she began to emerge as a power in her own right. During one late-night vote early in 2021, a group of Senate Republicans invited her to dine with them and Sinema accepted—provided she could enter through a back door and avoid being spotted by the press. She had bonded that evening with Mike Lee, the hard-line conservative Utah senator, about their shared Mormon upbringing and experience attending Brigham Young University. Displaying a side of herself she concealed from the press, Sinema confided that her family had tried to nudge her back to the faith she had long since abandoned.

Republicans quickly came to see Sinema as a steadfast ally on crucial structural matters in the Senate, most of all the preservation of the filibuster—the minority party's most valuable instrument for constraining Democrats.

Sinema's interaction with the White House, meanwhile, would only grow more awkward. In the spring, she became the first-ever lawmaker to argue with White House aides when they asked her to wear a face mask in the company of the president, repeatedly asking why that was necessary when she had been vaccinated.

Still, the White House had no choice but to deal with her, no matter how many red flags were flying.

House moderates conveyed a more deliberate message of unease to White House aides in a meeting on April 21. A month after Klain sat down with some of the most prominent leftists in the House, the chief of staff hosted lawmakers from the centrist New Democrat Coalition for a meeting that also included Ricchetti and Louisa Terrell, Biden's director of legislative affairs. The mostly genial session turned tense when the moderate legislators complained that they saw the White House catering too much to the left.

The White House seemed to see progressives as its natural allies, they said. But moderate Democrats shared Biden's worldview in a deeper way, and it had been their victories in 2018 that gave Biden's party control of the House to begin with.

"We're on your team," said Derek Kilmer of Washington State, a leader of the group, according to one person in the room. "You can trust us."

Chrissy Houlahan, a moderate military veteran from the purple suburbs of Philadelphia, pushed a bit harder. She had voted for plenty of party-line bills so far, Houlahan said, but she believed in bipartisanship and so did her district.

"Especially with such a slim majority that we have," Houlahan recalls saying, "we need to have the opportunity to be able to show the American people that we aren't just working with our side of the bench, but that we're working with everybody."

Klain tried to assure the group that the administration embraced their perspective—that the White House was not simply an arm of the Congressional Progressive Caucus. Biden and his team wanted to be seen as solving problems and doing big things, he said, not just veering ever leftward.

"I want to make it clear, we're a pragmatic operation," Klain insisted, according to one attendee.

As for bipartisanship, Klain pointed out that the White House was engaged in talks with Republicans on a major infrastructure bill at that very moment. The GOP was not interested in backing Biden's $2 trillion plan, but a group of senior Republicans in the Senate had opened negotiations about trying to meet in the middle. Ricchetti and other Biden aides had embraced the Republican overture, and Klain had put some work into reopening a bipartisan line of communication.

In Klain's case, that meant doing some cleanup after his role enacting the American Rescue Plan.

The chief of staff had been an unapologetic proponent of passing the rescue package on a party-line vote. He had shared his view on social media, retweeting columns that critiqued talks with Republicans as a waste of time and promoting an interview in which Schumer called it a "mistake" to negotiate with Susan Collins. The Maine senator had taken it personally, and she told Klain as much in a late March phone call.

Klain was quick to express regret, but Collins chided him on other matters, too. She had been the only Republican to vote for one of Biden's most contentious nominees, the low-profile health secretary Xavier Becerra, and she never got a single call of thanks.

If Biden wanted to work with Republicans, she suggested, perhaps his aides should act like it.

By the time the New Democrats visited the White House, Biden's staff was indeed acting like they were interested in dealing with the GOP. Earlier that week, there had been glimmers of progress on an infrastructure deal. A gang of Democratic and Republican senators was meeting the leaders of the House Problem Solvers Caucus, the New Jersey Democrat Josh Gottheimer and the Pennsylvania Republican Brian Fitzpatrick. The most committed deal-makers in the group hoped they could hammer out an agreement to spend about $800 billion on infrastructure.

But on April 22, the day after Klain met with the New Democrats, Senate Republicans made a formal offer to the White House that fell far short of that figure. They released an infrastructure proposal that totaled just $568 billion, barely a quarter of what Biden had proposed.

To people in both parties who wanted a deal, this looked like the rescue-plan talks all over again: a lowball offer that would anger congressional Democrats and make it easy for Biden to walk away.

As Biden's administration approached its one-hundred-day mark, the economy and the coronavirus case numbers both seemed headed in the right direction. Biden was considerably more popular than his predecessor, but there was no sign yet that his policies were attracting new support. In a poll released several days before his hundredth day, the *Washington Post* and ABC News found 52 percent of the country approved of his performance so far. It was an illustration of how polarized the country was that the opposition to Biden was already so cemented in place that he had not enjoyed the honeymoon in popular opinion afforded nearly every previous president except his immediate predecessor. Very few voters were up for grabs.

In private, Klain said the poll was somewhat disappointing, but he hoped the numbers would move with time. Perhaps, the chief of staff suggested, the public just needed more time to see the results of the administration's work.

Before his address to a joint session of Congress on April 28, Biden announced another multitrillion-dollar spending package to go along with the massive infrastructure proposal he had unveiled at the start of the month. This one, branded the American Family Plan, represented a massive expansion of American social-welfare programs, including universal pre-kindergarten, free community college, and a permanent extension of the child tax credits contained in the rescue plan.

It was a set of proposals that could only pass on a party-line vote, and even that seemed like a stretch. Republicans would not back Biden's plans, and the centrist wing of the president's party was giving every signal that he could not yet count on their support.

Yet in a meeting with news anchors hours before his address on the Hill, Biden said he had not given up on bipartisanship. By his own reckoning, he had already shown an unusual capacity for bringing together fractious political partners.

"I mean, we talk about, you know, can you unite the parties?" Biden told the group. "Well, I united the Democratic Party and no one thought it could happen, and pretty damn quickly."

* * *

As April turned to May, Joe Biden was still trying to find Republican support for his agenda. Despite their early disappointments with the GOP, Biden and his staff were still meeting on infrastructure with a group of old-guard Senate Republicans—seasoned legislators like Roy Blunt, Shelley Moore Capito of West Virginia, and Roger Wicker of Mississippi.

In one meeting, Biden showed just how determined he was to strike a deal during an unusually tense exchange with his vice president.

On May 13, the president hosted six Republicans in the Oval Office with Kamala Harris at his side. The group had not yet given Biden an acceptable counteroffer on infrastructure, and Biden was pressing them to support $1 trillion in new infrastructure spending. The group was resisting and pleading with Biden not to undo the corporate tax cuts they passed in 2017.

Harris thought there was something missing from the conversation and she spoke up to say so. What about the rest of the investments the administration wanted in infrastructure? In April alone, the White House had laid out proposals to spend more than $4 trillion on a combination of hard infrastructure and what it called human infrastructure—the social benefits and family-support programs so dear to Democrats.

Harris wanted the latter category of spending to be part of the conversation, and she began to make the case for a larger package than the one Republicans seemed to have in mind.

Biden dismissed her comment immediately.

That's all fine but these guys aren't going for that, the president said, according to two people present for the exchange.

It was such a terse response that even the Republican senators were taken aback. Biden wasn't wrong—they would never vote for the American Family Plan—but none of them had previously seen him shut down his vice president like that.

Biden was usually scrupulously respectful of his running mate. The two enjoyed a friendly if not close relationship, and Biden had been serious about keeping his campaign-trail promise to make Harris the last person in the room on major decisions. In April, Harris had told CNN that she had been the last person Biden consulted before finalizing his decision to withdraw from Afghanistan.

But beneath the two running mates' rapport, there was a deepening tension in the administration about Harris's political role and her place in Biden's insular operation.

Biden had chosen her as his running mate for tactical reasons: to help him win an election and bridge the gap to a new and more diverse cohort of voters. But Biden had also held up Harris to the country as a picture of the political future and vowed that she would be one of the most influential people in his White House.

That promise represented another test for the president and his administration: Could Biden show the country that there was a genuinely powerful place for the history-making figure at his side, or would Harris be relegated to a limited and largely symbolic role?

The question had been on Harris's mind from the start, even before the 2020 campaign was over. In a conversation before the election with Mary Kay Henry, the president of the SEIU (Service Employees International Union) and one of the most important women in the labor movement, Harris said she was determined to be known for more than just breaking identity-based barriers. She was proud to be the first woman of color nominated for vice president by a major party. But with Henry, a pathbreaking figure in her own right, Harris was thinking beyond that.

Harris said she wanted to get big things done, Henry recalls.

"She doesn't want the history-making aspect of her occupying certain seats to eclipse the job she does," Henry says.

During the campaign, Harris had resisted the apparent efforts of Biden's senior staff to contain her and stage-manage her. The Biden campaign had named a team of aides to manage Harris even before announcing her as the pick, in part to keep the vice-presidential candidate on a tight political leash.

But Harris was not accustomed to letting other people choose her staff for her. She had not gotten along with Karine Jean-Pierre, the forty-three-year-old aide designated by Biden's team as her chief of staff on the campaign, and almost immediately sidelined her. (After Election Day, Jean-Pierre went to work in the West Wing as Biden's deputy press secretary.)

Like many politicians, Harris would often pass along advice she got from her own outside advisers and donors, on matters from strategy to personnel, to the Biden team, a habit that grated on Biden's close-knit crew.

She lobbied the Biden team to bring in more Black senior advisers, urging them to hire the high-profile pollster Cornell Belcher and Karen Finney, a communications strategist with extensive experience on presidential races. Campaign officials passed on both suggestions, with some privately expressing annoyance that Harris seemed to be overlooking the sizable number of African American staffers on the campaign who were not as well-known as Belcher and Finney.

After the election, Harris was determined to recruit a formidable chief aide to run her operation. She told one political ally during the transition: I want my own Ron Klain.

She had found a forceful deputy in Tina Flournoy, a former top aide to Bill Clinton. Eight years Harris's senior, Flournoy was part of a tightly bonded network of Black women of her generation who had become an influential presence in Washington. As Harris's chief of staff, Flournoy would become something of a bridge between a set of important outside advisers to Harris— women like Donna Brazile, the former Democratic Party chair, and the veteran Democratic operative Minyon Moore—and Biden's predominantly white advisers who knew Flournoy better than they knew the vice president.

Yet as Biden and Harris were taking office, there was still no policy portfolio for her vice presidency, and it was not clear that Harris had one in mind for herself. In early December, the two running mates sat for a joint interview with the CNN anchor Jake Tapper. When Tapper asked Harris whether she would have ownership of any particular issues, the way Biden did with the 2009 stimulus, the president-elect interjected.

His running mate, Biden said vaguely, would deal with "whatever the urgent need is at the moment." Harris did not elaborate on her boss's foggy comment.

In the absence of a substantive assignment, Harris appeared to some Biden aides to fixate on perceived slights. And Flournoy found herself running damage-control errands that had little to do with important functions of state.

The first flash point of 2021 came the weekend after the mob attack on the Capitol, when an upcoming *Vogue* cover featuring Harris leaked on social media. The picture the publication had selected from a photo shoot with Harris showed her standing before a pink-and-green backdrop, clasping her hands and looking at the camera with a somewhat uncertain expression. It was an approachable but less than grand depiction of the incoming vice president.

Harris was wounded. She felt belittled by the magazine, asking aides: Would *Vogue* depict another world leader this way?

Four days after the January 6 riot, Harris's spokespeople were deployed to brief reporters about what they were treating as an act of perfidy by Anna Wintour, *Vogue*'s editor in chief. They had been expecting another photo, featuring a gold and regal-looking background and showing Harris in a confident, arms-crossed pose. The story of the backlash made the jump from Twitter to the *Today* show.

Symone Sanders, the strategist, still new to Harris's team, reached Wintour by phone to communicate the displeasure of the vice president–elect. The magazine editor protested that she had personally selected that image for the cover because she believed it made Harris appear "relatable."

Flournoy was caught off guard by the anger in Harris's circle and reached out to a senior Biden campaign official to ask what she should do.

The inauguration was less than two weeks away, Washington looked like a military encampment, and the House was racing toward impeaching Donald Trump. The Biden adviser told Flournoy that this was not the time to be going to war with *Vogue* over a comparatively trivial aesthetic issue.

Tina, the adviser said, these are first-world problems.

The exchange was the start of recurring tensions between the vice president and the West Wing.

The Harris team's initial attempt to claim a policy portfolio for her ran into skepticism in the White House, further stoking hard feelings between the vice president and some of Biden's closest aides. Hoping to carve out an international portfolio for Harris, her staff floated the possibility of the vice president overseeing relations with the Nordic countries—a low-risk diplomatic assignment that might have helped Harris get adjusted to the international stage in welcoming venues like Oslo and Copenhagen. White House aides rejected the idea and privately mocked it. More irritating to Biden aides was when they learned the vice president wanted to plan a major speech to outline her view of foreign policy.

Biden aides vetoed the idea. Why should a vice president have their own independently articulated view of global affairs?

Harris played only a minor part in the development of the American Rescue Plan. Though she'd served in the Senate with Manchin—unlike Biden—Harris had little relationship with him, and after her foray into West Virginia television she played no role in trying to secure his decisive vote. She had built few close relationships in Congress; like Barack Obama before her, she was off and running for president just two years after entering the body. Harris had not designed her Senate career the way other lawmakers did, carefully building friendships with an eye toward eventually becoming a committee chair or caucus leader.

Even to the new generation of progressive lawmakers, Harris was someone they mostly knew from afar. Jamaal Bowman, the New York progressive, had only seen the vice president on television when he arrived in Washington. Then he spent time with Harris at the White House and at a Congressional Black Caucus reception she held poolside at her residence.

"When you see her in person, she's incredibly impressive," says Bowman, lamenting that her engaging persona did not come through on camera.

At the White House, though, visitors from the Hill saw scant evidence that the vice president was actually shaping the administration's thinking. Her contact with lawmakers was mostly a matter of formalities: a thank-you call, for example, to Jim McGovern, the chairman of the House Rules Committee, for moving the legislation so speedily. Other calls, including with her former Senate colleagues, were heavy on small talk, with Harris asking about family but speaking little about policy or political strategy.

Larry Hogan, the Republican governor of Maryland, came away perplexed after a meeting with Biden and Harris about the relief package. Biden had been typically expressive in the meeting, buttering up Hogan and several other governors with talk of wanting to work together. The vice president's role, Hogan says, was "very strange."

"Harris did not say a word," he recalls, speculating that perhaps Harris was "just being deferential to the president—didn't want to step on him."

Harris was still figuring out what Biden wanted from her, and what she could do to develop real influence in his administration. In some ways, her challenges were distinctive and highly sensitive: Harris was the first woman and the first Black person to serve as vice president, and she was looking for a place of influence in a White House led by an elderly white man whose closest advisers were mainly white, male, and far closer to the president on a personal level than she was.

But the vice presidency was also a fundamentally inchoate job, one that had little actual power or relevance to day-to-day governing. For most of American history, it had been a largely ceremonial and often-mocked job. The string of more influential vice presidents around the turn of the century— Al Gore, Dick Cheney, and Biden himself—had been a departure from the historical norm. Harris was up against structural problems that went beyond personality conflicts with the West Wing.

She reached out to Gore for advice and spoke with Walter Mondale before his death in April, seeking counsel from the Minnesotan who as Jimmy Carter's running mate made the first great attempt to redefine the vice presidency as a governing role. She spoke, too, with former presidents—Obama, of course, but also with Bill Clinton.

And she began testing what she could do to shape the administration's agenda. If Harris had played a muted role on the rescue plan, she was more vocal internally on another subject: Black maternal health. As a senator, she had joined a group of lawmakers pushing for federal funding to address the alarmingly high rate of maternal death among Black women. Harris had lobbied other Democratic senators to sign on to a package of maternal-health legislation and made it an issue in her presidential primary campaign before Biden took up some of the same policy promises in the general election.

Lauren Underwood, the Illinois Democrat who worked with Harris on the so-called "Momnibus" measures in Congress, says it was clear from the start that the Biden administration was serious about helping vulnerable Black mothers. Underwood says she knew who to credit for that.

"I think that is 100 percent a function of Kamala Harris being the vice president," Underwood says, adding of Harris, "I think she's exceptional."

While Harris was determined not to be defined chiefly by her history-making identity, her race and gender had made her an especially meaningful leader for millions of Democratic voters. That was vividly apparent in the middle of March, after the massacre in Atlanta, when Biden and Harris flew down to meet with Asian American leaders. For a community that had faced a surge in hate crimes during the pandemic, it was a crucial sign of concern from the White House.

Biden began the meeting by telling the group that he was there to listen to their needs. Neither he nor the vice president said anything especially distinctive, but Harris's presence meant something important to the distressed people she was visiting. When she told them that it was up to them to be champions for "the community," the words sounded different than they might have coming from a previous vice president, like Mike Pence—or Joe Biden. It was Bee Nguyen, a state representative of Vietnamese descent, who said as much to Harris: It was comforting, she told the vice president, that Harris herself was an Asian American woman who grew up in an immigrant family.

Looking back on the event, Nguyen recalls feeling that it was important that the vice president "would understand the intersections of misogyny and sexism and xenophobia" at work in the attack.

When Biden finally gave Harris a new assignment at the end of March, it was not one she welcomed. Amid a surge in unlawful crossings at the country's Southern border, Biden tasked her with outreach to the three Central American countries where a huge share of migrants originated: Honduras, Guatemala, and El Salvador. Harris had no deep grounding in Latin America policy, but the so-called Northern Triangle had been one of Biden's assignments as Obama's vice president and now he was passing it on to her.

It was a politically undesirable task and Harris's staff knew it. Republicans had been battering the administration over the border situation, and even some Texas Democrats were openly critical of the president's team.

Harris was resigned to the assignment, but she and her team wanted to make sure her role was depicted in the narrowest possible way. She would take on the Northern Triangle, traveling to Central America and negotiating with governments there, but under no circumstances did she want to be branded Biden's "border czar."

Harris did not hesitate to chide Biden for characterizing her assignment in those terms.

When the two of them met in mid-April with leaders of the Congressional Black Caucus, Biden poured out praise for Harris, crediting her in particular for her passionate advocacy for Black maternal health. But the president also made the mistake of saying that he had given Harris the important assignment of handling immigration. Harris, he said, was going to do "a hell of a job."

The vice president corrected him at once.

Excuse me, she said, it's the Northern Triangle—not immigration.

Harris's concern about being depicted as Biden's border cop proved well founded. She came under immediate pressure to visit the border and struggled with media questions about when she would do so. On a trip to Guatemala, the NBC anchor Lester Holt interviewed Harris and pointed out that she had not yet visited the border.

"And I haven't been to Europe," Harris replied with a strained laugh.

The exchange dominated American coverage of her visit to Central America. To Biden's staff it was a strange and disappointing turn for the vice president. Holt's question had been entirely foreseeable, and yet Harris had seemed totally thrown. Had her staff failed to prepare her, or was the vice president just a very uneven performer?

The political fallout came in another form, too. Harris had carried a tough message on her trip to Central America, and at a press conference in Guatemala she addressed herself directly to potential migrants with a three-word message: "Do not come."

Harris had also acknowledged that many migrants were fleeing brutal violence and extreme poverty, but some leaders on the left had bristled at what they saw as a harsh admonition. Alexandria Ocasio-Cortez voiced her dismay, calling Harris's comments "disappointing" and arguing that migrants were legitimately fleeing instability inflicted on them in part by the United States.

It was a bruising hit from a wing of the party that Harris had courted on and off for years, and it enraged White House aides who saw it as a cheap shot at the whole administration by way of a convenient target. Cedric Richmond found it "despicable," and in an interview the former chairman of the Congressional Black Caucus questioned Ocasio-Cortez's motives.

"AOC's hit on Kamala was despicable," Richmond says. "I don't know if it's ambition. I don't know if it's intention. I don't know if it's clickbait. But what it did for me is show a clear misunderstanding of what's going on in the world."

After all, Richmond says, Harris "only said what Biden had already said."

Harris was unsettled after the Central America trip and Klain knew it. The chief of staff approached her after she returned to Washington and reminded her she was hardly the first vice president to endure tough coverage. It was the nature of the job, he said, and it had not stopped several of her predecessors like George H. W. Bush and, yes, Joe Biden, from ultimately attaining the presidency.

Klain was not entirely soothing, however. He also shared with Harris a candid view of political reality. Not every Democrat loved Joe Biden, he said, but people across the party saw their own success as closely intertwined with the success of the president.

Democrats, Klain explained, did not feel that way about the vice president.

Within weeks of Harris's trip, stories began popping up about dysfunction in the vice president's office. *Politico* reported that several aides had already quietly quit the Harris team and that some on the inside were blaming Flournoy for the internal friction. Some stories faulted Flournoy for hiccups in the operation, but the truth was that Biden's team regarded Harris's chief of staff as an indispensable steadying influence.

Kate Bedingfield, Biden's communications director, had grown weary of fielding questions about Harris's team and whether the White House was mismanaging her role in the vice presidency. In private, Bedingfield had taken to noting that the vice presidency was not the first time in Harris's political career that she had fallen short of sky-high expectations: Her Senate office had been messy and her presidential campaign had been a fiasco.

Perhaps, she suggested, the problem was not the vice president's staff.

Bedingfield was not the only Biden adviser whose patience was tested. West Wing aides had been annoyed for months about having to tend to Harris and what they saw as gaps in her operation, some of which generated bitter gripes from congressional Democrats. When Klain met in April with the New

Democrats, one lawmaker, Kathy Manning, had complained about being left out of parts of Harris's recent visit to her North Carolina district. Klain had not concealed his displeasure.

"That makes me want to vomit," he said, according to one person's account of the meeting.

Remarkably, comments like that had stayed private at the time. It was only after Harris's trip to Central America that a trickle of leaks began to accelerate.

No one was more frustrated by the leaks than Joe Biden. The president had known many of Harris's shortcomings when he chose her to be his running mate, but he was defensive of her and irritated by the unsightly drama spilling into view.

Calling his senior staff into the Oval Office, Biden gave them a warning.

If he found that any of them was stirring up negative stories about the vice president, Biden said, they would quickly be former staff.

*   *   *

By early June, Biden had given Harris another assignment that was no less difficult than the Northern Triangle but more central to the Democratic Party's agenda: voting rights.

Harris had asked Biden to give her a piece of that critical issue and the president had agreed. The vice president's office began convening meetings with civil rights leaders and state-level Democrats who were battling a wave of Republican legislation tightening voting laws in order to placate millions of Trump voters firmly and wrongly convinced that there had been election tampering in 2020.

House Democrats had passed a sprawling election-reform bill, known as the For the People Act or H.R. 1, that overhauled everything from voter-registration and early-voting laws to campaign finance regulation and the redrawing of congressional districts. But it had stalled in the Senate, where it did not even have support from all fifty Democrats.

Democratic congressional leaders had treated the bill as a kind of Holy Grail, a legislative prize-among-prizes that would keep elections safe for a generation. In an interview after her chamber passed H.R. 1, Nancy Pelosi said the democracy-reform bill was so important that the Senate should modify its voting rules to get it done, either by abolishing the filibuster or carving out an exception for voting-rights bills.

If the measure did not pass, then Pelosi said she believed American democracy was all but doomed and lawmakers might as well "go to the beach and forget the whole thing."

Some party officials acknowledged privately that H.R. 1 had originally been crafted as a so-called "message bill"—legislation aimed at fomenting a desirable debate on policy, casting Democrats as champions of clean government and forcing Republicans to vote against popular reform policies. It was not a piece of legislation that ever had a chance of clearing a fifty-fifty Senate as long as the filibuster was in place. But Democrats believed some new voting legislation was of vital importance, and they hoped some essential components of the bill—such as a ban on congressional gerrymandering and protections for mail-in voting—could pass in some form.

Pelosi was hardly the only leader in her party who believed the integrity of democracy itself was at stake. As the year went on, she grew frustrated that the White House was not doing more to lobby for action on the For the People Act.

In an Oval Office meeting, the speaker trashed Biden's adviser Anita Dunn—who was not present in the session—for questioning just how urgent the legislation really was. When Klain spoke up to defend his colleague, Pelosi questioned his commitment to the bill, too.

If Pelosi was incensed, Biden's advisers were equally annoyed at her attachment to the catch-all bill, especially some of the proposed campaign finance restrictions that they feared would actually hinder Democrats more than Republicans. Biden himself was somewhat ambivalent about the measure. The president's main concern was not gerrymandering or campaign finance reform but election subversion by foreign enemies or homegrown saboteurs. Pelosi's cherished bill did nothing to address that threat.

Yet by the late spring there had been no further movement on the bill or on any of the other Democratic priorities that could not necessarily be enacted through the budget-reconciliation process. The obstacles in the Senate were the same as ever: Republicans were not interested in helping Democrats overcome the filibuster, and Democrats did not have the votes to abolish the filibuster and make the Senate a majority-rule institution.

At the end of April, Chuck Schumer found himself confronted by a group of donors who wanted to know what the problem was. If Democrats really believed the bill could save democracy, why was it frozen in the Senate? Schumer pleaded for time. He had two main goals at the moment, he said, and they were advancing infrastructure legislation and passing the For the People Act.

Schumer did not quite say so, but the hope that had taken hold among Democratic leaders in Congress and the White House was that by doing the first of those they would unlock a path to doing the second.

Perhaps if Manchin and Sinema and the other Senate centrists felt that they had stood up for bipartisanship with an infrastructure deal, they could be persuaded to push through other legislation on a party-line basis and maybe even to abolish or weaken the filibuster.

But an infrastructure deal remained elusive, and Democratic frustration was mounting. Progressives in the House were starting to lash out, and with some justification. They had been promised a transformational agenda if they got on board with Biden, not a pandemic-relief bill and a bunch of excuses about Senate procedure.

In the middle of May, there had been friction between Pelosi and Mondaire Jones, the young New York progressive, in a meeting of the House Democratic leadership. When the subject of the Capitol Police came up, Jones voiced sharp skepticism of the force. Repeating a story he also told publicly, Jones said his chief of staff had noticed a copy of an anti-Semitic tract, *The Protocols of the Elders of Zion*, lying around at a security checkpoint on Capitol Hill. Jones remained convinced that some of the cops were a potential security threat.

In a moment of tension, the eighty-one-year-old Speaker of the House carefully pushed back on the young freshman from Westchester.

The Capitol Police saved their lives, Pelosi responded. It was obvious she did not want to discuss the subject further with her leadership team.

But the issue was not over. Jones was hardly the only lawmaker who worried about the integrity of the Capitol Police, and Black Democrats in particular had long expressed concern about racial bias within the force. Jim Clyburn, the eighty-one-year-old Democratic whip, had been outspoken on the subject for years. In the fall of 2021, a member of the Capitol force would be indicted on charges of obstructing justice for allegedly advising one of the January 6 rioters over social media to delete evidence of their activities that day.

Yet Clyburn and other older Black Democrats recoiled from the confrontational tactics of a younger, more left-wing generation. Indeed, Clyburn's open criticism of defund-the-police activists had so rankled a pair of newly elected progressives, Jamaal Bowman and Cori Bush, that a fourth Black lawmaker, the seventy-four-year-old progressive Barbara Lee, had to step in to mediate a truce between Clyburn and Bush early in 2021.

The activist left had not given up the cause, however.

On May 20, a handful of hard-line progressives decided to make a stand by declining to vote for legislation that included $1.9 billion in funding for the Capitol Police, leaving the measure teetering until it finally passed by a single vote.

It was a clear warning shot to Democratic leaders, and one the centrist wing of the party took as a grim omen of left-wing brinksmanship to come. While the measure was in limbo, Ron Kind of Wisconsin, a moderate Democrat from a pro-Trump district, approached one of his centrist colleagues on the floor and asked a demoralized question: "Why are we here?"

There was also growing Democratic frustration with the White House for less ideological reasons.

Biden and his advisers had talked a big game about promoting their economic-relief and vaccination programs, predicting that a shots-and-checks mantra could help Democrats stave off the defeat a president's party usually suffers in off-year elections. But with Biden's larger agenda slowing down and the president personally enmeshed in negotiations with Republicans, neither he nor Harris had spent nearly as much time as Democrats had hoped barnstorming the country to promote their achievements.

The president's aides had shielded him from the press to the best of their ability, even though Biden himself often seemed eager to engage the reporters who shouted questions at him. He did not hold a formal press conference until March 25 and did not conduct a second one until the end of his first overseas trip in June. By the spring, he had given just two extended television interviews, to CBS's Norah O'Donnell and George Stephanopoulos of ABC News.

Both demonstrated that Biden's staff had good reason to fear his interactions with the press. The president had never been known for his verbal discipline, but age seemed to loosen his tongue further, and his staff had to clarify his answers from each sit-down. With Stephanopoulos, Biden had spoken too freely for comfort on several sensitive topics, calling Vladimir Putin of Russia a "killer" and speculating that his friend Andrew Cuomo, the scandal-plagued governor of New York, could face prosecution for sexual misconduct. (As a result of moments like those, the former Obama adviser David Axelrod liked to joke that Biden's aides suffered from performance anxiety—the president performed, and they got anxious.)

The administration deployed other high-profile officials to go on television or tour the battleground states, from the first lady and the vice president to the transportation secretary, Pete Buttigieg. But in the middle of May one swing-state lawmaker, Stephanie Murphy of Florida, raised concerns about the White House message with the vice president face-to-face.

During a meeting in Harris's office with a group of Asian American Democrats, Murphy told Harris she was dismayed to see how her home-state governor, Ron DeSantis, was holding events that showcased initiatives he could only afford because of money in the American Rescue Plan.

The administration had pivoted away from the rescue plan too quickly, Murphy said. DeSantis should not be able to claim an ounce of credit for legislation the GOP opposed.

While none of them would say so publicly, some of Biden's political advisers had also begun to worry that Democrats were not doing enough to press their advantage on issues related to the pandemic and the economic recovery. Coronavirus cases were still falling, and while there were some worrisome signs of inflation, the overall trajectory of the economy was positive.

But on many days Biden was talking about issues that had fizzled in the Senate, or about infrastructure—an important subject with a dry and generic name.

Concerned that Biden was sacrificing a valuable political opportunity, John Anzalone, the president's chief pollster, urged the White House in May to stop talking about "infrastructure" negotiations and start calling whatever it was they were talking about "the jobs bill."

In a memo addressed directly to Biden at the beginning of June, Anzalone warned that Democratic economic policies were not selling themselves. In focus groups, voters in swing states were starting to bring up inflation as a concern, as well as the enhanced unemployment benefits that some businesses had begun to blame for their difficulties in hiring. The country was starting to worry about crime, too, Anzalone wrote: "Republican leaders are likely to attempt to ratchet up attacks and tie national Democrats to the trend."

Anzalone also noted a striking result from recent polling: Biden was the only national leader voters saw as genuinely interested in reaching across the aisle. That set him apart from his own party's congressional leaders, Schumer and Pelosi, as well as their opposite numbers in the GOP, McConnell and Kevin McCarthy.

But Anzalone said Biden's image as a conciliator was not an unalloyed asset.

"Voters of both parties largely share the view that bipartisan efforts result in the best policy," he wrote. "Still, there are indications that some Democrats are not willing to forgo action in favor of bipartisanship."

Starting in June, though, Biden would get a succession of encouraging election results in off-year primaries. To a White House concerned about divisions in the Democratic Party, it came as a great relief to see Terry McAuliffe, a gregarious centrist in the Joe Biden mold, win a primary election for governor of Virginia. In New York City, too, Democratic voters had chosen a moderate Black ex-cop, Eric Adams, as their nominee for mayor. In both elections, voters had spurned candidates who ran far to the left, including those who had campaigned on shifting money away from the police.

Adams, the Brooklyn borough president, was a charismatic but flawed politician who was facing serious questions about his financial ethics and his general credibility, and had mounted vicious attacks on other Democrats in the race. But Biden took his victory as a sign that his party was still with him. During a July meeting with Adams and several other city officials from around the country, Biden pulled aside the New Yorker to tell him how badly the Democratic Party needed leaders like him.

Adams, he said, was a "perfect match" for the moment—a figure who could talk with clear authority both about reforming the police and fighting crime. That combination, Biden said, was "something we've never had" in this country.

We will need your help in the midterm elections, the president told Adams.

The New Yorker was delighted to promise his assistance: "I'm going to work my ass off," he told Biden.

Less than half a year into his term, Biden could already feel the next campaign coming.

*   *   *

The midterm elections were still more than a year away, but the voting rules and congressional maps that would govern those elections would be set in a matter of months. And Democrats had still not made much progress toward a national election-reform law.

Joe Biden flashed sudden impatience on the subject during a trip to Oklahoma on June 1. The president was visiting Tulsa to commemorate the centennial anniversary of the 1921 massacre carried out by a white mob against the thriving Black neighborhood of Greenwood. It was the first time a sitting president had commemorated one of the ugliest episodes in modern American history. That event, Biden said in Tulsa, "can't be buried" in the country's memory.

In the speech, Biden addressed an onslaught of voting restrictions making their way through red-state legislatures. It was a "truly unprecedented assault on our democracy," Biden said, with the franchise of Black Americans at stake. Veering from the prepared text, the president acknowledged that he frequently heard people on television asking why he couldn't get a voting-rights law done.

The reason, Biden said, was that he "only has a majority of effectively four votes in the House and a tie in the Senate." And, Biden added, there were "two members of the Senate who vote more with my Republican friends."

It was obvious he meant Manchin and Sinema.

The president realized almost immediately that he had made a mistake. While Manchin and Sinema were the least cooperative Senate Democrats, it was not true that they mostly voted with Republicans. Antagonizing them would do nothing to help Biden advance his agenda.

Biden knew he would have to reach out to the senators to smooth things over. He told a senior aide: "I shouldn't have said that."

Cedric Richmond recalls that the White House hoped Manchin and Sinema would take Biden's remarks in the spirit he'd intended: as criticism of his skeptics in the press. Richmond says Biden and his team understood that Manchin, at least, was the best governing partner Democrats could expect from a state as red as West Virginia.

The alternative, Richmond says, "is a Republican and your agenda flat-ass stalls, it is dead in its tracks."

Yet there had already been months of hand-holding and smoothing-over with Manchin and Sinema and Biden did not have much to show for it. "Flat-ass stalled" was an apt prognosis for voting rights and a whole lot else.

Democrats close to Manchin still believed he was open to taking party-line action on voting rights, but he had not abandoned his support for the filibuster. He was in talks with Republicans on what he hoped would become a viable voting-rights compromise, but those efforts seemed doomed to nearly everyone but him.

The amiable West Virginian, always eager to burnish his image as a reasonable dealmaker, conferred with civil rights leaders in early June, telling them that he wanted to get something done—but he wanted any voting bill to be bipartisan. Pointing out that many Republicans would not even meet with civil rights groups, Marc Morial, the head of the National Urban League, asked if Manchin could connect them with his GOP allies.

A follow-up conversation with Republicans turned into a fiasco: Two of the civil rights leaders recall that Susan Collins asked them why she should support a federal election-reform law when the voting process in Maine worked well for her.

"Her statement just indicated what I had always believed—that this is not about our Constitution, this is about their political survival," says Derrick Johnson, the head of the NAACP.

There was seemingly no bipartisan way forward on voting rights, and without a major shift on the filibuster from Manchin and several other Democrats there was no backup path either. Johnson says that by this point his group had identified as many as seven Democratic senators who held Manchin-like positions on the filibuster, even if they were not willing to say so publicly.

If that math was right, it represented a terrible obstacle to most of Biden's remaining agenda.

When Johnson and his allies met with Biden on July 8, they came away uncertain of whether the president even had a theory of how to advance voting rights in Congress. Several civil rights leaders came prepared with tactical suggestions. Sherrilyn Ifill, the head of the NAACP Legal Defense and Educational Fund, proposed attaching voting-rights regulations to federal funding for elections.

Perhaps, she suggested, that could make it possible to include them in a reconciliation-style bill that could pass with just fifty votes.

Al Sharpton pushed Biden on the filibuster, telling the president that if the procedural roadblock remained in place then Democrats would suffer in the midterms.

Biden took notes laboriously, but he and his aides were noncommittal.

He agreed with Sharpton that there should be some kind of change to the filibuster, but did not say what that change should look like. In any event, Biden said, he did not want to make the filibuster the center of political debate.

Though Biden did not say as much himself, the Republicans with whom Biden was negotiating on infrastructure would certainly have been outraged by a sudden White House push to change the Senate rules.

So what did that leave the civil rights groups with, as they departed the White House?

Like so many other White House visitors in 2021, they collected praise from the president about the importance of their electoral constituency. Biden again hailed the role of Black voters in his campaign, telling Melanie Campbell, the head of the National Coalition on Black Civic Participation, that Black women were the reason he occupied the Oval Office.

It was a flattering and sincere sentiment. But flattery would not protect the franchise.

And just two weeks later, at another CNN-hosted town hall meeting, Biden again blurted out something his own base did not want to hear. He admitted he was deeply uneasy about the idea of ending the filibuster. Doing so, he told the network's Don Lemon in Cincinnati, could "throw the entire Congress into chaos and nothing will get done."

* * *

It would only be later, deeper into the summer, that Biden would reveal to a different set of White House visitors his apparent strategy on voting rights. Hosting an array of Asian American advocacy groups on August 5, the president found himself again challenged on the subject of election integrity.

One participant nudged Biden to consider the significance of Asian American voters to his own campaign. No group had improved its turnout numbers more, making a decisive difference in crucial states like Georgia where state-level Republicans had tightened the voting rules for 2022.

The president at first responded with the usual bromides about the electoral importance of his guests. At the mention of sky-high Asian American turnout, Biden cut in: Don't you think I noticed that?

But on the larger issue of his stalled agenda and the fate of voting rights, the president finally said out loud what he and other Democrats had been saying privately for months.

If I had done voting rights first, I would not have been able to get fifty votes for it in the Senate, Biden said. There would have been several Democrats out of reach.

But if we get infrastructure done, Biden said, then we will have the votes we need.

That forecast seemed as much a hope as it was a strategy. There was no hard guarantee even in the dead of summer that passing a bipartisan infrastructure bill would persuade Manchin, Sinema, or anyone else to support new legislation or new Senate rules that they did not already support.

But for Biden and his closest allies on Capitol Hill, it was the best shot left to get anything big done. The president was making an enormous bet that one major bipartisan deal on infrastructure would bring his party into line on a larger agenda that would transform the American social safety net, attack the climate crisis, and reform the rules of democracy.

As the summer wore on, that wager would prove to be an extraordinarily risky one.

* * *

The summer also brought a rare opportunity for Kamala Harris to interact with a woman who had walked the tightrope of world leadership longer and arguably better than just about any other person of her gender: Angela Merkel, the chancellor of Germany then nearing the end of her fourth term in office.

While Harris had made her own errors as a presidential candidate and as vice president, there was no question that she had faced sexism and racism throughout her career in national politics. Amid the legitimate critiques of

Harris there had always been cruel mockery and demonization of a kind male politicians seldom faced, most recently from snickering Fox News and talk-radio personalities who ridiculed her in grotesque language.

Perhaps just as grating to Harris, though, was the criticism that she knew circulated inside the building—from a White House full of people who had taken a negative view of Harris's political instincts and abilities since the Democratic primaries. Some of Harris's advisers believed the president's almost entirely white inner circle did not show the vice president the respect she deserved.

Harris worried that Biden's staff looked down on her; she fixated on real and perceived snubs in ways the West Wing found tedious. At one point she dispatched Flournoy, her top aide, to speak with Anita Dunn about a subject of concern to the vice president.

When Harris walked into a room, the White House staff did not stand up the way they did for Biden, Flournoy told Dunn. The vice president took it as a sign of disrespect.

When Merkel came to Washington for a state dinner in July, Harris wanted to connect with the most powerful woman on the planet, a role that Harris herself might occupy soon enough. At a White House meeting on infrastructure just before Merkel's visit, Harris sought out Phil Murphy, the New Jersey governor and former ambassador to Germany, for advice about interacting with the chancellor.

Murphy enjoyed a warm relationship with Merkel and her husband, and he told Harris that the German stateswoman and her country were desperate to believe that the Trump years had been an ugly but temporary experience for the United States.

Anything you can do to convince her that you and Biden represent the real America might go a long way, Murphy said.

Over breakfast at the Naval Observatory on July 15, Merkel raised that subject with Harris right away.

The chancellor asked: How can Europe be confident that Trump was an aberration?

Harris's answer was measured and vivid. Gesturing to her own arms, the vice president said sometimes people have an illness just beneath the skin. They can keep it under control with the right medicine, but sometimes it breaks out and appears on the surface.

Trump, she said, represented a bubbling-up of a contagion that had been in the American system for a long time. And Harris acknowledged that the underlying illness was likely not gone just because Trump had lost the election.

But lost he had, Harris reminded Merkel. Voters had turned out in immense numbers to reject him. America was ready for a change.

It was a delicate and partial version of reassurance that Harris offered, and an honest one. And Harris soon found that the German leader also had a mixed message of reassurance for her.

Merkel told the vice president she understood Harris's unique place as a woman in American politics and many of the burdens it carried, and spoke in some detail about the obstacles she had faced in her own rise.

If Harris needed advice in the future, Merkel told her, she would be glad to be in touch.

Chapter 11

A Purely Political Exercise

"HELLO, LINDSEY?"

Former President Donald Trump answered his cell phone during an interview for this book, smirking at the authors as he did so. He had ignored Graham's first call but picked up when the senator tried again a few seconds later. Trump did not step away from the two journalists with whom he was meeting. Instead, he put the South Carolina senator on speakerphone so the audience could hear him.

It was mid-April, well after the end of the winter season at Mar-a-Lago. Yet three months after leaving office, the former president was still greeting guests nightly at the buffet line like a winking maître d' who just happened to have recently commanded the world's largest nuclear arsenal.

Trump's main preoccupation, however, was not serving as the majordomo of his Palm Beach club. His chief mission in these days was maintaining his grip on the Republican Party. When Graham called, the former president recognized the chance to demonstrate to his guests that he was still controlling the GOP from his tropical retreat.

"Tell them about the Trump endorsements," he instructed the senator.

Graham, scarcely three months after renouncing his allegiance to Trump on the Senate floor, hopped to it.

"I've never seen it quite like this," Graham said, elaborating: "President

Trump's endorsement is the most consequential endorsement of any politician I've seen in my twenty-something years."

Trump looked delighted but not fully satisfied.

"Most importantly, would you tell them one thing," he nudged Graham. "Can Trump play golf?"

Graham happily expanded his testimonial, sounding like nothing more than an actor in a diet-fad commercial who tells the credulous viewer that he had been skeptical of the glorious product—until he tried it.

"I thought it was all bullshit, too," Graham said of the president's storied golf game. "If you don't believe it, go play with him."

The president took Graham off speakerphone only briefly, when the senator insisted that he had confidential political intelligence to share. As soon as the call concluded, a visibly excited Trump broke Graham's confidence to share the reason for the call. Graham had wanted to tell him that Herschel Walker, the famed football player and longtime friend of Trump, was likely to run for the Senate in Georgia.

Trump had no shortage of friends these days. He may have left office in disgrace, but unlike the last American president to exit under such a cloud—Richard Nixon—he did not suffer the sting of political isolation. By spring, Republican candidates were swarming his club in hopes of securing his support and the Republican National Committee was bowing to his request to hold a fundraising reception there, even paying to use his property.

Few Republican officeholders dared publicly criticize him. The voices that spoke out after January 6, declaring that it was time to move on from Trumpism, had largely gone silent. The scattered handful who continued to denounce Trump were increasingly treated as political lepers by their own party.

The Republican relapse was nearly complete.

From South Florida, Trump was presiding over a political faction that represented a rock-solid minority of the country that he believed would never abandon him. He would not be shunned, like Nixon in his San Clemente exile, because the country had changed in the intervening decades. America was divided in ways that made it impossible even to reach a common judgment against a president who refused to concede defeat at the ballot box and then incited a riot against the Congress.

To many Americans, including much of the Republican Party's old guard, this was hard to comprehend. Every other recent American president had set off on a life defined by some combination of family, philanthropy, and handsome speaking fees. Trump seemed to embody a different political model, one native not to the United States but to all manner of barely stable foreign countries with younger democracies.

Trump's Florida club was the temporary fortress of a strongman plotting his return to power. His gilded Elba was a languid and decadent redoubt, befitting the persona of its primary resident. Even the security seemed unserious: At the entrance, a single private guard asked for the names of visitors and whether there were weapons in the car, waving vehicles through without further inspection. A nearby Secret Service agent looked bored until he flashed his machine gun when a passing cyclist repeatedly bellowed, "Fuck Trump."

The often photographed interior of Mar-a-Lago was a shrine to the man himself, with framed magazine covers of the former president decorating even the men's room. Notices of club regulations doubled as tributes to his wealth and taste: Atop a 1927 Steinway baby grand piano in the club's great room stood a notice reading, "Please, do not place anything on this 1927 Steinway Baby Grand Piano."

The model of Air Force One on a coffee table in the center of the same room was not the only melancholy touch. Trump longed to be the center of attention and missed all the aggrandizing symbolism and ceremony of the presidency. He hungered for any news from the capital now controlled by his political opponents. In an interview with the authors that lasted more than an hour, he returned nearly every answer to his delusion that the election had been stolen from him.

Trump made no secret that he was plotting a return to power and a campaign of retribution against his enemies. He described his Republican critics with all the subtlety and nuance of a howitzer. Liz Cheney and Lisa Murkowski were "horrible people," he said, promising to defeat them both in 2022.

Mitch McConnell, Trump said, was the reason he was not "at the White

House having this conversation." In the early years of his term, Trump said, the Senate Republican leader and the last Republican Speaker of the House, Paul Ryan, had hindered his agenda. "Two real beauties," he called them. After the 2020 election, in his eyes, McConnell had simply failed to fight.

Not content merely to insult McConnell as a legislative leader and political tactician, Trump attacked the Kentucky senator's family in racist language, smearing a woman who had served in his own cabinet for all but the two final weeks of his presidency. Elaine Chao, Trump's Taiwanese American transportation secretary, was not "an innocent babe in the woods," the former president said, seemingly alluding to online conspiracy theories that McConnell's wife was compromised because of her family's shipping business and its commercial ties to China.

"Just ask China—ask China whether or not she is," Trump said.

Thousands of hours of slavish coverage could not spare Fox News from his insults, either. Trump said he had told Rupert Murdoch that the News Corp magnate was making a terrible mistake by not being more loyal. "They became much different as a network and, frankly, much less successful from the standpoint of what they represent," Trump said. "They've lost a lot of people that will never go back."

There was no indication at Mar-a-Lago that Trump was sharpening a set of political arguments or policy promises to fuel his return to the presidency. His worldview was as vague and primal as ever. Mere days after calling for a boycott of Coca-Cola products because of the company's support for voting rights, Trump sipped a Diet Coke that a waitress brought to him unbidden. Despite all his tough rhetoric about China, he was delighted to show off the room where he had served chocolate cake to Xi Jinping, and he appeared unfamiliar with one of the most basic and urgent political questions about the Asian superpower.

Asked whether he believed China was committing genocide in Xinjiang, Trump betrayed no sense that he knew what Xinjiang was or that the Chinese regime had been carrying out a barbaric campaign of ethnic cleansing against Uyghur Muslims there.

"Where?" Trump asked. "I'd rather not say at this moment, but I will let you know, maybe before your book."

The former president was far more voluble in discussing the personalities of foreign leaders, including Queen Elizabeth, whom he pronounced a "spectacular woman." In a private meeting with the British monarch, Trump said, he had quizzed her about all the American presidents she had known and what she thought of them. Her review of every one, Trump said, was the same: "I liked him very much."

In a moment of self-awareness, Trump hypothesized that perhaps Queen Elizabeth had not wanted to say anything that Trump could then blurt out in public.

"It was so genius," he raved.

Trump bragged that it was not only Republican politicians who had crawled back to his side after briefly rejecting him after January 6. One of the rejections that had bothered him the most had come from Bill Belichick, the legendary coach of the New England Patriots who had declined Trump's attempt to grant him the Presidential Medal of Freedom. In the immediate aftermath of the riot, it was just not possible for him to appear with Trump.

Back then, Trump said, Belichick had "chickened out." But get this, Trump confided: The coach had just a week earlier been playing golf at Trump's nearby course. Trump had run into him there on the second-to-last hole.

"He came up to me on the seventeenth," the former commander-in-chief recounted with relish.

Stretching credulity for anyone familiar with Belichick's gruff persona, Trump claimed: "He hugged me and kissed me."

For all his frivolousness and pettiness, there was also an obvious edge of menace to the hotelier-turned-reality-TV-star-turned-president-turned-hotelier. Even by then, his claims to having been cheated out of the election had ceased to shock. His vows of vengeance, too, were already tediously familiar.

But more alarming was his straight-faced rewriting of the events of January 6. The riot, he said, was spurred by "agitators in the crowd." The people responsible for the violence that day, Trump said, were "Antifa agitators and Black Lives Matter agitators."

In practically the same breath, though, Trump all but threatened right-wing violence if future elections did not work out better for him. The next election must "be honestly run."

"I think that people are very angry," Trump said, adding: "I think you're underestimating the anger of the people on the right."

The leaders of the Republican Party had felt the bite of that anger themselves. And in this early phase of Trump's post-presidency, most had opted to accommodate or embrace that anger rather than to fight back against it.

From the end of Trump's impeachment trial until the early summer of 2021, a succession of Republican leaders abandoned, muted, or even reversed their criticism of Trump as it became clear that most of the party's voters remained supportive of him.

Republican governors and state legislators overhauled their election laws in large part to placate voters wrongly convinced by Trump that there had been extensive fraud in 2020. Many of the same governors continued to ridicule and resist public-health measures like mask-wearing and vaccine mandates, mimicking the cavalier attitude toward the coronavirus pandemic that Trump had passed on to millions of his supporters.

In Congress, every single Republican leader save one attempted to minimize their differences with Trump as the months went on. For McConnell, that meant avoiding questions about Trump and averting his gaze from the former president's most outrageous behavior—the very strategies he had used to sustain their awkward partnership for the four years of Trump's term. In the House, Kevin McCarthy hugged Trump with such undisguised enthusiasm that it precipitated a decisive break with his onetime deputy, Liz Cheney, whose refusal to bow to Trump shone an even brighter light on the acquiescence of her colleagues.

And then there was Lindsey Graham.

Ninety-eight days earlier, Graham had been in a safe room in the Hart Building calling the White House counsel to threaten Trump's removal from office. But by the afternoon of April 14, he had reclaimed his role as a steadfast political servant. Graham thrived on attention and the perception of influence, and so far in the Biden era he had accumulated little of either. The new president was not interested in dealing with him—he had not heard from Biden except for their one uncomfortable post-election call—and Graham was not about to be left out in the cold.

When he returned to Trump's side, Graham told his colleagues he was doing it because Senate Republicans still needed a bridge to the former president. He began to use his speaking time at weekly lunches of Senate Republicans to brief his colleagues on Trump's latest thinking, share Trump's latest nicknames for them (the handsome John Thune was "pretty boy"), and to nudge them toward a posture of cooperation with the former president. This go-between role struck some in the Senate as another form of rationalization—similar to the excuses Graham had made for Trump during his time in the White House.

Trump had allowed Graham back into the fold, viewing him as a useful if unreliable ally. He told one Republican strategist that he could only count on Graham's support about 50 percent of the time—but when Graham was with him, Trump said, he was *really* with him.

"We gotta deal with the fact that Donald Trump is the most consequential Republican in the country and play that hand we've been dealt, and try to play it well," Graham insisted in an interview shortly after his phone call to Trump about Herschel Walker.

Out of Trump's earshot, in an interview later that day, Graham joked about the man he was trying almost daily to placate in some form or another. Trump, he said lightly, was always a good conversationalist when it came to his favorite topic: "As long as it's about him, it's a good thing," Graham said.

Attempting to explain his revived relationship with the former president, Graham said he was spending much of his time trying to broker a peace between Trump and McConnell and waving the former president away from his vendettas against other Senate Republicans, like John Thune. With some lawmakers, like Murkowski, Trump was simply implacable, Graham said.

What Graham did not say, and what most of his colleagues tried hard not to acknowledge, was that Trump was so powerful within their party to a great extent because so many Republicans who knew better continued to enable him. Except for a brief period after the Capitol attack, few made any attempt to lead their rank-and-file away from Trump rather than follow them back into his grip.

The re-embrace of Trump left his most prominent Republican critics crest-fallen and in some cases fearful for their safety. Ann Romney was one of those Republicans. She happened to be flying into Palm Beach on that same April day when Trump sat for an interview. Walking off the jet en route to her family's winter home, Romney volunteered how proud her five sons were of their father. But she also said they were unsure of whether they had a place in today's Republican Party.

Trump's dominance, she said, made it uncertain whether any of the boys could run for office as Republicans.

What she did not say was that her family felt at times that it did not even have a place in Palm Beach. According to a family friend, Mitt Romney had taken to wearing hats when he dined out in the wealthy vacation enclave. If he were recognized by Trump supporters there, there was a good chance he would be harassed.

* * *

The Trump forces began circling Liz Cheney again before the end of February.

The Wyoming congresswoman had won a strong vote of confidence from her Republican colleagues on February 3, when they opted to keep her in party leadership, and she had emerged quickly as a biting critic of the Biden administration, particularly on matters of energy production and national security. But exactly three weeks after turning back the revolt against her, Cheney committed the sin of standing beside Kevin McCarthy and speaking out against Donald Trump.

On February 24, at a news conference in the Capitol hosted by the House GOP leadership team, a reporter asked about the upcoming Conservative Political Action Conference, a long-running annual gathering of big names on the right. The reporter inquired: Should Trump be invited?

"Yes, he should," McCarthy replied without hesitation.

Cheney at first seemed to dodge the question.

"That's up to CPAC," she began.

But then she went on. McCarthy fidgeted nervously with papers folded in his hand.

"I've been clear in my views about President Trump and the extent to which, following January 6, I don't believe he should be playing a role in the future of the party or the country," Cheney said.

McCarthy jumped in to end the news conference. "On that high note . . ." he said, prompting laughs. The two left the event in opposite directions. They would never address reporters together again.

Almost always wary of direct confrontation, McCarthy spoke to Cheney in light terms in his office afterward, though his political point was serious.

"You're killing me," he told her.

Cheney held her ground, telling McCarthy no other president in history would even contemplate behaving the way Trump did, and the Republican Party could not tolerate it. McCarthy countered firmly: This is a different Republican Party now.

Away from Cheney, the House minority leader was more openly furious with her, and he told colleagues she had crossed a line by contradicting him and attacking Trump in the same breath. "We're a team," he insisted. "We stay as a team."

Cheney knew she was inviting backlash, and she seemed, at times, ambivalent about it. Speaking with one colleague after the February 24 news conference, Cheney allowed that perhaps she should have cut herself off after saying that CPAC invitations were a matter for CPAC to decide.

Yet her survival in the leadership vote had also emboldened her and inspired a flood of encouragement from sympathetic lawmakers in both parties. The outpouring of support from Democrats was particularly startling: Cheney could scarcely walk from the Lindy Boggs Room, a favorite gathering spot for female lawmakers near the Capitol Rotunda, to the House floor without a Democrat telling her how much they admired her. If the new respect from liberals was strange, Cheney still appreciated it.

And it wasn't just her House colleagues behaving that way. President Biden conveyed much the same sentiments to Cheney in a phone call and even conveyed his admiration to her father. In the late winter, telephoning the eighty-year-old Dick Cheney, his predecessor in the vice presidency, Biden told him that he was not surprised to see the man's daughter standing on principle.

After all, Biden told him, she's a Cheney.

Cheney's commitment to principle was less welcome in the House Republican Conference.

A few days later at CPAC, one of her ambitious colleagues attacked her from the stage. Jim Banks, an Indiana conservative who first came to Congress with Cheney after the 2016 election, denounced her sharply without saying her name. Hoping to move up in House leadership, Banks abandoned his past support for Cheney and played to the right-wing gallery. "The least popular" people in the House, Banks said, "are the ones who want to erase Donald Trump and Donald Trump supporters from our party."

Seated beside Banks on stage at the event was Kevin McCarthy.

Banks was emblematic of a certain kind of House Republican in those days, reading from the pro-Trump hymnal in public while indicating privately that he had misgivings. Trump used his own CPAC speech to berate the Republicans who had supported his impeachment, ticking through the seventeen names and exhorting the crowd to "get rid of them all." He singled out Cheney for derision, calling her a "warmonger."

Karl Rove, the former George W. Bush adviser, panned the speech in his *Wall Street Journal* column days later, warning that Trump's "divisive, controversial and embittered" message was dangerous to his party.

Reaching out to Rove with a message of appreciation was none other than Jim Banks.

"Many of us still recognize you as a voice of reason," Banks told Rove in a text message that he was certain Trump would not see. Banks, who had recently taken over the Republican Study Committee, a conservative faction in the House GOP, asked Rove for his help and advice elevating the group.

Banks was a particularly energetic practitioner of the politics of Trump appeasement. But he was far from alone. Anthony Gonzalez, the Ohio Republican, recalls that many of his colleagues approached him before the vote to certify the Electoral College results on January 6, confessing that they agreed with his view of the certification debate but felt they could not risk the backlash they might draw from approving Biden's victory. It was the ethos that came to govern the congressional GOP throughout the spring.

"There were a lot of people who said to me privately, 'You know, I wanted to be where you were but, you know, my district won't allow it,'" says Gonzalez. "To which I would always say, 'I don't know if my district is going to allow it for me either, but it's the right thing to do.'"

Even the Republican lawmakers who had voted to impeach Trump did not, for the most part, keep up their criticism of the former president as the season progressed. McCarthy encouraged them to keep their heads down and focus on other matters, and for the most part they obliged.

They did so in part because of the backlash they were confronting at home. Dozens of state and county Republican organizations approved resolutions censuring or scolding the lawmakers who voted for impeachment. Those resolutions carried no actual penalty, and some of them failed to pass, but they nevertheless sent an emphatic message from the worker-bee conservative activists who manned phone banks and knocked on doors every election year.

They were still with Trump.

The two Washington State Republicans who voted to impeach Trump, Jaime Herrera Beutler and Daniel Newhouse, got the message after their state party passed a measure criticizing them. The vote was almost unanimous: 111 votes in favor and two against. Herrera Beutler and Newhouse may have talked about punishing Trump or pressuring him to resign after January 6, but as the year went on they had less and less to say about him.

Liz Cheney still had plenty to say. And Kevin McCarthy would not stand for it.

* * *

For all his increasingly apparent shortcomings, the House minority leader had one great political gift. Kevin McCarthy had an easy time making friendships, or at least the kind of friendships party leaders make in politics, and he enjoyed easy relationships with the scores upon scores of Republican lawmakers who never asked anything particularly complicated of him. He had no deep expertise in policy and no distinctive vision for the party, but he traveled widely to his members' districts, kept in close touch with the ones in tough reelection campaigns and assured them they could count on his support when it mattered.

Liz Cheney had no such gift. While well versed on policy issues and fiercely committed to the cause of ideological conservatism, Cheney had not spent much time developing the buddy-buddy relationships with other Republicans that are important to party leaders. Though she had entered the House as something of a political celebrity on account of her name, Cheney had not spent long weeks barnstorming the country for her colleagues and using her star power to fill the coffers of those in difficult races.

To most members of the House Republican Conference, one of those profiles in leadership was considerably more appealing than the other.

By the spring, McCarthy was working around the clock to keep up with the transient issues that he saw as energizing the party base. It could have been a full-time job, chasing the weekly fixations of Fox News and, by extension, his party's popular constituency.

When the right was furious because some of Dr. Seuss's lesser-known and culturally outmoded books were taken out of circulation, McCarthy recorded a video reading from the children's book *Green Eggs and Ham*. Crusading against the cancel culture outrage du jour took McCarthy to Georgia, when conservatives were attacking Coca-Cola, Delta, and Major League Baseball for criticizing a restrictive voting law crafted by conservative state lawmakers.

It was not exactly high-minded stuff from a man hoping to capture an office once held by Sam Rayburn, the greatest Speaker of the House in the twentieth century. But McCarthy believed it was what his voters wanted—both the ones he needed to turn out by the millions in election years, and the two-hundred-some he needed to keep electing him to House leadership—and he was not without reason to think so.

McCarthy tried to ingratiate himself even with most of the Republicans who had voted for impeachment. When those lawmakers, and others who worried about the GOP's continued affiliation with Trump, complained about McCarthy's role rehabilitating the former president, the minority leader and his top aide, Dan Meyer, tried to mollify them. McCarthy, they argued, was only trying to protect them, ease Trump's wrath and put the party back in power after the next election.

But McCarthy's determined strategy of appeasement sent the most permissive of messages. And the most extreme members of the party chose to interpret that as a license to provoke and inflame, and sometimes to singe McCarthy in the process.

It was the middle of April when *Punchbowl News*, a newly founded outlet covering Congress, reported that a handful of far-right lawmakers were attempting to form an "America First Caucus" to protect what they called "Anglo-Saxon political traditions." The language in planning documents sounded dangerously close to that of a white supremacist group.

McCarthy knew he had to push back, but he did so gingerly. In a tweet, he said that Republicans were "the party of more opportunity for all Americans—not nativist dog whistles." But he never referred to the group or any of its ringleaders by name. After speaking with Marjorie Taylor Greene, one of the lawmakers identified as being at the heart of the project, McCarthy told people that she had been unaware of the plans. Her father had recently died, McCarthy told people, and she said she had not been involved in planning the new group.

It was just one more example of the culture McCarthy had encouraged by not taking a firm stand after January 6 against the extremism in his ranks. He would impose no penalty on Greene for her attacks on the legitimacy of the election or for her incendiary rhetoric around January 6, or for her harassment of other lawmakers or for comparing mask mandates to Nazism and calling people promoting vaccination "medical brown shirts."

By this point, McCarthy was even reversing his past support for a bipartisan commission to investigate the January 6 attack. Now the Republican leader was arguing that any probe into the attack on the Capitol should have a wider scope, also investigating the riots that broke out in a number of cities during the summer of 2020. It was a shift designed to minimize the unique horror of January 6 and shield Trump and his congressional allies from intensive scrutiny.

The one and only lawmaker McCarthy would punish publicly for speaking out of turn in the months after January 6 was Liz Cheney.

The House Republican Conference chair simply would not let up on Donald Trump. On the evening of April 10, addressing a Republican National Committee fundraiser that he had insisted on hosting at Mar-a-Lago, the former president railed against the 2020 vote and some of his party's most prominent leaders. The election results were "bullshit," Trump said, and Mike Pence lacked the courage to block them. As for Mitch McConnell, the ex-president called him "a dumb son of a bitch."

Cheney was already booked to appear the following day on the CBS show *Face the Nation*. She did not hesitate to decry Trump's unhinged tirade.

"The former president is using the same language that he knows provoked violence on January 6," she said.

Her position was irreconcilable with McCarthy's, and the rift between them became intolerable at a conference retreat later that month. Ratifying Florida's status as the capital of the Trump-era Republican Party, the House GOP gathered in Orlando for their spring conference. It was the same city where CPAC had convened two months earlier—an agreeable location for the party because of the sunny weather and the laissez-faire approach to public health favored by the state's governor, Ron DeSantis.

At a news conference during the retreat, McCarthy pointedly declined to call Cheney a good fit for the party leadership and said she was "not being productive" by continuing to criticize the seventy-four-year-old man living 170 or so miles to the southeast.

Cheney, meanwhile, conducted a series of interviews at the retreat, including one in which she directly repudiated McCarthy's latest position on the January 6 commission. She recognized his gambit for what it was—an attempt to downplay his party's culpability in the insurrection—and Cheney would not stand for it.

The events of January 6, Cheney said on April 26, were "unprecedented in our history," and any commission should be directed accordingly.

Her comments once again rankled McCarthy. The discomfort with Cheney had by now spread far beyond the Republican leader and the cohort of conservatives who had tried to depose her the first time around. After the retreat, when a group of Republican lawmakers repaired to Key Biscayne for a fundraiser, the talk among members was almost entirely focused on one matter: what to do about Liz Cheney.

John Katko, an upstate New York Republican, had been among the group that impeached Trump. But he had been one of those in the group that went on to mute himself almost entirely about the former president. Katko was working on bipartisan legislation to forge a January 6 commission, but he made a point of not commenting on Trump's ongoing acts of incitement.

Approaching a Republican official close to McCarthy in Key Biscayne, Katko shared misgivings about Cheney. Every time she talked about Trump, Katko said, it made it harder for him to get reelected.

By May, it was obvious that Cheney would be excommunicated from her leadership post. During a May 4 appearance on Fox News, McCarthy said there was widespread concern in the party about whether Cheney could effectively carry the Republican message, given her views on Donald Trump. He did not address the reality that Trump himself was defining the party's message with a constant barrage of conspiracy theories about the 2020 election. In any event, Cheney knew she was finished.

Unlike the last conference vote she faced, however, she would not put up a fight this time. Cheney preferred martyrdom.

"It was clear where it was headed," Cheney says, "and I made the decision that basically having to be in a position where you can't tell the truth about what has happened, if you want to stay in leadership—that was not a tough choice for me."

Cheney met her fate on May 12. The House Republican Conference was going to gather for a meeting on her leadership role and the outcome was a foregone conclusion.

Before Cheney even got to the Capitol that day, one of her Republican colleagues there gave voice to the reason she had to go, blaming Cheney for diverting attention from their efforts to take on Biden and forcing them instead to grapple with Trump.

"The fact that we're not talking about what's happening in the country, we're talking about an intra-party issue, I think is a disaster," said Jackie Walorski of Indiana, a conservative Republican who voted against certifying the results of the election.

Minutes later, Cheney arrived in the Capitol surrounded by the police detail she had been assigned for her protection after the impeachment vote. She swiftly entered an elevator but paused briefly to make a confident prediction to a reporter.

"The party is going to come back stronger," she said, "and I'm going to help lead the effort to make sure we do."

One of her friends trailing behind her made no attempt to put on a brave face. Tom Cole, the long-serving Oklahoman, complained that the House GOP was mishandling Cheney's ouster. The messy internal fight "could hardly be any worse," he said.

Yet Cole was candid about the difficult situation Cheney had created for her colleagues by continuing to confront Trump.

"She has put a lot of people in a tough spot," he said as he arrived at the labyrinthine Capitol Visitor Center, where the vote was to be held.

Cole had good reason to be dejected on the way in. As the top Republican on the Rules Committee, he had been given the grim task of presiding over the meeting.

It was over in sixteen minutes. Cheney did not insist on a recorded vote of members who were for and against her. Her colleagues removed her swiftly.

A number of House Republicans wanted to take Cheney's place at the top, including the hungry Hoosier Jim Banks. But McCarthy and his lieutenant, Steve Scalise, had arranged the succession in advance. The new conference chair would be Elise Stefanik, who had represented a sprawling district in New York's North Country since 2014, when she became the youngest woman ever elected to the House at that point.

A Harvard-educated former junior aide in the George W. Bush White House, Stefanik had extensive Washington connections and impeccable establishment credentials. She was also fairly bored as a House backbencher and made no secret of her initial distaste for life in Trump's Washington. By 2019, she had all but stopped going to Republican Conference meetings.

That all changed when House Democrats impeached Trump for the first time in 2019 and Stefanik rose to his defense. She became a star on Fox News and in the eyes of the Republican president, and millions of dollars poured into her campaign coffers in small donations from MAGA adherents around the country.

Her associates believed she wanted to vault into a top job in the Trump administration after the election, such as ambassador to the United Nations. Things had worked out differently in November, but Stefanik stayed loyal to Trump after his defeat, opposing the Electoral College certification and fanning Trump's conspiracy theories.

When she announced her desire to replace Cheney, Stefanik faced skepticism from more traditional small-government conservatives. Her voting record was hardly one of uniform conservatism: Stefanik had voted against Trump's signature tax law in 2017 because it would burden New York, and she was part of a group of younger Republicans who wanted the party to develop real policies around climate change. Chip Roy, a conservative hard-liner from Texas, stepped forward to oppose her.

But with support from McCarthy and Scalise—and most of all, Donald Trump—Stefanik won a lopsided victory days after Cheney's ejection. The former Bush Republican immediately hailed Trump as conservative voters' North Star—"the leader that they look to," she called him.

Right after her ouster, Cheney addressed reporters for less than two minutes, vowing to do her all to block Trump from reclaiming the White House. In a matter-of-fact fashion, Cheney said she did not feel betrayed by her colleagues because their actions reflected what the Republican Party had become.

Asked on her way up an escalator to comment on Kevin McCarthy, Cheney did not hold back.

"We're at a moment we need leadership in the party and he's not providing it," she said.

Well, why is that?

"Maybe he doesn't have it in him," she shot back.

With that, Cheney quickened her pace and forced her companions to keep up. One of them was the famed photographer David Hume Kennerly, a family friend, who was tagging along to document the momentous day and, perhaps, capture the start of something new. Awaiting Cheney in her office was the NBC anchor Savannah Guthrie, who was there to record an interview.

Stripped of her position, Cheney no longer had to maintain even the pretense of peace with her own party's leaders. The next phase of her career was under way.

* * *

Many of Cheney's colleagues were glad to have her gone. Some were gleeful about her ejection, while some more traditional Republicans viewed it as an unpleasant but necessary step.

It was deeply troubling, though, to a handful of lawmakers who thought her ouster said more about the party, and about McCarthy's submission to Trump, than it did about anything Cheney herself had done. To these Republicans, McCarthy's halting, indecisive, and ultimately obeisant handling of the situation was one more reason to be concerned about how he might conduct himself as Speaker of the House.

One of the lawmakers most disheartened was among the best-liked members of the chamber, Fred Upton of Michigan. A moderate first elected in Ronald Reagan's second term, Upton was widely regarded as one of the great gentlemen of the House: An heir to the Whirlpool fortune, he concealed his old money well and insisted on being called Fred.

On the afternoon of the Cheney vote, he was grabbing a sandwich by himself at the Subway kiosk near his office in the Rayburn Building. A usually cheerful personality, Upton was far more downcast than usual as he discussed the events of that morning.

One of the ten Republicans who had voted to impeach Trump, he pointed out repeatedly a fact that his colleagues chose to ignore in their scapegoating of Liz Cheney: It was not Cheney, but Trump, who insisted on keeping the party focused on the 2020 election and its shameful aftermath by spreading lies and attacking his critics.

As for McCarthy, Upton believed the Republican leader had made a bad bargain with an untrustworthy partner. During the campaign, Upton recalled, McCarthy would often tell members he had persuaded Trump of one important tactical consideration or another—the need, for instance, to stop trashing absentee voting methods that many Republican-leaning voters relied on—only to have Trump do something in public the very next day to show he had absorbed none of what McCarthy told him.

Trump, Upton said, "doesn't listen to anybody."

McCarthy might learn that the hard way, the Michigander noted. McCarthy's hopes for becoming Speaker would "depend on what Trump wants to do," Upton said. It was not difficult to imagine a scenario where the famously fickle former president kept McCarthy in his pocket through the 2022 campaign and then anointed someone else for the House's top job.

It just so happened that the day Republicans dumped Cheney was also the same day McCarthy made his first visit to the White House. Always eager to be in close proximity to power and fame, McCarthy had been anxious for an invitation, no matter what else he said about Biden in his daily attacks on the president. White House aides had not wanted to invite the House minority leader, but Mitch McConnell had intervened on his younger colleague's behalf. The West Wing, his aides conveyed, had to invite McCarthy for at least one meeting of the so-called big four: the top-ranking Democrat and Republican in each chamber.

The Oval Office discussion was focused on Joe Biden's hopes for an infrastructure bill. The president was deep into talks with a cluster of senior Republican senators about compromise legislation, and McConnell had blessed the negotiations on the Senate side. A few House Republicans were involved through the centrist Problem Solvers Caucus, but McCarthy himself had no role in the process.

Having become minority leader in 2019, the California congressman had only experienced such high-level gatherings during the Trump years. He came away struck by how, in the presence of a more conventional president, McConnell spoke more and Pelosi was far more congenial. It was a gathering of serious people, and McCarthy seemed to want to show that he was one of them.

He addressed reporters after the meeting. Speaking just hours after he and his colleagues had ousted Cheney for disputing Trump's lies about the election, McCarthy acknowledged that she was right on the substance of the 2020 vote.

"I don't think anybody is questioning the legitimacy of the presidential election," he said. "I think that is all over with."

Trump was, of course, questioning the legitimacy of the election on a near-daily basis. In an effort to balance his calculated coddling of the far right with his desire to present himself as a credible government leader, McCarthy simply had to pretend that was not the case.

The minority leader did not initially gloat over Cheney's demise. He had not relished the conflict, and he wanted to move on and put all the unpleasantness behind him. But his circle of advisers was delighted to be rid of someone they saw as a tedious distraction.

That circle included a lobbyist named Jeff Miller.

Miller had accrued clients and clout in Trump's Washington, and he went back a long way with McCarthy—all the way back to Bakersfield, where they had worked together in the office of Bill Thomas, McCarthy's mentor and the former chairman of the House Ways and Means Committee. Some McCarthy aides considered Miller the leader's best friend, and his rival lobbyists marveled at the access he enjoyed, while whispering about the two men blurring the line between business, politics, and friendship.

While Miller was representing companies like Apple, GE, and Pfizer, he attended House GOP meetings meant for elected officials at the Republican Club near Capitol Hill, and he hosted McCarthy's 2020 election-night party at his Washington condo.

The day after Cheney's defenestration, Miller was at one of his lunchtime haunts, Capital Grille, a popular hangout for lawmakers on Pennsylvania Avenue. Seeing two people he recognized at an outdoor table, Miller stopped long enough to give his view of Cheney's demise.

"Fuck that bitch," he said. "It's done."

* * *

Mitch McConnell found the whole Liz Cheney saga confusing.

For the life of him, the top Senate Republican could not understand why Cheney had kept criticizing Trump for months and months. By early May, when it was clear Cheney's ouster was on the way, McConnell told an adviser that the congresswoman had signed her own death warrant. In his mind, she was committing a cardinal sin—relinquishing power.

"When you're in leadership, the last thing you want to be is a liability for your members," said the man who had led Senate Republicans for fourteen years.

His counterparts in the House, he said, were "a mess."

McConnell was genuinely perplexed. Why, he wondered aloud, would Cheney willingly jeopardize her leadership post by continually condemning Trump? "Just ignore him like I do," he said.

The reality of McConnell's approach to Trump was more complicated than that. After pledging to banish Trump from American politics through the impeachment process, McConnell had relented and voted to acquit the former president at trial. He had castigated Trump from the Senate floor, and then, like so many other Trump critics, he had decided to go silent on the subject of the former president.

Or almost silent, anyway.

On February 25, less than two weeks after his jeremiad against the former president, McConnell was pressed in a Fox News interview to say whether he would support Trump in 2024 if he became the party's nominee for a third time. McConnell dodged at first, but when the anchor Bret Baier persisted McConnell gave a definitive answer.

"The nominee of the party? Absolutely," he said.

It was a turn that left anti-Trump Republicans demoralized. Cheney was particularly disappointed, and said so in an interview. To her, McConnell's strategy differed from McCarthy's in the particulars but not in the ultimate effect.

"Where Kevin is like, full-on public embrace, McConnell is: Ignore and hope he goes away. And that just doesn't work," Cheney says.

"McConnell is somebody who normally has really good political instincts," she argues. "He's one of the best, but I think he's completely misjudged the danger of this moment. This is about the Constitution. There is clear right and wrong."

Cheney said as much to McConnell in a private conversation, telling the Senate leader of Trump: "You can't appease him."

In their conversation, McConnell responded that he didn't need any more lectures about Trump. He had expressed his feelings on the subject, he told Cheney, and he was ready to move on.

Though he would continue to call himself a "Cheney admirer," McConnell would not attempt to disguise their disagreements, including in an interview with the authors of this book.

"We have a different approach to dealing with Donald Trump: I think we need to move on," McConnell says. He adds, with an evident note of skepticism about the value of thundering against the former president: "He goes away only when he doesn't have a following."

McConnell seemed to struggle in other ways to grasp the contours of the political moment. Unlike McCarthy, he was not so apt to chase the Fox chyron of the day. While he spoke out occasionally on subjects dear to the right wing—like the *New York Times*' 1619 Project, an account of American history that put slavery and racial inequity at the center of the national narrative—he sometimes seemed visibly ill at ease, particularly when the issues were of a racial nature.

The Senate Republican leader preferred an older and more staid version of political messaging. He and his lieutenants brought a series of outside advisers to the Capitol in the spring and summer of 2021 to share their thoughts on how Republicans could retake power. They were particularly keen on ideas for how Republicans could keep the support of Donald Trump's most enthusiastic voters without constantly embracing the former president.

It was former Senator Phil Gramm of Texas one day, and on another it was Karl Rove. Rove made the case to lawmakers that they should articulate a platform of conservative policies that voters could count on them to pass. If they did not say what they were for, Rove warned, then Trump and his agenda would fill the void. The former Bush adviser reached back into history to note that there had been a similar effort to elevate ideas over personalities in the 1966 midterm election after Republicans lost the 1964 presidential race in a humiliating defeat.

McConnell appreciated the help from Gramm and Rove, but his own intuition was that any success Republicans might have in 2022 would arise from voters' disapproval of how Democrats governed.

As silent as he was on Trump, McConnell was more outspoken on the other most polarizing subject in his party: the campaign to vaccinate all Americans against the coronavirus. As a polio survivor, McConnell was elated when the vaccine was authorized at the end of 2020. He posed for a photo after receiving the shot and used news conferences in Washington and hospital visits in Kentucky to promote inoculation.

By the spring, though, it was evident to him that Republicans were the biggest obstacle to the country reaching herd immunity. By early May, only about two in five people in his home state of Kentucky had received a dose of the vaccine. Poor people and conservative people were less likely to take it, and in McConnell's state those populations were large and heavily overlapping.

Bewildered that his own party was resisting a life-saving drug, McConnell aimed his pleas at the GOP.

"I'm a Republican man and I want to say to everyone, we need to take this vaccine," he said in April, noting that his demographic was lagging. It was the only way to get "back to normal," he said.

Addressing the right's loathing of Dr. Anthony Fauci, the infectious-disease expert Trump had belittled for more than a year, McConnell said that given Fauci's "history and background" he was "the most reliable witness I've seen."

By the summer, as the Delta variant surged, McConnell no longer bothered hiding his anguish.

"I'm perplexed by the reluctance of some to get vaccinated, totally perplexed," he said.

He ought not to have been. Some of his own colleagues were amplifying conspiracy theories about the disease and resisting the vaccine themselves. Steve Scalise, the second-ranking House Republican, waited until July to get vaccinated, by which point the disease was ravaging his home state of Louisiana.

For all his abiding partisanship, McConnell was out of step with his party on this singular issue, and closer in his worldview to the well-educated elites among whom he lived in Louisville and Washington than to the bulk of voters who kept electing him to the Senate.

Among those voters, Trump's dismissive attitude toward the coronavirus had taken root many months before. The president's endless complaints about masking had encouraged an attitude of resentment and disdain toward health officials, and right-wing media had increasingly depicted even basic instructions from public-health agencies as burdensome acts of a liberal nanny state. And Republican leaders around the country were not joining McConnell in challenging those attitudes, but rather tapping into them for their own political benefit.

"Don't Fauci My Florida," was Ron DeSantis's slogan on koozies and T-shirts, even as the Delta variant began tearing through his state. There were few better indications of the Republican Party's insular and angry turn than that a soft-spoken octogenarian physician had become a prime villain in the right-wing imagination.

In the summer of 2021, DeSantis and many other GOP governors were focused on passing laws to block localities from drafting or enforcing safeguards like mask mandates. By the fall, multiple governors would bar businesses in their states from requiring their employees to take the vaccine: Most prominent among this group was Greg Abbott, the governor of Texas, who was facing primary challenges from multiple far-right fringe candidates and seemed desperate to show that no one could outflank him in his contempt for public health.

Republican leaders in state capitals were using the spring and early summer to placate Trump's base in other ways, too. With much of the red-state electorate concluding that the election had been stolen, Republican governors and state legislators enacted new rules and regulations governing the casting and tabulation of ballots in some of the country's biggest states.

Some changes were aimed at eliminating emergency voting options that had been put in place for the pandemic: There would be no more drive-through voting or twenty-four-hour polling places in Texas, two novel procedures used heavily in Democratic-leaning areas in 2020.

But the most important new rules were flagrantly partisan in their intent or effect, and some of them threatened to make it harder for people of color and lower-income voters to participate in elections.

In Florida, where Republicans had long celebrated absentee and postal balloting as handy conveniences, DeSantis and the GOP state legislature limited the use of drop boxes for collecting those ballots and imposed stricter requirements on when and how voters must request mail-in ballots. In Georgia, Republicans also limited the use of drop boxes and absentee ballots, and a GOP-controlled state board was given the power to preempt local election officials on major decisions about election administration.

This legislative blitz, as much as anything Republicans did in the first half of 2021, represented an act of extraordinary fealty to Trump and the voters he gathered under his banner. After all, 2020 had been a surprisingly strong year for Republican candidates not named Trump. The existing election rules across the country had been favorable enough for Republicans to come within just a few seats of winning the House.

But Republican lawmakers did not have the fortitude to tell activists and Fox News viewers that, no, there had been no grand conspiracy that denied Trump victory but otherwise delivered a good year for the GOP.

Even Fox, the first network to call Arizona for Trump in a crippling setback to his election-night propaganda, showed signs of regretting that display of independence. The network had initially planned to air a documentary after Trump's defeat, hosted by the anchor Bret Baier, on how the president lost. Network executives had told Trump-skeptical employees to wait until after the election for the overall tone of coverage to change.

Then Trump began attacking the network, and Fox saw its audience dip as the former president's fans flocked to a pair of rival channels on the far right, Newsmax TV and One America News. Fox got the message. There would be no documentary on Trump's defeat. The politics editor who helped make the Arizona call was yanked from appearing on set and pushed out of the network in January.

By the spring, the network's opinion programming and on-air contributors were again an unbroken parade of Trump enthusiasts. As the cable-news powerhouse spewed forth a torrent of anti-Biden programming, stoking skepticism about vaccines and disseminating wild conspiracy theories about the January 6 attack, the Democratic president assessed Fox as one of the most destructive forces in the United States—and told an associate midway through 2021 that its corporate overlord, the Australian-born News Corp chairman Rupert Murdoch, was even more toxic than that.

Murdoch, Biden said, was "the most dangerous man in the world."

*   *   *

Not every Republican was cavalier about the coronavirus or the so-called Big Lie about the 2020 election, or a host of other, lesser conspiracy theories propagated on the far right. Many were appalled.

Larry Hogan, the Maryland governor, was one of them. Unlike many Republican governors who privately complained about their party's plunge into far-right populism, Hogan had built a reputation for saying so in public. Even still, he seldom said a cross word about his fellow Republican state executives. Governors considered themselves part of a select brotherhood, twice as exclusive as the Senate because there were half as many of them and exponentially more important because they did not spend their lives on markups and floor speeches.

So it was a mark of Hogan's boiling frustration that in an interview for this book he lashed out at DeSantis and other governors who chose to play Trump's game on the pandemic. On conference calls with other governors, Hogan says, he increasingly challenged his colleagues' resistance to public-health mandates, arguing, "This doesn't make any sense." But the party was shifting in the other direction and Hogan could not stop it.

"Mandating that businesses can't—like DeSantis going after the cruise industry, saying you can't require vaccines, when they're trying to get the cruise industry back—is crazy," Hogan says. "Telling school systems, you can't make kids wear masks, you decide in your schools—that's crazy."

The horror of moderate Republicans like Hogan had larger implications for the shape of the party. During the very phase when Hogan was losing his patience with his fellow Republicans over the pandemic, Mitch McConnell was recruiting him to run for the Senate in 2022 against the Democrat Chris Van Hollen. Hogan heard him out but was not enamored with the idea of a sure-to-be-divisive campaign in his deep-blue state, with the only payoff being a seat in what he saw as the world's most boring deliberative body.

But in resisting McConnell's overture, Hogan also made clear that he believed Trump was going to continue shifting the party in an ugly direction with his warlike interventions in primary season. Good people were going to lose primaries, Hogan believed, because Trump would make sure they did.

Hogan was not the only candidate McConnell was wooing for the Senate who had earned Trump's lasting enmity. Another was Doug Ducey, the Arizona governor Trump blamed for not overturning Biden's victory in his state. The former president had continued blasting Ducey well into 2021 for not supporting efforts by far-right state legislators to unearth supposed election fraud in his state.

Trump's attacks on Ducey and fellow Republicans had set the tone for other primaries across the country, and by springtime nearly every major nomination fight had been a contest for Trump's endorsement. Top-level Republican candidates tried to mimic Trump's smashmouth style and echo his views, claiming the election had been rigged and echoing his demand that states audit their returns.

Even the Senate Republicans' political arm, the National Republican Senatorial Committee, was consumed with placating Trump. McConnell had long controlled the committee, but after the 2020 campaign it was taken over by Rick Scott, the wealthy Florida senator with designs on the White House. Scott knew full well how McConnell felt about Trump. But that did not stop him in April from creating a new honor, the Champion for Freedom Award, and traveling to Mar-a-Lago to present a silver bowl to its inaugural recipient, Donald Trump.

In one key race, Trump quickly derailed the Republican Party's favored candidate. Senate Republicans had been delighted when Pat McCrory, the former governor of North Carolina, jumped into the race to fill the seat held by Richard Burr, the former Senate Intelligence Committee chairman who was retiring at the end of his term.

But Trump did not think McCrory was sufficiently loyal to him, so in early June he traveled to the North Carolina GOP convention to back another candidate, Ted Budd, a member of the House who voted against certifying the 2020 election. McCrory vowed to forge on in the primary, but Trump's intervention was a painful setback.

In Georgia, where Trump had just cost his party two Senate seats, he plunged the state party into a savage civil war. In the months after his defeat, David Perdue contemplated running to reclaim a seat in the Senate, but after a round of golf with Trump he decided against it. Trump was still obsessed with Brian Kemp, who would be running for reelection as governor in 2022. Perdue decided he did not want to mount a comeback campaign only to find himself caught between his governor and the former president. Citing personal reasons, he announced in February that he would not be a candidate in 2022.

A few months later, at Trump's urging, Perdue changed his mind—kind of. Perdue decided he would be a candidate in 2022 after all, but rather than running for Senate he would challenge Brian Kemp in the Republican gubernatorial primary. Trump endorsed his campaign right away.

The former president was consumed with resentment of Kemp, and in

April he used an RNC fundraiser at Mar-a-Lago to rail against the governor and make disparaging allusions to the senator Kemp appointed, Kelly Loeffler, who happened to be in the audience with her husband that night.

Some Trump vendettas verged on self-parody in their capricious pettiness. The former president decided at one point in 2021 that he needed to find a way to take retribution against the Republican governor of Alabama, Kay Ivey. The seventy-six-year-old Ivey had not spoken out against Trump or opposed him on matters of policy or strategy. Her sin was more parochial: Trump had wanted to hold a July 4 rally in a park housing the USS *Alabama*, a retired battleship preserved in Mobile, but the commission overseeing the ship had rejected the idea. Trump took it as a personal affront and blamed the governor, telling associates he wanted to see her face a primary in 2022.

There were still some mainline Republicans who held out hope that Trump's lock on the party might be diminishing. McConnell insisted to friends and aides throughout the spring that Trump was "losing altitude," with his popularity fading in ways that did not necessarily show up in opinion polls. Roger Marshall, the freshman senator from Kansas, relayed to his Republican colleagues that he had been keeping track of the number of Trump references voters and activists were making at party events back home; by the summer of 2021, Marshall claimed, the figure had dropped significantly.

Other leaders to the right of center believed otherwise and saw America's conservatives sinking deeper into Trump-inspired anger and paranoia as the year progressed. It was not only a phenomenon discernible in electoral politics: Russell Moore, a former high-ranking official in the Southern Baptist Convention, says that pastors had spent 2020 agonizing over how difficult their jobs had become because their congregants were so radicalized by the former president and the information they consumed on social-media binges.

At first, Moore says, they had hoped the fever would break after the election, or after Trump conceded, or after the meeting of the Electoral College.

"I think people are now starting to realize, with the Trumpism, it's not going to end," Moore says.

An outspoken Trump critic since the 2016 campaign, Moore decided in the spring of 2021 that he could not abide the concessions that he would need to make to stay in his role with the Southern Baptist Convention. In May, he stepped down.

That was a tempting option for beleaguered elected officials, too. As the year went on, a growing number of Republicans decided they had had enough of the high-wire act and chose to bow out of politics altogether.

The first was Rob Portman, the sort of well-credentialed, even-keeled, reliable conservative who was close to McConnell's ideal of a Republican senator. A few days after Biden's swearing-in, Portman blindsided his colleagues by announcing he'd had enough.

"The rewards in politics have changed," he told the conservative writer Stephen F. Hayes. "The days of bipartisanship being viewed as a positive versus a negative have shifted."

McConnell implored the next retiree to stay: He and Graham enlisted other Republicans, from Karl Rove to Trump himself, to lobby Roy Blunt to run for a third term. But Blunt could not be persuaded. After spending much of his adult life in politics, Blunt, who served in the House and Senate leadership, had become deeply disenchanted.

Perched in the office once occupied by his fellow Missourian Harry Truman, Blunt spoke plainly in a July interview about the challenge Republicans like him face with their base. A champion of public-health spending who had pleaded with Missouri voters in McConnell-like terms to get vaccinated, Blunt deplored the way voters were increasingly rewarding the wrong politicians for the wrong behavior.

Blunt noted that in a previous fundraising period, his highly respected friend Tom Cole had raised a modest sum for his reelection campaign while his flame-throwing junior colleague in the House, Marjorie Taylor Greene, had brought in $3.2 million. When that happens, Blunt says, "something is dramatically wrong with the system."

In both Ohio and Missouri, the vacancies quickly gave rise to crowded primary contests full of Republicans desperately seeking Trump's support. The Senate hopefuls from Ohio were so hungry for Trump's support that a number of them submitted to a joint meeting with the former president at Mar-a-Lago that became a sort of political spinoff of *The Apprentice*. One of the leading candidates, Josh Mandel, acknowledged to Republicans in Washington that he was parroting absurd rhetoric in the primary campaign out of a desire to court Trump and his supporters—but that was simply what he believed it would take to win.

In fact, even as he publicly mimicked Trump's incendiary rhetoric, Mandel would privately reach out to McConnell's top lieutenants to alert them each time one of his top rivals, J. D. Vance, criticized Washington Republicans—effectively trying to have it both ways with Trump and the GOP leaders he derided.

In Missouri, a disgraced former governor, Eric Greitens, tried to win over Trump with a highly targeted hiring decision: He enlisted Kimberly Guilfoyle, the conservative media personality dating Donald Trump Jr., to work on his campaign. Trump balked, however, at the idea of backing Greitens, who had been forced to resign as governor after accusations that he had assaulted and threatened blackmail against a woman with whom he was having an affair. Trump said he could never back Greitens—because he resigned.

There were only a few candidates who stepped forward in major races to try running without Trump's blessing. The most formidable candidates from the traditional, center-right Republican establishment largely passed on running for office because for the time being they saw it as a hopeless errand. Bill Haslam, the popular former Tennessee governor who twice declined McConnell's efforts to recruit him for the Senate, said Republican politics had been so warped by the Trump years as to make it thoroughly unappealing for people like him to serve.

"Due to the polarization of Trump and Covid, and maybe those two things are related, it's no fun anymore," Haslam says. "It's just not—I mean, it's not fun to be a governor, it's no fun to be in the Senate."

Trump, he says, had been "the first post-truth candidate," inventing an alternate reality for his voters to live in.

Through the spring, summer, and fall of 2021, they were still living there.

* * *

On May 14, the top Republican on the House Homeland Security Committee, John Katko, and the committee's Democratic chairman, Bennie Thompson, announced they had reached a deal to form a panel that would investigate the attack on the Capitol. There would be ten members, half appointed by Democratic congressional leaders and half by Republicans, and the panel would have subpoena power.

Katko had negotiated the deal with the blessing of Kevin McCarthy. The Republican leader had proposed a bipartisan commission back in January, and while he had gradually shed his enthusiasm for the idea, he could not deny that the Democratic negotiators had accommodated Republican demands regarding the size, scope, and powers of the panel.

But McCarthy's initial reaction to the deal was equivocal, with the minority leader promising only to "look through" the agreement he had authorized Katko to negotiate.

It did not take a mind reader to see where McCarthy was headed. The following week, after Trump issued a public demand that Republicans block the commission, McCarthy came out against his own member's carefully crafted agreement. He issued a murky statement referring nonspecifically to "political misdirections that have marred this process" and complaining that the commission would be solely focused on January 6 and not other political violence, such as the riots of the previous summer.

More galling, still, to Republican supporters of Katko's deal, McCarthy and Scalise actively whipped votes against creating the bipartisan panel of inquiry. They did not even pretend this time that they trusted their members to cast votes of conscience. They were determined to deny the commission the weight and credibility of a bipartisan probe, or at least show Trump that they had done their best toward that end.

The Thompson-Katko deal still easily cleared the House, with thirty-five Republicans voting aye, including all ten who voted to impeach Trump. The roll call of ayes included the stunned and humiliated Katko.

A Syracuse-area lawmaker who had worked for years as a federal prosecutor, Katko was the sort of Northeastern, center-right Republican who once flourished in the House. In more partisan and polarized times, however, his was a dying breed, and McCarthy's reversal on the commission was helping speed it to the grave.

The person in Washington least surprised by McCarthy's betrayal of Katko may have been the president of the United States.

For all his nostalgia yearning for a Washington where ideological opposites could work together, Joe Biden had quickly taken the measure of Kevin McCarthy. It had not taken long for him to assess the grasping Californian and assign him about the same level of regard that Nancy Pelosi did—which is to say, none.

When a friend asked Biden in May if McCarthy was really so craven and so desperate to become Speaker that he'd even torpedo the January 6 panel he once supported, the president answered without hesitation.

"Do not overestimate the motives of the people I have to deal with," Biden said.

* * *

Biden had more respect for the person who killed the commission in the Senate.

Mitch McConnell did not try to hide his motives. He believed a credible, bipartisan commission would prolong the nation's scrutiny of the darkest days of the Trump era and make it harder for Republicans to win back power in 2022. On May 25, McConnell walked out of the Senate Republicans' weekly luncheon and said so before a bank of cameras.

Democrats, he argued, want to "litigate the former president into the future." A commission, he said, would be "a purely political exercise."

Speaking with an author of this book on the same day, McConnell was even more explicit. "Trump is fading," he said. Why would he let Democrats make him and January 6 central to the midterm elections in 2022?

There was more than a dash of wishful thinking and self-justification in McConnell's argument.

If Trump was already a spent force, then McConnell could just, well, move on. He would not have to do the hard work of fulfilling his late-night vow after January 6 to crush Trump's lackeys at the ballot box in 2022.

McConnell's opposition to the commission was a blow to the proposal's chances of winning the sixty votes it needed to clear a filibuster in the Senate. Few lawmakers were more upset than the band of Democratic and Republican senators who still hoped to restore bipartisanship and collegiality to the Capitol. Some of them believed they were nearing a breakthrough in their infrastructure talks with Biden at that very moment.

Susan Collins, the Mainer who had won reelection in 2020 after refusing to endorse Trump, had worked with Democrats to structure the commission in a way that she hoped could pass muster with her more conservative colleagues, and she gave a rosy prognosis to Democrats about the number of votes it could win in the Senate. She told Nancy Pelosi she believed it could still survive a filibuster, perhaps with a few votes to spare.

"They thought they could have thirteen," Pelosi recalls. "Just needed ten."

On May 28, only six Republicans voted to break a filibuster, leaving the Senate short of the votes needed to move the bipartisan deal toward passage. Collins told Pelosi that she thought they could engineer a different result if they kept working for another week and then tried voting again.

Another week slipped to a few more and Collins's kindred spirit on the Democratic side got involved. Manchin had been so optimistic on the morning of January 6, as he went to get the vaccine and forecast a golden age of bipartisanship under the new president who was a moderate veteran of the Senate. Now Manchin was upset by the raw partisanship of his Republican colleagues. He was as desperate as Collins to create a commission and treat the tragic day with the gravity it demanded.

He approached John Thune, the man who a few months earlier had wooed him at dinner about changing parties, and asked him: "Can't you do something?"

But Thune had no good answer for Manchin. "It's Mitch's decision," Thune told him.

Manchin kept working his Republican colleagues to try to come up with a potential compromise. He floated a classic congressional move, putting off something today that can be done tomorrow, and proposed a commission that could begin its work in January of 2023, after the midterm elections that Republicans were so worried about.

He relayed the idea to Pelosi. Though the two had wildly different policy priorities and assessments of the Republican Party, Pelosi and Manchin shared a bond over their Italian Catholic heritage (the name Manchin is an Americanized version of Mancini) and their commitment to old-school Democratic constituencies like mining unions. On June 23, Manchin approached Pelosi at the funeral of John Warner, the former dealmaking and intrigue-loving Virginia senator who died in late May 2021 at the age of ninety-four.

Speaking in the narthex of the National Cathedral, the small anteroom at the entrance to the vaulting sanctuary, Manchin said putting off the commission to 2023 was the best he could do. That was a nonstarter for Pelosi: The investigation was a consuming preoccupation for her, and she also felt political pressure to make sure Republicans face the results of a probe before the midterms.

"Well, you know, I can't wait," Pelosi told him, according to her recollection.

Manchin already understood that. The bipartisan January 6 commission was dead.

* * *

The demise of the commission put an exclamation mark over all the other mounting evidence that January 6 would never be the kind of traumatic national event that could even temporarily jar the country from its ultra-factional politics. There had been no extended period of unity after January 6 as there had been after the September 11, 2001, terror attacks. Nor would there be a 9/11-style commission to investigate an attack on democracy.

The congressional inquiry into January 6 would rise again in another form, however.

Nancy Pelosi was not about to let the attack on her Congress disappear into the past without an honest-to-goodness reckoning for the people who planned, incited, and executed it. She and Bennie Thompson believed they had given Republicans a good deal: a bipartisan commission that would do the work of investigating that lamentable day with balanced membership and extensive input from the House minority.

And Republicans had rejected that deal.

On June 30, the House voted by a margin of 222 to 190 to create a select committee investigating the attack. It would not be an evenly split panel with equal input from Republicans. It would have Republican members, but it would be directed by the Democratic majority. Only two Republicans voted in favor of its creation, Liz Cheney and Adam Kinzinger.

The legislation gave Pelosi the power to name eight lawmakers to the panel and left five slots for Kevin McCarthy, should he choose to fill them. After several weeks of deliberation, McCarthy announced a slate of choices that represented a middle finger to the whole enterprise: Among his selections were Jim Jordan, the far-right Ohioan who was one of Trump's most reliable footmen in the House, and Jim Banks.

He named three other Republicans, too—more evenhanded members that Democrats might have managed to work with. But Pelosi could not tolerate including Jordan and Banks in the committee. On July 21, she called McCarthy and told him she was rejecting those two choices. Reading from a prepared text, Pelosi told him his handling of the committee was beneath the dignity of his office. McCarthy was incensed, telling the Speaker that she was abusing her power.

But he had no power to stop her, so McCarthy announced there would be a full Republican boycott of the committee and pulled back all five of his appointments.

Pelosi understood that there was value to giving the committee at least a patina of bipartisanship, and that it would be better to have even one or two Republicans involved than zero. But it would take a special kind of Republican—one who enjoyed all the freedom of having nothing left to lose—to defy McCarthy and Trump and take a seat on the select committee at the Speaker's invitation.

Pelosi had expressed her admiration of Liz Cheney before, and had approached her at a service for a Capitol Police officer killed in April by an attacker driving a car—a new blow to a badly frayed force. At a reception in the Capitol's Rayburn Room, the Speaker had sought out Cheney with a message of appreciation and praise.

"Thank you so much for your courage," Pelosi had told her then.

The call Pelosi made to Cheney in July was a more momentous act.

Liz Cheney was accompanying her father to a doctor's appointment when Pelosi called. She told Cheney that the committee would hunt down the truth about January 6 and follow the evidence wherever it led. And she wanted Cheney to be part of it.

"Thank you for your patriotism," Pelosi told her.

Cheney accepted her invitation on the spot.

Chapter 12

Amateurs

As Joe Biden stood in the White House driveway just past noon on June 24, he was practically glowing with excitement. With Kyrsten Sinema, the nettlesome Arizona Democrat, to his left and Rob Portman, the sober Ohio Republican, to his right, the president announced a breakthrough in bipartisan negotiations. A group of ten senators in both parties had forged an agreement to spend $1.2 trillion to repair and modernize the nation's tattered infrastructure. After months of negotiations, a deal was in hand.

"This reminds me of the days we used to get an awful lot done up at the United States Congress," Biden crowed. "We had bipartisan deals. Bipartisan deals mean compromise."

The infrastructure deal had emerged from painstaking, late-night talks between an independent-minded group of Republican senators and centrist Democrats in the Senate and the White House. Of the five Republican negotiators, all but one had voted to convict Donald Trump at his impeachment trial earlier in the year. The fifth, Rob Portman, had already announced his plans to retire from the Senate, putting him beyond reach of conservative primary voters who loathed Biden.

Like the president, many of these lawmakers pined for the old days of dealmaking in the Senate. Several of them had attended the funeral of John Warner that very week, and before they went out with Biden to announce the deal, both Susan Collins and Mark Warner invoked the spirit of the late Virginia centrist. Let's get this done, they told Biden.

In meetings with the Senate negotiators, Biden had spoken effusively about the importance of reaching a deal: Collins recalls Biden saying that friends and adversaries across the globe "kept questioning whether America's institutions were still strong and working." He said Emmanuel Macron, the young French president, was among the world leaders who had told Biden that America's leadership role was at risk because of the country's inability to get anything done at home.

Biden dreamed of proving Macron wrong. And for a moment outside the White House, he basked in what he saw as the realization of that dream.

Then political reality reasserted itself in the form of the Speaker of the House.

Nancy Pelosi thought the infrastructure deal was pathetically unambitious. She did not share Biden's sentimental view of bipartisanship as a mode of governing or of the Senate as an institution. Her party was assembling a massive package of social-welfare and climate programs in a reconciliation bill even larger than the American Rescue Plan. The emerging bill was a colossal piece of legislation that would pour money into clean energy and grant the American people robust new benefits ranging from government-backed childcare to dental insurance for the elderly. One version of the package, drafted by Bernie Sanders as the chairman of the Senate Budget Committee, totaled $6 trillion in spending over a decade.

On a personal level, Pelosi also seemed to feel the infrastructure deal was just too small to serve as a capstone achievement in her epic career. She had not held on to the Speakership into her eighties—and held her party together through the grim days of the Trump administration—to fill some potholes.

Pelosi knew, too, that her caucus was not about to curb its ambitions in order to pass an infrastructure deal that reflected Mitt Romney's priorities better than their own. That was not just an assessment based on intuition: Earlier the same month, Pramila Jayapal, the chair of the Congressional Progressive Caucus, had informed Pelosi that her ninety-six-member bloc had taken an internal vote and a strong majority would not vote for an infrastructure bill before the larger reconciliation package was complete.

In a small meeting with the heads of other Democratic factions, Pelosi had asked Jayapal: "You don't trust the president?" The Speaker reminded Jayapal, a third-term lawmaker, that this was her first time serving under a Democratic president. Dealing with Biden was not the same as dealing with Donald Trump.

"Of course I trust the president," Jayapal replied. "But I don't trust my colleagues in the Senate."

Speaking to the press on June 24, shortly before Biden's festive turn in the driveway, Pelosi said the House would not take action on an infrastructure bill until the Senate passed the much larger reconciliation package that was still being negotiated.

"In fact, I use the word 'ain't,'" Pelosi said. "There ain't going to be an infrastructure bill, unless we have the reconciliation bill passed by the United States Senate."

Pelosi issued that public ultimatum without consulting the president.

And in a private interview the following day, on June 25, she seemed pleased about that fact, chuckling softly when asked if she had given Biden a heads-up.

"Oh, no. I just said it."

Biden heard her loud and clear.

Little more than an hour after his appearance with the infrastructure negotiators, Biden struck a new tone in the East Room of the White House. Appearing with prominent members of his own administration involved in the deal, Biden again hailed it as an important breakthrough that would prove to the world "that we can function, deliver and do significant things."

But he added a Pelosi-like caveat: He would only sign the bill if it came to his desk alongside separate social-welfare and climate legislation.

To Biden's Republican interlocutors in the Senate, it was a stunning addendum. They had seen themselves as negotiating a stand-alone bill, one that represented a set of spending priorities on which both parties could reach consensus. Now it sounded like they had been lured into endorsing one appendage of an expansive Democratic agenda.

Steve Ricchetti, the Biden adviser who had led negotiations for the White House, rushed to calm the Republican bloc. Phoning moderates on the Hill, he acknowledged that Biden had blundered.

We're fixing this, he told them.

In a few cases, Ricchetti asked the president to make his own calls of reassurance to senators. Biden spoke for twenty minutes with Portman, explaining to the Ohioan that he planned to issue a statement walking back his comments and inviting Portman to offer edits on the draft via Ricchetti, a fellow Ohioan.

The Republican infrastructure negotiators let Biden off the hook. Senators like Portman and Collins and Romney earnestly wanted a deal, and they were not about to walk away because of a verbal blunder by a president known for making them.

Biden's comments had exposed an authentic political tension that his damage-control efforts could not erase. He had staked his presidency on twin promises to ease the country's partisan warfare and to deliver comprehensive economic and social change. By the end of June, he had devised a pair of legislative vehicles to achieve both goals.

Now Biden had to convince his entire party to support both bills, and he wanted to do it without alienating the Republicans who were willing to lend their backing to the more modest of the two proposals. He attempted to do so by keeping his legislative strategy awkwardly opaque and, for months, never definitively articulating when and in what order he wanted to pass the pieces of his agenda into law. This approach allowed both liberals and moderates to imagine that Biden was, in his heart of hearts, on their side.

It was a statement on the Democratic Party's fractious internal politics that Biden and his advisers believed such deliberate vagueness was necessary to avert sharp conflict between the party's factions. But in the absence of clear direction from the president, Biden's party sank into an anguished, months-long standoff on Capitol Hill.

Combined with grim developments overseas and in the domestic economy, this stalemate badly sapped Biden's political momentum. In the summer of 2021, Biden and the Democratic Party's congressional leaders had to navigate that extraordinarily delicate process amid a darkening national mood and a calamitous sequence of events in Afghanistan that badly damaged the White House's image of studied competence.

At every step, the president would be pulled between his impulse toward seeking consensus and his hunger for titanic achievement—between the centrist wing of his party in which he had spent most of his career, and the left wing that now seemed far more invested in the greatness of President Biden.

*　*　*

If the opening months of Biden's presidency felt like a season of relief from the darkest days of the Trump era, the period from July into the early autumn came as a stark reminder of profound national defects that transcended any one presidency.

The national vaccination campaign slowed due to hesitancy among conservative and lower-income Americans, and the Delta variant of the coronavirus tore through poor communities, especially in red states where Republican governors pandered to vaccine skeptics. With the debate fully politicized, disputes over public health restrictions were leading to screaming matches in retail stores and county government buildings and death threats against local health officials.

The resurgence of the disease led to a slowdown in the country's economic recovery and stoked fears that many consumers might feel the pinch of inflation before they reaped the benefits of new prosperity.

As early as late June, some of Biden's counselors were already contemplating the possibility that Republicans could retake Congress in 2022. When an adviser to Bernie Sanders contacted Ricchetti to warn him that the midterms could get ugly if Biden did not pass his most ambitious domestic policies into law soon, the presidential aide gave a less-than-reassuring response.

You know, Ricchetti said, a lot of people around Biden weathered the

1990s and did battle with Newt Gingrich. We know how to handle a Republican Congress.

He sounded like a man anticipating a divided government.

About six months into his tenure, Biden was starting to wonder if he was approaching the end of the most productive phase of his presidency. During a visit in Delaware with Chris Coons, the state's respected junior senator, Biden wondered aloud whether the reconciliation package would be the last landmark legislation of his term.

Coons was worried about his friend, the president. In Coons's reckoning, Biden's return to electoral politics had been a monumental personal sacrifice.

At age seventy-eight, the president deserved to be playing golf and hanging out with his grandchildren, Coons felt, rather than striving daily to save democracy. The president was deeply involved in raising his grandkids: He was known to put aside his work to take their calls, include them at White House gatherings, and make a point of attending their athletic events or bringing them out golfing when he returned to Delaware. In his brief time as a private citizen after 2016, Biden had directed a large chunk of the money he earned from paid speaking engagements toward funding their college tuitions.

Though none would say so openly, Biden's age was a constant subject of private discussion among Democrats, particularly those who had known him for a long time. Biden's voice remained sharp and authoritative on matters of policy, but his stories were longer and more repetitive. He tired more easily, traveled less, and took longer to recall people's names. The president knew it, too: Catching up with one friend over the summer, Biden briefly drew a blank on the name of one of the new, firebrand House Republicans whom he found so deplorable, and sighed to his guest that recalling such things used to be easier.

During his visit with Biden in Delaware, Coons told the president that he saw great promise in the remaining years of his presidency. Biden, he said, could use the convening power of his office to gather congressional leaders and encourage grand compromises on issues like immigration, gun violence, and labor law. The president could keep creating the space for dealmaking, Coons said, much as he had done with infrastructure.

Biden heard him out. He wanted to believe it was possible.

"I'm holding on to that hope," Biden said.

But the president could not conceal his skepticism. The path to a bipartisan infrastructure bill had been hard enough.

And Biden knew that bill was still a long way from reaching his desk.

* * *

Joe Biden and his aides had resurrected bipartisan talks over infrastructure through willpower and persistence after they had seemed to fall apart altogether in early June. The president's talks with Senate Republicans led by Shelley Moore Capito of West Virginia had stalled so long that they no longer seemed useful. Capito confided to Biden during the extended talks that her Republican colleagues called her "the dreamer" for thinking she could strike a deal. Then, in a phone call on June 8, Capito acknowledged to the president that things were not working out.

"I was worried we were headed to a breakup," she joked gamely, according to a person briefed on the conversation.

Yet as soon as Capito was sidelined, a different set of Senate centrists rushed into the void—including her fellow West Virginian Joe Manchin, who seldom passed up the chance to upstage his Republican colleague. Weeks of furious talks had yielded the package Biden announced on June 24. It was now likely to pass the Senate in a matter of weeks.

Across party lines, the group of negotiators shared a conviction that getting something done on a bipartisan basis was an inherently good thing, even if it left all participants somewhat dissatisfied. Mitt Romney had told his colleagues that he was willing to vote for a good bit of policy he did not like simply for the sake of showing the country the Senate could actually function as the collegial body it was meant to be.

On July 14, Biden met with a bipartisan contingent of mayors who found him luxuriating in the breakthrough. The city executives, including David Holt of Oklahoma City and Nan Whaley of Dayton, Ohio, were ostensibly there to talk with Biden about what the legislation would do for their cities. But in the Oval Office they heard Biden captivated with the bill's secondary purpose: restoring an image of functionality to the American government.

The very same day, Biden attended a lunch of Democratic senators on Capitol Hill and reiterated that point. The Trump years had been a humiliation for the United States in the eyes of the world, Biden said, according to notes from an attendee. The president told the assembled lawmakers that when he attended the G7 summit in the United Kingdom, he had faced painful questions about January 6. The credibility of the American system was on the line.

But Biden conveyed to that group that the infrastructure bill alone would not be enough to redeem American democracy. The country had to master climate change and restore the public's confidence in the fairness of the economy. Republicans, he said, were trying to win the blue-collar voters by campaigning on "culture" and "the prejudice game."

Briefly affecting a southern accent and alluding to his home state's rural element, Biden allowed that Democrats would never win "wacko racists." But he argued there was a real political opportunity for his party if they could pass major legislation to "give working people a break." The infrastructure bill alone would not do that.

Eight days later, with the bill nearing Senate approval, Biden gathered an assortment of business federations for a meeting in the Roosevelt Room. With Cedric Richmond at his right elbow and Steve Ricchetti to his left—a visible display of centrist political muscle—Biden hailed the infrastructure deal as a consensus-based plan for economic growth.

But the president also confided to the assembled business leaders that the politics were complicated. He could not talk about the legislation as a big victory for Democrats, lest he alienate Republicans whose votes he wanted. Nor could he talk about it as a huge win for the GOP, because his side did not want to strengthen Donald Trump's party.

As Biden hinted to Chris Coons, he suspected the infrastructure bill might be the one and only great bipartisan legislation of his presidency. Opposition even to that legislation was already gathering in the House. When Kevin McCarthy met with the Problem Solvers Caucus on July 1, a week after Biden announced the deal, the House Republican leader predicted that the legislation would flop among his members. There would be fewer than ten GOP votes for the bill in the House, McCarthy promised. He was not afraid House Republicans would pay a political price for voting against the popular bipartisan measure.

McCarthy's counterpart in the Senate was handling the moment differently. To Mitch McConnell, long loathed by Democrats for his obstructionism, the infrastructure bill looked like a moment for cooperation. He had assured members of his conference that if they struck a deal he would not stand in its way, but now the Senate leader was thinking of going beyond merely not fighting the legislation. He was thinking of actually voting for it.

McConnell had political motives, beyond any sense of graciousness or assessment of the legislation's merits. He knew well that the most moderate members of the Democratic caucus were intensely invested in the infrastructure deal. If Republicans helped it become law, it would be a validation of the centrists' worldview—proof that the Senate could work through consensus and compromise. By approving the deal, McConnell believed, he could help armor the Senate's rules against liberal reformers who wanted to end the filibuster and free themselves to govern on a party-line basis.

He had said as much in private earlier in the summer, telling a group of GOP donors in June that the bipartisan legislation was a way of defanging restive elements of Biden's party: "There are many, many Democrats in the Senate, and I'll bet the same in the House, that are pulling for these bipartisan negotiations to fail," McConnell said. "So they can say, again, don't waste your time with the Republicans."

If that argument carried the day on the Democratic side, then there might be no stopping the reconciliation package that McConnell feared far more than anything in the infrastructure bill. By the middle of July, he was using stark language to describe his alarm about that developing legislation.

McConnell's view, as he articulated it then: "If they succeed with this massive bill, we won't ever be able to undo it and I think it is a turning point for the country. And this is going to be one big fight."

For McConnell to have even a shot at prevailing in that fight, he needed the most devoted centrists on the Democratic side to hold their ground and maintain their faith in bipartisanship. On August 10, the Senate voted by a margin of sixty-nine to thirty to approve the Infrastructure Investment and Jobs Act. Among the lawmakers voting aye was the senior senator from Kentucky.

Some Republican senators facing reelection in 2022 held back from voting for the infrastructure bill, apparently out of concern that Trump would attack them in their primaries if they supported it. When John Thune, the pragmatic South Dakotan, voted against the measure, McConnell remarked to him drily: Well, I guess you are running for reelection.

It was a triumphant day for Biden, though not an unblemished one. As the Senate delivered a great victory for Biden's agenda, the president got upsetting news from elsewhere: In New York, Andrew Cuomo announced he would step down as governor in the face of detailed sexual-harassment allegations, marking the abrupt demise of a close Biden ally. More ominously for Democrats, Ron Kind, the centrist Democrat from Wisconsin who had grown weary of left-wing grandstanding in the House, announced he would retire at the end of his current and thirteenth term.

If Biden hoped policies like the infrastructure bill would help save Democrats from defeat in 2022, Kind's district—a stretch of western Wisconsin where the lawmaker had endured even as rural whites fled to the GOP—would soon put that proposition to a difficult test. Far from unifying Democrats and handing them a powerful message for the midterms, the infrastructure deal helped trigger a standoff between the left and the middle that would come close to tearing the Democratic Party apart.

* * *

The crunch for Biden's domestic agenda began with a standoff over the rights of tenants and landlords.

At the height of the coronavirus pandemic, the federal government issued a series of temporary bans on evictions, citing a severe risk to public health if tens of thousands of people were turned out of their homes. The latest moratorium was set to expire on July 31, and Biden did not intend to renew it. The Supreme Court had signaled it would look unfavorably on another extension, and White House lawyers did not want to lose in court.

The left revolted. Cori Bush, a former Black Lives Matter activist in St. Louis now serving her first term in the House, held a sit-in on the steps of the Capitol to protest Biden's acquiescence. Equipped with an orange sleeping bag, Bush held a vigil that stretched on for days and drew several colleagues to her side, including Alexandria Ocasio-Cortez.

As progressive activists rallied to Bush's banner, the White House scrambled to placate them. Nancy Pelosi wanted to avoid a full-scale panic on the left, and she said so to the White House, urging them to get new legal advice. She suggested reaching out to Laurence Tribe, the prominent Harvard professor, who had his own theory of how to survive the courts. Badgering reluctant White House aides to take action, Pelosi asked them whether they even cared about the impact of evictions on children.

Biden relented and the Centers for Disease Control issued a new moratorium. But the president made his ambivalence plain, noting that the renewed renter protections would certainly face tough legal challenges.

His fatalistic tone upset liberals further. Biden's language was "not the commentary of someone who is actually trying to help people," said Mondaire Jones, the New York progressive.

The episode put the White House in a sour mood. Biden advisers were annoyed with Pelosi, first for pushing them to issue a moratorium they saw as flawed and then for leaking to the press that she had directed them to Tribe. The White House, after all, was stocked with well-credentialed lawyers, including a chief of staff who had known the Harvard professor for decades. Pelosi's effort to force Biden's hand generated a raw moment of tension between the Speaker and the West Wing.

Ron Klain, however, was angrier with the left. In private, Klain fumed that the administration had laid out a set of political imperatives for the party and the left was helping nothing by lashing out at the White House.

It was not only in the halls of the West Wing where resentment of the left was starting to boil. In the House, lawmakers who had rejoiced at Biden's infrastructure deal were growing exasperated that the bill was stuck in a state of suspended animation while Pelosi awaited a reconciliation deal.

A large group of House moderates and members from vulnerable districts wanted Pelosi to skip a drawn-out standoff with the Senate and pass the bipartisan deal immediately. In the reckoning of these Democrats, average voters did not know what reconciliation was, or who Joe Manchin or Kyrsten Sinema were. But they did know what roads and bridges were, and they would understand components of the bill like funding for rural broadband and electric buses.

"It's an easy win," explains Chrissy Houlahan, the Pennsylvania Democrat who nudged White House aides in the spring to turn toward bipartisanship. "It's an easy thing to tell people about."

These Democrats knew, too, that there was a faction in Biden's White House that agreed with them. Among Biden's aides, there was real disagreement about the next stage of the legislative strategy. Ricchetti, for one, wanted to move the infrastructure bill expeditiously, arguing that it would bolster Biden's popularity and please the centrist Democrats whose support he would need on reconciliation.

Klain saw things differently, as did several other key Biden aides. To them, the infrastructure bill was an important piece of a larger agenda that would prove to the country that this was an administration of action. On a practical level, Klain saw no chance of getting robust support from House liberals on infrastructure without simultaneously advancing the rest of Biden's domestic spending plan. If centrists wanted the left to support the infrastructure deal, then the surest way to do that would be for them to support a progressive reconciliation package.

These tactical disagreements had a larger ideological component to them. Ricchetti was seen in the White House as an avatar of Biden's centrist core— a pragmatist who shared the preference for consensus-seeking and incrementalism that had defined most of Biden's career. Klain was a more partisan figure, openly skeptical of working with Republicans for its own sake and more invested in Biden's aspiration to record achievements on the scale of the New Deal and the Great Society. Their work histories, at least between government jobs, illustrated their differences: Ricchetti spent years as a high-powered, deal-seeking lobbyist while Klain worked in venture capital and did a stint writing sharp-edged and often thoughtful columns for the *Washington Post*.

What was still unclear to almost everyone in Congress was how Biden himself wanted to proceed. His mixed signals and false starts had created a situation where centrist lawmakers could reasonably claim to be standing up for Biden's agenda by demanding a quick vote on infrastructure, and liberals could just as credibly claim to be championing Biden's cause with their both-or-neither stance on infrastructure and reconciliation.

In Congress, Josh Gottheimer was among the lawmakers who had lobbied Pelosi back in July to take quick action on infrastructure. The former Clinton White House aide had helped negotiate the deal from his perch atop the Problem Solvers Caucus, and he was willing to be a thorn in the side of leadership. Pelosi had politely dismissed his initial plea for a vote—"Thank you, dear," she told him—and as August progressed, he marshaled a more combative strategy.

A group of nine moderates came together—a combination of ideological centrists, like Kurt Schrader of Oregon, and lawmakers in vulnerable districts, like Vicente Gonzalez, whose Rio Grande Valley district in Texas nearly turned red in 2020, and Carolyn Bourdeaux, a first-term member from the Atlanta suburbs.

On August 12, they issued an ultimatum to Pelosi.

Either hold an immediate vote on the infrastructure bill, they wrote in a letter, or the group would withhold their support for a budget resolution coming up for a vote at the end of the month. The budget resolution was a kind of placeholder for the multitrillion-dollar domestic agenda Democrats aimed to pass through reconciliation. Once Congress passed the budget resolution, it would allow negotiators to fill in $3.5 trillion in spending plans, a figure that had been negotiated down from Sanders's original blueprint of $6 trillion. The sooner the House approved the resolution, the sooner Pelosi and the White House could finalize the details and push their social-welfare and climate plans into law.

The demand from Gottheimer's Group of Nine was ostentatiously brash, to the point that even sympathetic lawmakers saw it as obnoxious. It was one thing to press for a speedy vote on infrastructure. It was another matter entirely to threaten to derail the largest remaining piece of Biden's agenda.

Pelosi and her leadership team reacted initially with a combination of eye-rolling and disbelief. They did not believe it was a serious threat. In private, Pelosi had a scornful description of the belligerent group.

"Amateurs," she called them to her friends.

Amateurish or not, the members meant what they said, and they were getting encouragement from outside the chamber. The two senators holding up Biden's reconciliation package in the Senate, Manchin and Sinema, had begun to reach into the House in an unusual way, seeking to dislodge the infrastructure bill they had helped negotiate. They urged Gottheimer and his group to hold firm in their demand for a speedy vote.

"Stay strong," Manchin told one of them in a phone call on August 12. The West Virginia senator said he was fed up with the left wing of his party and he wanted the infrastructure vote to happen quickly.

"These people are crazy," Manchin said.

On August 20, the House renegades issued a collection of statements reiterating their ultimatum. If Pelosi did not bend, then this group was willing to break the path forward for the reconciliation package.

The White House was reaching out to the Group of Nine and urging them to back down from their demands, at first gently and then in more menacing language. Ricchetti, normally among the more congenial White House aides, came down hard on them. He still wanted an expedited vote on infrastructure, but the centrists' act of legislative hostage-taking offended him. A handful of House members of any ideology could not be allowed to undermine Biden as the author of his own political destiny.

The longtime Washington operator voiced a sense of betrayal with the group of backbenchers that was attempting to strong-arm party leaders.

"Anybody opposed to the resolution, it's a dealbreaker with the administration forever," Ricchetti warned one of them.

In private, Ricchetti vented anger at one in particular: Jared Golden, the thirty-nine-year-old Marine from a pro-Trump district in rural Maine. Golden was one of two Democrats who voted against the American Rescue Plan, and now he was messing with Biden in a more dangerous way.

Golden was practically a Republican, Ricchetti told one associate. The Biden adviser floated the idea of recruiting another Democrat to run against Golden in 2022.

A week into the standoff, Pelosi was still projecting confidence that the dissenting Democrats would back down. At a weekend retreat for her donors in Napa Valley, the Speaker conveyed no sense of fear or anxiety. The party, she told donors, had one strategy for governing and then fighting the midterm campaign in 2022: Stick with Joe Biden. (As if to prove her point, Biden phoned Pelosi during a luncheon; the Speaker put her iPhone on speaker and held it to a microphone so the president could address her contributors for a moment.)

Biden tried delivering the same stick-with-me message to one of the troublesome centrists that very weekend.

On the evening of Sunday, August 22, Biden placed a phone call to Stephanie Murphy. A leader of the moderate Blue Dog Coalition, Murphy had pursued a job in the Biden administration and contemplated a campaign for Senate before opting to stay in the House and serve on the January 6 committee. She also happened to be close personal friends with Kyrsten Sinema. A persuasive overture from Biden might have useful ripple effects.

It was not a successful conversation.

Biden told Murphy that she and her allies needed to back down. The White House was trying to move the infrastructure and reconciliation bills toward passage side by side, and the Group of Nine was not helping. The forty-two-year-old Floridian pushed back, telling Biden that she favored changes to the reconciliation bill and objected to progressives stonewalling the infrastructure deal. Still, Murphy told the president she wanted to get both bills done—she wanted to support his agenda.

The president bristled. To him, supporting the White House's agenda meant backing his strategy.

Don't kid yourself, Biden told her. You're the opposition.

The call ended on an unpleasant note.

But then, it had begun that way, too. Biden had opened his chat with Murphy by alluding to another subject entirely, the ongoing American withdrawal from Afghanistan and the messy process of trying to evacuate Afghans who had helped the United States.

Then he had asked Murphy, who came to the United States as a child refugee from Vietnam, when her family had arrived. Murphy told him they had made it to America in 1979, four years after the fall of Saigon. Her parents had worked for the United States and the South Vietnamese government, but they had not been evacuated when American troops left in 1975. Vulnerable to Communist reprisals, they had to cut their own desperate path out.

It was a story that echoed uncomfortably with the ragged retreat unfolding at that moment in Kabul, events that left scores of Democratic lawmakers as downcast about the Biden administration as they had ever been.

*   *   *

John Anzalone's memo on August 20 was clinical in its tone, but the conclusions were grim. The president's pollster diagnosed an abrupt drop in Joe Biden's approval ratings as Americans absorbed the Taliban's rapid conquest of Afghanistan. Voters did not disagree with Biden's decision to end the twenty-year war, Anzalone wrote, but they believed the withdrawal was poorly executed and they were blaming Biden.

In a document circulated to the White House and a collection of outside allies, Anzalone cautioned that it was too soon to say if the chaotic pullout would take a lasting toll on Biden. His approval numbers had been falling even before the withdrawal, the pollster wrote, "in part because of the spread of the Delta variant in the U.S."

Biden did not need Anzalone's memo to know that the collapse of Afghanistan was a blow to his administration and to his own stature as a practitioner of global affairs.

The president had decided long ago to end the war altogether, overruling some of his senior military commanders who favored keeping a small American force on the ground. In July, he had dismissed the possibility that the Afghan government might crumble, rejecting a reporter's comparison to South Vietnam. The Afghan government and military were far more robust than those of South Vietnam in the 1970s, Biden said. "They're not remotely comparable in terms of capability."

On August 15, the Taliban swept into Kabul as the last remnants of Afghanistan's government disintegrated and the president, Ashraf Ghani, fled the country—just after telling Tony Blinken he would fight on to the end. The Afghan military had surrendered territory to the Taliban across much of the area, while formerly pro-government factions cut deals with the Islamist forces rather than fight and risk a gruesome defeat.

In private Biden expressed feelings of disappointment with his own team. The president felt he had represented the situation in Afghanistan based on the best advice of his intelligence services, military commanders, and handpicked national security aides. In his view, their guidance had turned out to be wrong.

This is not what you guys have been telling me, he told his advisers as the situation in Afghanistan deteriorated.

The outcry on Capitol Hill was ferocious and bipartisan, but muddled on the substance of the withdrawal. Senior Democrats delivered scathing criticism of the pullout but almost uniformly backed Biden's decision to leave Afghanistan. Hillary Clinton sought to reach Biden because she was concerned about the execution and totality of the pullout: The former secretary of state believed there should have been some residual American force left in place in the country. Clinton and Biden had not been close for years, and they had nurtured a quiet but intense rivalry ahead of the 2016 campaign, when Biden felt that Clinton and his boss, Barack Obama, effectively boxed him out of the race. But Clinton had still been irked not to hear from Biden in the early months of his presidency, and told people she believed the president should be consulting with a wider range of voices.

Lawmakers in both parties, including a cohort of Democratic military veterans elected in 2018, were working around the clock to help their own

Afghan contacts escape the country, and their patience with Biden and his appointees was wearing thin.

Republicans were more brutal than Democrats in their criticism of the president and his team, but far more divided on the underlying issue of the Afghan War. While some, like Mitch McConnell and Lindsey Graham, favored keeping thousands of troops in the country, many Republicans had cheered on President Trump when he called for bringing home the whole American contingent. Kevin McCarthy had been one of those Republicans.

In August, the would-be House Speaker sounded incoherent as he blasted Biden for negotiating with the Taliban while defending Trump for doing the same. He chided the administration for pulling troops back from Bagram Air Base while maintaining that he still believed in a full withdrawal from the war.

Trump himself jeered at Biden from the sidelines, ridiculing the new president and insisting he would never have allowed such a humiliation to unfold on his watch—a dubious claim given that Trump's demands for a hasty pullout and his administration's talks with the Taliban laid the groundwork for withdrawal in the first place.

Yet in American politics, the sitting president is typically held accountable for overseas chaos and military defeats that happen on his watch, irrespective of whether his opponents are critiquing him in an honest and sophisticated manner. Biden's career was a case in point: He had been elected to the vice presidency in 2008 amid backlash against George W. Bush's war in Iraq, which Biden had supported for years.

In his August 20 memo, Anzalone noted that the American people had tangled views on Afghanistan, with three in five Americans favoring withdrawal on Biden's end-of-August timetable and 51 percent saying it would have been worth it to keep troops there for another year—two positions that were irreconcilable with each other. In any event, he said, the political cost was real.

"Much like the Delta surge, the events in Afghanistan have drowned out some of the news around the President's Build Back Better Agenda," Anzalone wrote, stating the depressingly obvious for the White House.

On August 26, an explosion at Kabul's Hamid Karzai International Airport overwhelmed everything else in the life of the Biden administration. A suicide bomber had targeted the throngs of people massed outside the airport in a desperate quest to leave before the United States abandoned them entirely. Scores of Afghan civilians were killed—along with thirteen American service members.

The fiasco deepened further after Biden vowed to take retribution. On Sunday, August 29, the military launched a drone attack in Kabul against a vehicle it said it believed to be carrying an ISIS bomb. Mark Milley, the country's top general, described it as "righteous." Within weeks, the *New York Times* and other news organizations would expose the drone strike as a horrifying atrocity: Its victims had not been terrorists but an aid worker and his family, with seven children among them.

On the same day as the drone strike, Biden traveled to Dover Air Force Base to receive the remains of the American soldiers slain at the Kabul airport. The somber occasion became yet another illustration of how the country's political divisions were infecting nearly every element of American life. Shana Chappell, the mother of a slain Marine, berated Biden on the tarmac and accused him of having her son's blood on his hands.

Afterward, she went on social media to call Biden a "traitor" and claimed that he had become president through "cheating." Chappell invited Trump to attend her son's funeral.

Biden left Dover in a dejected state and returned to Washington. There, he drove to Holy Trinity Catholic Church, the Jesuit parish near Georgetown University that had been a place of worship for the nation's only other Catholic president, John F. Kennedy, six decades earlier. Making his way into the pews by himself, Biden eased into a seat one row behind a familiar parishioner: Gina Raimondo, the secretary of commerce, who was attending mass with her teenage daughter, Cecilia.

Raimondo, noticing the president was alone, invited him to join her and her daughter, and Biden accepted, moving up one row to sit beside them. They prayed together quietly, and then at the sign of peace—a moment at mass when parishioners greet each other—Biden turned to the cabinet secretary who was young enough to be his daughter.

"Thanks," he said, "for being a good friend."

* * *

Gina Raimondo was one of a few prominent figures in Biden's administration who never deviated from selling his domestic agenda. With a wide-ranging economic portfolio and no responsibility for the war in Afghanistan, the former Rhode Island governor spent August and September on a determined campaign of persuasion aimed at an array of congressional moderates in the House and Senate whose support Biden needed for both his infrastructure and social-welfare policies.

Leveraging her own credentials as a business-friendly centrist, Raimondo was reaching out to a range of vocal lawmakers, including Manchin and Gottheimer. Since she did not have to address them across an ideological divide, Raimondo seemed to feel free to give the lawmakers something of a hard kick.

Like the president, she believed Democrats would do better in the 2022 elections if they had a portfolio of compelling achievements to wave around. But Raimondo also made a forthright case to centrists about getting stuff done for its own sake, even if Democrats suffered in the short term.

After bonding with Manchin over their shared Italian heritage and background as former governors, Raimondo pointed out that he was famous for complaining about the Senate. Why, then, was Manchin worried about placating his Trump-loving home state?

You don't like this job that much, Raimondo told him. You liked being governor better. Take the vote, get booted out, wear it as a badge of honor.

With Gottheimer, she was even more direct. The two were just four years apart in age, and both had endorsed Michael Bloomberg for president out of a determination to beat the hard left in the Democratic primaries. The hard left had been beaten, no thanks to Bloomberg, and now Raimondo was prodding Gottheimer to help the mainstream president pass a daring version of the reconciliation package.

You have a moment right now to do something historic to help America, she told Gottheimer. If you do the right thing and don't get reelected, so be it.

In the last days of August, the Group of Nine cut a deal with Pelosi to let the budget resolution go through in exchange for a crucial promise from the Speaker. Pelosi committed to hold a vote on infrastructure by September 27. That left just a month for the White House and Democratic congressional leaders to negotiate a deal on the reconciliation package that could clear both chambers.

The agreement brought Democrats no closer to real consensus on the strategy or substance of their legislative agenda. It left an almost comically compressed timeline for the various parties to strike a deal on the reconciliation package and then write the actual text of an immense piece of legislation. There was little reason at the end of August to believe Democrats could succeed in doing all of that so quickly.

The White House understood that, and so did Democratic leaders in Congress. Negotiations over the reconciliation package had been under way for months already, and no one felt much closer to a breakthrough that would resolve the Democratic Party's serious internal divisions.

Manchin and Sinema both wanted to cut the reconciliation price tag from $3.5 trillion to less than half that figure, but they had separate priorities for the remaining spending and had major differences on the subject of fighting climate change.

Progressives felt they had already been more than reasonable by lowering the size of Sanders's initial reconciliation draft from $6 trillion to $3.5 trillion. They did not want to scale back their ambitions any further or lose cherished New Deal–style social programs, like free community college for all Americans or government-backed dental coverage for the elderly.

Embedded in those two negotiating positions were two different views of how to turn the page on the Trump era. To the centrists, Trump represented a decisive turn into politics as a form of warfare, with every issue, every presidential action, and every congressional vote treated as combat. They believed that dealmaking and bipartisan cooperation would restore a mood of normalcy and calm in the capital, and eventually in the nation at large.

From the perspective of the Congressional Progressive Caucus, that was a sucker's view. Even if voters told pollsters they cared about bipartisanship, liberals believed Americans cared far more about tangible improvements to their lives—improvements like the funding for childcare and paid-leave programs contained in the reconciliation bill. To the left, purging Trump from the political system meant showing the electorate, including lower-income whites who supported the former president, that government could transform their lives for the better.

The left wing believed that Democrats had missed too many chances to do that in the past. As Andy Levin, the House progressive from Michigan, puts it, his wing of the party was now determined to pass an agenda so bold that it would wind up "making working-class white people say, 'I'd never vote for Donald Trump, I'm voting for the party that puts money in my damn pocket—the Democrats.'"

Most Democrats, including the president, did not want to choose between those two approaches. A large majority of Democrats in the House and Senate wanted to vote for both a robust reconciliation package and the infrastructure deal. The question was whether Biden and his congressional allies could steer those bills around the obstacles thrown up by the feistiest factions of their party, which viewed each other with bitter distrust.

On September 10, Anzalone gave the White House another bracing update on public opinion. Voters still favored Biden's Build Back Better agenda, but the president's job approval rating was underwater and stuck there. Most concerning were Biden's falling numbers on the coronavirus pandemic. A slim plurality of Americans now said that the president had not communicated a clear plan of action.

"As the Delta variant of the novel coronavirus continues to spread, American confidence in communications from the CDC and President Biden about the public health threat has dropped," Anzalone wrote.

The public had good reason to be confused. Despite the government's sustained vaccination campaign, the daily count of coronavirus fatalities and new cases was far higher on Labor Day in 2021 than the previous year. The worst outbreaks were still concentrated in areas where Republican governors had reopened their states rapidly and defied federal public-health guidance, but there were also communities of color across the country where vaccination rates were lagging and case counts were comparatively high.

It was not only the Biden administration and many other Democrats running out of patience with the unvaccinated, many of whom were marinating in a toxic brew of social-media conspiracy theories and anti-vaccine rhetoric on Fox News and other television outlets. On September 8, Jim Justice, the Republican governor of West Virginia, railed against the "crazy ideas" of Americans who were ingesting conspiracy theories such as the idea that vaccines were a way of implanting people with tracking devices.

"For God's sakes a livin', how difficult is this to understand?" an exasperated Justice said during a livestreamed health briefing.

On September 9—one day after Justice's outburst and one day before Anzalone's memo—Biden made his own move. For the first time ever, the president mandated vaccination for all federal employees, and he directed the Occupational Safety and Health Administration to impose vaccine mandates on private businesses with more than one hundred employees. Another arm of the government would require vaccination for health-care workers, while still another would increase fines for airline passengers who flouted masking requirements.

Taken together, it was a dramatic use of federal power to force the vaccination campaign forward.

Up until this point, Biden had hesitated to employ blunt-force tactics with the unvaccinated, leaving it instead to states and municipalities to implement coercive measures and watching from afar as they did so unevenly. But by the fall the great majority of the country was vaccinated, the Delta variant was still spreading quickly, and Americans were desperate to get out of the pandemic once and for all.

Among vaccinated Americans, there was a mounting spirit of resentment toward people who by then had had more than half a year's time to get inoculated and had chosen not to do so.

That dynamic burst into view in mid-September with a statewide election in California. Conservatives in the state had engineered a recall campaign targeting Gavin Newsom, the Democratic governor who had implemented strict lockdowns throughout the pandemic and mandated vaccination for state employees earlier in the summer. The leading Republican candidates opposed those measures and caricatured Newsom as a left-wing busybody.

Newsom campaigned on his assertive public-health strategy, warning in ads that the election was "a matter of life and death." National Democrats seemed to agree: Biden broke with his strictly limited travel schedule to campaign for Newsom in the days before the vote, marking his first trip west of the Central Time Zone since taking office.

On September 14 voters rejected the recall effort by 24 percentage points—a decisive outcome even by the standards of solid-blue California.

In his victory speech, Newsom cast the election as a referendum on public health.

"We said yes to vaccines," he declared. "We said yes to ending this pandemic."

Newsom had come a long way from his tense conversations with Donald Trump about cruise ships and forest maintenance. The California governor had acted faster than Biden to force compliance from the unvaccinated, and voters had seemed to reward him. White House aides hoped the country would respond the same way to Biden's new mandates.

But to run as the party of public health and effective government, Democrats still needed to prove they could get big things done with their power in Washington.

As Pelosi's reluctantly imposed September 27 deadline for an infrastructure vote approached, those ambitions were hanging by a narrow thread.

* * *

On September 22, a Wednesday, Joe Biden summoned the two major ideological factions of his party for meetings in the Oval Office. In the space of a few hours, the president met face-to-face with a set of congressional centrists and then a group of House and Senate liberals, all with an eye toward breaking the impasse around his agenda.

The centrists went first. Joe Manchin and Kyrsten Sinema were there, of course, and the House contingent included Josh Gottheimer and Stephanie Murphy.

For most of the year, Manchin had been the most conspicuously challenging senator for the White House to work with, and he entered the session as one of the toughest holdouts. He had repeatedly stated his preference for a $1.5 trillion bill, a fraction of what progressives wanted. In an unusual ploy, Manchin had presented Chuck Schumer over the summer with an outline of his red lines for the reconciliation package, making explicit that he would not commit to voting for anything that cost more than $1.5 trillion.

The West Virginian had asked Schumer to affix his signature to the document to confirm he had reviewed it—a tactic seemingly designed to shield Manchin against any claims later on that he had misled party leaders about what he would or would not be willing to support. But Schumer kept the document secret from other Senate Democrats, leaving them in the dark while he tried to change Manchin's mind.

Democrats who negotiated with Manchin throughout the summer felt that he was stiffening his conservative instincts on certain social policies. Manchin complained to some Democrats that the child tax credit would effectively pay people to have children, when so many people in his state already had families too big for them to afford.

Even more pointedly, he told Cory Booker, one of the architects of the tax credit, that he remained convinced that people would use the money for malign purposes.

"Everybody just takes this check and buys drugs," Manchin claimed in one meeting of Senate Democratic leaders, prompting Booker to counter that plenty of people would use the money to buy diapers and other essentials.

Manchin had been argumentative with White House aides, objecting to components of the reconciliation package that he viewed as far-left ideas foisted on the party by Bernie Sanders. Biden advisers tried to disabuse Manchin of that notion by personally emailing him an itemized list of reconciliation items that had been in the president's own campaign platform.

It was a familiar and frustrating negotiation with the conservative Democrat. But it was not a hopeless one: Manchin had also been emphatic about wanting to pass a reconciliation bill with generous new spending paid for with tax increases. He believed the rich had gotten off too easy during the Trump years and he had said so often in public. The administration was confident there was a version of the bill he would support.

Biden was not sure the same could be said for everyone in the Oval Office that day.

For the most part it was a polite session. Biden had an overarching message for both factions he was meeting with that day: His administration, and the party as a whole, wanted both major domestic-spending bills enacted, and it was up to them to figure out a way to do it. There was another tense exchange between the president and Murphy as the Florida congresswoman told Biden he needed to do a better job calibrating liberals' sky-high expectations for the reconciliation bill.

We need you to show leadership on this, Murphy told Biden.

The president grew defensive, bristling at the suggestion that he had not done so already.

I wrote this thing, Biden told Murphy. These are my ideas and they are popular across the country.

It was a telling boast. Biden was hardly the intellectual architect of the reconciliation package. Dating back to the spring of 2020, he had borrowed many of his biggest proposals from other Democrats, like Bernie Sanders and Elizabeth Warren on the left and Michael Bennet and Cory Booker in the middle. But he now felt a level of ownership over the legislation that verged, in his mind, on authorship.

That may have been why the president was so frustrated with Sinema for demanding that he narrow the legislation considerably, and why Biden could not help making that plain in the meeting.

At one point Biden floated a budget number for the reconciliation bill that he hoped everyone present could accept. Perhaps, Biden said, it could end up around $2 trillion. He acknowledged that Sinema was pushing for a much smaller package.

In fact, Biden told the group, the Arizona senator had set her limit at $1.1 trillion.

The room froze.

Until then, Sinema had been a uniquely opaque character in negotiations—a far more difficult quarry than even Manchin. In private conversations, White House aides felt she often sounded more like Mitt Romney than a member of Biden's own party, telling the president that people in her state liked corporations and she did not want to support tax policies aimed at their bottom line. Speaking with Republicans, Sinema happily boasted that she was willing to stand up to the left in ways her fellow centrist Democrats were not: She told one Republican senator she believed there were five or six other moderates who typically agreed with her on policy but preferred "hiding behind my skirt."

Few of her fellow Democratic senators knew her well, and Sinema abruptly left some caucus lunches when policy debates grew tense. Much of the intelligence the White House got on Sinema came from her former House colleagues, many of whom regarded her as a slippery character: "To know her is not to trust her," says Hakeem Jeffries, the possible Speaker-in-waiting who had entered Congress with her in 2013.

The Arizona senator had refused to outline her negotiating parameters in public, as Manchin had done. That was partly because the White House had asked her not to. Biden aides believed her demands were not reasonable, and they feared that if Sinema drew a public red line at $1.1 trillion—a miserly sum by liberal standards—then the party would erupt in open war.

Now Biden had exposed to some of Sinema's colleagues the very position his aides had asked her to conceal. The senator was visibly angry.

"Mr. President," she said, "that was a private conversation."

Sinema began to stand up. She asked Biden: "Do you want me to leave?"

The president hastened to calm the situation. Of course he did not want Sinema to leave. If Biden resented her theatrics, he did not say so in the moment. He could not afford to lose her vote.

Biden's meeting with a liberal delegation later that day was considerably more agreeable. With his guests arranged in a horseshoe around the Oval Office—Bernie Sanders to one side of the president and Pramila Jayapal on the other—the president listened intently as Jayapal laid out the case for holding up the infrastructure bill. Both the infrastructure deal and the reconciliation package were components of Biden's agenda, but one of them was vastly larger and more important than the other, she said.

We aren't going to allow us to leave behind 85 percent of your agenda, Jayapal told the president. Invoking her own family's experience immigrating from India, Jayapal told Biden that his Build Back Better agenda would restore the American dream they had crossed a world to pursue.

When the meeting broke up, the president pulled Jayapal to the side. The two had struck up an unlikely political partnership since the end of the Democratic primaries, when Jayapal had energetically supported Bernie Sanders over Biden. Just the previous night, Biden had called her up to wish her a happy birthday and cheer her for an appearance on Rachel Maddow's MSNBC show.

Now in a private conversation, Biden riffled through some papers and came up with a copy of his speech to Congress earlier in the year articulating his grand agenda for the country.

"This really is my agenda," Biden said, according to Jayapal's recollection. Handing her the speech, he said: "I'd like you to have this copy."

Jayapal asked the president to sign it and Biden gladly obliged.

The two most intransigent factions of Biden's party were not getting closer together. But after those meetings at the White House, it seemed that one of them was growing far closer to Biden than the other.

*　*　*

For all the new warmth of her relationship with the president, Jayapal was keeping Biden and his advisers as hemmed in as the centrists were. The promised vote on infrastructure was now only days away, and the White House did not believe progressives were bluffing about taking down the bill. Ron Klain was adamant that the administration could not afford to let the House vote if they were likely to lose.

The top Democrat in the Senate was starting to confide to allies that he worried his fellow party leaders had mishandled the situation. Chuck Schumer had taken a different view of the infrastructure-and-reconciliation challenge from the start. He had been telling senators, donors, and activists for months that the infrastructure deal was linked to the rest of the Democratic agenda—not just the social-welfare bill but also voting rights and other major issues.

It had been a mistake for Biden to pretend otherwise, Schumer began to tell people, because it had created an unsustainable ambiguity about his priorities. He had to clear things up one way or another or the party would never find a path forward.

But in the eyes of some fellow party leaders, Schumer did not have much standing to complain about the situation. The Senate majority leader had receded as a force in negotiations, and members of his caucus had begun to grumble to each other that he did not seem to have a plan to bring the two wings of his party together. Sensing that Schumer did not have a clear strategy for corralling Manchin and Sinema, Pelosi began to deal with them directly herself in an effort to reach a deal.

There were only a few options left for the president and Democratic congressional leaders. One was to strike a last-minute reconciliation deal on paper and persuade the progressives to trust Manchin and Sinema to keep their commitments, thereby allowing the infrastructure bill to go through. Another option was to cancel the infrastructure vote, reneging on Pelosi's commitments to the Gottheimer gang in a concession to the power of the left.

Some lawmakers hoped for a third option: an intervention by the White House to back the infrastructure bill and call on progressives to help pass it. If Biden told his party that he needed them to pass the bipartisan deal straightaway, that could make it harder for the Congressional Progressive Caucus to hold together the votes to block the bill.

After all, Biden was the head of his party and an architect of the infrastructure package. Perhaps it was time for him to start acting like it.

But so far, Biden had not attempted to test his powers of command on the diffuse Democratic caucus. As the deadline approached, he gave no sign that he was about to change that.

For at least a few days, Democratic leaders opted for delay. On Monday, September 27, there was no infrastructure vote. Pelosi and her lieutenants urged the caucus that day to be patient. A deal with the Senate was still possible, they said, and a vote on infrastructure was imminent in any case. Holding up the bipartisan bill any longer, the Speaker said, was "just not a reasonable thing."

In a caucus meeting, Pelosi told her members that the party was confronting a great test of its relevance—of its ability to deliver for the American people.

"What breaks your heart is when you knock on a door and people say: My father didn't have a job under a Democratic president or a Republican president, what difference does it make?" Pelosi said at one point, adding: "What we talk about is essential: Does government work? Do Democrats make a difference?"

Several mainstream Democrats—none of them ultimatum-issuing renegades on the left or in the center—spoke up during the meeting to plead with their colleagues that it was time to stop the standoff and get something done. Susie Lee, a vulnerable lawmaker from Nevada, warned that if the party failed then "we can kiss the majority goodbye for ten years." Colin Allred, the Texas Democrat, conjured an even bleaker prospect.

"We cannot let these two bills go down," Allred pleaded. "Because if they go down, President Biden goes down, American democracy goes down."

As September 27 came and went without a vote, the rogue moderates who had forced Pelosi to set that deadline did not rebel immediately. They had all taken heat from Democrats in their districts for their brinksmanship in August, and they did not want to risk open war with the Speaker—or the

White House. Besides, it seemed to them like some kind of deal really might be within reach: an agreement with Manchin and Sinema on the broad strokes of a reconciliation bill that might satisfy House progressives enough for them to let the infrastructure bill go through.

But dealing with Manchin and Sinema was not getting any easier for Biden's team.

On September 28, between negotiating sessions at the White House, Kyrsten Sinema held an afternoon fundraiser with a collection of Republican-leaning business groups, including lobbies for the grocery and roofing industries. Several of the organizations had spoken out against the reconciliation bill. In a space above the Capitol Hill pub Bullfeathers, Sinema showed them exactly why Biden found her so exasperating.

There were parts of the reconciliation package she liked, Sinema told the group. She liked its biggest climate measures and she liked some of the social programs, such as the child tax credit. But Sinema expressed intense skepticism of taxation and spending overall and played up her differences with the rest of her party.

"I come from a fiscally conservative state," she said. "And I'm interested in maintaining pro-growth tax policies that ensure that we can get through this pandemic without losing ground."

To the delight of her audience, Sinema sounded more like a Republican as she went on: "Arizonans don't like taxes, and we don't really like government. We love our country. And we love our military. And that's about where it ends."

Had Sinema's Democratic colleagues been in the room, they might have been startled to hear her speaking warmly about several House Republicans whom Democrats regarded as among the worst of Donald Trump's henchmen.

Kevin McCarthy and Steve Scalise, she said, were "friends of mine." Andy Biggs, a far-right lawmaker from Arizona who had peddled outrageous lies about the 2020 election, was a "dear friend."

"I love Andy Biggs," Sinema said. "I know some people think he's crazy, but that's just because they don't know him."

Her remarks went unreported at the time. But Sinema did not spare her

Democratic Senate colleagues, complaining that Bernie Sanders had stoked House progressives' blockade of the infrastructure bill and speaking dismissively about Ron Wyden, the Oregon Democrat who chaired the Senate Finance Committee.

In a final insult, Sinema could not resist tweaking Biden before the supportive crowd. Aside from his talks with Democrats, the president was also locked in a standoff with Mitch McConnell over an upcoming deadline for Congress to raise the statutory limit on government debts. The Republican leader was insisting that Democrats raise the debt ceiling without any help from the Senate GOP. Biden called that position irresponsible.

But Biden, Sinema mused, did not exactly have clean hands on the issue.

"Many of my colleagues, including the president, have at one time or another voted against the debt limit," she said. "Perhaps that makes it a little bit harder for folks to be, you know, kind of righteous on this issue."

She did not sound like a senator moving toward a deal.

* * *

By Thursday, September 30, it was clear to the main negotiators that there was not going to be a breakthrough on the reconciliation package. Democratic leaders had to decide what to do about the infrastructure vote that was already three days overdue. They had delayed a day of reckoning with their own internal divisions for about as long as they could.

There were a few centrist Democrats who wanted to take a vote even if it meant losing. Josh Gottheimer believed it would be useful to members in swing districts to vote for the infrastructure bill, even if progressives blocked it, so that they could tell voters back home that they had stood up for jobs and bipartisanship. In a leadership meeting that Thursday, Steny Hoyer echoed that view with a sigh.

I know no one agrees with me, Hoyer said, but I think we should take the vote.

The Speaker of the House believed she had a better option than either losing or pulling the vote. She had kept another plan secret from members but seemed to show her hand in a meeting with the centrist New Democrat Coalition on Thursday. Pelosi was holding sessions with the major ideological factions in her caucus, trying to keep people calm and divine a way forward. The New Democrats were as confused as anyone about how the current standoff would get resolved.

At one point, Pelosi leaned over to Chrissy Houlahan, a leader of the moderate group, and touched her elbow as though she were about to share a confidence.

"Your idea of bringing Biden here—that could happen," Pelosi said, according to Houlahan's memory.

The Pennsylvania lawmaker had not actually suggested to the Speaker that she bring in Biden, but Houlahan took it as a reference to the wishes of the group. Pelosi knew that many centrist Democrats were holding on to hope that Biden might show up on the Hill and give the House caucus a stirring pep talk that would sweep his infrastructure bill into law. Pelosi was leaning into the idea that this might really happen.

So was Steve Ricchetti. The Biden adviser was sensitive to the tangled dynamics of the president's wide-ranging agenda, but he had always believed that getting infrastructure done would only strengthen Biden's hand with Congress. Manchin and Sinema had grown harder to deal with during the protracted standoff, not easier, in part because of their resentment toward House liberals holding up the infrastructure bill. Ricchetti had gone as far as asking his old boss, Bill Clinton, a Democrat who spoke centrism as his native tongue, to help him lobby Manchin and Sinema. The former president had not managed to move either one of them.

Ricchetti knew, too, from his contacts in the House that support among Republicans for the infrastructure bill was plunging. After winning nineteen GOP votes in the Senate, the bill was at risk of winning less than half that support among House Republicans—just as Kevin McCarthy had predicted. In the Senate vote, no less a Republican partisan than Mitch McConnell had been able to claim that the infrastructure deal was distinct from the rest of Biden's agenda. Now the linkage was all too apparent.

Some Republican House members open to voting in favor were surprised that the White House was not reaching out to seek their help. Even GOP lawmakers with a record of taking on the right, like Fred Upton and Adam

Kinzinger, heard nothing from the president. That treatment was reserved for a few select Senate Republicans.

On Wednesday night, September 29, Biden had attended the congressional baseball game, cheerfully greeting lawmakers on the diamond at Nationals Park. He sat for a time with Andy Levin, and the liberal lawmaker came away convinced that the president was not interested in strong-arming progressives or speeding up a vote on infrastructure.

"This is your agenda," Levin recalls telling him, "and we're sticking up for it."

Biden replied with a message of encouragement.

"I know it," the president said, according to Levin. "And I appreciate it."

*   *   *

On Friday, October 1, Ricchetti told one member of Congress that the president was likely headed for Capitol Hill in a matter of hours. White House aides had been drafting remarks for Biden to make to the Democratic caucus leaning in hard to the value and urgency of passing the infrastructure bill.

Pelosi wants him to come in and close the deal, Ricchetti told this lawmaker.

In a meeting of the Democratic caucus on Friday morning, some lawmakers spoke up to deplore the bleeding fissures within their own party: Lois Frankel, a seventy-three-year-old Democrat from South Florida, lamented that there seemed to be "total war between these different caucuses and factions," even though in reality "the differences are slender." Another, Sara Jacobs, a thirty-two-year-old freshman from Southern California, invoked the attack of January 6 in a plea for unity.

"I literally almost died with twenty of you, across the ideological spectrum," Jacobs said. "The insurrectionists didn't care if you were in the Blue Dogs or the Progressives, I'll tell you that."

Hakeem Jeffries, too, sought to direct his party's ire outward, toward the GOP: The most important division at the Capitol, he said, was "patriots versus traitors."

The Speaker of the House did not signal she was about to bring in Joe Biden in a bid to unify her party behind the infrastructure bill. While Pelosi said it was time to move ahead with the legislation—"It's very important for this bill to pass today," she said—the Speaker sounded highly sympathetic to her party's progressive wing and its grievances. They did not like being pushed around by hostage-taking centrists in the House or the Senate, and neither did Pelosi.

Those centrists, Pelosi told her caucus, had forced her to promise a vote and then reneged on their side of the bargain. In her telling, Pelosi had struck a simple deal with them in August: She would promise to bring up infrastructure for a vote by September 27, and they would promise to vote for a $3.5 trillion reconciliation bill. But then, the Speaker claimed, moderates had broken that deal, teaming up with Sinema and Manchin to shrink and revise the reconciliation package in a way that delayed the process.

"We read in the paper that there are members of our caucus joining with members of the Senate that reject the 3.5," Pelosi said. "The very same people who are demanding a vote on a certain day are making it impossible for us to have a vote on a certain day."

There were uncomfortable murmurs going up in the room, getting louder as the Speaker went on. "I'm just stating fact," Pelosi said, adding: "This is a family discussion. Families can get rough sometimes."

To the moderates Pelosi was deriding, it was a very rough family discussion indeed. The Speaker was mischaracterizing the deal she had made: Gottheimer and his Group of Nine had never committed to support a $3.5 trillion reconciliation bill, along the precise lines Pelosi envisioned. They had agreed to support the $3.5 trillion budget resolution—an important intermediate measure—but they had all understood that the final deal on reconciliation was a work in progress.

Pelosi had known that in August. She surely knew it on October 1, too. Within the centrist group, it felt like Pelosi was trying to make them take the fall for the chaos of the week.

Carolyn Bourdeaux, the Georgia freshman, texted the other eight members of the Gottheimer-led moderate bloc before the meeting adjourned.

"Oh dear lord this whole thing is going to collapse," she wrote.

Kurt Schrader, the Oregon centrist who had voted to keep Pelosi as

Speaker because he saw her as a safeguard against the far left, wrote back in biting language. The former veterinarian had never intended to vote for a multi-trillion-dollar reconciliation bill at all. Pelosi's claim was absurd.

"Truly a terrible person," Schrader said of the most powerful Democrat in the House.

A third lawmaker, Jared Golden of Maine, reported that he had tracked down Steny Hoyer. According to Golden, Pelosi's longtime deputy had looked directly at Golden and said of the Speaker's remarks: "That's bullshit."

Yet Golden also mused that perhaps there was a method to Pelosi's apparent madness. Perhaps, he suggested, Pelosi was blaming their little crew for the mess at hand as a way of placating progressives before she asked them to do something they did not want to do—vote for the infrastructure bill.

"So she can't take the embarrassment so she tells them we screwed her and now the whole caucus has to pass the BIF," Golden said, using an acronym for Bipartisan Infrastructure Framework to refer to the infrastructure bill.

In a sign of the distrustful mood gripping Democrats, the young Marine from Maine speculated that perhaps Pelosi would hold a vote and root for the progressives to block it.

"Maybe she hopes it fails?" he wrote.

* * *

Nancy Pelosi was not planning to lose a vote on the infrastructure bill. And the president of the United States was not going to Capitol Hill to watch his cherished bipartisan deal disintegrate.

As word spread of Biden's plan to meet with House Democrats, a surge of optimism rippled through the centrist wing of his party, and party leaders were projecting a full-speed-ahead attitude about the vote. Speaking with reporters at the Capitol, Hakeem Jeffries publicly predicted that the infrastructure bill would pass into law within twenty-four hours.

Anticipating a possible shift in the stalemated negotiations, Pramila Jayapal announced that the Congressional Progressive Caucus would meet after Biden addressed House Democrats. If the president came down hard on liberals with a demand to pass his infrastructure bill, they would have to regroup quickly.

Before Biden left the White House, he conferred one last time with Mike Donilon, his longtime political adviser and speechwriter, about what he wanted to say. The president was clear about the message he planned to deliver, but on the Hill there was a swirl of rumor and speculation. Ricchetti's description of Biden's intent was spreading quickly, but that was just one adviser's confidential description of the situation, and the White House had not formally notified its negotiating partners of what Biden was going to do.

Jayapal reached out to Ron Klain ahead of Biden's speech. She asked the chief of staff: What is he going to say?

I think you'll like it, Klain replied, without elaborating further.

Jayapal did not think Klain would have said that to her if Biden was about to twist progressives' arms on the infrastructure bill.

Klain himself was intensely skeptical that strong-arming the left would get the infrastructure bill passed that day. In the White House's whip count, there were still about thirty-two Democrats who planned to vote no on the bill, including fifteen whose position could be more accurately described as "hell no." The chief of staff did not want Biden to go all-out for the legislation and then lose.

Neither did the president.

By the time Biden entered a spacious conference room in the Capitol basement around four o'clock in the afternoon, Democrats were braced for a moment of political climax. The president of the United States was in their midst, standing before the same flags and mahogany-colored paneling where House Democrats were accustomed to seeing their own leaders and committee chairs.

Surely a decisive moment was at hand.

Or perhaps not.

Biden addressed them in broad and encouraging terms. He wanted to pass both the infrastructure bill and the reconciliation bill, the president said. He knew the vast majority of them did, too. They were on their way to making transformational change in America. The policies they were putting forward—immense new benefits for children and families, the elderly and the sick, and the largest-ever investments in clean energy and decarbonization—would rank among the great achievements of the Democratic Party over the centuries.

But Biden reminded them he lacked the huge congressional majorities that other transformational Democratic presidents had enjoyed. Franklin Roosevelt and Lyndon Johnson had not been working with an evenly split Senate and a four-seat margin in the House.

The party would have to compromise to get what it wanted, Biden added. He believed he had support for his entire domestic agenda from forty-eight senators, but there were two he had not yet been able to bring along. Concessions would have to be made. That would take some more time, and the infrastructure bill would have to wait.

The president had decided October 1 was not the day to demand a vote.

Biden did not say when he hoped to reach terms with the Senate holdouts, or what those terms might be, or when he expected to hold a vote on the infrastructure bill.

If Biden had a plan, he did not share it.

The president did share a story about Satchel Paige, the legendary Black pitcher who played baseball deep into his forties in a career that spanned the integration of Major League Baseball. Paige, Biden said, had once been asked about his capacity to play at such an advanced age. The pitcher's retort had been that age was an abstraction: "How old would you be," he supposedly asked, "if you did not know how old you were?"

It was not clear what message Biden intended to convey with that story. Some members had heard it from him before, in the more appropriate venue of the Democratic dugout at the congressional baseball game the previous night. As lawmakers filed out of the meeting room Friday after an anticlimactic presidential address, Biden's yarn about an aging pitcher was not altogether reassuring.

On their way out of the building, Biden and Pelosi strolled past a throng of reporters who bellowed questions at the president about when he would get his agenda passed.

"We're going to get this done," Biden said, raising his outstretched hands to shoulder level in an appeal for calm. "It doesn't matter when. It doesn't matter whether it's in six minutes, six days, or six weeks. We're going to get it done."

*   *   *

The president's speech did not resolve the standoff within his own party, but in an odd way it managed to defuse some of the accumulated tension around Pelosi's deadline on infrastructure. By declining to demand a vote, Biden shouldered some of the blame for missing that checkpoint. The Group of Nine was still mad at the Speaker, but that anger was diluted somewhat by their confusion about the president's role.

Pelosi was angry, too, and in private she vented about the progressive blockade that had forced her to cancel the infrastructure vote. She told another House Democrat that Jayapal and Ocasio-Cortez were vying to be the "queen bee" of the left, but that their reward might be serving in the House minority after the next election.

Progressives, though, took Biden's appearance in the Capitol as a validation of their position: no vote on infrastructure until there was a reconciliation deal in place. The president, Jayapal exulted on MSNBC, "affirmed the need to do both bills together and made it clear that where we are is that we will not be able to do the infrastructure bill without the reconciliation bill."

Yes, she allowed, Biden had affirmed the need to trim back the legislation to win over the Senate holdouts. But in the process, he had effectively aligned himself with the left.

The weekend after Biden's speech, an odd calm settled over the surface of the party. With the September 27 deadline on infrastructure voided, Democrats were no longer captive to a maddening set of interlocking procedural and policy disagreements. In theory, they could take a few weeks just to focus on the substance of their negotiations. Surely, many of them believed, the party would be able to converge on some number and some set of programs that everyone from Jayapal to Sinema could agree on.

As Biden said, it might only be a matter of time.

Or it might not.

For some lawmakers, however, time was a precious commodity.

It was one thing for the president and congressional leaders to let negotiations drag on indefinitely. Most of them were at the end of their careers,
focused on cementing their legacies. Pelosi herself had raised eyebrows at a
news conference when she described the reconciliation bill as "a culmination
of my service in Congress"—the closest she had ever come even to implying
that the end was near.

The long delays were also safe enough for Joe Manchin and Kyrsten
Sinema, who did not have to face the voters again until 2024, and for Jayapal,
who held a solidly Democratic seat, to engage in a months-long staring contest. There was no chance they would face repudiation in the midterms.

But scores of other Democrats were anticipating difficult reelection campaigns in 2022. If the party wanted to shape the political landscape with massive
legislative achievements, then the negotiations could not go on forever and ever.
Already, candidates in the 2021 off-year elections feared they would suffer from the
deadlock in Washington: Terry McAuliffe, the former Virginia governor seeking to
reclaim his old job, was repeatedly calling his friend Ricchetti with pleas to get the
infrastructure bill done and buck up the president's approval rating.

On October 5, four days after his visit to the Hill, Biden gathered yet another group of House Democrats for a meeting, this time in a virtual setting.
It was a contingent chosen specifically for their political vulnerability. All were
so-called "frontliners," lawmakers from marginal seats whose victory or defeat
in 2022 would likely determine control of Congress. They were Democrats
enveloped in political danger.

They were also Democrats who had been on the front lines of danger on
January 6.

Joining Biden for the meeting were Susan Wild and Lizzie Fletcher, survi-
vors of the House gallery evacuation, and Lauren Underwood, who had been
locked out of her own office without a phone as rioters rampaged through the
Capitol. There was Colin Allred, the former football player who had brandished a metal pole in self-defense, and Abigail Spanberger, the former intel-

ligence officer who had warned Alexandria Ocasio-Cortez in the days before January 6 that she should dress in plain clothes for her own safety.

The meeting was mainly about the two pending pieces of domestic legislation, and Biden asked the members to lay out their priorities for the reconciliation bill. Spanberger, for one, told him that the final version ought to focus on climate change, the child tax credit, and lowering the cost of prescription drugs—a recommendation that reflected something of an emerging consensus among left-of-center Democrats in the House and Senate.

But to some members of this group, the fine details of the reconciliation package mattered somewhat less than the urgent imperative that Democrats finish the deal—and fast. Voicing the feelings of many Democratic colleagues, Colin Allred stressed to Biden that if Democrats did not prove that they could make government work, then the party—and the country—would pay an awful price.

"The alternative is a Republican Party that doesn't believe in democracy in the same way," Allred told Biden, according to his memory.

It was Susan Wild, the last member to speak, who most thoroughly addressed the raw politics of the moment.

The Pennsylvania litigator had been a voice of straight talk throughout her two years and ten months in the House, criticizing Biden's slothful campaign, urging Pelosi to stop holding show votes on legislation that would never pass the Senate, and sharply rebuking the White House for the summer disaster in Afghanistan.

Now she was face-to-face with the president of the United States, albeit in a video meeting. Wild chose her language carefully.

During the long season of negotiation and posturing between Democrats in Washington, the White House had not done all that much to promote its achievements or sell the contents of the reconciliation bill to the American people.

Addressing Biden, Wild said it was time for all that to change. Voters needed to know that the administration was about to deliver meaningful and specific benefits for them, not just the amount of money it was about to spend.

Just as important, Wild said, Biden had to spend more time explaining to voters how the legislation would be paid for. Many Democrats, including the president and the Speaker of the House, had been pushing the line that the reconciliation bill would not cost a nickel—a glib and inarticulate way of expressing that taxes on corporations and the wealthy would cover the cost.

Wild said voters were "incredulous" when they heard that a multitrillion-dollar bill would not cost them anything. They needed to be persuaded that it was true.

"The more people can understand it, the more they're able to sift through the opposition's talking points and recognize them for being false," Wild said, by her own recollection.

That candid moment with the president represented a painful reality check on many of the political aspirations of Biden and his team. They had begun the year by boasting that they would move faster, fight harder, and sell their accomplishments more aggressively than Barack Obama ever did. Now it was autumn, and a vulnerable member of the House—one with down-to-earth Pennsylvania roots like his own—was telling the president things had not yet worked out that way.

Biden did not get defensive or argue with Wild.

In fact, the president agreed with her.

"I feel the same way," Biden replied, according to Wild. "We've been talking about this—we really need to change some of our messaging."

To the whole group, Biden made a larger commitment. On that autumn day, eleven months after he defeated Donald Trump at the ballot box, Biden acknowledged that the fight for control of the country was about to go to the voters once again. His domestic agenda was still hanging in the balance on Capitol Hill, but the ultimate fate of his presidency would be decided in the midterm elections.

I know that I need all of you, Biden told his guests. I know that I need you all to hold your seats in order for the second two years of my term to be productive.

The president promised: I'm going to be there for all of you.

The next campaign was already approaching.

Epilogue

A Very Important Battleground

ON NOVEMBER 15, a bipartisan delegation from the House and Senate gathered on the South Lawn of the White House to celebrate the signing of the infrastructure bill. In a proud, sober address, President Biden reminded the country that he had run for president in the first place "to make sure our democracy delivers for you—for all of you."

"We're the only country that's always come out of great crises stronger than we went in," Biden proclaimed, calling the law proof that America could still do big things.

The nation, and many of Biden's fellow Democrats, could be forgiven for receiving that resolute message with skepticism.

The House had finally approved the Senate's infrastructure bill late on the night of November 5, more than a month after Biden's first trip to the Hill when he disappointed Nancy Pelosi by declining to demand the immediate support of House Democrats. The president's hesitation to break the standoff between centrists and progressives in his party had left Democrats in a painful state of suspended animation. Biden's approval ratings continued to slide as he appeared frozen in indecision over how to resolve the deadlock in his party.

Pelosi had hosted Biden on the Hill a second time, on October 28, just before his trip to a crucial climate summit in Scotland. The White House again seemed to be setting up a pivotal moment for the president, releasing a framework for a slimmed-down version of the Build Back Better plan that it believed could clear the Senate. The two most intransigent Democratic senators had given Biden reason to be optimistic: Kyrsten Sinema told House Democrats in confidence that she could back the framework now that it lacked the tax hikes she so reviled. Joe Manchin, meeting with Biden at his home in Wilmington, had given the president permission to tell progressives he expected to be able to get Manchin's vote, too.

With a seemingly improving path for Build Back Better, Pelosi hoped Biden would use his second visit to the Hill to demand an immediate vote on infrastructure. Surely progressives would recognize they were on track to get what they wanted and do as Biden asked.

But again, Biden had declined to make a direct plea to progressives to pass his infrastructure deal that very day. He left it to Pelosi to speak up in the meeting and urge her members to vote straightaway. Biden's hesitation enraged and bewildered the Speaker. In private, she blamed Ron Klain for coddling progressives. But she blamed Biden, too, asking with irritation why he could not tell Manchin he absolutely needed to vote for Build Back Better and be done with it—a profound misreading, Biden knew, of how such a command would likely go over with a proud senator.

It had taken a sharp kick from the voters to stir the White House into action. The off-year elections in New Jersey and Virginia had loomed for months as a distant consideration, but by late October the two big states were poised to deliver a judgment on the country's ruling party. The mood of the country was sour after twenty-one months of battling the coronavirus and all the restrictions on schooling, commerce, and leisure activities that entailed. Biden's approval ratings had sagged in both states.

In Virginia, Terry McAuliffe's attempt to reclaim the governorship looked highly imperiled. The playbook Gavin Newsom had used in California was not working quite as well in a more closely divided state. Deriding Republicans as Trump stooges and public-health saboteurs was not proving a surefire strategy for Democrats who controlled the state and federal government in a moment of roiling public discontent.

Epilogue: A Very Important Battleground

Both McAuliffe and Pelosi pleaded with the White House to do whatever it could to dislodge the infrastructure bill and secure a win for the party after months of political starvation. McAuliffe even used his after-hours time on the campaign trail to call up Joe Manchin and lobby him to support Biden's larger social-welfare agenda, in the hope it would help liberate the infrastructure bill from the House.

A week before the election, Abigail Spanberger, the outspoken moderate congresswoman from Virginia, cornered Biden backstage at campaign rally in Arlington and lobbied him to put pressure on House progressives.

Mr. President, she told Biden, it's time to "turn the screws."

But Election Day came and went on November 2 without a victory on infrastructure. Phil Murphy narrowly held on to the governorship of New Jersey, while Republicans swept Virginia. When Biden called McAuliffe afterward, he did not attempt to deflect the blame.

The president told McAuliffe: I screwed you and I'm sorry.

McAuliffe kept his political resentments private, but another Virginia Democrat did not. The day after the election, Spanberger blamed Biden's grandiose policy ambitions for the defeat.

"Nobody elected him to be FDR," she said. "They elected him to be normal and stop the chaos."

The sting of defeat became the catalyst Democrats needed to make some hard choices. Facing an avalanche of criticism for allowing his great legislative priorities to languish, Biden finally told House progressives he needed them to vote for infrastructure immediately. Leaders on the left made it clear they resented the demand, but some of the most influential House progressives appeared to recognize that holding out any longer was untenable.

As the infrastructure bill moved to the House floor, Pramila Jayapal was nervous about what would happen in the Senate. But she said she would take what the president might call his word as a Biden.

"We're going to trust the president that he's going to get 51 votes in the Senate," she said on MSNBC's *Morning Joe*.

It took all the muscle of the president and the Speaker to get the bill passed. Pelosi called in favors from the conservative-leaning building trade unions to lobby their Republican friends and asked Josh Gottheimer, a New Jersey Democrat she had privately derided for months as a "renegade," to help deliver as many GOP votes for the legislation as possible. On the night of the vote, Democrats were still short of a majority when Steny Hoyer called Klain and asked him to personally lobby key progressives for their support.

In the end, a half dozen left-wing lawmakers rebelled against Biden, including Alexandria Ocasio-Cortez and Jamaal Bowman—enough to deny Pelosi a party-line majority to pass the legislation. Had only Democrats voted for the bill, it would have died on the floor.

But thirteen Republicans broke ranks with their side to support the bipartisan infrastructure package, giving the legislation the votes it needed to reach Biden's desk. Among the GOP "aye" votes were several members who had been scolded and threatened by their party for voting to impeach Donald Trump—lawmakers like Anthony Gonzalez and John Katko and Fred Upton, who had little left to lose in defying the Republican base.

A bill worth more than $1 trillion in upgrades to the nation's roads and bridges, mass transit, and electric-vehicle systems was at last headed to Joe Biden for his signature.

As Biden gazed out on the crowd on the South Lawn on that November day, he had in hand a legislative trophy that seemed to embody so much of what he had aimed to do as president. Much of his own party had belittled the bipartisan deal as an inadequate down payment on Build Back Better, but the legislation was consequential in its own right—a vast and overdue investment in infrastructure, achieved with bipartisan majorities in both chambers of Congress and the personal support of Mitch McConnell, the most fearsome Republican legislator of the age.

Biden had pledged as a candidate, and as president-elect, to bring the country together in a spirit of consensus and show that American democracy could improve the lives of average voters. If one law could capture the conciliatory spirit of that pledge, the bipartisan infrastructure bill might be it.

For the first time in months, Biden seemed aglow with the pride of achievement and the conviction that his personal theory of presidential leadership really did have merit. Deal-making was hard, but it was still possible. The country was divided, but there were still areas of common ground—provided the right leaders were there to seek it. In the hopeful flush of victory at the White House that day, the president approached Lisa Murkowski, the anti-Trump Alaska Republican who had helped negotiate the law, and told her he was ready to help her in any way she needed. The president knew she was facing a tough reelection campaign in 2022, with Trump crusading for her defeat.

The day, however, was a less than complete vindication of the Biden presidency.

After all, the president had promised not just to rebuild America, but to build it back as a better, stronger, more equal country than it had been before the pandemic—and before Donald Trump. He had promised not just to repair bridges and railways but to master climate change and attack racial injustice with sustained resolve.

Having spent half a century reaching for the political middle, Joseph R. Biden Jr. had finally entered the presidency determined not merely to tinker but to transform.

He had made so many promises that he had not yet kept, so many plans still not enacted. The unresolved Build Back Better agenda was chief among them.

When Abigail Spanberger lashed out at Biden after the Virginia election and belittled his Rooseveltian ambitions, the president had taken rueful note. He knew he was dreaming big—as big as he had ever dreamed—but he had come to like it that way. Biden wanted to make the most of his presidency, however long it lasted. He was not about to abandon his grandest aspirations in the face of an off-year electoral setback or another round of cranky commentary from Sinema or Manchin.

Or because of a scolding from an aggrieved House sophomore.

Not long after Spanberger's tart remark, Biden placed a phone call to her. When she picked up, he greeted her in a light and knowing tone.

"Hello, Abigail," the president began. "This is President Roosevelt."

After a pause, Spanberger answered: "Hello, Mr. President."

Biden chuckled, telling Spanberger he was glad she had a sense of humor.

"No," she quickly replied. "I'm glad *you* have a sense of humor, Mr. President."

* * *

At the end of Biden's first year as president, the America he governed was unquestionably in better condition than the one he inherited.

The nation's economic recovery had seemed so halting for months, but by the end of 2021 the United States had enjoyed the fastest single-year economic growth since the Reagan era. The coronavirus was still circulating widely—the latest known variant, Omicron, had appeared around Thanksgiving—but a large-scale vaccination campaign had blunted its deadliest effects. The White House and Congress were tangled in painstaking legislative negotiations, but the federal government had already delivered economic and public-health aid on a gargantuan scale.

Now, a generational upgrade to American infrastructure was on the way, too.

After a trip to Asia in the fall, Gina Raimondo had reported back to her colleagues in the White House that at every stop—in Japan, Singapore, and Malaysia—foreign dignitaries had hailed the infrastructure bill as an imposing triumph for the new American president. For all its sometimes humiliating dysfunction, American government truly could work, at least up to a point.

There were reasons for optimism, of a kind. Under the pressure of multiple terrifying crises, the United States had shown no small measure of political resilience. American democracy would not pass away quietly into history's night.

The system had wobbled and creaked—but it had not failed.

Yet it had not thrived, either.

For all the other signs of national recovery, the country's political architecture remained fragile.

The American two-party system cannot function well unless at least one party is politically powerful, internally coherent, and serious about governing, all at the same time. At the end of 2021, it was impossible to describe either the ruling Democrats or the Republican opposition in those terms.

On the Democratic side, every major party leader ended 2021 weaker than they started it. Biden's party had been given a chance to govern by an expansive coalition of voters opposed to Donald Trump, but those voters and the lawmakers they elected harbored deep disagreements on so much else. The president and his friends in Washington had employed a range of tactics to mute those differences, but they had not managed to do away with them. The anti-Trump forces that granted power temporarily to Democrats had not morphed into a durable progressive alliance.

In Congress, both Pelosi and Chuck Schumer were badly diminished figures, sapped by a year of navigating their party's internal rifts.

In the House, Pelosi had lost the faith of centrists who once saw her as a fail-safe against the left, and she had angered progressives who once hoped her experienced hand would deliver their greatest aspirations. She had exasperated the White House, too, as she veered between placating one side of her caucus to appeasing the other. Ron Klain expressed his bewilderment to White House colleagues when Pelosi shifted from villainizing Gottheimer and his allies over the summer, to treating them as cherished partners in governing once it became clear the left flank of her caucus had become even less cooperative.

Pelosi's grievances with the White House had deepened, too, and at the start of 2022 she was increasingly open about her frustrations with Biden. By then, the House had approved Build Back Better and voting rights legislation. The Senate had done neither and the Speaker was openly doubtful of whether Biden had a strategy to change that. In January 2022, Pelosi startled the White

This Will Not Pass

House by twice criticizing Biden for his public remarks on voting rights and the legislative strategy for Build Back Better, in both cases chiding the president for rhetoric she saw as ineffective.

The eighty-one-year-old Speaker had long shrouded her future plans in mystery, including from members of her family. In the spring of 2021, her husband, Paul, had told the governor of California over dinner that even he did not know how long she would choose to stay as Speaker. But as the year came to an end there was more open conversation among Democrats about whether Pelosi might make way for a Speaker from the next generation—Hakeem Jeffries, most likely, or maybe Katherine Clark, the Massachusetts progressive.

Dozens of other Democrats were retiring from Congress ahead of a difficult midterm campaign, including senior members of the party who had served with Pelosi for decades. It seemed possible that after years of being led by people born before the invention of color television, the congressional Democratic Party was headed for a stark generational transition.

Chuck Schumer was no less depleted. The Senate leader who had approached Biden during the transition with a strategy for strong-arming Mitch McConnell, and who had successfully lobbied the White House to support a party-line version of the American Rescue Plan, now seemed bereft of ideas for getting anything else done. He had not managed to forge a unanimous consensus among Democratic senators on either Build Back Better or on voting rights. To many Senate Democrats, Schumer looked to have played a dangerous game—placating both Bernie Sanders and Joe Manchin at the same time, trusting that he would ultimately be able to jawbone a compromise out of both men—and lost.

So many other Democratic plans had cleared the House only to wither in the Senate, including immigration reform, a gun-control package, and the George Floyd Justice in Policing Act. With the filibuster intact, these liberal aspirations appeared all but doomed.

On voting especially, Schumer seemed adrift, bringing up multiple versions of election-reform legislation and hoping that eventually the holdouts

416

in his caucus would relent amid relentless lobbying from advocates. It was an empty strategy: The notion that two maverick senators who delighted in bucking their party would bow to that kind of pressure was folly. White House officials thought Schumer was consumed with "protecting his left flank," as one of them put it, focused as much on avoiding blame for defeat as he was on crafting a plan to win.

Defenders of Schumer insisted that he deserved more credit for political adroitness than that. By year's end he had lined up every Democratic senator save one—Manchin—behind a version of the Build Back Better plan. All but two—Manchin and Sinema—now supported changing the Senate rules to allow a voting rights bill to overcome a Republican filibuster. Forty-eight or forty-nine votes was not what these measures needed to pass, but it was awfully close.

Yet close was not good enough, and Schumer's inability to manage Manchin risked becoming a fatal obstacle to the rest of Biden's agenda.

The West Virginia senator grew frustrated throughout the fall with Biden aides and liberal lawmakers who he felt did not take his cautious instincts and conservative home state seriously. In one conversation with Jayapal, Manchin asked the Seattle progressive to describe her House district to him. When she detailed the cosmopolitan, highly diverse seat she called home, Manchin replied that he had a different base: Trump won his state by nearly forty points.

Biden and Schumer had relented to Sinema's preferences on taxes, agreeing to remove from Build Back Better the upper-income tax hikes that she opposed and Manchin favored. But they were holding fast to a set of big-spending programs that were structured in a way Manchin found highly suspect. The West Virginian had maddened the White House and, increasingly, his Senate colleagues with a fluid set of policy demands and gut-level misgivings on the domestic-spending package. And there was also a real consistency to some of his objections—most significantly, his opposition to extending the newly expanded, newly expensive child tax credit by only a year or two and leaving it to a future Congress to devise a longer-term way to fund it.

Republicans were still trying to court Manchin and Sinema into switching parties, though without much success in either case. Sinema rebuffed one GOP overture by noting that her bisexual identity made that a nonstarter.

I have a girlfriend, she told one Republican senator. That's not going to fly with Arizona Republicans.

Manchin was not quite as dismissive, but he was no closer to defecting than he had been at the start of the year. Republican senators wooed him again over a second dinner at Bistro Cacao in November, and while Manchin heard out their evangelizing he made clear that he was not about to convert.

In December, Manchin was even blunter with Mitch McConnell, telling the Republican leader that he saw no political benefit in joining the GOP. Trump, Manchin predicted, would come after him in 2024 no matter what party label he had next to his name. He had voted twice to convict the former president in his impeachment trials.

To one fellow senator, Manchin mused that he would never formally leave the Democratic caucus, but he could imagine switching his party label to independent while still aligning himself overall with Democrats, à la Bernie Sanders.

Chuck Schumer had few tools for dealing with a man so unmoored from the institutional Democratic Party, and it showed.

It came as a brutal disappointment to the White House when Manchin announced on Fox News in mid-December that he could never vote for the version of Build Back Better approved in the House—or anything that closely resembled it. He did not entirely rule out supporting a greatly reconfigured bill, leaving some room for future negotiations, but his announcement infuriated Biden.

The president felt that Manchin had misled him before the infrastructure vote, giving Biden his blessing to tell liberals the White House could likely deliver Manchin on Build Back Better—and then making a liar out of Biden by dooming the bill, at least in its existing form.

The president felt his word as a Biden had been tarnished by Manchin. In the House, liberal lawmakers were inclined to agree, feeling they had been goaded into supporting Manchin's beloved infrastructure bill in exchange for a promise that had quickly expired.

Biden dispatched aides to issue a scorching statement on Manchin's reversal, then quickly regretted the harsh tone. He still needed Manchin's vote to get anything done.

In a phone call, the two men agreed to let things cool off a bit.

You made a commitment to me, Biden told the senator. If I can't trust your word, what do I have?

Manchin told Biden that he had no problem with the president himself, but the White House staff had become too difficult for him to deal with.

You and I are just fine, Manchin told Biden. We're okay.

It was not clear that either man knew what that was supposed to mean.

*　*　*

It was not only Joe Manchin troubling the president as he neared the end of his first year in office. After pursuing the White House for most of his lifetime, Biden found himself ill at ease in the executive residence, uncomfortable with the lack of privacy and the pervasive presence of servants and aides. He left for Delaware or Camp David many weekends, seeking a kind of refuge with his family.

The political climate was still worsening for Biden, as the coronavirus surged once again, inflation kept climbing, and congressional Democrats continued battering each other over the details of his stalled agenda. Deaths from the pandemic were disproportionately afflicting counties that voted for Donald Trump, where the most lethal coronavirus variant was a culture of vaccine denialism. But Biden knew it was his job to master the disease, and his administration had not yet managed to do that.

Like most presidents, Biden was keenly aware of public criticism; and, unlike his former running mate, Barack Obama, he did not pretend to ignore the scolding of opinion columnists and television pundits.

I shouldn't watch it, Biden would tell aides. But you know how it is . . .

A devoted viewer of MSNBC's *Morning Joe* and CNN's *Don Lemon Tonight*, Biden was stung by the barbs of various talking heads with a sensitivity his aides found unfortunate. Even more vexing to his aides was when Biden would then invite his cable-news critics, like the foreign policy scholar Richard Haass, to meet with him in the Oval Office.

There was not much to cheer up Biden on the shows, nor was the political guidance of his aides much more encouraging. His polling numbers had never recovered from the plunge they took after the fall of Afghanistan. By some measures, they had worsened. A few days after the signing of the infrastructure law, his pollster John Anzalone circulated another downbeat memo. Voters, Anzalone wrote, "are not just feeling sour about the economy and inflation now, but voters also feel things are moving in the wrong direction for the future."

Biden's problems, Anzalone warned, were not just about the big-picture plight of the country. "The President's personal traits have also taken a tumble since the summer," the pollster wrote, citing surveys conducted by *Politico* and the intelligence firm Morning Consult.

The polling found particularly grim results for Biden on the question of whether he was a clear communicator.

It was not a new problem for the Biden White House, but it had grown more dire with time. As early as the spring of 2021, Anzalone's polling firm had assembled a presentation for top Democrats urging Biden to better educate the public about his support for raising taxes on the wealthy, and to explain how his administration intended to secure the border with Mexico.

In a forty-page document, Biden's pollsters warned then that "most voters have not heard anything" about how the president aimed to pay for his agenda and that voters in general "do not feel he has a plan to address the situation on the border." The White House, they wrote, had to develop a "drumbeat" of messaging about Biden's plans to create jobs.

That drumbeat had never materialized—on jobs, taxes, immigration, or nearly anything else. For the voting public, Biden's voice had been a faint and distant one over the course of 2021. Following two presidents who were, in different ways, outsize public figures, Biden made only sparing use of the bully pulpit afforded to him and conducted far fewer interviews than Obama and Trump did in their opening year.

Despite his many vows not to repeat the mistakes of the Obama administration, Biden had recapitulated one of the overarching political errors of Obama's first year: immersing himself in arcane legislative strategy at the cost of large-scale political salesmanship.

Biden had failed to trumpet his own accomplishments, advertising the successes of the American Rescue Plan only in fits and starts. He had done vanishingly little to explain to the country what his Build Back Better plan would actually do, because he and his congressional interlocutors had never really decided what would ultimately be included in it. For much of 2021, there was a quiet clamor on the Hill for Biden to get out more in public: Pete Buttigieg, the young transportation secretary, frequently relayed pleas to the West Wing from politically vulnerable Democrats desperate to see Biden and prominent officials like Buttigieg hit the road to sell their achievements.

Some Democrats delivered those appeals to Biden directly. During a trip to Michigan in October, the Democratic lawmaker Dan Kildee had nudged the president to be more visible and more expressive with the country. At a union facility, Kildee, who hailed from a local political dynasty, approached Biden and told him: "It makes a difference when you get out there."

Biden had agreed, but then weeks more had gone by without a major shift in the White House's approach to communicating with the country. More ominous, by the start of 2022 some high-profile Democrats were dodging Biden when he came to their states, and members of the cabinet conceded that Biden's unpopularity had made some parts of the country political no-go zones.

Frustrating Democrats, for months Biden had done almost nothing to delineate a sharp contrast with Republicans and persuade voters to punish the GOP for opposing the most popular elements of Biden's agenda. Republicans were trapped in their own civil war and they had yet to articulate anything resembling a policy platform of their own. But the White House had not made that reality clear to voters.

In the fall, the prominent Democratic strategist Paul Begala contacted Klain to tell him just that. The president, Begala said, was too Olympian, too prone to putting himself above the partisan fray, just as Obama had done.

Biden, Begala said, needed to remind people every day that Democrats favored popular programs like universal prekindergarten and the child tax credit, and Republicans opposed them. He needed to drum into the country's consciousness the threat it still faced from Trump and his insurrectionist allies.

Offering Klain a ready-to-go attack line, Begala proposed Biden tell Americans that Republicans "fear Trump more than they care about you." It was a smooth line easy to imagine coming from Begala's most famous client, Bill Clinton.

Well, Klain replied, that approach isn't this president's comfort zone. That's not his brand.

Biden had long told advisers that he intended to seek a new term in 2024, with the caveat that at his age the ultimate decision would partly rest on factors beyond his control. When one senior adviser pointed out to Biden that he had described himself during the campaign as a transitional leader, Biden batted away the observation. He had not meant to imply anything about 2024 with that remark, he said. As Biden saw it, there was still so much work left to be done.

But at the moment, Biden looked less like a transformational president than one of those sturdy workmen of history who steps into the job at a dark time and carries out his duty with a kind of quiet determination, but no evident gift for connecting with the public. In the self-deprecating automotive metaphor favored by an earlier crisis-era president, he looked at the moment more like a Ford than a Lincoln.

Yet four years is a long time in politics, and Biden was only a quarter of the way through his term. Promisingly, the start of Biden's second year brought with it the chance to fulfill his vow to elevate the first Black woman to the Supreme Court, an appointment that would at once cement a key part of his legacy and energize the dispirited voters who had helped deliver him the Democratic nomination and the presidency.

It was one more way for Biden to go further and push harder—to realize more of the plans that had inspired wary liberals to support his campaign and stoked Biden's own dreams of transcendent historical greatness.

Even more than a chance for action, Biden felt he had an obligation to succeed. Trump was still out there, plotting a comeback that could tear the country apart for good. Someone had to defend American democracy in 2024.

If Biden was not that person, then who was?

* * *

Few Democrats had confidence that it was Kamala Harris.

The first woman ever to be a heartbeat away from the presidency ended the year as politically isolated as she had ever been.

Harris's voting rights portfolio had become another dead end. The vice president had held a series of meetings with voting rights advocates and state legislators battling Republican voting restrictions in the states. But she had never become a leading actor in the Democratic effort to pass a voting bill on the Hill, or to marshal public support for that effort through mass communication. Months after taking on the assignment, Harris had never spoken directly about the issue with Manchin, the most important Democratic holdout, or with Murkowski, the lone Republican who had backed any version of voting rights legislation in 2021.

Harris remained studiously loyal to Biden, but on the issue of voting rights she cast some blame on the president for her predicament. How was she supposed to communicate clearly about voting-rights legislation, Harris asked West Wing aides, when the president would not even say that he supported changing the Senate rules to open the path for a bill?

Biden had said he was open to such a step during a town hall–style event on CNN in the fall, but Harris told the president's aides his position was still too ambiguous. She was in a corner, she argued—unable to make a forceful case for getting legislation done until voters knew that Biden himself was willing to back the procedural steps required to make that a real possibility.

The president ultimately called in December for narrow changes to the filibuster, specifically on issues related to voting rights, but by then any political momentum on that front had nearly vanished.

Harris's relationship with Biden remained friendly but not close, and their weekly lunches lacked a real depth of personal and political intimacy. The vice president seemed eager to relay concerns to Biden from political donors and activist leaders, but she seldom went further than acting as a conduit. She told Biden several times that there was widening dismay in the party about the weak condition of the Democratic National Committee; she did not share suggestions for strengthening the DNC or volunteer to dive into the issue herself.

Aware of her own unsettled place in the administration, Harris grew impatient with her own aides, blaming the latest configuration of staff around her for letting her down. She told an ally in the fall that she had initiated an audit of her office to make it function better. Soon after that a series of advisers departed, including Symone Sanders, the fiercely loyal Biden campaign aide who had been at Harris's side for only about a year.

The vice president had one vocal and unyielding defender in the West Wing: the president's chief of staff. Klain would brook no criticism of Harris. He had lobbied Biden to pick her as his running mate in the first place, and colleagues detected a certain defensiveness from Klain at any implication that perhaps Harris had been the wrong choice.

Yet even Klain understood that something was not working. He told Harris in the fall that she had erred by holding her Latin American assignment at arm's length: Yes, he acknowledged, it was a politically delicate portfolio, but there had been an opportunity there for her to take full ownership of something, sink into the policy details and produce results.

That, Klain told Harris, was the way to succeed as a vice president.

He urged her, too, to get in front of the media more and do more interviews. Up to that point, Harris had been on a feast-or-famine schedule of media appearances, going weeks without having a sustained exchange with a reporter and then sitting for a burst of interviews all at once. That was a recipe for getting out of practice and making mistakes, Klain told her, and when you interact with the media infrequently, people only remember your mistakes.

Harris absorbed the advice, but she continued to resist the exhortation to pick some signature issues, partly out of concern that she would be restricted to handling subjects closely linked to her personal identity. She told West Wing aides she was open to taking ownership of a few subjects, but they had to be broad-spectrum issues. Harris said in frank terms that she did not want to be restricted to a few subjects mainly associated with women and Black Americans.

Harris knew well enough that she had a political problem. One senator close to her, describing Harris's frustration level as "up in the stratosphere," lamented that Harris's political decline was a "slow-rolling Greek tragedy." Her approval numbers were even lower than Biden's, and other Democrats were already eyeing the 2024 race if Biden declined to run. And Harris had done almost nothing to gird herself for such a contest: Far from the right-wing caricature of her as a hidden hand already plotting a takeover, Harris had built no independent political operation for herself and had yet to make courtesy calls to some of the most powerful Democrats in early primary states.

Buttigieg was a favorite of wealthy donors who wanted an alternative to Harris for 2024 or beyond. Several major governors who had battled Trump—including Phil Murphy, JB Pritzker, and Roy Cooper—were making the rounds with Democratic contributors. And when Biden named

Mitch Landrieu, the former mayor of New Orleans, to a major federal job overseeing infrastructure spending, it stirred a ripple of speculation that the eloquent southern Democrat might soon act on the presidential ambitions he had harbored for years.

Harris began seeking out advice from beyond her inner circle, taking counsel from longtime veterans of the Washington scene like Rahm Emanuel, the Chicago mayor-turned-ambassador to Japan, and Joe Scarborough, the congressman-turned-MSNBC star, as well as some of her old campaign consultants and other administration appointees. The advice she got was emphatic and consistent: Get out of the bubble of the vice presidency and stop agonizing so much about the ornate internal politics of her dysfunctional party.

Just be there for Biden. Get out in public. Talk to the country. Own some issues and get stuff done.

It was all easier said than done.

In several candid conversations, Harris admitted to confidants that she simply did not know Washington all that well. She had only arrived there after the 2016 election, and the insular nature of the White House had made it difficult for her to make new friends and figure out how the nation's capital really worked.

It was a sobering acknowledgment of her own limitations from a politician not overly given to self-criticism. If Harris had a path to recovery, then perhaps admitting she had a problem was a useful first step.

* * *

As the leaders of the Democratic Party entered another dark winter, their counterparts on the Republican side were feeling somewhat more optimistic, at least where raw electoral politics were concerned. Biden's tribulations could only lift them in the 2022 campaign, and the midterms were already looking like they could be a replay of the backlash elections that had greeted nearly every other recent president halfway through his term.

If Democrats ultimately failed to pass Build Back Better, then the ultimate impact of Biden's presidency might be more limited than conservatives had feared it might be.

Yet the Democrats' season of agony had not done much to strengthen the two men tasked with leading the national Republican Party, Kevin McCarthy and Mitch McConnell. Nor had Republicans managed to escape the shadow of Donald Trump and his failed presidency. It was still impossible to discern what the Republican Party stood for as a whole, besides channeling Trump's grievances and opposing Joe Biden. The party members most sincerely interested in governing, many of them apostates who had broken decisively with Trump, had already announced plans to retire or would likely never run again.

McConnell was not quite one of those Republicans, but he was close. While retaining the support of his Senate colleagues, McConnell was increasingly isolated from his party outside the walls of the Capitol, detached from the rank-and-file and locked in seething conflict with a former president who demanded his ouster on a routine basis.

The Old Crow, as Trump had begun calling McConnell, was laboring to recruit candidates for the 2022 elections who mirrored his own conventionally conservative instincts and sensibilities about the role of the Senate. By year's end, he was confronting the dispiriting prospect that he might have to settle for Senate nominees like Mo Brooks, the extreme-right Alabaman who had addressed Trump's mob on January 6 before they rioted, and Herschel Walker, the Georgia football legend whose history of mental health issues and domestic violence allegations had not deterred Trump from recruiting him as an opponent for Raphael Warnock.

McConnell attempted to shake off the worst of the indignities Trump visited on him. At social events he hosted, he displayed a bottle of Old Crow, the cut-rate whiskey, as a wry joke on the whole situation. But in unguarded moments he confessed to colleagues that he had not expected Trump to continue dominating the party for so long after leaving office in humiliation.

Of McConnell, Lisa Murkowski says: "It's fair to say that he also has been surprised by the hold, if you will, that the former president continues to have over so many in the Congress—his level of continued influence."

There was scant appetite among Republican senators for dethroning McConnell, but many suspected the elderly lawmaker would give up his post in the not-distant future. McConnell understood that, too.

The Senate minority leader was fully aware of his own mortality, and at times dropped hints that he knew the end—of his career, or perhaps more— could be approaching. Early in 2021, Tom Cotton had approached him on the Senate floor with a bracing inquiry. With the Senate so evenly divided, the clinically tactical Arkansas conservative had done a little research into where his party might risk losing an additional seat or two if elderly legislators were to die. Cotton found one conspicuous state with an aging Republican senator and a Democratic governor empowered to name a replacement in the event of his death or resignation.

That state was Kentucky, and the senator was Mitch McConnell.

As Cotton raised the matter, the Republican leader cut in: I know, I'm taking care of it.

Within months, by McConnell's design, the Kentucky legislature had changed the succession laws in his state to restrict the ability of Andy Beshear, the Democratic governor, to name a replacement if McConnell's seat suddenly became vacant. If McConnell went on to his eternal reward, he wanted to en- sure that Democrats would not reap more temporal benefits.

McConnell was making preparations for the final curtain in less morbid ways, too.

In December 2021, when his well-liked deputy John Thune was agoniz- ing over whether to run for reelection in 2022, McConnell nudged him with a word of encouragement.

I'm not going to be around here forever, McConnell told him, dangling the prospect that Thune could be the top man in the Senate soon enough.

Thune believed that was likelier to be after the 2024 election than in the immediate future, but some Republican senators had begun talking quietly about offering McConnell the political equivalent of a gold watch after 2022 if they did not take back the majority.

Of all the political setbacks he faced in the fall of 2021, the most stinging for McConnell might have been the rejection he faced in New Hampshire from the state's popular governor, Chris Sununu, who toyed for months with a Senate candidacy before abruptly trashing the idea in early November. In the Senate, Sununu complained, "frankly too often doing nothing is considered a win." It was a brash pronouncement that McConnell's advisers took as a direct insult.

McConnell did not believe he was in the Senate to do nothing.

The Kentucky legislator was proud of having voted for the infrastructure law. In early November, just three days after House Republicans furiously tried to block passage of the bill, McConnell had traveled to northern Kentucky to hail the billions of federal dollars that would soon pour into his state. There would be so much money coming to Kentucky, McConnell boasted, that they might even be able to replace the notoriously dilapidated Brent Spence Bridge spanning the Ohio River.

That trip—and that pork-barrel boast—revealed once again the gulf separating McConnell from his party's angry base.

Trump had railed against the infrastructure package, calling it a political gift to Biden that would empower the Democratic president to sweep the rest of his policy agenda into law. McConnell and thirty-one other Republicans in the House and Senate had ignored Trump, but the hundreds of other Republicans in Congress had opposed the measure. They had cited a hodgepodge of reasons for voting against it.

For the most part, Republicans shared a simple motive for opposing the bipartisan measure: An infrastructure law would be a win for Joe Biden and Republican primary voters back home would not countenance that.

Kevin McCarthy was one of those Republicans. He had never considered voting for it.

Rob Portman, the Ohio Republican who helped negotiate the deal in the Senate, called McCarthy several times to urge the House minority leader not to put up a wall of resistance to the bipartisan measure. Portman did not expect McCarthy to support the infrastructure deal, but he could at least decline to crusade against it. McCarthy quickly stopped taking Portman's calls. The House minority leader knew what his party's activist base wanted and that was reflexive opposition to anything with a whiff of the Biden administration on it.

But if a wall of resistance was what right-wing voters wanted, McCarthy did not manage to erect one. The roll call on the infrastructure bill was an embarrassment for McCarthy, who had predicted throughout the summer that the count of Republican "aye" votes would number in the single digits. As the vote unfolded, McCarthy urged Republicans who were tempted to support the legislation to hold back from voting until it became clear whether Democrats could get it over the finish line on their own. If Democrats could not get it done, he argued, then Republicans should not bail them out.

Thirteen of his colleagues rejected that appeal, including several who made a point of voting early as a personal rebuke to McCarthy. One of those lawmakers was John Katko, whom McCarthy had betrayed over the January 6 commission. These Republicans ignored their nominal leader to help secure a landmark bipartisan victory backed by a Democratic president.

McCarthy's swerving opportunism was starting to catch up with him.

As 2021 neared its end, McCarthy was clinging to the same political strategy he had followed all year: sticking close to Trump and bowing to the far right, trusting that they would ultimately give him the support he needed to become Speaker of the House. It was not a fanciful scheme. If Republicans won the House by a huge margin in 2022, then even McCarthy's internal critics knew it might be hard to deny him the most important job in Congress.

But Republicans were not guaranteed a thumping victory, and McCarthy's shortcomings were blazingly apparent to members of all ideological stripes. His failure to thwart the infrastructure bill enraged hard-liners and drew threats of retribution from them. A few even suggested that Trump himself should be made Speaker of the House after 2022, rather than the House minority leader who was so desperate to please him.

Closer to the political middle, McCarthy was viewed even more scornfully. Over the summer, a gathering of mainstream GOP lawmakers known as the Republican Governance Group—the Tuesday Group, to longtime members—had broached the subject of McCarthy's feeble leadership. A succession of Republicans who had clashed with McCarthy over the previous year spoke out against him, including Katko; Peter Meijer, the young Michigander who voted for impeachment; and Steve Womack, the conservative military veteran whom McCarthy had spurned in his attempt to punish Mo Brooks after January 6.

Set against McCarthy, Womack proposed another Republican as a future Speaker: Steve Scalise, McCarthy's second-in-command. The conservative Louisianan was imperfect, Womack acknowledged, but he was well liked by his colleagues. And he was not Kevin McCarthy.

Beyond the halls of Congress, a man who knew the Speakership better than nearly anyone else alive was floating another alternative to McCarthy.

Toward the end of the year, John Boehner, who had spent half a decade as Speaker of the House, was telling friends in Washington that Patrick McHenry of North Carolina, the top Republican on the House Financial Services Committee, could make a fine substitute if McCarthy struggled to lock down the job. The forty-six-year-old McHenry was thoroughly mainstream, respected by his Republican colleagues, conservative in his roots but pragmatic in his disposition. Most of all, he was a seasoned man of the House, having entered the chamber well before his thirtieth birthday.

McCarthy faced another threat from beyond his party. Democrats, too, were beginning to talk about thwarting the rise of a man they regarded as craven to the point of seditiousness.

It has long been customary for the House to choose a Speaker by a simple majority vote, with each party's members voting for their side's anointed contender. But if Republicans were to capture the House in 2022, a handful of Democrats had begun to talk about crossing the aisle to support another Republican for Speaker in order to block McCarthy from taking the job. Letting

Kevin McCarthy occupy an office in the presidential line of succession, they believed, would imperil American democracy itself.

The House minority leader had done much to encourage that assessment of him. In his thirst to appease hard-line figures on his own side, he had become one of his party's leading apologists for a growing strain of violent extremism in the Republican conference.

Over the summer, McCarthy had done nothing when Mo Brooks put out a statement expressing sympathy for a man who issued a bomb threat against the Capitol. During the same week Biden signed the infrastructure bill, the House minority leader was working to shield Paul Gosar, the extreme-right Arizona Republican, from official sanction after he posted a cartoon video on Twitter that showed a stylized version of Gosar murdering Alexandria Ocasio-Cortez.

House Democrats voted to censure Gosar and strip him of his committee assignments, but only two Republicans supported them: Liz Cheney and Adam Kinzinger, both GOP outcasts.

The culture of menace that McCarthy tolerated had implications far beyond the outrageous stunts of a few attention-seeking Republicans. A year after a bloodthirsty mob sacked the Capitol, too many lawmakers in both parties remained fearful that violence would strike again. They had good reason to be concerned: members targeted on social media sites or on right-wing television networks, or in public statements from Donald Trump and his loudest advisers, could expect to receive a flood of harassment and death threats that went far beyond the long American tradition of political heckling.

As Trump's most daring critic within the party, Liz Cheney received an inordinate share of those threats. Her chief of staff, Kara Ahern, had taken to conferring every week with the Capitol Police and the House sergeant-at-arms about threats against her boss. Every week, there were hundreds, many of them pouring in during the Fox News prime-time shows hosted by Tucker Carlson and Laura Ingraham.

Cheney was proud of her role prosecuting the case against Trump, and as a leader of the January 6 committee she was one of the chief figures issuing subpoenas for documents, summoning testimony from Trump's inner circle, and referring multiple uncooperative Trump loyalists for possible criminal prosecution.

Cheney's political future was highly uncertain. She faced a strenuous re-election fight at home against an opponent backed by Trump. But unlike other dissident Republicans who had chosen to retire from Congress—including Kinzinger, Katko, and Gonzalez—Cheney appeared determined to go on to the end. She had already traveled to New Hampshire, teasing the possibility of a Cheney 2024 candidacy, and told people in private she was determined to stop Trump from reclaiming the White House at any price.

Trump's cadre was unanimous in its hatred for her, and she welcomed their hatred.

Yet the air of violence in American politics touched not only natural brawlers like Cheney but also scores of other legislators and candidates who had entered politics to govern and serve, and who had not envisioned political office as a kind of warfare.

One of those lawmakers, the young Illinois nurse Lauren Underwood, told the authors of this book midway through 2021 that the atmosphere in Congress was so toxic that the prospect of renewed violence seemed almost an inevitability.

Few of her colleagues could honestly have disagreed.

"Someone," Underwood said then, "is going to get shot."

* * *

And then there was Donald Trump.

The former president had been defeated and disgraced, impeached twice by the Congress and held responsible by the voters for dividing America and mismanaging the coronavirus pandemic. By the end of 2021 he was facing a tangle of legal probes that threatened his businesses, his political future, and perhaps even his personal freedom. The January 6 committee was probing his inner circle of advisers for information about any links to the attack, while prosecutors in New York were investigating Trump for financial fraud and a district attorney in Georgia was scrutinizing his efforts to overturn the 2020 election.

As unpopular as Biden had grown over the course of the year, he was still better liked than the man he defeated. While Trump maintained a large and passionate following, there was no sign that most of the country missed having him as president.

There was also no sign that Trump had gotten the message.

On the night of November 2, he had watched the election results in Virginia with glee, taking them as a personal validation of his own far-right politics. Glenn Youngkin, the victorious Republican candidate for governor, had kept a wary distance from Trump, courting his supporters but deploying emissaries like Newt Gingrich and Lindsey Graham to plead with Trump not to visit Virginia. It was a Democratic-leaning state and Trump was still reviled by most voters there.

Yet as the results trickled in, Trump called Graham in a mood of delight, telling him to turn on the TV and marvel at the strong turnout from Republican voters.

He had commanded Graham: Watch, watch, watch! Those are my people!

There were other Republicans girding to run for president in 2024, but Trump did not believe that any of them would stand a chance against him. Across the party, there was a widespread assumption that the 2024 nomination was his for the taking, if he wanted it.

Yet there were hints of Trump fatigue among mainstream Republican voters; the tumult always surrounding him was exhausting even to some admirers. The midterm campaign would test Trump's influence, and his campaign of vengeance against fellow Republicans, in ways that could be less than fortifying for the former president.

But rather than swelling, the ranks of Republicans willing to battle Trump openly had thinned over the year. McConnell, after thundering against Trump in February, had taken pains to avoid even discussing the former president. In the House, many of his Republican critics had opted to retire rather than face the primary voters again.

Even George W. Bush, the only living former Republican president besides Trump, declined to wage a public effort to cleanse his political party. He told a group of allies over the summer in 2021 that it was essential for Republicans to get rid of Trump, but with the exception of a much-lauded speech on September 11, 2021, about domestic extremism, Bush all but silenced himself in public. He was more willing to tinker in partisan politics in private, as he did at a fall fundraiser for Liz Cheney in Dallas where he said his party needed to speak the truth and embrace new leaders.

Bush's former vice president, Dick Cheney, offered his own gesture of solidarity with opponents of Trump's faction, visiting the Capitol on the anniversary of the January 6 attack to sit on the House floor with his besieged daughter. As they took their seats for the commemoration of the attack, the elder Cheney looked around with disappointment.

It's really sad, he told his daughter, that there are no other Republicans here.

* * *

In Washington and in friendly capitals around the world, there was no more fearful prospect than a Trump comeback.

At a NATO assembly in Portugal late in 2021, Brendan Boyle, the Pennsylvania congressman close to the White House, found himself barraged with nervous questions about a president who by then had been out of office for nine months. Boyle's conclusion: "The nervousness and freakout about American democracy is still alive."

As long as Trump maintained his grip on one of the country's two major parties, there could be no true confidence in the United States or abroad that the American political system was secure and healthy. Far from a vibrant and enduring republic, the country looked far too often like a weary and incoherent jumble of regions, capable of spending huge sums of money in times of emergency or war but otherwise incapable of resolving its most important and intractable domestic problems.

The question Angela Merkel posed to Kamala Harris in July was still on the lips of leaders around the world: Was it really over? Had the threat from Donald Trump really passed?

To some of America's closest friends—and to the authors of this book—it was obvious that the answer was no.

The January 6 attack, after all, had not organized itself. Nor had Trump conjured the rioters out of thin air. The former Australian prime minister Malcolm Turnbull, a moderate conservative in beliefs and temperament, made that observation in penetrating terms during an interview for this book, as he deplored the mob riot as the work not just of fringe crazies but of "doctors and nurses and teachers and lawyers and small business owners and policemen." Goaded by Trump and Fox News, Turnbull said, those people had given expression to a hideous strain in the American identity.

"You know that great line that you hear all the time: 'This is not us. This is not us. This is not America,'" Turnbull said. "You know what? It is, actually."

"It was too broad a section of the community to be complacent about," he said.

Just as unsettling was the view of Bob Rae, Canada's ambassador to the United Nations, who confessed sadly that it was simply impossible to view the United States in quite the same way after the chaos and horror of the Trump years.

"He's an authoritarian," Rae said of Trump. "I don't believe the Republican Party believes in democracy."

The Canadian diplomat, a longtime leader of his country's liberal party, cautioned that the threat to American democracy from within was far from defeated. Far from a singularly durable democratic power, the United States looked in some ways more like other countries around the world that had battled strongman-style populism—nations like Italy and Brazil and many others. The temptation to surrender freedom and democracy was not a new or distinctively American phenomenon.

But there was still something exceptional about the struggle under way in the United States.

"America," Rae said, "is a very important battleground."

Acknowledgments

WHEN WE FIRST conceived of this book at the end of 2019, we envisioned a richly reported account of what was sure to be a memorable presidential campaign. That was then. As we lived through and covered the events of 2020, the extraordinary aftermath of the election and the tumultuous months since, it became clear that our original concept was inadequate. This period of crisis in American politics, in the years 2020 and 2021, deserved something more.

So we set out to craft a work of history—to capture the campaign yet also the equally important story of how the election and its violent conclusion shaped this country and its two political parties. We were determined not just to present portraits of Presidents Trump and Biden, but to render a more comprehensive picture of the crucial political actors of this moment, from Washington to state capitols to city halls.

This was, and is, the political story of a lifetime, and we felt well positioned to tell it. We know many of the main characters and have covered them for years. How, though, would they fare in this moment of trial? The great historian Robert A. Caro says that power reveals the core of a person. So, too, does crisis.

Our hope is that we have fully portrayed how those with political power wielded it in these harrowing times, when democracy itself was—and still is—in the balance.

We feel privileged to have the opportunity to tell this story, and to do so together. The 2020 election was the fourth presidential campaign we covered together, in a partnership that began at *Politico* and continued at the *New*

York Times. That's to say nothing of the many elections and assorted political dramas we have written about since becoming colleagues and friends fourteen years ago. It was, as they say, love at first sight. We share a passion for politics, history, and journalism. This book is a grand way to marry all three.

It was a joy to write, even if much of the material was sobering, and it came at a time of tumult in our own lives. This project spanned repeated waves of a global pandemic, multiple moves, illness, full-time newspaper jobs, and the arrival of a newborn. It also took us to the West Wing, to every nook and cranny of the Capitol complex, three of New York's boroughs, even more statehouses, and one of the prettiest islands in Maine. This book could not have come to fruition without the support of a number of people.

Our agents, Keith Urbahn and Matt Latimer, enthusiastically and immediately embraced our idea, and then helped us reshape it as events steered us toward pursuing something broader than a campaign book. Keith and Matt were invariably candid, insightful and encouraging. Every book writer, and particularly first-time authors like us, should have professionals like them in their corner.

And we only wish every author could be lucky enough to have Priscilla Painton as their editor. From the first moment we talked to her (via Zoom!), it was like talking to a close colleague and friend. That's because, while she is now a gifted and sought-after editor, Priscilla is still a political reporter at heart. She was enthused about the news in these pages, and she knew just how to frame it for the reader. Working with Priscilla was a delight, and most every week we said to one another that we seemed to have won the editor lottery.

The same could be said, actually, for all of Simon & Schuster. We could not have asked for a better publisher, and we are grateful to the entire team there. We are especially appreciative of the trust and confidence we enjoyed from Jonathan Karp, a visionary leader, and Dana Canedy, our former *Times* colleague with whom we were happily reunited. We want to offer special thanks to Hana Park, a crucial ally and unfailingly attentive and thoughtful partner in this long project.

We are thankful to senior production editor Mark LaFlaur and copy editor Rick Willett for their eagle-eyed attention to our manuscript; jacket

Acknowledgments

designer Jackie Seow and interior designer Wendy Blum for designing this beautiful volume; managing editor Amanda Mulholland for shepherding this complicated project to publication; publicity director Julia Prosser for helping a pair of reporters navigate the world of PR; and attorney Elisa Rivlin for giving this whole thing a close and careful review.

While it is our names on the cover of the book, there is a third person who could just as easily appear there given all the work she did to bring this project to completion: Christine Mui, our immensely talented and indispensable lead researcher. Christine painstakingly transcribed hours of interviews and meetings, meticulously fact-checked much of the book, advised us on the structure and organization of the narrative and came to know the materials and characters herein as well as the two of us. She is wise far beyond her years and will, if she so chooses, be a fantastic journalist and a tremendous asset to any organization smart enough to recruit her.

We are indebted, too, to Luke Tomes, who joined Christine midway through the project and immediately became a trusted and skilled researcher. His enthusiasm for politics reminds us of why we also love it so much, and we know his future is bright, even if he is a Notre Dame fan. We remain very grateful to two researchers who helped us early in the project, Meena Venkataramanan and Dylan Hu, who helped us transcribe and organize our interviews and notes at a vital stage of this undertaking.

All of their invaluable work was made possible by the Institute of Politics at the Harvard Kennedy School, which generously supported our work. Our friend Amy Howell, the former executive director, embraced and encouraged this project from the moment we first described it to her, and we are deeply in her debt. Our great thanks go to Mark Gearan, its always thoughtful director, and Setti Warren, the current executive director, who backed this project to the end. Thanks also to Sadie Polen and Kimberly Peeples for all their help.

Thanks also to our meticulous lawyer, Andrea Cohen, who helped us with our contract and was upbeat, patient, and thorough every step of the way.

We have two professional homes, the *New York Times* and CNN, that value our reporting and have supported us as we have written this book.

Acknowledgments

We want to thank our editors at the *Times* who steered us through the Trump era and the 2020 campaign, led by two children of the Bay State, Carolyn Ryan and Patrick Healy. They are everything a reporter could want from an editor, and they share the same glint in their eyes when you tell them about a developing scoop or story. We are just as appreciative of their extraordinary deputies and editing partners, including Bill Brink, Rachel Dry, and Jonathan Weisman, who have made our copy sing and were more indulgent of us than we deserved.

We are grateful to the leadership of the paper for entrusting us with the responsibility of covering national politics for a truly great American institution, and for giving us an enthusiastic green light to pursue this book.

At CNN, we're thankful to work with an all-star team of news executives, anchors, producers, and reporters who care about politics the way we do.

We have been very lucky to work with a host of colleagues and friends too numerous to name. But we want to express our special appreciation to an editor and mentor we both share, and who is more responsible than anyone for creating our partnership: John F. Harris, our editor at *Politico*, is a friend whose wit, wisdom, and deadpan never get old. (Well, okay, some of his Mel Laird material is a little dated.)

We are thankful to two colleagues whose friendship, partnership, and relentless group text-messaging exceed the boundaries of any one journalistic institution: Sasha Issenberg, whose gifts as a chronicler of modern political history are matched only by his Twitter fastball; and Maggie Haberman, the best reporter and most loyal colleague with whom we've ever worked.

Lastly, we want to jointly thank the sources, named and unnamed, who made this book possible. We care deeply about reporting and gathering information and ideas from a wide variety of people. That would not have been possible if you, dear source, had not agreed to talk and then put up with our calls, emails, and texts—clarifying, pushing, and perhaps even badgering for more.

Thank you. We promise to leave you alone—for now.

—*A.I.B.* and *J.L.M.*

Acknowledgments

* * *

Any worthwhile reporting career is built on the help of teachers and friends, and I have had more than my fair share. In addition to those already named, I want to thank a few who played a vital part in steering me toward and through a life of storytelling, reporting, and the study of history: Maralee Schwartz, Carl Cannon, Danielle Jones, Bill Nichols, Doris Kearns Goodwin, Maya Jasanoff, Rachel St. John, Brad Carson, Fredric Smoler, Jim Cullen, Michael Cook, and Jerry Raik. I would not be the journalist I am today without them.

When I was a twenty-two-year-old research assistant at *Politico*, a far more experienced reporter praised a story I'd written and told me encouragingly: Just imagine what you'll be doing when you're thirty. I'm a bit older than that now, but the answer, it turns out, is that I'd be writing a book with that same encouraging colleague, Jonathan Martin. Jonathan is a reporting partner like none other, a total force of nature in every sense and one of the great friends of my life. He and Betsy did so much to help me manage becoming an author and a father at the same time, and my whole family is in their debt.

I am more grateful than I can ever say to my parents, George Burns and Lisa Goldfarb, who are the most caring people, the best teachers, and the sweetest grandparents in the world. They taught me to love storytelling, reading, and writing from the youngest age and counseled me throughout the process of bringing this book to life. Thank you to my sister, Rachel, with whom I've spent a lifetime sharing those same passions and who is the most voracious reader and the most gifted young writer I know, and to her husband-to-be, Aaron Segal.

Thanks also to Stephen and Jane Lee, and Paul and Lillian Lee, who rooted for this book since long before the first words were typed. I am so fortunate to have them as my family.

Four people who are no longer with us have my deepest thanks: Benjamin and Pearl Goldfarb and Albert and Mary Burns, who unwittingly laid the foundation of my reporting career through many hours of watching The McLaughlin Group and debating William Safire columns as I toddled around and periodically switched off the television, much to Grandpa Ben's consternation. I wish so much that all of them could be here to read this work.

No one believed in this book, and no one believes in me, more than my wife, MJ. She was an unflinching, patient, empathetic, and thoughtful ally from the moment this project began, and through a long reporting and writing process that coincided with the birth of our daughter and the first eleven months of her life. Every page of this book reflects MJ's contributions; she is not just the greatest partner a person could hope for, but also one of the finest journalists and most patriotic Americans I know.

Though she is too young now to read this book, I hope it will one day make Penelope Lee Burns proud of her father. Thank you, little girl, for the happiest time of our lives.

Finally, a special thank you to the best friend on three paws a man has ever had, our boy Bandit, who has always been there for us, especially when we needed him most.

—A.I.B.

* * *

I've often joked that while other kids went to the beach or mountains for vacation, my parents dragged my brother and me to battlefields, museums, and just about every historic site imaginable. I couldn't be more thankful they did. Beyond their unconditional love, the best gift they gave us were those trips to Appomattox and Yorktown, the arrival of *TIME*, *Newsweek*, *U.S. News*, and *Sports Illustrated* in the mail each week and a recurring reminder: You'll never be bored if you have a book. They are the best parents a guy could ask for.

And Jeremy is the finest big brother, my compadre from the get-go and the guy whose order I'd copy at Roy Rogers. All these years later, we're still the best of friends and fishing, quite literally, in the same boat. Making life even better, we're now joined by Jill and Josie, who complete the California Js triumvirate and make life as sunny as a spring day in Solana Beach.

Acknowledgments

Also brightening my days is the inspiring example of my paternal grandmother, Priscilla Martin, who has lived through two pandemics, can still recall the voice of Al Smith on the radio and, at nearly one hundred and five, loves this country as much as she did when she saw her only son off to war over a half century ago. I'm so glad she could hold this book, and I wish Sally, Boppa, Grandma Nette, and Grandpa Mal could do the same.

I feel the same about my favorite professor, Ronald Heinemann, a true Virginia gentleman gone too soon. But I'm thrilled that so many others who nudged me along this life of bylines and datelines can read our biggest heave yet: Jeff E. Schapiro, Bob Lewis, Amy Walter, Charlie Mahtesian, Chuck Todd, Danielle Jones, Rich Lowry, Bill Nichols, Mike Allen, and Adam Nagourney. Thanks, also, to Jake Sherman and John Bresnahan, Capitol Hill reporters nonpareil, who welcomed an interloper to their own hideaway.

My career in journalism would not be nearly as fun or fulfilling had a recent Harvard grad not come to *Politico* in 2008. Hillary Clinton's line about meeting Bill Clinton comes to mind when I think of Alex Burns: We began a conversation, and fourteen years later we're still talking. Alex is the smartest person I know, a gifted journalist and the best partner and pal I've had in my career. He made this book what it is and I'm so grateful for him and MJ.

The best years of my life started when I met Betsy and Ella. My favorite girls make everything more fun. Thank you, B, for pushing me toward this project and for your ideas, encouragement, and support. I could not have done this without you. Thanks, also, for understanding all the popping to and from interviews, more interviews, and even a few more after that. How's this for output? Love you!

—J.L.M.

Index

About the Authors

ALEXANDER BURNS is a national correspondent for the *New York Times* and a political analyst for CNN. He has covered politics at the *Times* since 2015, including as a national political correspondent in the 2020 campaign. Prior to joining the *Times*, he was a reporter and editor at *Politico*. Born and raised in New York City, he is a graduate of Harvard College, where he edited the *Harvard Political Review*. He and his wife, MJ Lee, live in Washington, D.C., with their daughter, Penelope, and their dog, Bandit.

JONATHAN MARTIN is a national political correspondent for the *New York Times* and political analyst for CNN. Before joining the *Times* in 2013, he served as senior political writer for *Politico*. His work has also been published in the *New Republic, National Review, National Journal,* the *Washington Post,* and the *Wall Street Journal.* A Virginian, Martin is a graduate of Hampden-Sydney College. He and his wife, Betsy, live in New Orleans and Washington, D.C.